Y0-BCC-894

320-1
24

SOCIAL WORK
with FAMILIES

SOCIAL WORK
with FAMILIES
Theory and Practice

Edited by
Carlton E. Munson

THE FREE PRESS
A Division of Macmillan Publishing Co., Inc.
NEW YORK
Collier Macmillan Publishers
LONDON

Copyright © 1980 by The Free Press
                A Division of Macmillan Publishing Co., Inc.

All rights reserved. No part of this book may be reproduced or
transmitted in any form or by any means, electronic or mechanical,
including photocopying, recording, or by any information storage
and retrieval system, without permission in writing from the Publisher.

The Free Press
A Division of Macmillan Publishing Co., Inc.
866 Third Avenue, New York, N. Y. 10022

Collier Macmillan Canada, Ltd.

Library of Congress Catalog Card Number: 79-7851

Printed in the United States of America

printing number (hardcover)

1 2 3 4 5 6 7 8 9 10

printing number (paperback)

1 2 3 4 5 6 7 8 9 10

Library of Congress Cataloging in Publication Data

Main entry under title:

Social work with families.

Includes bibliographical references and index.
1. Family social work—United States.
I. Munson, Carlton E.
HV.699.S62   362.8'2'0973   79-7851
ISBN 0-02-922300-8
ISBN 0-02-922310-5 pbk.

823890

LIBRARY
ALMA COLLEGE
ALMA, MICHIGAN

This book is dedicated to my mother, Katherine Lewis Munson, who knew what families are all about, and to whom I never expressed this sentiment directly during her short life.

I come of a Family that has thought very well of itself for 300 years, and with some reason.

H. L. Mencken

There are six people in my family, and I am one of them.

Comment by 7-year-old boy to the author

Contents

Preface

Today many aspects of family functioning are changing or are under attack. Boehm suggests that such changes and stresses call for a response from social work that will enhance interaction between the family and other social institutions.[1] Policy and practice must be integrated into work with families if it is to be effective. Kamerman and Kahn, noting the gap between social change and social policy, assert that the United States has only a piecemeal social policy regarding the family and that the lack of a coherent approach is attributable to societal values and norms antithetical to a systematic family policy.[2]

That the practice and policy concerns of social work theory conform to the prevailing societal perspective on the family is evidenced by the decline in attention to family issues in the social work literature over the past five years and, at the same time, by the increase in specialized journals dealing with family therapy.[3] By contributing to the tendency to equate family policy with family therapy, this trend leads us further away from a comprehensive perspective. Most social work educators perceive and label social work courses concerned with the family as "family therapy." Thus a recent study of the social work curricula of 160 schools found that 59 percent of these schools offered primary content in the area of the family and that at all levels of education (BSW, MSW, and DSW) the principal content area was "family treatment."[4] Generally, theories used by social workers relate to specific aspects of family functioning, particularly to family therapy.

While students and practitioners often find these theories intriguing, they do not address the range of problems social workers face in working with families. Family therapy is an essential component of social work education and practice, but it is only one component of a comprehensive view of the family to which all social work practitioners should be exposed. To deal effectively with the range of problems families face today, social work practitioners must develop a broader view of the family and its function in society.

This book is designed to provide a view of the family that is unified and comprehensive instead of the psychological, individual dysfunctional, micro-sociological approach of most other family texts. Developmental theory[5] was selected as the organizing principle of the book because it is the most comprehensive theory of the family available in that it permits analysis from multiple orientations: the family as a social institution, the family in relation to other social institutions, the family as an interacting unit, and the individual within the family. At the same time the concepts are easy to understand and cover most aspects of family dynamics with which social workers are concerned. Further, because the developmental approach to the family takes into account the individual and the institutional aspects of human behavior, it offers a particularly useful framework for dealing with ethnic-minority issues in practice.

Social work places much emphasis on the use of theory to guide practice; our weakness has not been a scarcity of theories but failure to make full use of the theories that exist.[6] Turner asserts that theory is of value in practice because it allows the practitioner to predict outcomes; to identify, understand, and explain new situations; to relate and transfer knowledge from one situation to another. Further, it permits us to explain our efforts to others, to assess other theories, and to be evaluated fairly.[7]

Since theory is a means of classifying and organizing events, explaining past events and predicting future events, and understanding how and why events occur,[8] a good theory contains assumptions that are clearly stated, verifiable, and interrelated; is comprehensive in treatment of phenomena; fosters and influences systematic and heuristic generation of research; and brings complex events within the range of understanding.[9] Developmental theory of family functioning meets all of these tests. The theory contains clearly stated assumptions that can be verified and interrelated, is comprehensive and allows treatment of family functioning from several levels of analysis, has influenced a broad range of systematic and heuristic research, and through the use of precise and interrelated concepts permits understanding of complex interactions and events.

Using developmental theory to organize the readings produced a very simple and effective design. The three major components of developmental theory as applied to the family are conceptualized by Roy Rodgers in Chapter 1. All of the following chapters address some element of social work practice with families. Parts II–IV are based on the three facets of developmental theory. Thus Part II deals with the family in relation to government, economics, religion, education and other societal institutions. Part III looks at the family internally as a self-contained unit. The chapters in this section address issues social workers confront in helping families with their internal interaction. The material presented in Part IV aids the worker in situations where individual functioning impacts on the family, as in the case of retardation, health problems, mental illness, alcoholism, and death. The extensive bibliography suggests additional resources in the various areas covered in the text.

This collection of articles is designed to meet the learning needs of undergraduate and graduate students preparing for social work practice with families. In addition the readings themselves and the organizing theory can be helpful to practitioners in specialized settings and has been found quite effective in the training and education of nonprofessional, paraprofessional, and volunteer workers.

The theoretical concepts have broad applicability, for theory building and curriculum development as well as classroom teaching and practice. The parallels between theory building and curriculum building can be drawn from the introductory section, and developmental theory can be used by social work educators to plan relevant and substantive curriculum and course content. Using the three main facets of the theory, appropriate and integrated content for social welfare policy, human behavior in the social environment, and social work practice courses can by systematically planned.

References

1. Werner W. Boehm, "Social Work Education: Issues and Problems in Light of Recent Developments," *Journal of Education for Social Work* 12 (Winter 1976), p. 21.

2. Sheila B. Kamerman and Alfred J. Kahn, "Explorations in Family Policy," *Social Work* 21 (May 1976), pp. 181–183.

3. See Michael W. Howe and John R. Schuerman, "Trends in Social Work Literature: 1957–1972," *Social Service Review* 48 (June 1974), pp. 283–284.

4. Joe Rollo et al., personal communication. For details of this study see Danuta Mostwin, ed., *The American Family: Continuing Impact of Ethnicity* (Washington, D.C.: The Catholic University of America, 1977).

5. For a detailed discussion of this theory see Roy H. Rodgers, *Family Interaction and Transaction: The Developmental Approach* (Englewood Cliffs, N.J.: Prentice Hall, 1973).

6. Francis J. Turner, ed., *Social Work Treatment: Interlocking Theoretical Approaches*, Second Edition (New York: Free Press, 1979), p. 4.

7. Ibid., p. 8.

8. Jonathan H. Turner, *The Structure of Sociological Theory* (Homewood, Ill.: Dorsey Press, 1974), p. 2.

9. Calvin S. Hall and Gardner Lindzey, *Theories of Personality* (New York: John Wiley and Sons, 1970), pp. 9–15.

Acknowledgments

I would like to acknowledge the help, support, and assistance of several people in the preparation of this book. I thank my wife, Joan, for typing the manuscript. I appreciate the support, encouragement, and editorial assistance of Gladys Topkis, senior editor at The Free Press. I am indebted to Roy Rodgers, whom I have never met and know only through his skilled writing. Dr. Rodgers has helped me in organizing my courses and this book much more than he can know. His conceptual approach has made my work much easier over the years. I am appreciative of proofreading done by two of my teaching assistants, Debra Wymore and Jamie Gluck. I appreciate the advice, criticism, encouragement, and ideas provided by my students throughout the years as I was struggling to put this material together and to have it make sense. Finally, I want to acknowledge the help given me in the past by William B. Snyder, the late president of Hagerstown Bookbinding and Printing Company, Inc. Bill died as this manuscript was being revised for publication, and his death came as a shock. I owe a debt to him for supporting publication of the first book I ever wrote. He taught and helped me a great deal. He will be missed.

The Contributors

MARCIA ABRAMSON, Ph.D., is assistant professor of social work at Columbia University.

DONALD R. BARDILL, D.S.W., is dean and professor, School of Social Work, Florida State University.

ELLEN BASSUK, M.D., is assistant professor of psychiatry at Howard Medical School and director psychiatric emergency services at Beth Israel Hospital, Boston.

ANDREW BILLINGSLEY, Ph.D., is president of Morgan State University, Baltimore.

JEAN LIPMAN-BLUMEN, Ph.D., is fellow-in-residence at the Center for Advanced Study in the Behavioral Sciences.

WILLIAM E. BOUTELLE, M.D., is assistant chief, Psychiatry Service, V.A. Medical Center, Bedford, Massachusetts.

ROBERT M. BRESSLER, M.S.W., is executive director of the East Plains Mental Health Services, Jericho, New York.

ROBERT A. BROWN, D.S.W., is a clinical social worker in private practice.

CATHERINE S. CHILMAN, Ph.D., is professor, School of Social Welfare, University of Wisconsin—Milwaukee.

DONALD A. DEVIS, M.S.W., is assistant professor of psychiatry, Emory University School of Medicine, Atlanta.

NORMAN EPSTEIN, Ph.D., is director of transitional services, Children's Psychiatric Center/Community Mental Health Center, Red Bank, New Jersey.

DOROTHY R. FREEMAN was formerly associate professor of social work at McGill University, Montreal.

JOSEPH H. GOLNER, Ed.D., is co-director of Interactive Therapies, Needham, Massachusetts.

DAVID HALLOWITZ, M.S.W., is associate director and chief psychiatric social worker, Child and Adolescent Psychiatric Clinic, Buffalo, New York.

ALEXANDER HERSH, D.S.W., is associate dean, University of Pennsylvania School of Social Work.

DONALD F. KRILL, M.S.W., is associate professor of social work, University of Denver Graduate School of Social Work.

GEORGE KRUPP, M.D., is assistant professor of clinical psychiatry, School of Medicine, State University of New York at Stonybrook.

JOHN L. LAUGHLIN, M.S.W., is a family therapist in private practice.

MARY W. LINDAHL, M.S.W., was formerly assistant professor of psychiatry at Tufts University School of Medicine, Boston.

ELIZABETH HERMAN MCKAMY, M.S.W., is psychotherapist and psychiatric social worker at the Menninger Foundation.

JOHN F. MUELLER, M.S.W., is director of alcoholism training, Malcolm Bliss Mental Health Center in St. Louis.

CARLTON E. MUNSON, D.S.W., is associate professor, Graduate School of Social Work, University of Houston.

ANN MURPHY is director of social work, Developmental Evaluation Clinic, Children's Hospital, Boston, and clinical assistant professor, Boston University School of Social Work.

CAROL NADELSON, M.D., is associate professor of psychiatry, Howard Medical School.

SIEGFRIED M. PUESCHEL, M.D., is director of the Child Development Center at Rhode Island Hospital and associate professor pediatrics at Brown University.

MARGARET E. RAYMOND, M.S.W., is a clinical social worker in private practice.

KATHLEEN HICKEY REED, M.S.W., is a clinical social worker in private practice.

ANDREW E. SLABY, M.D., is professor of psychiatry and human behavior at Brown University.

MARTA SOTOMAYOR, D.S.W., is special assistant to the administrator for alcohol, mental health and drug abuse, Department of HEW.

ROBERT SUNLEY, M.S.W., is associate director of the Family Service Association of Nassau County, New York.

SOCIAL WORK
with FAMILIES

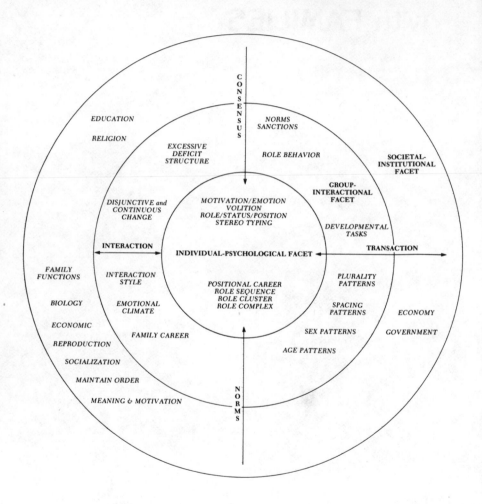

CONSENSUS

EDUCATION

RELIGION

NORMS
SANCTIONS

EXCESSIVE
DEFICIT
STRUCTURE

ROLE BEHAVIOR

SOCIETAL-
INSTITUTIONAL
FACET

GROUP-
INTERACTIONAL
FACET

DISJUNCTIVE and
CONTINUOUS
CHANGE

MOTIVATION/EMOTION
VOLITION
ROLE/STATUS/POSITION
STEREO TYPING

DEVELOPMENTAL
TASKS

INTERACTION

INDIVIDUAL-PSYCHOLOGICAL FACET

TRANSACTION

FAMILY
FUNCTIONS

INTERACTION
STYLE

PLURALITY
PATTERNS

BIOLOGY

EMOTIONAL
CLIMATE

POSITIONAL CAREER
ROLE SEQUENCE
ROLE CLUSTER
ROLE COMPLEX

SPACING
PATTERNS

ECONOMY

ECONOMIC

FAMILY CAREER

SEX PATTERNS

GOVERNMENT

REPRODUCTION

AGE PATTERNS

SOCIALIZATION

MAINTAIN ORDER

MEANING & MOTIVATION

NORMS

PART I
Developmental Theory and Family Analysis

Introduction

Developmental theory contains three broadly defined *facets* for use in assessing family functioning. The *societal-institutional* facet relates family functioning to various institutions such as educational, religious, economics, etc. The *group-interactional* facet deals with the individual family unit and how it functions through meeting or failing to meet the needs of its members. The *individual-psychological* facet is concerned with the individual as a unique biological and emotional being, as well as with social functioning through role performance based on transactions with the family and social institutions. These three facets are interrelated through the concepts of *transactions* and *interactions*. Transactions refer to activity between and among facets while interactions refer to activity within a given facet.

THE SOCIETAL-INSTITUTIONAL FACET

The family is itself a major social institution, but as an individual unit it is influenced, impinged upon, and at times threatened by other social institutions. The family as a social institution and as a recipient and carrier of societal values and norms is most relevant to social welfare policy issues. In this context the family is constantly giving up and taking on functions to meet

2

cultural needs. In this process there is always a cultural lag between family functioning and societal needs. The family is always playing a game of catch-up in cultural evolution. Some families manage to keep pace, while others fall behind and turn to agencies for aid. Social workers need knowledge of this process of family struggle for survival in a cluster of governmental, educational, economic, and religious institutions that profess to serve the interests of the family but in actuality often *transact* with the family in ways that weaken it emotionally, financially, and structurally. Government supports the family through tax exemptions for children, home owning, medical expenses, and disability, but at the same time family benefits under the Social Security Act recognize divorce in only a limited way, favor the nuclear family over the extended family, and favor the husband as an income source.[1] Families that keep pace economically, socially, and emotionally in society take advantage of the supports just mentioned, and families that fall behind are the recipients of the "benefits" that often aggravate existing handicaps.

The government usually lags behind in trends affecting the family regarding human rights.[2] For example, legislation safeguarding women's rights was not passed until private groups mounted demonstrations, protests, and lobbying campaigns. Legislation on this and similar matters has a direct impact on family roles, but whether this impact is viewed as positive or negative depends upon one's orientation. The equalitarian model of the family has high professed value in American society, but sex role designation and segregation of much family activity persist.[3] Practitioners need a framework for assessing the conflicts among the needs and expectations of society, institutions, families, and individuals. The developmental theory of the family provides such perspective.

In the economic sphere there is a reciprocity between the family and the economic system in that the family is the supplier of workers for the marketplace, and the economic system is the source of exchange for services and goods that provide security for family members. Changes in the needs of the labor market directly impact the family. Since 1940 married women have entered the labor market in increasing numbers, depending partly on the number and ages of their children and the level of their husband's income. The more children, the younger the children, and the higher the husband's income, the less likely women will enter the labor force.[4] At the same time the high inflation of the past decade has forced more women into work outside the home. As the divorce rate and the age at first marriage increases and the life expectancy for males decreases, more women can be expected to enter jobs. These factors produce pressures for further institutional changes such as expansion of day care centers and repeal of "blue laws" to accommodate Sunday shopping. All of these issues have direct implications for social welfare policy and social work practice that need to be addressed by social welfare planners and social work practitioners.

Historically the family and the church have had close ties, but the influence of institutionalized religion on the family is decreasing.[5] The decline in religious influence is correlated with geographic factors, socioeconomic status, and ethnic orientations, and often these factors interact in a complex manner that practitioners must take into account. For example, geography and socioeconomic status have an impact on mate selection and interfaith marriage,[6] but in rural areas the church generally has more influence on the family than in urban areas. This rural-urban differential becomes particularly acute for certain ethnic groups, such as Mexican-Americans, as they turn to the church in urban locations, where traditional cultural supports deteriorate more rapidly than in rural areas.[7] The urban church is admittedly unprepared to respond in the manner and at the level needed.[8] Such institutional weaknesses must be recognized in family practice since many families will not seek help from outside agencies without the support or recommendation of a clergyman.[9] In dealing with troubled families, collateral contacts with clergy can often be as significant as direct intervention.

THE GROUP-INTERACTIONAL FACET

This aspect deals with interactions that take place among members within specific family units or groups of families with common characteristics. Social workers in the areas of public assistance, protective services, juvenile delinquency and adult crime, health, and mental health must have knowledge of individual family functioning. This facet has numerous organizing concepts for understanding families dynamically such as *development tasks* to be mastered at all stages of the *family career*. Families have *interactional styles, emotional climates,* and *facilitating mechanisms* which contribute to the development of the individual and to the forms of interaction the family evolves. There are *plurality, spacing, sex,* and *age patterns* that are important in understanding family operations. Families devise their own unique *norms* and *sanctions* that must be known to the worker before effective intervention can take place. Families have excessive and deficit structures related to missing members or multiple generations residing together.

Little effort has been made to apply these concepts directly to social work practice, but when the concepts are applied they are valuable tools in organizing practice. For example, excessive or deficit family structure can be utilized to conceptualize the structuring of family interviews. When a significant family member is absent (deficit structure) from the treatment or from a given session, the interaction and the outcome can be significantly affected. In the case of large families, having relatives or all the children present can create excessive structure that makes the situation interactionally too complex for the worker to manage. These group-interactional concepts have various levels of utility that can be valuable to the practitioner in organizing family practice. All of these concepts are illustrated in detail in the first selection, by Rodgers.

Families have myths, secrets, and interactional rules that determine communication, and they engage in mystification to keep others in the dark regarding what goes on. When one studies family interactional styles, internal dynamics become more unclear and external comparison more difficult.[10] In dealing with such a complex system, a theory to organize and guide intervention is needed. Systematic application of the concepts derived from developmental theory is helpful in analyzing the internal and external tasks, structures, styles, careers, emotional climates, norms, sanctions, patterns, and changes over time. Many modern theories of family therapy grew out of development theory, making them compatible with teaching family treatment as a component of a more comprehensive theory of the family. This is essential if we are to avoid the pattern of teaching family treatment exclusively from a negative, dysfunctional view.

Minuchin's structural theory of family therapy exemplifies a model of family treatment based on developmental theory in that it presents "a body of theory and techniques that approaches the individual in his social context" and "starts with a model of normality against which to measure deviance."[11] Utilizing this approach, Minuchin views the family as a "social unit" that faces a series of "developmental tasks" which "differ along the parameters of cultural differences, but . . . have universal roots."[12] He draws heavily on the concepts of developmental tasks, transactions, interactions, and societal and institutional imprints on individuals and families. The practitioner who begins family therapy after being exposed to the developmental theory of family is better equipped to understand the forces that shape, mold, and determine the functioning of individual family units regardless of the specific theory of family therapy they utilize.

THE INDIVIDUAL-PSYCHOLOGICAL FACET

Sociologists have been accused of neglecting individual determinants of behavior, while psychologists have been accused of failing to take group influences into account. The developmental theorists use a social-psychological approach that includes group as well as individual concepts. What makes developmental theory unique in this regard and of special value to social work practitioners is that the concepts are defined and explicated within the context of the family.

In our culture we tend to see the family primarily as a center from which the individual operates.[13] It is in this area that the individual-psychological facet can be explored in relation to the two previously discussed facets. In the legal system emphasis is placed on the individual. Even in family law, the marriage contract is treated as a contract between individuals, and the same conception applies to divorce. In the economic sphere, employment is based on individualistic orientations; some organizations in fact have restrictions on employing more than one member of a family. Government services and programs are geared to individuals. Often these conceptions work against both the individual and the family. Many public welfare programs exclude intact families from benefits and support only splintered, fractured, individualized families. At the point of contribution, social security programs collect from family members individually, but at the point of receiving benefits honor only one family member's participation. In a society founded on a philosophy of individualism, the social, political, educational, and economic examples of preference shown to the individual are many. Through developmental theory these preferences can be analyzed systematically. The developmental conceptualization of the individual can be used to explore issues and dilemmas encountered in social work practice; for example, whether it is appropriate for a caseworker to refer a teen-age client to a public clinic for birth control information and contraceptive services without involving or notifying the parents.

The developmental theory of family can be used to organize major theoretical approaches to the individual within society. The varying degrees of emphasis placed on the individual and the group by psychoanalytic, existential, behaviorist, structural functionalist, symbolic interactionist, or any of the many other psychological and sociological theories of human behavior currently in use can be explored systematically using developmental theory as a unifying framework.

The developmental perspective views the individual as a unique genetic organism but at the same time never loses awareness of society[14] in one form or another. As has been argued here, society, for the individual, most often manifests itself within the family, where the individual must adjust, adapt, and reconcile his unique being with the expectations he encounters both external to the family and from within the family. There are several sources of possible conflict. Perhaps because we have not had a theoretical framework to guide our analysis of the families we see in practice, we are not very clear about what produces conflict and what does not. We have made many assumptions about how modern, complex society has given rise to role conflict and role strain, but there has been a great deal of role accumulation and role adaptation that can lead to more healthy functioning of the family and the individual[15] that has not been explicated in practice.

In family treatment the recent trend has been away from emphasis on the individual and toward greater concern for the family as a unit or system.[16] This trend could have a negative impact for the individual given the stance of developmental family theory. The importance of not losing sight of the individual has been pointed out by Otto Pollak, who believes the most important function of the modern family is to provide a sanctuary from the bureaucracy—a place where family members can let loose the rage they've built up in their daily contacts with the educational, military, governmental, or corporate bureaucracy. In some cases an individual will choose "protective alienation" from others to protect a family member; for example, a person may withdraw from social contacts to avoid the risk of exposing a spouse's alcoholism. Often in such cases the importance of the family is increased for the individual,[17] and the social worker who does not take this function into account could deepen rather than alleviate problems through intervention.

Luthman and Kirschenbaum have developed an interactive model of intervention based on the work of Satir, Jackson, Bateson, Haley, and Perls that integrates the family system and an individual focus. It is their philosophy that "for the individuals within the family to achieve their maximum growth potential, families must also have ways to maintain the stability of the family unit; and, at the same time, adapt to the continually changing growth needs of individual members."[18] If the worker fails to focus on the individual as well as the family unit and views intervention as a means to adjust the individual to the family system, then the family becomes merely one more institution to which the person must accommodate, forgoing the self for the sake of the group. This is the essence of the not so flippant witticism, "They say the family is an institution, but who wants to live in an institution?"[19] Although this book takes an institutional approach to the family, it is important to remember that in practice we are always dealing with individuals struggling to cope with difficult social situations.

USE OF THE DIAGRAM

The diagram on p. xviii shows the concepts used in developmental theory that are explained in this introduction and Chapter 1. The diagram allows the reader to have a unified image of the theory. It is recommended that the reader refer to the diagram before, during, and after reading each section for assistance in readily understanding how the readings relate to the theory.

The diagram presents all of the concepts from developmental theory. Each facet is shown within a circle. The outer circle shows the societal-institutional facet, the second circle the group-interactional facet, and the inner circle the individual-psychological facet. The terms transaction and interaction are used to differentiate between activity within a facet and between facets. Interaction refers to activity within a facet; for example, between educational and religious institutions regarding families involves an interaction. Transactions refer to activity between facets, as when a family relates to the educational or religious institutions. Interaction can occur within any of the facets, and transactions can occur between any or all of the facets. The concept of norms refers to generally agreed upon behavioral expectations of individuals and groups; consensus refers to agreement between individuals and groups about the behavioral expectations. The other concepts are specific to the facets under which they are listed. All of these concepts are defined in detail in Chapter 1 by Rodgers.

Notes

1.   For a detailed discussion of the Social Security Act and the family, see Ellen Guillot, "Congress and the Family: Reflections of Social Processes and Values in Benefits in OASDI," *Social Service Review* 45 (June 1971), pp. 173-183.

2.   For a detailed analysis of this governmental lag, see Catherine S. Chilman, "Public Policy and Families in the 1970s," *Social Casework* 54 (December 1973), pp. 575-585.

3.   Rodgers, *op. cit.*, p. 31.

4.   Linda J. Waite, "Working Wives: 1940-1960," *American Sociological Review* 41 (February 1976), pp. 65-80.

5.   Ira L. Reiss, *The Family System in America* (New York: Holt, Rinehart and Winston, 1971), pp. 410-411.

6.   David A. Schulz, *The Changing Family: Its Function and Future* (Englewood Cliffs, N.J.: Prentice-Hall, 1976), pp. 147-148.

7.   T. Lynn Smith and Paul E. Zopf, *Principle of Inductive Rural Sociology* (Philadelphia: F. A. Davis, 1970), p. 347.

8.   See John J. McRaith, "Why the 'Call to Action' Process was Worthwhile," *Catholic Rural Life* 25 (December 1976), pp. 11-12.

9.   Floyd M. Martinson, *Family in Society* (New York: Dodd, Mead, 1972), p. 233.

10.   Arlene Skolnick, *The Intimate Environment* (Boston: Little, Brown, 1973), pp. 2-3.

11.   Salvador Minuchin, *Families and Family Therapy* (Cambridge, Mass.: Harvard University Press, 1974), pp. 2-15.

12.   Ibid., p. 16.

13.   Rodgers, *op. cit.*, p. 33.

14.   See Richard Sennett and Jonathan Cobb, *The Hidden Injuries of Class* (New York: Vintage Books, 1973), p. 192.

15.   For a discussion of confusing role strain with role accumulation, see John D. Photeadis and Richard A. Ball, "Patterns of Change in Rural Normative Structure," *Rural Sociology* 4 (Spring 1976), pp. 62-67.

16.   Diane I. Levande, "Family Theory as a Necessary Component of Family Therapy," *Social Casework* 57 (May 1976), pp. 291-292.

17.   Sennett and Cobb, *op. cit.*, pp. 196-198.

18.   Shirley G. Luthman and Martin Kirschenbaum, *The Dynamic Family* (Palo Alto, Calif.: Science and Behavior Books, 1974), p. 3.

19.   See Ernest W. Burgess, "The Family as a Unity of Interacting Personalities," *Family Therapy: An Introduction to Theory and Technique*, ed., Gerald D. Erickson and Terrence P. Hogan (Monterey, Calif.: Brooks-Cole, 1972), p. 15.

1

Three Facets of Family Dynamics

Roy H. Rodgers

The behavior of families is a very complex whole. Any analysis of it necessarily takes a particular perspective and, in the process, ignores other possible ones. If someone were inspecting a cut diamond with its many facets, each turn of the diamond would reflect a different character, though the stone would always be the same one. Undoubtedly, there exist many facets to family dynamics. The developmental approach focuses its particular attention on three of them.

Much family behavior has its origin in the society's expectations concerning what family ought to be. There always exists a certain set of institutional norms which govern family behavior. And so, throughout a family's career there is a *societal-institutional* facet to its conduct. What is equally true is that many activities occurring in families arise out of expectations which develop within the groups themselves concerning the appropriate rules for interaction within them. This evolved aspect can be called the *group-interactional facet*. Finally, every group is made up of individuals with their own physical-psychological makeup. The unique qualities of individuals also determine to some extent the kinds of interaction which take place in families. This last level may be labeled the *individual-psychological facet*.

One of the problems to which the developmental approach addresses itself is a more adequate way of dealing with analysis of families in all three facets. Each level has something significant to tell us about how families behave. The more information we include in our theoretical approach about each of these aspects, the greater the explanatory power of the theory. The developmental approach has attempted to incorporate into its theoretical

Source: From Roy H. Rodgers; *Family Interaction and Transaction: The Developmental Approach,* pp. 23–65. Copyright © 1973. Reprinted by permission of Prentice-Hall, Inc., Englewood Cliffs, New Jersey.

framework concepts which will deal adequately with each of the facets and also concepts which will tie the three facets more closely into an integrated whole. Let us take a closer look at each of the facets.

The Societal-Institutional Facet

Every society develops a fairly systematic and conscious set of expectations concerning what it considers right and what it deems wrong about the way families should be formed and function.[1] In American society there are expectations that individuals should possess a certain maturity before they enter into a marriage, that sexual relationships should occur within wedlock, that husbands should be the primary providers, that husbands should be the "head of the household," and many others. Although these expectations generally are recognized in the society, it also is quite clear that there are ranges of conformity to them which vary in different cultural groups of the society or in certain regions of the country. Nevertheless, as one observes family life throughout the American culture, one finds a clear common thread of behavior running through it that is based on societal-institutional expectations about which all members of the society know and to which they conform to a considerable degree.

The developmental theoretical approach deals with the societal-institutional facet from two perspectives. One view treats the family as a major social system in the society. This approach stresses how the family system is interrelated with the other structures of the society as a functioning whole. The other standpoint deals with the structuring of the family institution in terms of a broad range of cultural values and goals. In a very real sense, the primary emphasis of the social-system aspect is on the role of the family within the larger society, whereas the institutional perspective emphasizes the influence of the larger society on the family structure. These distinctions are primarily analytical ones which help us to clarify the complex interrelationships which exist. In the day-to-day functioning of the society, they are not so clearly distinguished.

FUNCTIONS OF THE FAMILY SYSTEM FOR THE SOCIETY

Social-system theorists usually have talked about the functions of a system for the society or, alternatively, about the development of structures to carry out certain duties the society considers necessary. Several sets of these "necessary" functions have been developed by various writers.[2] One such set, which seems to capture the functions most adequately, was presented several years ago by Bennett and Tumin.[3] It includes: (1) maintenance of biological functioning of group members; (2) reproduction or recruitment of new group members; (3) socialization of new members; (4) production and distribution of goods and services; (5) maintenance of order; and (6) maintenance of meaning and motivation for group activity. As a convenient way of classifying group activity, it seems useful to examine the family relationship in light of these functional prerequisites.

Robert Bierstedt[4] has defined an institution as an organized procedure for carrying out some societal task; that is, an institution is the set of rules which defines the way in which something ought to be accomplished. If we tie this idea of an institution to the functional prerequisites of Bennett and Tumin, we can see that there are major institutional structures—that is, organized procedures in the society—which are designed to meet each of these necessary tasks. Or, to put the point in another way, every group either has such a procedure as a part of its own system of roles or has available to it some other group or system to carry out these tasks. The family may be seen as an institution of the society which carries out some of these obligations. Exactly which functions are handled by the family depends on the structure of a given society. For American society, reproduction and a great share of the socialization function are the responsibilities of the family structure. In an earlier period of American history, when the society was largely agricultural, it is probably true that the family had a larger responsibility for several other functions than now. Other structures have taken these over to a large degree, however, as the society has grown larger, has become more industrialized and more urbanized, and as the family has changed from an extended to a nuclear form. The essential point is that part of the family system's position and role structure will carry out whatever functions are its responsibility in the society and, at the same time, will provide those functions for its own family members.

Reproductive Roles.   In most societies, reproduction is a family function with some very clearly defined roles specifying how it is to be carried out. There is, first of all, the limitation on entry into the function, which is usually handled by a minimal age specification before which reproduction is viewed as inappropriate. There may be puberty rites or defloration rituals which indicate that a person is eligible for the reproductive role. There may be certain designated ages which the individual is viewed as eligible for marriage and when he is considered not eligible. These ages may be very formally specified in laws or may be informally formulated.

The second kind of normative structure encourages individuals who have reached eligibility for reproduction to begin to have offspring. In American society, young married couples who delay childbearing find increasingly that their associates and kin begin to raise questions concerning the immanence of their "starting a family." As a matter of fact, the term applied to a married pair without children is more likely to be *couple* than *family*. Having children, not simply being married, becomes the significant criterion for qualifying as a family. Couples who find that they are biologically incapable of having children also feel pressures placed upon them to adopt children to attain family status. There is a quality of evaluation toward childless couples which implies that they have not totally fulfilled themselves until they have reproduced. In other societies, similar behaviors are noted—even to the extreme of legitimizing divorce on the grounds of the failure to bear children or of the failure to bear children of a given sex.

Patterns appear in many societies which put pressure on single persons to get married. These configurations may consist of frequent questioning of single individuals about their plans for marriage, thinly veiled matchmaking, the application of terms to marriage-eligibles which have negative connotations, or economic features which encourage families to marry off their children or stimulate individuals to marry. All these are expressions of norms designed to influence people occupying positions in which reproductive behavior is defined as desirable to demonstrate the appropriate role behavior.

The third aspect has to do with exit from the reproductive role. There are often negative norms which discourage individuals who have reached a certain point in their career from having any more children. Especially in societies which emphasize the nuclear-family pattern, older couples—especially older men—may be discouraged from reproducing, since they may not live long enough to care for the children to maturity. The nuclear-family system has little provision for the care of orphaned children and, therefore, they place a special burden on the system.

From a developmental point of view, then, the reproductive role contains clear time elements. There are periods when reproduction is appropriate and is encouraged, and there are periods when it is inappropriate and is discouraged. These periods usually are tied to the role sequences of positions in the family system in a way that designates when reproduction is fitting in the sequences and how it should occur. These indications by the society may be communicated formally and informally.

Maintenance of Biological Functioning.   The human infant has one of the longest periods of dependency on others for its nourishment and shelter needs. Societies do not always assign this function to the family system, as the case of the Israeli kibbutz system demonstrates.[5] But it is also clear that a great many societies have placed this responsibility within the family system. Reciprocal role complexes are incorporated into the role structure of the family careers requiring certain actors to provide for the protection and sustenance of the young and for persons at all age levels above childhood. The assignment of the biological-maintenance function is highly variable. The familiar Western pattern of the wife-mother having primary responsibility for the domestic activities of food preparation and for personal care, while the husband-father is accountable for physical protection and for obtaining the food and other goods to be utilized in physical maintenance, is only one type of approach to this task. Some societies turn these matters over to actors other than the mother or father of the child. Older children may be assigned the responsibility of child care so that the mother and father are released to carry out some other role, such as working in the fields to produce food or other desired products. An older female, a grandmother or aunt, may have this role as a part of her position in some extended family systems. Still another common pattern is to wean the child early from the mother's breast or to transfer the nursing of the infant to another individual, not necessarily a family member, which allows the mother to meet other role expectations. Indeed, the American nursery school, often involving children as young as two years, has this last function.

There are a number of legal aspects to the maintenance function which appear in American society. Child-support laws require fathers to provide for their minor children in cases of divorce, separation, and out-of-wedlock reproduction, even though the mother may have remarried. There are also laws dealing with child neglect by which parents may be criminally prosecuted for failing to provide adequate maintenance for their offspring. In American society, however, there are considerable ambivalence and ambiguity in the role definitions of the wife-mother concerning her responsibility for the care of the young. Although it is generally viewed as highly desirable that a mother care for her own young, and mothers who society thinks neglect their children in favor of other roles are frequently negatively evaluated, the industrialization of the society has developed alternative roles for women which compete with this traditional family role. The data on the behavior of American women indicate that there are periods in the role sequence of mother when it is less obligatory for her to play the child-care role. Mothers of infants and preschool children are less likely to be found among the ranks of the gainfully employed, implying some sort of role prescription which keeps them in the home, but an increasing number of mothers go to work as the ages of the children increase.[6]

The evidence shows a clear developmental quality to the maintenance-function norms which ties the maintenance role to certain periods of the role sequences of actors in the system. Although we have focused on the child-care period, similar data exist with respect to the care of individuals throughout the family career.

Socialization of New Members.   Data similar to those just discussed appear for the socialization function. Societies differ in the amount of socialization assigned to the family system, the roles it is allotted, and the various segments of the role sequences in which the function is concentrated. However, Reiss[7] argues that this is probably the single function universally attached to the family system.

The characteristics of the socialization function are reflected in both the objects of socialization and the roles of the socializers. Some societies, expecting that children will receive a great share of their total socialization experience within the family system, assign the roles of socializer to the positions of the mother, the father, and/or the older siblings. Other societies assign this function to the family only in certain portions of the role sequence of the child, turning over major portions of the socialization experience to other systems of the society. The kibbutz, for example, places a heavy burden upon child-care units with professionally trained individuals who specialize in socializing all of the children from infancy to adulthood. The parental socialization role becomes one narrowly confined to a kind of emotional nurturance role, similar to the grandparent role in American society. Parents do not have responsibility for the discipline of the children in the American sense but spend time with children in recreation and on holidays, when the quality of the relationship is considerably more expressive than it is instrumental.[8]

In contrast, American society concentrates the socialization function in the roles of parents in the early years of the role sequence of the child but divides the responsibility between the family and the school system in later childhood until, finally, the school becomes the primary socialization experience in late adolescence and young adulthood.

Another side of the socialization function is seen in societies which have given a considerable amount of the duty to the elders of the society, often segregating the sexes, with the elders of the same sex as the children teaching them their appropriate roles. In such a system, an adult male or groups of males, not necessarily the parents of the boys, will teach appropriate masculine skills to the entire group of boys who are of the suitable developmental level. Meanwhile, adult women will be providing appropriate experiences for the girls of the society.

Frequently, the society sets up finely divided age-graded experiences, with special rites of passage accompanying the movement from one category of socialization experience to the next. Our own society, though it places some emphasis on the movement from school grade to school grade (especially on the transition from grade school to junior high school, from junior high to senior high school, and graduation from senior high school), generally focuses less on this kind of ceremonial occasion than do other societies. There is considerable blurring of the movement through the role sequences and their attendant socialization experiences. Even such fairly significant events as reaching the age of twenty-one, with its supposed symbolism as the attainment of adulthood, do not change sharply the role relationships which the individual experiences. The role sequences in American society are considerably more continuous in nature than the disjunctive character of role sequences in some other societies. Nevertheless, by the time the child reaches the later portion of his role sequence in the family career, his socialization experiences with respect to the family are rather minimal, and the parents are not expected to treat their offspring as "children" at this point in life.

All these examples have more of an informal quality to them, though some have strong moral aspects which place them in the general area of the mores of the society. Examples of legal definitions of socialization functions are not as frequent in this area as in some others. In American society, aside from laws which deal primarily with the maintenance function, most statutes tend to limit the socializing responsibility of the family by placing obligations on the parents to turn their children over to the school system. A number of court decisions and interpretations of law have ruled that even parents who are formally trained and certified as schoolteachers may not attempt to educate their own children but must send them to the public schools or to approved private schools for this experience.

The major developmental aspect of the socialization function appears in the way the socialization experience is tied closely to the maturational level of the child. Indeed, the role of socializer is almost always defined by the role sequence of the recipient of socialization. Thus, the age and developmental status of the socializer may vary from a relatively young person with only minimal adult status for himself to that of a quite aged senior person with many adult responsibilities. Yet, their socialization roles in the same society with respect to a child of the same developmental status will be quite similar. This example is a particularly good one of how the role obligations of a given actor are defined by the reciprocal role and contain little discretionary behavior.

Production and Distribution of Goods and Services. Industrialized societies usually place little responsibility on the nuclear family for this function. Even the agricultural activities of such societies are highly developed technologically so that the farm family unit is less important than having a few trained workers to operate the complex equipment utilized in agricultural production. Furthermore, only a minority of the population of an industrialized society is involved in farming. Most productive activity is located in highly complex industrial organizations which deal with the individual as a working unit rather than in a family which constitutes the unit of production. In such a societal setting, the family contributes individual workers to the productive system, but the family unit is a consuming, not a productive, one.

The productive role in the American family is focused on the adult male husband-father position as provider, which is closely associated with the maintenance function. Likewise, the adult female's productive roles are devoted to preparation of food, to provision for personal needs, and occasionally to production of items of wearing apparel, which are also more identified with the maintenance function than with the productive responsibility. For the male children of the family, the productive role appears primarily in anticipatory socialization. It consists of pointing them toward adulthood, when they will be expected to take on a provider role in their future position as husband-father, rather than with respect to any current role they might be expected to play. Female children may experience very little normative pressure either of an anticipatory socialization kind or with respect to any current productive expectations. It is probable, though, that American girls begin to experience quite early some ambiguity over the conflict between domestic and productive roles in their future positions as adult women in the society.

Societies which do assign productive roles to the family members may do so in a variety of ways. Some societies place no productive expectations on occupants of the young-child positions but suddenly may inject normative anticipations into the position at a given developmental level. Others attach expectations very early with increasing responsibility as the child matures. Similarly, the wife-mother position may have productive roles associated with it. These may vary depending upon whether the woman is also expected to bear and care for young children or whether she is released quickly from the child-care role in order to meet productive-role expectations. Though not universally true, the adult male position in a great share of all societies appears to have the most clearly defined expectation for productive activity and for the direction of the other members of the family in carrying out their productive roles.

Another aspect of the production-and-distribution function relates to how productive roles are assigned *within* the family group. Family division of labor has been researched heavily in the United States. There exists a very strong age-sex element exhibited in the data, which show that certain kinds of tasks are clearly "man's work" or "woman's work." Although the equalitarian model tends to be highly valued in American society and, indeed, there is considerable evidence of some sharing of certain tasks, the sex designation of a great part of the family activity remains. A similar pattern is exhibited in the tasks assigned to the child positions. Male children tend to be expected to participate in the so-called masculine kinds of activity—lawn mowing, trash handling, and the like—whereas female children are assigned the domestic duties involved in food preparation, washing, ironing, and cleaning the house.[9] Non-American cultures also tend to have strong age-sex definitions of family division of labor.

Maintenance of Order. Two types of order maintenance are of concern to the developmental approach. There is internal regularity, which focuses on the way authority and decision-making roles are defined within the family. Some characteristics of order maintenance are seen in patterns of patriarchal, matriarchal, equalitarian, and democratic authority structures. For American society, although the dominant value orientation appears to be a democratic or equalitarian one, there is considerable evidence that the entire range of patterns is present in family behavior.[10] The strong tradition of patriarchy, probably rooted in Puritan patterns of the colonial era and in the period of westward expansion, remains a very real force in modern American families. Even very middle-class households, when pressed to indicate who should make the final decision on a given issue, tend to respond that the husband is the ultimate authority. Both upper- and lower-class families tend to select patriarchal authority as the standard value orientation more frequently than their middle-class counterparts. Developmental researchers try to emphasize how increasing amounts of authority for decision making may be incorporated into the role sequences of the child positions and how the relative weight of authority in family positions would shift over the family career.

The major sources of authority and decision-making patterns are found in the more informal folkways and mores of most societies. There are some formal legal aspects, such as laws which give American parents major control over the behavior of their children until they reach the age of majority. Children apparently hold some rights as indirectly indicated in the laws of inheritance. These laws often provide for the division of an estate in proportions which may leave the widow with as little as one-third to one-half of the family property where no will has been executed, even though the children may still be below the age of majority. In contrast, traditional Japanese law provides for all kinds of power for the patriarch and upon his death, for the passing of this power to the oldest son. Thus, distinctions between the amount of authority granted to male children versus female children and the division of authority between the husband-father position and the wife-mother position over the career of the family may be found in a variety of societal normative structures.

Another area of interest is what the society expects of the family for maintaining external order. It is clear that the more urbanized societies assign less responsibility to the family, placing the function in the hands of the government. Punishment of family members for violations of societal laws falls less to the family than to the courts in most of these systems. On the other hand, less urbanized societies (present and past) expect considerably more of the family in order maintenance. A classic example is the ancient Judaic society, in which the family system was the primary source of order in the society with the patriarch holding almost absolute power, even to the point of death, over family members. Traditional Japanese and Chinese societies exhibited a similar pattern of strong control by the family, as did our own early American culture. In each of these, there were clearly defined roles associated with authority which were assigned to familial positions and which changed as the occupant moved through his positional career in the family system. This power continued to be exercised over members long after they had reached adulthood, since they were still members of the extended family where power was located. The power was expressed in both formal legal and informal moral codes of conduct.

Maintenance of Meaning and Motivation.   This function has to do with the issues often treated under the heading Religion or Philosophy in Societal Life. The degree that the society assigns the task of providing the basic meaning in life to the family system is the basic focus of this section. In one sense, we may view the matter under consideration as discerning societies which are to a greater or lesser degree "familistic" in their orientation; that is, some societies or subcultures place great emphasis upon the family system as the primary source of meaning in life. Once again, the ancient Judaic, Japanese traditional and Chinese traditional societies are excellent examples. In these societies, a great share of all the role definitions for individuals have their source in their particular position in the family system; to be cut off from the family system is to be cut off from a place in the society in general. This means, that developmentally, throughout the life of the individual, a basic reference point for the various role sequences in his career is his family position. The legal systems of Judaic, Japanese, and Chinese societies all carry heavy family aspects in them.

In contrast, our own American society tends to see the family more as a center from which the *individual* operates. This orientation takes place during the socialization process, when basic values are taught to the child. These values do not tend to be familistic in their focus, but individualistic. The child is' taught to find meaning for himself as an independent actor', not necessarily in the context of the family system. The American legal system reflects this encouragement by how it treats the individual as an independent actor. Family law demonstrates this orientation both in treating marriage as a contract between two individuals and divorce as based on offenses of one individual party toward the other. In addition, a well developed religious institutional structure exists where a great deal of responsibility is placed by the society for interpreting the basic meaning of life. In American society, the legal separation of church and state has the effect of reserving to the church certain matters concerning individual meaning in life.

The consequence of these facts for the developmental approach is that nonfamilistic societies have few clearly defined family role sequences related to meaning and to motivation. In familistic societies, a great many role sequences as defined by the society are directly concerned with this function.

Summary.   The functional prerequisites just discussed show that the family affects the society in a number of ways, even in modern industrialized settings. Developmental theorists have been attempting to identify the way positional and familial careers are structured with respect to various functions. This work is not fully developed by any means. What I have tried to describe in this section are some of the possibilities which exist when the societal-institutional facet of the family is approached from the developmental vantage point. There remains the analysis of how the society affects the family during its career.

THE IMPACT OF THE SOCIETY ON THE FAMILY SYSTEM

A major impact of the society on the family system has already been treated in the discussion of the societal definitions of roles designed to carry out societal functions. No further elaboration of that aspect is necessary. In addition, there are the major relationships which exist between other systems of the society and the family. Although there are many such relationships which could be cited, the discussion to follow will be restricted to some of those intersystem relationships which influence the family over its entire career. This area is not one which has had a great deal of attention from developmental analysts. Therefore, as above, the discussion is intended to provide some indication of the possibilities which exist more than of the accomplishments attained.

Government and Family. One way that the governmental institution has a strong influence on the family system is through its legal authority. In societies with highly developed formal legal systems, there are many aspects of those systems which bear directly upon family structure and functioning. Matters dealing with meeting the qualifications for marriage, property rights, care of children, inheritance laws, divorce, and a host of others all influence the family at various points in its career.[11]

Another way the government affects the family system is through the various facilities which are developed and may take the form of direct or indirect services to family units. For example, the entire social welfare effort of many societies is directly intended to provide for family stability. In the early and middle years of the family career, this aim may take the form of financial aid for the welfare of children or the provision of food, clothing, and medical care through governmental financing. In the later years of the family career, programs for the aged such as social security and medical care for the aged are provided. Throughout the family's career, programs to provide housing or financing for housing may be made available. Other types of governmental service deal with the production and consumption activities of the family. In the United States, the Departments of Agriculture and of Commerce are particularly concerned with these activities.

More indirect in their effect, though no less real, are the many services associated with the provision of streets, sewers, street lights, parks, police protection, fire protection, postal service, and so on. To cite one illustration, the massive system of state and interstate highways has made possible the distribution of goods and services in a more efficient and less expensive manner than before. These same roadways have allowed families to move about more easily, which accounts in part for their increased spatial mobility, while at the same time the transportation system makes possible contact between various units of the extended family even though they are widely separated.

Of course, a major governmental impact on families is its taxing power. The U.S. federal income tax system uses the family as a major taxing unit, and the family has differing tax statuses at various points in its career. The provision for dependency exemptions and for deductions for items essential to family life, such as excessive medical expenses and interest payments on mortgages and consumer purchases, is a recognition of the impact of the taxing power on the family. Similarly, provisions for special tax considerations for the aged and disabled are also recognitions of the pervasive effect of this governmental authority.

Finally, there is the military function of the governmental system, which has a great effect on the family system. Families with children approaching the age of military eligibility are acutely conscious of this governmental relationship. During times of national emergency, the husband-father may be called to military service, providing a severe impact on the family system. Once again the military system recognizes its important relationship to the family structure through its provision for dependency allotments, medical care for dependents, certain kinds of exemptions from military service related to the dependency status of the eligible individual or exempting the "sole surviving son" from military service.

The developmental approach recognizes the intricate relationship which the family has with the government in numerous phases of its career and attempts to take these into account where they appear significant.

Education and Family.   I have already mentioned that many societies turn over a great share of the socialization function to agencies other than the family. Educational systems of various cultures are structured in many ways; but regardless of their unique characteristics, they are a major factor in the life of the families of the society. One of the more obvious facts concerning the educational system is that it removes members from the family setting for major periods of time and exposes the members to new ideas and to fresh ways of behaving which they may not have known before. The outcome is that these members may adopt ways of thinking and acting which may vary with those considered appropriate within their family. Although parents may value highly the educational experience, there most likely exists some ambivalence in their response to the effect that it has on their offspring. In a society like the United States, with its high value on education as the route to success, the educational system may produce some fascinating conflicts in the family's role relationships. The educational system is a major factor to deal with through a large portion of the family career as it envelopes much of the life space of the children and, reciprocally, as it involves the parents to a high degree.

The economic factors associated with education also have considerable importance. Even in societies with "free" public education, there exist some major economic burdens related to taking advantage of the educational opportunities provided. This fact becomes particularly true where college education is involved. Many families invest a large proportion of their economic resources in providing the formal education of their children, which cannot help but to have profound effects on other areas of their life together.

A third consequence of the educational system is the mobility in the social structure which it may provide. Children may enter new socioeconomic classes as a result of their experience in school. Their relationships with the parental family may be affected so that they find it more difficult than before to relate to their parents in the roles they had played as young persons or in the roles which their parents believe to be appropriate. College students are frequently heard to remark that they can no longer find a common ground with their parents because of their educational experience. As this process is extended into the kind of life style to which they and their parents may have aspired, the ability to relate to their mothers and fathers from their new positions becomes increasingly difficult.

The developmental consequences of the educational system are long term, carrying far beyond the schooling years in the effects that they have on the later positional careers of family members.

Economy and Family. In societies with a highly developed economic system, the family is involved with this structure in two distinct ways. As already noted, the family becomes the unit which supplies occupants for all manner of positions in the economic system. The occupational roles have a heavy influence on the way in which they are able to carry out their familial roles. From the period that children begin to enter this system as part-time workers through the span when they as adults play a full-time worker role, they are constantly having to balance off the demands of the work setting with those of the family. In a family with which I am familiar, a sixteen-year-old son took a summer job in a grocery super market. Almost immediately, a number of family activities were affected. Mealtimes were adjusted to fit with the work schedule of the son, even to the extent of modifying the work schedule of the father so that common meals might be taken occasionally. The family found itself taking weekend trips and other excursions without the son, whereas these had always been family group experiences before. Adjustments were made in the division of labor in the home, with the assigning of tasks formerly carried out by the oldest son to the other two children in the group. The new-found economic "independence" of the oldest son provided him the opportunity to be more active in extrafamily events which further separated him from the family. The relatively recent affluence of the oldest sibling also provided some pressure on the parents from the other two children as they recognized his ability to make expenditures beyond their ability. In these and a number of other ways, the oldest son's participation in the economy directly affected the family's role structure. Another effect was a kind of anticipatory socialization experience for all of the members of the family. They began to recognize the ultimate fact that he someday would be totally outside the household structure. More than once, the remark was made, "Well, I guess we'd better get used to the idea that he won't always be with us." The long-term consequences of participation in the economy were recognized, even though the complete break with the family would not occur for a number of years.

Another major impact of the economy, shown by the example above, is the place of the family as a major unit for the consumption of the goods and services produced. One need only analyze the advertising media to recognize the importance of the family unit in the functioning of the economy. Although much advertising is directed to individuals, a great share of it emphasizes the family unit as its target. Family themes are appealed to in sales techniques, and family values are frequently utilized as a means for making a given product appear attractive. A widely advertised cold salve carried out a campaign which emphasized the parent-child unity which could be achieved through the use of the preparation as opposed to the so-called impersonal quality of decongestant pills. Children were pictured as receiving the loving attention of their mothers as the salve was rubbed on their chests at bedtime. Similar approaches have been used to sell all kinds of products. Thus, the family becomes a major target of the business world, and marketing techniques are developed to appeal to families at various points in their careers. There exists a very real reciprocal relationship between these two societal systems, since it is true that the family finds its needs for certain kinds of products vary at differing points in its career.[12]

Religion and Family.   The long history of the Judaic-Christian traditions reflects a continuing close relationship with the family system. In early Judaism, of course, the family and religion were essentially coterminous with the patriarch of the family, who also had the role of religious elder. With the institutionalization of Judaism as a separate system complete with its own independent priests and other officials and later, with the coming of the rabbi, the emphasis on the family character of the religion was not lost. Thus, in modern Judaism the most important religious observances, such as Passover, are still family observances. Furthermore, depending to some extent on the particular branch of modern Judaism, the day-to-day life of the family is strongly affected by its religious tradition.

Similarly, though Christianity emphasized the faith of the individual believer to a much greater extent than Judaism, the Christian church has maintained a strong tie with the family unit. The New Testament frequently uses family themes and, indeed, the apostle Paul likens the relationship between husband and wife to the affinity between Jesus Christ and the church. American Christian churches have been family-unit oriented from the earliest days; and, significantly, one of the major problems of the contemporary Christian church has been dealing with the changing family structure. Urbanization and the individualization which has resulted has made it increasingly difficult for the church to meet the needs of the family as a unit. Older traditions, such as daily family devotions, have almost vanished in all but the most conservative families. With this disappearance has gone the participation of the family as a whole in many of the church activities. One major denomination has abandoned an approach to religious education which emphasized the joining of the parents in home study with their children because it became clear that the great share of families were not utilizing the materials made available for use in the home. This experience and others has caused the denomination to initiate an intensive study of its relationship to its member families along a number of dimensions of church programs including worship forms, educational activities, and various smaller group programs.

Catholicism, of course, has a long history of influence on the family. In terms of the basic issues of reproductive behavior, the validity of marriage, the naming of children, the grounds for divorce, and many other considerations, the Catholic Church has clear ecclesiastical legal positions. Indeed, the Sacraments of the Catholic Church are in a very real sense a series of rites of passage in the life cycle of the individual. Although they are not related directly to the family for the most part, they nevertheless have great significance in the life careers of family members and in the career of the family itself.

Religions outside the Judaic-Christian tradition vary in the extent of their involvement in the family. Some, such as Confucianism in classical China or Shintoism in Japan, are strongly family oriented and have a great impact on the family career. It is interesting that, in both China and Japan, Buddhism is also quite strong. This extremely philosophical and individualistic religion often is practiced at the same time as the worship of ancestors. Taoism in China is also considerably more philosophical and individualistic in focus than Judaism or than Christianity. Hinduism has some strong family influences due especially to its caste structure. Finally, Islam has very strong familistic principles. In fact, much of Muslim law deals with family matters.

There exist, of course, a great many sects and cults both within and outside Judaic-Christian traditions some of which have strong family influences and others which have little or no family implications. Thus, for example, the Old-Order Amish are strongly familistic, as is the Church of Jesus Christ of Latter-Day Saints (the Mormon Church). On the other hand, there appears to be very little familistic quality to Christian Science (Church of Christ, Scientist). Another cult, the Shakers, had difficulty because of a rather basic family attitude that it held—a strong prohibition against sexual intercourse. Lacking any biological means of reproduction, the Shakers ultimately were unable to recruit enough members from the outside society to flourish. Recent attempts at revitalization are not meeting with great success.

In summary, we can see that there are wide variations in the degree of relationship between religious systems and the family. Some of these structures have extremely strong effects on the family from its initiation to its dissolution. Others seem to have little or no impact at all.

Other Systems and the Family.   The four systems which we have examined appear to be the most frequently encountered in a broad range of societies. There are other structures, but they do not appear as universally. Thus, for example, the system of recreation in American society undoubtedly has a major influence on the family. Increasingly, as the time devoted to productive labor is decreased, nonwork time becomes an important element in the life of the American family. A whole new area of sociological concern is developing around this factor in modern industrialized societies. As a greater body of research and theoretical literature is developed, it may soon become possible to indicate in greater detail how this important area affects the family career.

Likewise, we may cite effects of the system of health maintenance on the family. Medicine, nutrition, and sanitation are all well developed areas in the more technologically evolved societies. Indeed, one of the most significant single factors in the changing demographic characteristics of the "developing societies" is health maintenance. The impact of this area on the birth-rate and the death-rate characteristics of a society are massive. Inevitably, the family system is caught up in the resulting changes.

I have mentioned these two additional areas only to indicate the addtional possibilities for analysis of the relationships which may exist between the family and the broad society. In any developmental examination, these factors play an important part in a satisfactory explanation of the family phenomena being studied.

EXPLANATIONS AVAILABLE IN THE SOCIETAL-INSTITUTIONAL FACET

The ultimate goal of theory is explanation. In concluding this section let us attempt a brief identification of the kinds of explanations of behavioral phenomena made possible by attention to the societal-institutional facet in the developmental approach.

A review of the kinds of issues identified in this section should show that the societal-institutional facet is quite helpful in explaining patterns of familial role structures that may be found in a given society; that is, analyses in this area are going to be most productive in showing the dimensions of the structural boundaries within which familial behavior takes place. It will be possible to point out the sources of basic intrafamilial relationships in the broadest terms as the kinds of positional and role structures appropriate for a given society are identified. Explanations for the types of transactive relations which are observed between the family group and other groups in the society, as well as between individual positional occupants in their nonfamilial positions, may also be discovered. In a very genuine way, the societal-institutional facet provides the explanation for the themes observed in familial behavior. On this basis, it is possible to explain the *variations* on the themes which may be observed. Certainly the identification of the basic boundaries for familial behavior is a significant foundation for the explanatory process; however, much will remain unexplained if the analysis is carried no further.

The Group-Interactional Facet

Each individual family group plays its own variations on the theme of the societal-institutional expectations for family life. These modifications may have their source in a particular tradition which one or the other of the marital partners brings from his or her parental family, in some combination of such customs, from some unique set of circumstances which develop and solidify into a normative pattern in the family's own history, or from some other internal or external source. Whatever the origin, it is clear that families do develop their own distinctive style of operation which, when viewed by the outsider, may seem deviant to a greater or lesser extent from the dominant family expectations. It is probably true that the degree of individual variation is related to the kind of societal setting in which the family is located, with the more traditional or authoritarian societies providing less opportunity for deviation than the less rigid ones. These distinctive styles are of considerable significance to the theorist who tries to account for a variety of outcomes in family behavior in his research. The degree of patterning or systematic development of these variations is also a theoretical problem of considerable importance.

In defining the family from a developmental point of view, we found that part of the definition dealing with the unique quality of the positional and role definitions in a given society actually represents a set of boundaries for the family. Now in turning to the group-interactional facet of development, we shall select only that part of the definition which treats the familial behavior incorporated within its boundaries. In other words, we shall analyze both the way in which the interrelated positions and roles are structured to result in the semiclosed system of actors and how this structure changes through time.

But already a roadblock looms, and we must clarify a difficult, though common, analytical distinction in sociological analysis. In sociological work, there exists a continuing tension between the *structure* and the *dynamic process* of social groups. They are inseparable; we cannot observe family behavior outside the family. Observed behavior provides the raw data from which the structure is abstracted, but this structure must already exist as a concept in the minds of the actors or no orderly behavior will take place. Therefore, we must oscillate back and forth between the structural concepts of norm, role, position, and so on and the role behaviors related to and partially explained by these structural concepts.

THE FAMILY AS A SEMICLOSED SYSTEM

The central core of the developmental theory lies in the view of the family as a *system*. Superficially, it seems easy enough to define a *system* as a set of parts structurally tied together, but then we have only examined the tip of the iceberg. Below the surface, we find that a system also involves a process of feedback, in which changes in one part of the system activate changes in another element or elements of the same system. Ben Franklin's old potbellied stove is a good example. Neither it nor our grandfather's original central heating furnaces with their heat ducts, registers, and dampers were heating systems in the technical sense. (And they were not very effective in the practical sense.) There were no automatic changes due to feedback except on the human level; when the temperature dropped, someone had to rush to the basement to refuel the furnace. A heating system was created only when thermostatic controls were linked to an automatic fueling device, such as a mechanical coal stoker. Then people could relax. When the temperature rose by a certain number of degrees, the stoker stopped. The system was interconnected so that changes in one part triggered changes in another part.

When we shift our attention back to the family, we see that it is more than just a complex set of related roles and positions. It is a *system,* and when changes occur in the roles of one position, it changes the roles of other positions. And to further refine the point, the position itself is a system to a certain degree, since a change in one role of a position often means that other roles of that position are also effected.

But why a *semiclosed* system? Most discussions of systems involve some notion of their boundaries. We have seen that the societal-institutional facet tends to identify the confines of the family. The definition of the family we have used states that the content of the positions and the roles assigned to the family are unique to the family structure. This assertion is a way of setting limits. But there also are notions of kinship in the family which do not apply to other systems of the society. These facts notwithstanding, all behavior which occurs within families is not motivated by other family behavior, and all behavior of family members is not directed toward other family members. The system of the family "opens and closes" to deal with other systems, to be influenced by them, and to allow certain actors to act in other structures both as family representatives and without any reference to their family status. Therefore, *some* change and *some* behavior in the family is related to outside factors, i.e., the system is semiclosed.

Another look at our definition of the family will illuminate a critical difference between the developmental approach and other sociological approaches. "The family is a semiclosed system of actors occupying interrelated positions defined by the society of which the family system is a part as unique to that system with respect to the role content of the positions and to ideas of kinship relatedness. The definitions of positional role content change over the history of the group." If our definition ended with the first sentence, it would be quite time bound. But, as we have seen, the great advantage of the developmental approach is that it does not limit itself to the narrow time dimension of the interactional perspective but instead tries to explain the dynamics of change in family behavior through family history. The historical perspective makes the developmental approach unique.

We use one set of descriptive terms with the static structure, namely, norm, role, position, and group, as well as another set for changing structure, that is, role sequence, positional career, and family career. In addition, the terms *role cluster* and *role complex* are utilized as bridging concepts;[13] they provide a method of reflecting the time element in the static structure. At any given time, a specified position will be composed of a set of roles which will differ from the roles in that position in another period. Using the idea of *role cluster* allows us to make this distinction. Similarly, the reciprocal roles of a given group will change at various times; so, we may use the term *role complex* here. (We are using *position* and *group* as generic terms, whereas we are using role cluster and role complex to specify a content for these general terms at a given point in time.) The concepts of *role behavior* and *sanction* provide us with a way of dealing with the behavioral expressions of the normative structure, and most essentially, with a way of accounting for the changes due to the interactional experience of the family members. These concepts are now our operational tools, and they will enable us to examine minutely the structural characteristics of the sytem they describe.

STRUCTURAL CONDITIONS

Structure initially is defined normatively by the cultural expectations of a given society. In a structure, there are a specified set of positions with given role content. These roles also are defined by a stated set of norms. In one sense, this structure is the ideal family group. Although this model varies from society to society, the perfect Indian family is much larger than the ideal American family and even may have subcultural variation, it is always possible to find both a core structural definition for the family and a number of conditions which provide for change in the family structure.

Excess and Deficit in Structure.   An amusing anecdote from some of the initial attempts of American technological experts to aid the Indian government's efforts to control the population growth, will illustrate this idea: The specialists used colorful before-and-after pictures as one of their methods. The before picture showed a large, badly undernourished family that wore tattered clothing, whereas the after picture showed a three-child family, two girls and a boy, who were considerably healthier and wore much better clothing. The caption read, "WHICH WOULD YOU CHOOSE?" Unexpectedly the widespread reaction was in favor of the larger family. Most people said of the smaller family, "Look how poor that man is. Only three children and only one boy at that!" According to Indian family values, this group was incomplete in structure. Not only were there too few children, but the highly valued male child was nearly absent. This father was a failure. The Indian family structure demanded not only a certain number of children but also a number of boys in the ideal family. If either expectation is unfilled, the family has a deficit structure.

A deficit structure raises a number of implications for familial behavior. Most obvious is the fact that certain roles may be shifted to other positions in the family organization, may be played by nonfamily members, or may not even be played at all. We all have heard comments made about households in which one or the other parent is absent: "She has to be both mother and father to the children." "His oldest daughter was like a mother to the other children." These statements simply describe the shifting of certain roles from one position to another; however, the consequence of this kind of shifting causes a change in the so-called normal characteristics of the related roles in the other family positions. Clearly, while an older daughter may act like a mother in a family, she cannot play the role exactly as a mother would play it. Neither her role relationships with her siblings nor with her father are the same as those of a real wife-mother. Her roles as a daughter-sister modify the wife-mother roles to a considerable extent. Her father cannot play the same type of reciprocal role that he played with his wife, nor can the children play their reciprocal roles as sons and daughters in the power manner when their mother is missing. Certain roles of the wife-mother, such as sex partner, cannot be shifted to some other position in the family, or, in this society, even to some outside member. Other roles, though moved to a new position, are modified as a result of the presence of other role expectations normally a part of this position. Occasionally, there exists some tension between the normal expectations of the roles constituting the original position and the new expectation of the shifted roles. For example, an outside male may attempt the father role for a set of fatherless children, but the roles of his own position as outside male may cause some problems which will undercut the adequacy of his function as a father-substitute. He cannot always be both father-disciplinarian and objective pal. Thus, a deficit structure modifies both the internal and external patterns of the family.

At the other extreme, there may be actors present in the family for which there normally are no designated positions. In the American nuclear family system, the presence of an aging parent or an unmarried sibling of the husband or wife disrupts the usual structure. Although the roles of grandparent and aunt or uncle form a part of the extended family sytem in American society, the neolocal characteristic of the system provides no place for such a position *within* the nuclear family. When such an actor is present, the position may be almost devoid of any role content. A grandmother, while allowed to play an affectional role toward her grandchildren, would be infringing on the role content of the wife-mother if she disciplined them or if she took over certain housekeeping duties. Thus, in this type of excess in structure, there is also a necessity for a reallocation of roles to the position of the extra member. No societal norms currently exist for dealing with the situation. Each family must solve its own problems.

There are other types of excessive structure which have various implications. A daughter's illegitimate child is one example. The moving in of a young married couple with either set of parents is another. The failure of a grown child to leave the parental home is another. In each case, the presence of additional actors, for whom no position is defined normatively, leads both to a reallocation of roles within the family structure and to a change in the interactional patterns of the group.

These excessive and deficit structures have longitudinal implications; that is, they dramatically change the role sequence and positional careers of all the family members, and sometimes their effects last long after the superfluity or the lack has disappeared.

Plurality Patterns.   The impact of size on group functioning is so obvious that often it is taken for granted. Everybody knows that large families are different from small ones. Years ago, Bossard[14] pointed out the mathematical quality of family size with the formula $X = Y^2 - Y/2$. In this formula X is the number of paired interpersonal relations, and Y is the number of persons. Thus, in a family of five people there are ten pairs of relationships, whereas in a family of eight, there are twenty-eight combinations. The formula only begins, however, to capture the complexity of size. There are also possibilities for coalitions of three persons, four persons, and so on up to the maximum size of a given family. Kephart[15] attempted to deal with this problem. According to his method, a family of five has a potentiality of from four to ninety different interpersonal relationships.

However, neither Bossard nor Kephart's formulas deal with a very important aspect of size as it relates to the family, which fluctuates in such a way that the additions and the subtractions from membership precipitate notable and far-reaching reorganizations to the role and positional structure of the group. This result brings up three additional structural factors: spacing patterns, sex patterns, and age patterns, all intimately tied to the plurality issue, all interrelated and conveying implications of their own.

Spacing Patterns.   A common American folksaying goes, "The first pregnancy takes any amount of time; all the rest take nine months." Although humorous, this pithy saying does contain a kernel of truth. The first child may be conceived premaritally, but after that the minimum biological limit is nine months. Exceptions to this fact are premature births, multiple births, and adoptions. Maximum theoretical spacing involves the birth of the first child early in the marriage, with the second child not appearing until shortly before the onset of the mother's menopause. This extreme pattern is not as common as other ones, and there exists an almost infinite set of possibilities. It depends on the number of children in the family, but they may be bunched close together early in the marriage; they may be clustered at some other time during the childbearing period; they may be distributed rather evenly over a portion of the childbearing period or over the entire span; they may be concentrated in two or more periods; they may be concentrated at one point with one or more children born during earlier or later isolated periods, and so on.

It is probably true that there are some societal and group normative expectations concerning child-spacing patterns, although I am aware of no studies which have dealt with normative issues and relatively few which have presented data on this subject.[16] In a study of three-generation families carried out in the late 1950s,[17] the spacing patterns of the grandparent and of the parent generations who were presumed to have completed their childbearing were tabulated. In a total of 854 individual births in 182 nuclear families which ranged from one to sixteen births per family, arrangements covering from less than one calendar year to over nine calendar years occurred. The model for grandparent families spanned 24–35 months, whereas the one for parent families extended over 12–23 months; however, the overall spread in the distribution of the data made it difficult to determine what normative patterns may have governed the child spacing of these two groups. Regardless of what normative patterns there may be, a given spacing pattern places certain important structural influences on the developing role structure of the family. As in the case of plurality patterns, the longitudinal impact of a given spacing configuration has its most profound effects on the interactional experience of the family.

Sex Patterns.   As might be expected, a family of all female children has a remarkably different set of role characteristics than one composed of all males. Various combinations of the two sexes provide for additionally interesting variations in role structure. Here again is an area where very little research has been done, although the sexual composition of a family is highly significant, as is the influence of sex on role expectations. To date, developmental research tends to ignore the element of sex, treating role development as if it were the same regardless of the gender of the child. This view is surely inadequate.

Age Patterns.   Role structure is further modified by the existent pattern of ages which prevail at any point in the family career. This factors is tied closely to the spacing, the size, and the birth order of the children. There is a considerable body of research on certain factors related to the birth order of the children, but it basically is oriented to the personality variables of the individuals or with variables essentially treated as an extension of a particular personality, such as the impact of ordinal position on occupational preference.[18] Most of the research done deals with the characteristics of the roles of the oldest and youngest children and ignores all the middle ones. Furthermore, the impact of the change in roles associated with a change in the relative position resulting from the birth of additional children remains relatively unexplored.

Another important factor concerning age is the relative gap between the ages of the parents and the ages of the children. Middle-aged parents with young children do not have the same role relationships as young parents with young children. Placed in longitudinal perspective, these differences continue throughout the family career; parents who delayed having children still have their offspring at home in their later years, whereas parents who had children soon after marriage find themselves childless at a relatively early age. In the late sixties and in the early seventies, the concern and the anguish that people felt about the generation gap may be explained partly by a systematic analysis of this kind of age differential between parents and children. This section concludes our highlighting of the key structural conditions necessary for an interactional analysis of a family; the fact that they must be seen in dynamic terms has significant implications for the whole set of role sequences and of role complexes which develope over the family career.

CHANGE IN THE FAMILY SYSTEM

During our discussion dealing with the important areas of change in the family structure over a period of time, we shall begin with the nature of change, shall move to a treatment of the interactional alteration arising from varying normative content of positions, and shall conclude by examining the modifications springing from societal sources. Remember we shall separate these three factors only for analytical purposes. In reality, they are not distinct entities.

The Nature of Change.   Western industrial cultures measure change in terms of chronological time; that is, we talk and think about periods— years, months, days, hours, and minutes. Close examination reveals that chronological divisions are imposed on the process of change. Frequently, these units break a process of change into artificial elements which are inadequate reflections of what is happening. Any college student knows that midterms occur in a spread which may begin in the third week of a ten-week term and which may not end until the eighth week; or, if they do take place at midterm, there is frequently an awkward division of the course material which has little to do with logical units of time. Similarly, the job hours of a day may impose an awkward break in the work process, with certain tasks remaining incomplete. On other days, all work may be done before quitting time, and the employee finds himself trying to appear busy when there is nothing to do. In other words, social processes and chronological time do not necessarily coincide.

This point is very important to understanding the developmental view of change and of time. The focus of the developmental analysis is on processual not on chronological time. Thus, a developmental period is identified by a distinctive processual character which may be separated from another span of a different character, regardless of the chronological time dimension. The chief criterion for a given developmental period is the identification of a distinctive role complex structure. Therefore, we speak of divisions in family development as the "Establishment Stage," the "Childbearing Stage," the "Childrearing Stage," the "Launching Stage," the "Postparental Stage," and so on. These periods are identified not because they have the same chronological length nor because they occur during the same chronological era in all families, but because they have a distinctive role structure which separates them from other periods in the family career. Thus, they are measured in processual time.

It is important to understand qualitatively the process of change as well as the nature of the alteration of time. Some of the variations in social structure are precipitious, unanticipated, and almost revolutionary in essence. Others occur in a much slower evolutionary manner. The former type of change has been termed *disjunctive,* since it involves a radical and sudden reordering of the role structure of the system. The latter type of change may be seen as *continuous*, including considerably less disruption of the sytem and allowing for a somewhat more leisurely adjustment of the structure.

There are certain specific problems in dealing analytically with these two kinds of change. At first glance, it may appear relatively easy to distinguish between them. When we begin to think of examples of disjunctive changes, however, it becomes clear that we must deal with a more or less disjunctive quality. Some examples may be marriage, the birth of a child, the departure of a member, the death of a member, or the sudden disability of a member. On close examination, it becomes possible to see a continuous quality to most of these events. The courtship process is in actuality a period during which a couple gradually takes on marital roles. In a very real sense, the marriage ceremony symbolizes what has already occurred to a great extent—the couple already has taken on the marital roles. The situation is analogous to academic commencement exercises. The granting of a diploma or of a degree represents what a person has *become* over a period of time. He does not reach the platform as an uneducated person and does not suddenly become educated when he is handed his diploma. Neither do the great share of couples approach the marriage ceremony in our society totally devoid of marital roles and, upon pronouncement of the marital vows, suddenly incorporate these combinations of norms into their role complex. The couples have been in the process of taking them on for some time. Of course, it is true that they continue to modify and to adjust the normative content of these roles during the postceremony. This practice occurs, however, throughout their marital history, not simply during the "period of adjustment." Similarly, birth is preceded by pregnancy, which carries with it the beginning of a readjustment of roles anticipating the addition of the new member; departures of members are often anticipated and role relationships subtly adjusted; even death is frequently anticipated.

Probably there are some relatively pure cases of disjunctive change. It is also most likely, however, that a great many of the changes which appear disjunctive at first contain a clear, continuous element. Furthermore, some changes, such as the entry into adolescence, often are thought of as disjunctive but in actuality are continuous in nature. Artificial "benchmarks" expressed by a given chronological age may be established in a given culture. They, however, frequently are inadequate indicators of the actual role situation. But this fact does not mean that they are insignificant. Indeed, they may serve to explain a given kind of behavioral phenomenon in which certain role expectations are focused on an actor and in which he is unable or is unwilling to incorporate the new roles into his position. Some of the problems of American society associated with adolescence, reaching adulthood, and retirement may be explained in these terms.

Yet another kind of difficulty occurs that has to do with how the analyst can determine when enough change in a role structure has taken place so that he is justified in stating that a "new" role structure exists. If the analyst compares the role structure which exists between parents and a child of age seven and the one which exists between these same parents and their child at age eleven, he can see some clear differences in the two systems. But *when*, that is, at what point in the process, is he justified in stating that an analytically genuine change has taken place in periods of a considerably shorter length? In American society, there are no rites of passage during this time that mark a dramatic shift in role expectations, but they do occur. Clearly, it is theoretically unjustified to treat the role complexes at the two periods as identical, but it is also difficult to ascertain empirically when the shifts take place. This fact is generally the case with continuous change situations.[19]

Changing Normative Content of Positions. Within the interactional facet of analysis, there are four key sources for the change in normative content of positions over time. The first source is a variation in structure. When this change occurs, adjustments in the normative content of positions follow. Normative change is implied where there exists an excess or deficit in structure, in plurality pattern changes, in spacing patterns, in sex patterns, and in age patterns. It would be redundant to carry our discussion of these effects any further than we have above.

The second source of change, the shifting importance of roles, can be explained best by Bates'[20] article on the concepts of position, role, and status. He points out that in each position there are both dominant and recessive roles, which also can be called obligatory-discretionary or manifest-latent roles. Each variation provides us with the conceptual equipment to account for various kinds of change in the interactional patterns of the family. Throughout the family career, roles change. Dominant ones become recessive, and recessive ones become dominant. The role of the wife is certainly dominant at the beginning of the marriage. With the onset of children, however, it must compete with the role of mother, and, thus, the role of wife becomes recessive. The same result occurs when the husband becomes a father. At a later point, these parental roles become less dominant as the children become more independent of their parents. This example also provides us with an excellent case if a latent role, the parental one, becoming manifest, and when the children leave home, it returns to a relatively latent state. Both the parent and the spouse roles are obligatory, but other ones are discretionary. For example, the wife may be a wage-earner. In early marriage, before the children arrive, she may work in order to obtain material goods or to build up some savings. Then, too, when the children are older, she may return to work. Nothing in the societal-institutional norms, however, defines such a role as obligatory, unless the husband should die or the couple should separate. Then the role of wage earner may become obligatory. Although the family changes in its career, it is possible to analyze the resulting variations in roles from the perspective of the dominant-recessive, latent-manifest, and obligatory-discretionary natures they possess, and this kind of approach becomes a powerful tool in examining the changes.

The third source, involving the concept of *developmental task* has been closely associated with the type of examination mentioned above and has been a major focus of developmental material almost from the beginning. Robert J. Havighurst defines developmental task in the following way:

> A developmental task is a task which arises at or about a certain period in the life of an individual, the successful achievement of which leads to his happiness and to success with later tasks, while failure leads to unhappiness in the individual, disapproval by the society, and difficulty with later tasks.[21]

Later work in developmental theory seems to call for a modification of Havighurst's definition. In an early analysis, I concluded that in reality the developmental task phenomenon is only a special case of the incorporation of a given role into the role cluster of a position at some given point in the role sequence of a positional career. Viewed another way, it is the process of making manifest one of the latent roles of a position. I therefore redefine the developmental task phenomenon as follows:

> A developmental task is a set of norms (role expectations) arising at a particular point in the career of a position in a social system, which, if incorporated by the occupant of the position as a role or part of a role cluster, brings about integration and temporary equilibrium in the system with regard to a role complex or set of role complexes; failure to incorporate the norms leads to lack of integration, application of additional normative pressures in the form of sanctions, and difficulty in incorporating later norms into the role cluster of the position.[22]

Thus, one explanation for a certain kind of interactive process in the family may be associated with the actors in the system imposing normative pressures on one of the members to take on a certain role at a particular point in his positional career. These influences usually are associated with age and sex norms which provide the broad pattern of the positional career in the system. Thus, when infants reach a certain age in a given society, normative pressures are brought to bear with respect to the basic drives of food intake and elimination. Children are weaned and are switched to culturally appropriate foods. Children are "toilet-trained" in a certain manner. Later they are the focus of normative pressures to take on particular roles which may be associated with the division of labor in the family or with some set of roles which they may be expected to play in the larger society. As the developmental task concept notes, this process has a cumulative character. If the role is incorporated inadequately, it has implications both for the role complexes in which the actor is involved and for the role sequence of his own career. The process we have been describing here is, of course, socialization within the family. Broom and Selznick[23] divide socialization into four elements: (1) concern with the basic physical and emotional disciplines—eating, elimination, control of emotions, sexual drives, sleep, and so on; (2) imparting the culturally accepted aspirations; (3) acquisitions of the necessary cultural skills; and (4) learning the appropriate social roles. Elements of this process involve the kind of focused normative pressure at a given point in the positional career identified in the developmental task concept. The first and third elements probably are most easily identifiable in this respect. The second and fourth elements probably are associated with a more continuous kind of role development, and the kind of heightened normative pressure points involved in developmental tasks is not observed readily.

There is a danger in associating developmental tasks only with the child positions in the family system, for socialization clearly is a life-long process, and developmental tasks can be identified in the adult positions. Developmental tasks, however, are less likely to be so dramatically obvious as in the concentrated socialization experience of the child positions. Certain aspects of the husband-father position, particularly those associated with his role of supporting the family, have strong developmental task implications as his occupational career unfolds. Similarly, the wife-mother roles, such as those identified with the shift from the primary focus on mothering as the children leave the nuclear family, have equally strong developmental task associations. The movement into the postparental period, the movement into retirement, and similar major shifts in the role clusters of the adult positions are possible points of emphasis of a developmental task type.

Finally, there is another aspect of the developmental task that deals with certain points in the family career when major role shifts involve the entire family role complex. Here, instead of stressing one role in the system, the entire organization constitutes the unit of emphasis. Duvall states: "Family developmental tasks are those growth responsibilities that must be accomplished by a family at a given stage of development in a way that will satisfy its (1) biological requirements. (2) cultural imperatives, and (3) personal aspirations and values, if the family is to continue to grow as a unit."[24] Although these major role adjustments may be precipitated by the developmental state of one position in the system, their impact is so widespread that it involves a radical reorganization of the role structure of the system. Obviously, such a radical role change has dramatic effects on the interactional patterns of the family. These radical role changes can explain the phenomenon of a total reorientation of a family in their interactional experience, which often is observed in research but is difficult to explain.

The fourth major source of change in the normative content of positions is related to the day-to-day interactional experiences of the family. In contrast to the kinds of normative shifts tied to particular points in the career of a position or linked to the family as a total system, these normative changes occur out of a given interactional experience. The experiences may be idiosyncratic to a specified family. They may be treated in a general fashion, however, by noting that in all social systems certain normative structures are established as a result of the interactional history of each system. A certain circumstance or event may arise in the family experience in which the normative structure that prevails proves inadequate. The sociological term to identify such a situation is *anomie*—normlessness. There are several types of anomie: (1) a situation in which there are no norms to guide the actors in their behavior; (2) a situation in which the norms are ambiguous so that it is unclear what behavior is called for; (3) a situation in which there are conflicting sets of norms requiring mutually exclusive kinds of behaviors; and (4) a situation in which more than one set of appropriate norms are acceptable. Thus, in any of these types of circumstances, a series of interactions must take place which will serve to define the norms for the roles of the actors. Such a series of interactions may then serve as a precedent which will guide future behaviors in similar situations and, thus, will incorporate a new role into one or more role clusters in the system.

A crisis provides a conspicuous example of anomie. (We must be cautious not to think that anomic situations occur only in obvious interactional experiences.) If a crisis arises which the family has never faced before and for which there seem to exist no clearly defined roles, modifications are made in the role expectations of one or more positions in the family. Thus, the family equips itself to meet the situation when it arises again. Similarly, but often at a less emotionally charged level, a certain set of expectations involving two or more reciprocal roles may prove inadequate in meeting the kinds of goals which those role definitions were intended to serve. As a result, subtle or more obvious redefinitions of the roles will take place to deal more satisfactorily with the situation in the future interactional experience. Such role shifts may involve reassigning certain areas of responsibility in the division of the labor of the family system or in the decision-making process. The areas of responsibility may include such mundane matters as who takes out the trash or some major issues such as who allocates the money. Regardless of the sphere to which they refer, the essential point is that these normative changes arise from the interactional experience itself, which is how a relatively unique family subculture is built and is modified over the family career. Old agreements concerning role relationships are abandoned, and new ones are reached in order to carry out more satisfactorily the day-to-day operations of the system.

We have identified the four major areas of changing normative content of positions: the structural changes of the family system, the manifest-dominant-obligatory nature of certain roles, the developmental state of a position or of the total family system, the interactional experience of the actors in the system. We turn now to another area of potential variation in the normative structure of the family—societal change.

Societal Change as a Source of Familial Change. We already have pointed to the way societal norms set boundaries for family interaction. One obvious source for an explanation of change in family interaction is a variation in the character of the boundaries, for example, as a result of the direct and sometimes dramatic effects of historical changes. Our goal here is not to detail the kinds of modification that have occurred in a particular society but simply is to sensitize ourselves to the fact that one explanation for the change in internal dynamics of families is historical in its nature.

Thus, both the long-term historical changes involving industrialization, urbanization, and the like, and the short-term historical events involving wars, economic depressions or inflations, disasters, and so forth, have an important impact on interactional patterns and the variations which may occur. As we noted in our discussion of the societal-institutional facet, these matters are not central to the developmental process per se, but they may so change the thematic content of the family so as to divert the developmental process in a new direction which can be explained in no other way.

EXPLANATIONS AVAILABLE IN THE GROUP-INTERACTIONAL FACET

Although the societal-institutional facet depends on an analysis of the basic characteristics of the society, an analysis of the family group provides the explanation of behavior in the group-interactional facet.

First, the fact that the family is not a closed system explains some familial behavior. Roles and positions occupied by family members in other social systems affect the conduct of these same members in their household positions.

The second point is derived from the various aspects of the structural characteristics of the family. Some proportion of the variance in behavior can be accounted for by analyzing families according to common sets of structural characteristics.

The third point is derived from the process of change which is an inherent characteristic of the family system. These changes can be disjunctive or continuous. One explanation of a particular kind of interactional phenomenon is related to the quality of change. Another explanation is related to one of four major kinds of change: (1) those associated with structural conditions; (2) those associated with the dominant-recessive, manifest-latent, and/or obligatory-discretionary character of roles; (3) those associated with changes arising at a critical period in a family, which we called developmental tasks; and finally, (4) those arising from the interactional experience of the family.

The fourth point providing the explanation for interactive characteristics of families is related to long-term societal change and to particular short-term historical events which change the thematic quality of family roles.

The Individual-Psychological Facet

Students in the behavioral sciences often despair of ever making any scientific generalizations because of the unique quality of the individual human personality. This quality is certainly a powerful influence on the functioning of most groups. Certain combinations of personalities found within a group probably determine to a considerable degree the nature of group interaction. It also must be noted that the group provides considerable influence on the development of individual personality, so that we see a complex process involving the group and the individual. Ignoring either group or individual influence reduces the explanatory power possible. Sociologists frequently have been guilty of neglecting individual influences. Psychologists often fail to take account of group effects. This fact is one major reason for the rise of interest in the social-psychological perspective in the behavioral sciences. Indeed, the developmental approach is explicitly social-psychological, since it includes individual, as well as group, concepts in its framework.

In turning attention to the individual-psychological facet of analysis of family careers, we become most acutely aware of the incomplete character of the developmental theory. Although some family development theorists have identified this aspect as a necessary element in the overall theory, they have paid very little concentrated attention to creating the necessary conceptual scheme to reflect processes occurring at this level. The essential bridging concepts which would tie this facet to the other two also have received little effort. There are several interlocking reasons for this neglect: The great share of theorists have their primary expertise and interest in the sociological aspects of the developmental approach. Consequently, they have neither the necessary scholarly background nor the interest in the kinds of problems typically associated with individual-psychological matters.* Those theorists who have the necessary professional background have tended to be more concerned with the strictly individual developmental problems than with the group context of these issues.

The goals of this section, then, are considerably more limited than the objectives of the two immediately preceding divisions. All that will be attempted is an identification of the kinds of problems which the individual-psychological facet must handle, some possible concepts to deal with these difficulties, and some of the kinds of explanations which may result from an adequate analysis of the individual-psychological facet.

In their article on family conceptual frameworks, Hill and Hansen state

---

*I fully recognize my limitations in this respect and take full responsibility for the inadequacies in the treatment of this area which others with greater expertise are sure to find. In my opinion, however, one way to stimulate work in a field is to present it in its incomplete state so that others may see what needs to be done.

five assumptions of the developmental approach. Three of these assumptions are relevant here:

1. The human is actor as well as reactor.
2. Individual and group development is best seen as dependent upon stimulation by a social milieu as well as on inherent (developed) capacities.
3. The individual in a social setting is the basic autonomous unit. [25]

Perhaps the implications of these three assumptions may be stated best as follows: The developmental theory does not view human behavior as a simple and automatic stimulus-response chain but posits between stimulus and response an intervening step in which characteristics of the individual come into play to process the stimuli as well as to add new elements resulting in a unique response. In addition, the individual himself may be the source of new stimuli to which others respond in the same manner. [26]

THE INDIVIDUAL AS ACTOR—IMPACT OF THE INDIVIDUAL ON THE FAMILY

Earlier we distinguished between the concept of *role*, the group expectations for behavior, *and role behavior*, the way a given actor carries out the expectations. The disparity between the expectations for behavior and the actual behavior of the individual is one reason why a simple stimulus response model is inadequate to explain human conduct. We shall look for these explanations in the characteristics of the individual.

Each individual is born with a unique genetic makeup. The implications of this fact are far-reaching. It is apparent that no two individual human beings are exactly alike in their physical or psychological composition. Yet, it is equally apparent that there exist many physical and psychological similarities among all humans. For purposes of illustration, we know that the ability to see is generally alike in all human beings, though we also know that it has a range, with some people having better sight than others. On a purely physical level, then, the ability to sense light stimuli emitted from a book page is essentially similar among individuals, though there is a scope of ability around this likeness.

Returning to the family setting and to the occupant of a position in the family, we already have seen that each occupant has certain roles assigned to his position. When persons holding reciprocal roles pressure an individual to behave in a particular way, we observe a particular kind of role behavior. Rarely is this conduct precisely that prescribed by the role. It may be very close, but it may also be a wide variance. There are three possible reasons for this variation between the expected and the actual behavior: First, the actor may not have grasped fully what was expected of him. Second, although he may have comprehended what was expected, he may have been unable to respond in the anticipated way. Third, having understood what was expected, he may not have desired to respond in the anticipated way.

Assuming adequate communication of clearly defined normative expectations, if the actor fails to understand them, he is unlikely to respond in a satisfactory manner. His lack of comprehension may result from his inability to receive adequately the full range of stimuli addressed to him, from his inability to process these stimuli in sufficient manner, or from his reaching a set of conclusions concerning the stimuli which bring a behavioral response other than the one anticipated. In this latter instance, it is apparent that an element of *anomie* is present, since it is assumed that the stimuli have been received and have been processed adequately; but it is still possible to come to more than one conclusion concerning the appropriate behavioral response. Summarizing this first source of deviation between role and role behavior accounted for by characteristics of the actor, we see that they result either from inadequate reception, processing, or interpretation of the expectations by the actor. Concepts developed for the individual-psychological analysis should be able to take account of these various types of "slippage" in the interactive process.

Turning to the second situation, we shall assume that the expectations have been fully grasped but that the actor is unable to respond appropriately. Inability to act in the anticipated manner may result from the failure of the actor to have incorporated the necessary repertoire of behavioral skills into his role, that is, from the lack of success in achieving certain prerequisite developmental tasks or from some basic lack of physical or psychological ability. In the first case, we can assume that the potential ability is present to behave in the appropriate manner but that the individual has not yet developed the suitable skills for the conduct. There are situations in which expectations may be placed on an individual before he has developed physically and/or mentally to a point of being able to accomplish a particular act, for example, asking for a level of hand-eye coordination which is beyond his developmental level. In the second situation, we assume that the individual simply is incapable of behaving in the expected manner due to some inadequate physical and/or psychological equipment. These are elements of mental or physical retardation or disability which affect the capacity to respond appropriately. In either circumstances, the role behavior deviates somewhat from the role expectation.

In the third situation, we posit a mental process in which the role occupant chooses to act in a manner other than what he concludes is expected of him. There may be various explanations for this decision. Among them may be a desire on the part of the actor to avoid an experience which he has found unsatisfactory in previous circumstances. He may have responded appropriately at some time and may have found that the consequences were displeasing to him. Thus, he fails to respond as expected since he wishes to avoid the same distasteful situation. Or, perhaps, although he has no particular aversion to the kind of behavior expected of him, he envisions an alternative which he anticipates will be even more satisfactory. Another possibility may be that, while recognizing that a particular kind of behavior is called for, he also understands that it will result in certain responses from those in reciprocal roles which he does not want. Therefore, he may react in some other way that gains a response which is more satisfactory to him. The case of deviation between role expectations and role behavior calls attention to the social time element in human interactions. In responding to expectations, actors take into account both past interactive experience and anticipations of future experiences.

Three types of situations which may account for deviations between role and role behavior have been identified. It is improbable that they ordinarily occur in their pure form. It is likely in the day-to-day interactive process that these situations will occur in combination with one another. We can anticipate situations in which inadequate reception and/or processing are combined with unwillingness and/or inability to respond in the manner which the actor concludes is expected. The analytical problem is a very complex one. It is amazing that we find as much correlation between role and role behavior in daily experience as we do, given the many possibilities for variation!

What are the consequences for the family of the individual as autonomous actor in the system? The behavior of a role occupant may be the source for initiating new role expectations, for modifying existing ones, or for eradicating them all together. If a given actor consistently fails to play his role as defined by those in the reciprocal roles, the possibilities for response by the reciprocal role occupants are limited to four: (1) to continue to persist in placing the same expectations on the actor, even though he does not conform to them; (2) to modify the expectations in the hope of gaining conformity; (3) to cease to place the expectations on the actor; or (4) to adopt a set of expectations that the role occupant has indicated are desirable to him. Any of these reactions represents a modification of the normative structure of the system.

Further complicating the situation is that those in the reciprocal roles may misinterpret the actions of the role occupant. They may assume that he is unable to respond when, in fact, he has not understood their expectations or has been unwilling to respond. Any of the other combinations of misunderstanding also may occur. The character of the response to the actions of the role occupant will be quite different depending on how the meaning of his actions is interpreted.

What has been analyzed is not a matter of the role occupant as *reactor*. Instead, what has been highlighted is the fact that the actor in a role does not simply react but that he introduces new elements into the situation as a result of his own genetic characteristics and social experience. A child who says to his parents, verbally or behaviorally in some nonverbal fashion, "I can't," or "I don't want to," or "I don't understand," or "I'd rather do this," is not *reacting*, but *acting*. The child has introduced a new element into the system which instigates a response on the part of the parents. Although the normative expectations placed on the child by the parents has triggered the sequence of events, the youngster's behavior is not a simple reaction but would be only if a fully conforming response took place. The actor plays a most important part in the role sequences of the reciprocal roles as well as of his own role, and he plays a most imporant part in the family career as an entire system. The phenomenon of central interest is not the unique case of a failure of role behavior to conform to expectations. This topic is of interest when the failure leads to a modification of expectations and a new direction in the role sequences and positional careers of the family.

What makes these processes *developmental?* First, they are more likely to occur at points in the positional career where societal or group norms place new role expectations on the occupants of positions. An actor is more likely to introduce his own particular characteristics into a *new* or into a *revised* situation than into one that has been in force for some time. Although he may certainly change his behavior with respect to a relatively stable role, there is greater opportunity to act autonomously when new role expectations are placed upon him. New role expectations have not been set into a habit pattern in which all parties act in a more uncritical manner. In the very situations where the occupants of reciprocal roles are most conscious of the actor, the actor is also most conscious of the expectations being placed upon him.

These new role expectations often occur in a family career context which already may be encountering other modifications, either in the roles of the other family members or in a general alteration of the system. For example, while a child in his late teens is dealing with increasing independence in his role behavior the following may be happening: The wife-mother actor may be facing playing the roles of middle age; the husband-father may be trying to adjust to leveling off his career aspirations; and a younger sibling may be facing the first experiences of adolescence. If one or more of these actors tends to reject or attempts to modify the expectations placed upon him by the other actors in the system, this behavior only adds to the complexity of an already changing situation.

The individual-psychological facet does not isolate the processes associated with an individual actor in a family position. Rather, the analysis is carried out in relation to the processes occurring in other sectors of the system. It is, therefore, a *social* psychological, not an individual psychological, approach.

THE INDIVIDUAL AS REACTOR—IMPACT OF THE FAMILY ON THE INDIVIDUAL

The other side of the individual-psychological coin turns attention back to the family group. As opposed to the previous discussion in which the concern was with group characteristics and how they affected the group career, the attention focuses now on group characteristics as they affect the positional career. Many of the same elements are relevant here. The factors of excess or deficit in structure, plurality patterns, spacing patterns, sex distribution, age distribution, ordinal position, the various change elements associated with the system, and those changes associated with the society all call for reactions from the actors in the various family positions. There are, however, some additional factors. The features to be discussed arise out of widely observed, though not universal, characteristics of the interactive and normative styles of individual family systems.

Families sometimes assign to particular positions in the family special definitions which have little association with the characteristics of the actor or with the position itself. The occupant of the oldest-son position, for example, may be designated as the one to carry on the family business, not because the occupant has demonstrated any particular ability or any interest in this goal but because the oldest son is considered the appropriate one to head the organization. As a consequence of this general expectation a great many specific role expectations evolve. The response of the role occupant, both active and reactive, may have unique character. In his interactive experience, he does not have a repertoire of role models related to these particular anticipations. His peers may be experiencing some of the same normative pressures related to common roles played by individuals of his particular age and sex. But in this particular role, he has little guidance other than the expectations and behavioral responses of those in his family system; so, the family becomes the dominant influence on the individual.

More closely associated with the actual or assumed characteristics of an actor role occupant are a set of processes which might be best termed *stereotyping*. Labeling a particular actor "the brain of the family," "the queen," "the lazy one," "the athletic one," "the stupid one," or "the scatter-brained one" affects the role definitions of that actor. These assessments may be accurate or inaccurate, but the consequences are real. They demand response from the actor. A body of evidence has been building which indicates, for example, that mentally retarded children who have role expectations placed upon them more applicable to mentally normal children, tend to peform at a level above the one usually observed in their previous behavior. This finding has led some observers to conclude that the mentally retarded child may be responding to role expectations placed upon him by occupants of reciprocal roles who are aware of his slowness. There are also studies which have shown that erroneous information about student's intelligence given to teachers tends to result in the student's performing at the level of expectation set by the incorrect knowledge. One conclusion to be drawn from such findings is that these role expectations have elicited role behavior at variance with the true ability of the child. An alternative explanation is that the teacher's *evaluation* of the performance, rather than the performance itself, has been influenced by the erroneous information. The basic point is that stereotyping demands a response from the actor.

Another impact of the family on the individual results from special patterns of relationship which may develop between one or more actors in the system. There is nothing, generally, in the normative structure of the family which dictates these specific alliances. An exception, perhaps, is the husband-and-wife relationship. Nevertheless, cliques of various types may occur, or a certain actor may become an isolate. Being a member of a particular intrafamilial clique or being an isolate may have a major effect on a given actor.

There are various phenomena with a similar quality which may be called the family's *interactive style*. Jacobsen,[27] in his analysis of family occupational socialization, identified certain "modes of socialization" of families. He noted that some households emphasized verbal approaches with their children; others referred them to sources where information might be gained; whereas still others emphasized the necessity for their children to gain experience. Some families used more than one mode and, indeed, some used all modes. There were certain differing styles typically utilized by families in this socialization area. It seems safe to assume that these approaches also were utilized in other kinds of socialization and that, in general, families develop typical interactive styles associated with certain types of activities.

Other interactive styles may involve focusing by the family on certain principles or values—philosophical, religious, political, economic, or the like. Hill[28] observed that families seemed to follow certain "policies" in their economic decision making. We all know families who hold strong moral or religious values which seem to dominate much of their household life. Or we know families who place a high premium on education, social service, or economic wealth. Such orientations have a major influence on the individual actors and on the way they play the various roles in their positions.

Another family characteristic is the type of psychological or emotional climate which prevails. Such qualities as warmth, coldness, affection, hostility, optimism, pessimism, fatalism, happiness, sadness, acceptance, rejection, and similar attitudes may pervade the general approach to life taken in a family.

Finally, there are a set of characteristics which may be called *facilitating mechanisms*.[29] The presence of such material things as books, tools, magazines, or the like may aid an actor in playing a particular role. The willingness to help or to give instructions or to talk about experiences or events which have occurred—or the lack of such willingness—can have a similar impact.

In summary, we have identified general effects a family may have on its individual actors: the special definitions of role occupants, the stereotyping of role occupants, the formation of cliques or isolates, the peculiar interactive styles, the particular psychological or emotional climate, and the presence of various facilitating mechanisms.

SOME CONCEPTS FOR
INDIVIDUAL-PSYCHOLOGICAL ANALYSIS

In determining the concepts needed to carry out family developmental analysis at the individual-psychological level, what criteria should such concepts meet? Our discussion above provides a good guide for developing these criteria.

First, we need concepts to capture the basic psychological processes associated with the apprehension and processing of stimuli from other actors in the system and from the general social environment. Second, we need concepts which handle the physical and psychological capacities to act and to react as a result of the reception and the processing of these stimuli. Third, we must bridge the gap between the individual-psychological facet and the other two facets. Fourth, we must use terms which handle the way actions and reactions of the individual actor are converted into part of the normative structure of the system. Fifth, we should have concepts available to capture the kinds of family characteristics pertinent in their impact on the individual actor. Sixth, and the final requirement, we should choose only concepts that have longitudinal process dimensions.

Sample concepts associated with the reception and processing of stimuli would include *perception* and *cognition*. Perception involves receiving or becoming aware of stimuli taken in through the senses of sight, hearing, taste, and touch. Cognition is the thinking and knowing process with respect to stimuli received from outside and stimuli which arise from within the actor. During cognition the actor places the stimuli into some sort of structure of meaning and identifies possible behavioral alternatives.

To deal with the response to the perceptual and cognitive processes, the term *ability* denotes both the physical and psychological capacities for behaving in a given manner. Two concepts to explain some of the behavior observed are *motivation* and *emotion*. Motivation denotes the elements which arouse or direct a given behavioral response, perhaps as the result of drives or needs of a physiological, psychological, or social origin. Emotion designates a quality of feeling or an affect concerning current perceptions and cognitions as well as toward contemplated behavior. Finally, to signify the autonomous character of certain types of behavior, it may be useful to introduce the idea of *volition*.

There are other classical psychological and social-psychological concepts which also need to be added to the ones suggested. Ideas such as definitions of the situation, values, attitudes, self-concept, internalization, and identification come readily to mind. Beyond pointing out the relevant concepts, there is the more demanding task of determining how they are related to one another. This latter activity is the process of constructing a conceptual framework. Such a foundation should reflect empirical reality as far as possible. To list only a set of possible concepts which may be applied falls considerably short of developing a theoretical base for analysis.

Concepts needed to bridge the gap between the societal-institutional, the group-interactional, and the individual-psychological facets may include a concept such as *consensus* to identify the process by which an individual behavior response becomes accepted as normative by the group. Other ideas must deal with such matters as the relative power or influence a given actor may have in achieving recognition for his particular approach to playing a role. Some of the work in social psychology dealing with exchange theory and balance theory will be valuable in determining other appropriate concepts.[30]

In developing concepts to deal with the group characteristics affecting the individual actor, such ideas as *idiosyncratic role, stereotyping,* and *coalition* appear useful. Perhaps *modes of interaction,* to generalize Jacobsen's term, may cover processes involving themes, policies, or orientations which characterize particular families. Similarly, the label *emotional climate* may be applied to the other qualitative style of interaction. The term *facilitating mechanism* seems useful to designate the kinds of aids available to individual actors in their roles in a given family setting.

A word of caution is in order at this point. What we have just done may be a bit deceptive. The underlined terms may or may not be authentic concepts. If each word or group of words refers to clearly identifiable phenomena which possess the same qualities, then it probably is valid; however, it may be only a label grouping together a conglomeration of phenomena which do not share the same characteristics and, consequently, which do not carry the same significance in the analysis of behavior. Determining what is actually the case forms another part of the exacting work of constructing conceptual frameworks for a theoretical system.

EXPLANATIONS AVAILABLE IN THE INDIVIDUAL-PSYCHOLOGICAL FACET

The explanatory focus of the individual-psychological facet centers on the *role-role-behavior* comparison. If individual actors were observed to conduct themselves in exact correspondence with the societal-institutional and group-interactional normative structure, then no explanatory problem would exist. Interpretations of their divergence are sought in an analysis of the characteristics of the individual actor and of his unique experience in the family setting. Rather than basing these explanations on the *absolutely* "unique personality of an individual," we look for generalizeable characteristics which we expect exist in the makeup of all role occupants. We then may be able to advance propositions stating that in a given set of circumstances, particular actors possessing a specified set of characteristics can be anticipated to behave in a designated way.

The conceptual development for the individual-psychological facet remains incomplete. As work progresses, additional analytical problems may become evident. While this will further the complexity of the theory, it will strengthen its explanatory power.

Interactional and Transactional Arenas of Behavior

Throughout the discussion of this chapter, we have been discussing behavior inside and outside the household, especially in the discussion of the family as a semiclosed system. To distinguish between the internal and external behavior, the terms *interaction* and *transaction* have been developed.[31] We have, then, two *arenas* in which we may observe family conduct taking place.

In the interactional arena of family dynamics, the emphasis is on analysis of the processes which occur within the family system. Explanations of behavior observed are derived from other behavior or from normative patterns of a particular family. If there is a certain pattern of decision making observed, for example, the explanation for its sources are based on other elements internal to the system, such as normative structure which attributes to some actors authority or expertise in decision making and to others less authority or expertise.

We already have established, however, that the family is only more-or-less a closed system. Many internal processes have their explanations partially, if not wholly, in external elements. In this situation, then, the transactional arena becomes involved. For example, a great deal of discussion and interaction may take place in certain families over how to handle a situation with an aging parent. The norms and expectations governing such an interaction are not found totally within that system. Some of them are derived from expectations based in relationships with other relatives, including the aging parent, or with friends and acquaintances. In addition, there are certain societal norms concerning relationships of this sort. In other words, this particular issue does not exist in the vacuum of the nuclear family system but is involved intricately with other relationships external to it.

There is a broader aspect to the transactional arena in family behavior. A number of components of the internal relationships are almost totally dominated by relationships external to the family. A husband's occupational role strongly will influence a great many areas of his family life. Ability to spend time with family members, some of the recreational pursuits followed, participation in certain types of community organizations, and a host of other elements of his occupational life-space govern his ability or his inability to relate to family members.

Hill and Hansen use a third term, *action,* to refer to "behavior of the single unit with iself or another object or unit as referent."[32] This element is certainly an analytically distinct one in family behavior. We are not interested primarily in the individual's behavior except as it has a transactional or an interactional referent. Those aspects appear to be adequately captured by the interactional and transactional arenas, even though there may be merit in certain circumstances for abstracting out the actional element.

References

1. John Sirjamaki, "Cultural Configurations in the American Family," *American Journal of Sociology* 53 (May 1948), pp. 464–470.
2. See Ira Reiss, "The Universality of the Family: A Conceptual Analysis," *Journal of Marriage and the Family* 27 (November 1965), pp. 343–353; Norman W. Bell and Ezra F. Vogel (eds.), *A Modern Introduction to the Family* (New York: The Free Press, 1968), pp. 7–34.
3. John W. Bennett and Melvin W. Tumin, *Social Life* (New York: Knopf, 1948), p. 49.
4. Robert Bierstedt, *The Social Order* (New York: McGraw-Hill, 1963), p. 341.
5. See Melford Spiro, *Kibbutz: Venture in Utopia* (Cambridge, Mass.: Harvard University Press, 1956); Melford Spiro, *Children of the Kibbutz* (Cambridge, Mass.: Harvard University Press, 1958).
6. Ivan F. Nye and Lois W. Hoffman, *The Employed Mother in America* (Chicago: Rand McNally, 1963), pp. 3–16.
7. Reiss, *op. cit.*
8. Spiro, *op. cit.*
9. Robert O. Blood and Donald M. Wolfe, *Husbands and Wives* (Glencoe, Ill.: The Free Press, 1960), pp. 47–74.
10. *Ibid.,* pp. 11–46.
11. See Max Rheinstein, "Motivation of Intergenerational Behavior by Norms of Law," in Ethel Shanas and Gordon F. Streib (eds.), *Social Structure and the Family: Generational Relations* (Englewood Cliffs, N.J., Prentice-Hall, 1965); Joseph Goldstein and Jay Katz, *The Family and the Law* (New York: The Free Press, 1965); and Samuel Mencher, "Social Authority and the Family," *Journal of Marriage and the Family* 29 (February 1967), pp. 164–192.
12. See Lincoln H. Clark (ed.), *The Life Cycle and Consumer Behavior,* Vol. 2 in the *Consumer Behavior* series (New York: New York University Press, 1955); Nelson Foote (ed.), *Consumer Behavior: The Models of Household Decision-Making* (New

York: New York University Press, 1961); and Reuben Hill, "Decision Making and the Family Cycle," in Shanas and Streib, op. cit., pp. 112–139.

13. Reuben Hill and Donald A. Hansen, "The Identification of Conceptual Frameworks Utilized in Family Study," *Marriage and Family Living* 12 (November 1960), p. 301.

14. James H. S. Bossard, "The Law of Family Interaction," *American Journal of Sociology* 50 (January 1945), p. 293.

15. William M. Kephart, "A Quantitive Analysis of Intragroup Relationships," *American Journal of Sociology* 55 (May 1950), pp. 544–549.

16. See Harold T. Christensen, "Children in the Family: Relationship of Number and Spacing to Marital Success," *Journal of Marriage and the Family* 30 (May 1960), pp. 283–289.

17. See Roy H. Rodgers, *Improvements in the Construction and Analysis of Family Life Cycle Categories* (Kalamazoo, Mich.: School of Graduate Studies, Western Michigan University, 1962); and Reuben Hill, *Family Development in Three Generations* (Cambridge, Mass.: Schenkman Publishing Co., 1970).

18. See John A. Clausen, "Family Structure, Socialization and Personality," in L. W. Hoffman and M. L. Hoffman (eds.), *Review of Child Development,* Vol. 2 (New York: Russell Sage Foundation, 1966); Kenneth Kammeyer, "Birth Order as a Research Variable," *Social Forces* 46 (September 1967), pp. 71–80; Edward E. Sampson, "The Study of Ordinal Position: Antecedents and Outcomes," in Brendan A. Maher (ed.), *Progress in Experimental Personality Research,* Vol. 2 (New York: Academic Press, 1965); Aida K. Tomeh, "Birth Order and Kinship Affiliation," *Journal of Marriage and the Family* 31 (February 1969), pp. 19–26; and Gerry E. Hendershot, "Familial Satisfaction, Birth Order, and Fertility Values," *Journal of Marriage and the Family* 31 (February 1969), pp. 27–33.

19. See Anselm Strauss, "Transformations of Identity," in Arnold M. Rose (ed.), *Human Behavior and Social Processes* (Boston: Houghton-Mifflin Co., 1962), pp. 63–85.

20. Frederick L. Bates, "Position, Role and Status: A Reformulation of Concepts," *Social Forces* 34 (May 1956), pp. 313–321.

21. Robert J. Havighurst, *Human Development and Education* (New York: Longmans, Green, 1953), p. 2.

22. Rodgers, *op. cit.,* pp. 54–55.

23. Leonard Brown and Philip Selznick, *Sociology* (New York: Harper and Row, 1968), pp. 86–87.

24. Evelyn M. Duval, *Family Development* (Philadelphia: J. B. Lippincott, 1971), p. 150.

25. Hill and Hansen, *op. cit.,* p. 309.

26. See Lawrence Kohlberg, "Stage Sequence: The Congitive-developmental Approach to Socialization," in Daniel Goslin (ed.), *Handbook of Socialization Theory and Research* (Chicago: Rand McNally and Co., 1969), pp. 347–380; and Harriet L. Rheingold, "The Social and Socializing Infant," in Goslin, *op. cit.,* pp. 779–790.

27. R. Brooke Jacobsen, "Intrafamily Models of Socialization: Theoretical Develop-

ment and Test," unpublished doctoral dissertation, Eugene, Oregon, University of Oregon, Department of Sociology, 1968.

28. See Reuben Hill, "Patterns of Decision Making and the Accumulation of Family Assets," in Fotte, *op. cit.*, pp. 57–80; Reuben Hill, "Judgement and Consumership in the Management of Family Resources," *Sociology and Social Resources* 47 (July 1963), pp. 446–460; and Reuben Hill, "Family Development in Three Generations," *op. cit.*

29. Roy H. Rodgers, "The Occupational Role of the Child: A Research Frontier in the Developmental Conceptual Framework," *Social Forces* 45 (December 1966), pp. 217–224.

30. See John N. Edwards, "Familial Behavior as a Social Exchange," *Journal of Marriage and the Family* 31 (August 1969), pp. 518–526; and Stephen Richer, "The Economics of Child Rearing," *Journal of Marriage and the Family* 30 (August 1968), pp. 462–466.

31. Hill and Hansen, *op. cit.*

32. *Ibid.*, pp. 301.

PART II
The Societal-Institutional Facet

Introduction

    The articles in this section explore the transactions between the family and various societal institutions. Kamerman and Kahn first explore the transactions between the family and governmental institutions through a relationship that manifests itself as family policy. It is their view that the United States has no coherent, clearly articulated family policy but instead has an "unacknowledged policy" that, when analyzed, raises serious questions about our commitment to the establishment of a consistent, focused, "deliberate" point of view clearly defining what government should and does do for the family. The authors give a brief history of U.S. family policy and its European antecedents, explaining the social service implications of family policy as well as the political obstacles to it. They speculate about the future potential for a comprehensive and clearly articulated family policy.

    Chilman explores public social policy for families as the basis for her argument that policy makers' concern for the family has diminished during the past decade while the family during the same period has undergone increased cultural, societal, and technical stress. Like Kamerman and Kahn, Chilman believes that the United States must develop a more effective family policy, and that this policy must strike a balance between individual rights and family welfare. She calls for a comprehensive policy that recognizes the complex connections between the family and political, economic, religious, and educational institutions. The practical obstacles to developing a family policy are identified, such as structure and operation of government, desires of special-interest groups, the legislative process, funding, and administrative resources and methods.

While the articles by Kamerman and Kahn and by Chilman deal with the comprehensive aspects of a family policy, Guillot focuses on the specifics of the relationship between the family and policy through an analysis of family benefits under the program of Old-Age, Survivors' and Disability Insurance since its enactment in 1935. She shows how societal values and processes are reflected in this program, and how these values frequently work against many families. The program emerged as a fragmented and categorical approach based on the family subsystems of husband and wife, parent and child, and adult son or daughter and parent. Guillot demonstrates how legislation at times has taken into account and at other times has lagged behind such social changes as the shifting roles and rights of women, the increase in divorce, and the role of the extended family.

Lipman-Blumen uses national demographic trends to explore changing sex roles and their implications for family structure. The facts that women are living longer, marrying later and less often, divorcing more and remarrying less frequently, having fewer children, and increasingly planning not to have children are discussed in relation to major societal institutions such as education, economics, the mass media, and housing. The article goes on to relate these trends to the specific elements of developmental theory that deal with biological functioning, reproduction, socialization, production and distribution of goods and services, maintenance of order, and meaning and motivation in the context of the family. All of these activities are explained in relation to changes that the author believes will occur in the family during the next two decades.

The article by Sotomayor explores the transactions between Mexican-American families and various societal and cultural institutions. The author explains how the Mexican-American family has been prevented from transacting with many societal institutions. Where transactions do occur, Mexican-American families have been discriminated against and assigned an inferior status that affects the healthy functioning of the family and of the individual within the family and the community. These patterns of transactions are discussed in relation to educational, economic, and legal institutions. The author offers guidelines for the social worker in working with Mexican-American families to enhance their functioning and transactions with institutions.

Billingsley discusses the black family in relation to the institutions of a "white racist, militaristic, and materialistic society." It is his view that analysis of black families has failed to take into account the societal-institutional impact but instead has mistakenly traced their problems to the role of the family itself in the black community. He cites research that refutes this view and demonstrates that when blacks and whites exist under similar economic and social hardships, the black family actually undergoes less disintegration and manifests less deviance. The research also suggests that there is more variation in family functioning in the black community than has been recognized by the dominant white culture.

The article by Sunley offers guidance to the individual caseworker in dealing with specific families that are not faring well in their transactions with various societal institutions. Sunley emphasizes the advocacy role of the caseworker and offers fourteen forms of intervention that can be used in working with families with grievances against or problems in transacting with social institutions. The author depicts the worker as an advocate and the institutions he deals with as adversaries, but not necessarily as enemies. A system of advocacy for an entire agency structure is also described.

2
Explorations in Family Policy

Sheila B. Kamerman
and Alfred J. Kahn

Is America about to rediscover the family? Various television programs have featured inquiries into the American family. Congressional hearings have examined changes in the family, and additional forums are promised, including one by the Senate Subcommittee on Children and Youth.[1] Newspaper columns and editorials exhort government to intervene to reverse patterns of family disorganization and the loss of our children. Many express concern about the growth of one-parent, female-headed families and the increasing rate of participation in the labor force among mothers of young children. At the same time, however, there are those who herald the arrival of new social patterns. Repeated everywhere are the climbing statistics on divorce, separation, out-of-wedlock childbirth, and out-of-wedlock sex. The search for optimum approaches to raising young children continues, as conventional wisdom changes and new approaches emerge.

The family is at center stage, so the issue now is not whether the family can attract the necessary attention, but what this attention will yield. The questions are these: What is, or might be, the nature of the discussion, and will there also be action? Sermons, political speeches, and popular articles so far reflect no more than interest and concern, and no clear consensus about the meaning of the trends or the consequences of recent developments has yet emerged. There is certainly no coherent program for the family and even if there were, it appears that there is major opposition to the government's participating in the formulation of a policy on the family.

Although this country has no conscious or coherent approach to the family, related issues arise daily in public forums, and actions are proposed or taken that have obvious, if often unarticulated and largely unexplored, consequences for family life. Meanwhile, the broader considerations sur-

Source: From *Social Work* 21:3 (May 1976), pp. 181–186. Copyright © 1976, National Association of Social Workers, Inc. Reprinted by permission.

rounding such issues and actions struggle for attention. Perhaps if there were more deliberation on the broader issues, policy choices might relate more closely to emerging social realities. There might be a more systematic consideration of potential consequences and alternatives, and even the question of how individual policy decisions relate to one another might receive discussion.

In the absence of a national debate on these broader considerations, legislation providing extensive child care programs is vetoed because

> good public policy requires that we enhance rather than diminish parental authority and parental involvement with children.... For the Federal government to plunge headlong into supporting child development would commit the vast moral authority of the national government to the side of communal approaches to child rearing over against the family centered approach.[2]

Yet despite these convictions, mothers of young children are entering the labor force in increasing numbers. One-third of all children under 6 have mothers who work—this represents 50 percent of the women with children of that age—and most of these mothers work full time. Sixty-one percent of the mothers of school-age children work.[3] Does organized child care, given existing realities, undermine the family, or does it support the family in fulfilling its role?

Unacknowledged Policy

Although Congress encourages or pressures mothers receiving Aid to Families with Dependent Children (AFDC) to place their children in care and take jobs, day care cost analyses and reports on actual and potential earning patterns raise serious questions about the economics of such policies. And if pressuring AFDC mothers to work is not a way to save money, then what is it? Should these, of all mothers, be separated from their young children through public policy? If all mothers deserve an option, is it possible to design a neutral policy? Does this line of exploration not need to be carried further to the question of whether our social goals would be better achieved if government provided family allowances (that is, demogrants based solely on the number of children) or income supplements for intact poor and working class families as well as broken families, or if government supported higher minimum wages? What would be the impact of each approach on the family, child rearing, the labor market?

Although the evidence for concern is mixed, child development experts worry about the absence from home of mothers of infants. They would, if necessary, rearrange the location and hours of work to facilitate parental coverage, but they also want to reestablish the status of parents who remain in the house. Feminists show increasing interest in the viability of the child-rearing option. The question also arises of whether this country should give attention to European developments in guaranteed maternity benefits of extended, paid maternal or parental leaves after childbirth and of special child care allowances during the first several years of life.

The consideration of these possibilities necessarily involves a host of related questions. How, for example, would the adoption of any such policies affect larger objectives in the various movements for equality? How would they affect children? What are their implications for the social security system?

Still other developments in the fields of foster care and child care raise issues that touch eventually on tax policy. Foster home care is much needed; it is better than and even more economical than many other options. Yet it is difficult to achieve a high degree of success in a program of foster care, and there are shortages of foster homes. Recently, various sacred cows of foster care have come under attack as practice has changed and new questions presented themselves. Does it, for example, make sense for government to pay strangers but not relatives to provide foster care for children? Or to pay more to unrelated foster parents than what public assistance provides for a mother to care for her own child? Or to permit tax deductions for child care expenses only when paid to a nonrelative, although sometimes a loving grandparent could provide the best quality of care at lower cost?

Government policies also have consequences for family members other than children. The numbers of elderly are increasing rapidly, especially those aged 75 and over. Rates of functional impairment, chronic disease, and institutionalization increase with age. There are scandalous abuses in nursing homes, and the costs are horrendous. Congress and the states are in the midst of a search for remedies. Is it a deliberate attempt to destroy the family when government programs pay for institutionalizing an elderly parent, but not for caring for that parent at home? What does it suggest about the government's motives when there is an implicit requirement that, if long-term nursing care is needed, couples divorce or a spouse be pauperized in order to be eligible for Medicaid? Is it supportive of the family to pay strangers to care for an elderly parent but to forbid assisting family members to do so? This is an approach that is permitted in some countries. Alternatively, could standards be maintained and service provision monitored if relatives were paid to function as homemaker—home health aides for elderly family members?

Everywhere there are new preventive programs and pilot projects addressed to one-parent, female-headed households. Is it always accurate and is it wise public policy to see such families as symptomatic of social pathology, to see them as requiring intervention to stop the formation of such families, and to adopt a therapeutic posture toward such mothers and children? Or should this society consider new approaches to such families, approaches that could adapt to the transitory nature of this status for some families and that might in other situations foster the emergence of a viable living pattern for such households?[4] If new ways were developed to support such families so that they could become viable and sound child-rearing environments, what would be the social consequences of such policies?

Here is one final illustration of the confusions and contradictions that arise in the absence of a coherent principle for policy development. New national and state legislation establishes costly systems for the identification and reporting of battered and abused children. The organizational and professional problems involved in such programs are many, and the results thus far are modest. Other programs mandate medical screening of AFDC children, but these have proved difficult to implement despite the financial penalties levied on states for noncompliance. Furthermore, the identification of defects in children has not led automatically to effective follow-up.

What would occur if, as is the case in many countries, national policy were to reflect the obvious connection between routine medical screening and the identification of abused children—if there were a national network of child health centers that offered frequent, mandated, comprehensive check-ups in the first several years of life? What would the consequences be of establishing such a child health program? Could one effect be to undermine the need for a general reform of medical care in the United States and for a program of family medical care?

Deliberate Policy

This listing, however long, is a mere sample. Related illustrations from such program areas as housing, food stamps, or education readily come to mind. Clearly, government is doing a great deal that has consequences for families, and even more is currently being suggested or debated. Furthermore, significant dilemmas, inconsistencies, and even outright contradictions are evident from policy to policy and nonpolicy to nonpolicy. There is some alertness to the need for concern not only with what is specifically proposed, but also with possible unintentional spin-offs, and amid the quest for action, there is a growing awareness of the gap between social changes and social policy.

It is because of these elusive and intangible elements of public policy that the authors propose serious exploration of the potential values and disadvantages of more deliberate attention to the family. It is necessary to take seriously the question of whether it would be helpful to focus on the family as such, both as an object of governmental actions and as a criterion for social policy? Related questions also present themselves. What would it take to achieve such focus? Are there undesirable consequences? Is it possible to consider "the family," with all the traditional connotations associated with this term, while at the same time acknowledging the social changes that have modified the family and defining family in a way that responds to current realities?

Although the authors are far from having firm answers to these questions, analysis to date suggests that there is little choice stated or unstated; family policy does exist, and consequences relevant for the family are inevitable concomitants of policies at every level of government. The issue is whether to turn aside and avoid noticing or to develop a more systematic approach to analysis and action. Because families and their place in society are changing, because current and planned governmental actions do and should affect families as well as individuals, and because deliberate policy is often better than stumbling and coherence better than contradiction and fragmentation, the authors propose more systematic attention to the family. They propose the discussion of family policy.

What follows is a brief introduction to such a discussion. The focus is on how the term has been used and how it might be defined in the light of present-day realities. The obstacles that exist in this country to a discussion of family policy need attention in this context, as does an agenda for future work.

Defining Family Policy

"Family policy" means everything that government does to or for the family. Preliminary thinking suggests several distinctions within family policy that may be useful:

• Situations in which government undertakes specific programs and policies to achieve explicit, agreed-on goals regarding the family.

• Situations in which, although there are no agreed-on overall goals, there are programs and policies that nevertheless do things to and for the family.

• The secondary consequences for families of governmental actions and policies that are not specifically or primarily addressed to the family.

These distinctions require further elaboration. Some actions—such as day care, child welfare and family counselling, income maintenance, family planning, some tax benefits, some housing policies, and the like—involve consequences for the family that are deliberately structured into the policies. These may be thought of as falling into the category of "explicit family policies." Other actions may be addressed to quite different targets, but they also affect families. Examples are decisions on industrial locations, the building of roads, trade and tariff regulations, and immigration policies. These actions contain elements of "implicit family policy."

The purposes of family policy may be "manifest" (revealed or stated) or "latent" (not immediately visible or perhaps even hidden). Consequences may be "intended" or "unintended," "direct" or "indirect." Family policy includes both the effects on the family of all types of public activities and the efforts to use "family wellbeing" as an objective, goal, or standard in developing public policy. Family policy, then, is both a field of activity and a perspective.

Implicit in all the foregoing forms of family policy is yet another element that merits consideration. It is probably essential in the analysis of family policy to differentiate the interest of the family as a unit from those of particular roles and statuses within the family. It is quite possible, for example, that programs will have differential consequences within the family affecting some members more than others, even perhaps advancing the interests of some and impeding those of others. Policy on behalf of the family unit may not necessarily be constructive for every member, and family policy will have to learn to cope with those tensions.

The Literature

Although there has been little systematic work in the United States, family policy is hardly a new concept. In the sense suggested in this article, it was first used in Europe, usually in the context of proposed transfer payments favoring large families or of population policy in a broader sense. There is an extensive and valuable tradition of research and writing in this field, particularly in England, France, Germany, and Scandinavia.[5]

The first classic in family policy, which was actually written in the United States and with this country in mind even though it talks about Sweden and what was then a threat of depopulation, was Myrdal's *Nation and Family*. Responding to those who told government not to interfere with family life, Myrdal, who is paraphrased here by Moynihan, argued that in a modern industrial society no government can avoid policies that influence family relationships:

> For, the only option is whether these will be purposeful intended policies or whether they will be residual, derivative, in a sense concealed ones. . . . *A nation without a conscious family policy leaves to chance and mischance an area of social reality of the utmost importance, which in consequence will be exposed to the untrammeled and frequently thoroughly undesirable impact of policies arising in other areas.* [italics in original].

It is far better to face the facts and the real value issues and to choose.[6]

More recently Wynn, writing in a firmly established British tradition that includes Sir William Henry Beveridge, has stressed the consequences of government policies for the economic security of families with children, indicating how the costs of rearing children vary over time and over the life cycle.[7] Rodgers, discussing this issue from a somewhat broader perspective, defined family policy as "how state action, government policies, are actually affecting families and the quality of family life.[8] She compares French and British family policies, focusing on social insurance benefits, the political significance of the family, and the relationship of family policy to social change. Myrdal, writing for the Swedish Social Democratic Party, connects family policy with the "equality debate."[9]

Although literature on family policy in this country is far thinner, it both follows the European interest in population policy and life-cycle income transfers and goes somewhat beyond these issues. Family policy is an underlying issue in Burns's major work on policy analysis.[10] A relatively early and still important essay was published by Schorr in 1962 under the title "Family Policy in the United States." It conceptualized family policy as "consensus on a core of family goals toward the realization of which the nation deliberately shapes programs and policies."[11]

Several years later Winston made a plea for the establishment of a family policy in the United States based on such agreed-on goals, but reported the cultural and historical obstacles to consensus or to adopting a policy.[12] Recently, several of the reports issued by the Subcommittee on Fiscal Policy of the Joint Economic Committee as well as the findings of the Michigan longitudinal study of five thousand American families have highlighted the interrelationships between family well-being and public policy in such areas as income maintenance, employment, housing, and population.[13] From the perspective of a psychologist and child development expert, Bronfenbrenner has written about the consequences of income, health, employment, and housing policies for children and child development and has engendered considerable response.[14]

Yet another strand in the literature concerns family policy in the social services—in supportive and substitute care and in remedial services for the poor and homeless, the handicapped and the endangered. Beginning with interventions on behalf of the deviant and troublesome, countries have moved somewhat more in the direction of prevention and increasingly have launched universal services. The literature on this subject is extensive. A discussion of new trends in service provision for average families is the objective of a recent book by the authors.[15]

The concerns of the women's rights movement that began in the late 1960s represent another component in family policy. The literature that has emerged from this movement is voluminous and covers the issue of equality in several domains, including such family-related questions as social insurance benefits for working mothers and housewives, child care programs and other social supports to facilitate women's dual roles, part-time work, and the parenting roles of fathers. Among the works with particular relevance to family policy are those of the Rapoports and Fogarty in Britain and of Cook, whose writings are concerned with a large number of countries, and the works of Hilda Scott on Eastern Europe and Isabel Sawhill on the United States.[16]

Family as Perspective

Traditionally, then, family policy regarded as a field of activity has parameters that include population policy, family planning, cash and "in kind" transfer payments, and, in more recent years, employment, housing, nutrition, and health policies. Personal social services, child development, and the whole field of social policy for women have all been defined by some analysts as part of the family policy field.

If one adopts family well-being as a criterion of social policy and uses family policy as perspective as well as field, the relevant policy areas become even more extensive. Policies regarding taxes, the military, transportation, land use, and the environment all have major consequences for the family. In fact, applying the well-being of the family as a criterion could affect every policy arena. Family policy has rarely been conceptualized this way, but Bronfenbrenner in the United States and the leadership of the equality movement in Sweden have argued the desirability of doing so. Such analysts would relocate industry, change working hours, and inaugurate many other measures on the assumption that social relations and the quality of family life should dominate labor market considerations.

The general but not unanimous response elsewhere has been skepticism about invoking family well-being as a perspective, as a criterion for policies in many other fields that bear on family life. Although few analysts deny the extent to which public policies on such matters as taxes, road building, or land use directly affect the well-being of families, skeptics nevertheless question whether the society is willing to have family interests predominate. Alternatively, some argue that family policy could merge with the whole constellation of policies affecting people, thus becoming social policy and nullifying the family component as a useful subcategory.

If family policy is field and perspective, it is also instrument. Government sometimes uses the family as a means of achieving objectives vital to other institutions or policies. The family thus becomes an intermediary. The most important, long-standing, and familiar illustration is in the field of labor market policy.[17] There is now widespread familiarity in this country with the use in Eastern Europe, Cuba, and China of child care facilities, maternity allowances, and child care leaves to recruit women into the labor force.

The incentives and disincentives used in many other countries are more subtle and are not as readily acknowledged. Their subtlety has given rise to debate about whether the desire of women to work or some policy decision to make work feasible and attractive has come first in a given country at a given time. There is, however, no doubt that at one time or another most countries have seen the family as an important vehicle for achieving broader political or social goals, which have ranged from achieving political indoctrination to controlling the labor market.

Particularly interesting in this category of using the family as instrument are recent discussions about supporting the family in its social service role.[18] These discussions have centered on using the family either in conjunction with formally organized social services or as alternatives to further costly expansion of such services. After all, the family has always absorbed and cared for the aged, the handicapped, and the deviant. It still is the major child welfare institution. Among the questions now being raised are these: Is the social service role of the family declining or is it changing? Can and should the family's capacity to fill these roles be strengthened or updated? How could this be done?

Recent trends in community care of the aged and child care are enough to identify these as major questions. Social agencies expanded, in part, in response to changing family roles. Future projections for the social services depend on certain assumptions about the validity, effectiveness, and costs of policies that will affect the family's ability to carry out these functions. There is obviously a reciprocal relationship between the formal expansion of social services and the enunciation of new family policies.

Obstacles to a Policy

It will not be easy to launch deliberations or actions under the banner of family policy in the United States. In a fundamental way, such policies run counter to the national ethic. The American myth is that family and government are completely separate entities. The national ideology is that the welfare of this basic institution should not be tampered with.

According to Moynihan, the American ideals of democracy, individualism, and humanitarianism "each seem to militate against accepting the subject [of family policy] as a legitimate one, and the interactions between them are notably negative in this respect."[19] At the same time that American conservatives perceive family policy as unacceptable government intervention into individual and family functioning, liberals often label anything concerned with the family as reactionary. Or they fear—and not without reason—that the definition of the family reflected in public debates and policies will always be restrictively traditional. Yet the facts remain: governmental actions do have enormous and far-ranging impact on the family, and the family in all its various forms remains the primary socializing environment.

It is possible to move away from the historical definition that identifies as a family only the grouping that includes both a man and a woman who are married and have one or more children. Some initiatives toward a more realistic definition include all types of families as meriting concern and support: one parent, two parent, married, and contractual. Perhaps the simplest definition for the future would be one adult and one dependent other.

Toward a Policy

Concern with policy outcomes is growing, and people are beginning to search for ways to make policy choices more conscious and deliberate. There is some acceptance of the notion that even family forms can change. There is mention in Congress and elsewhere of the desirability of developing a review process and statement that would assess the potential impact on families of proposed legislation or regulations.

Despite the fears and objections to adopting a family policy, Myrdal's argument is being rediscovered and applied to the current situation. The real choice is not whether to have a policy, but the kind of family policy to have. The society may choose a series of fragmented and conflicting family policies or a coherent and consistent one. Or it may continue deliberately with fragmentation and inconsistency because that too serves some purposes.

Family policy is discussed formally and enacted in some European countries and is a consideration even where not so named in others. Departments and bureaus are specifically concerned with family policies and programs, and there are several biennial and annual governmental reports. New, serious research is currently being undertaken, especially in England and France.

Much is to be gained from a broader debate in the United States. Social workers, social scientists, and policy analysts are needed to participate in the discussion and research, and there is also need for sharing of experience and for formulations of issues across national borders.

The arena for action is broad. At present the authors are organizing, with foundation and government support, an International Working Party on Family Policy, which will include participants from East and West European countries. In addition, in several interrelated projects, the authors are conducting (1) an exploration of the feasibility of conceptualizing and operationalizing a "family impact statement" as a routine element of policy development (Kamerman), (2) a systematic study of the interplay, in the daily life of working mothers, both of formal social services and child care programs and of informal social networks (Kamerman), (3) a comprehensive study of American family policy (Kahn).

The authors recognize that urging explorations of family policy as an instrument and criterion for social policy analysis and development has its risks. As was noted above, the concept could be applied in conservative or regressive ways. What is "good" or "bad" for the family might be perceived in a rigid, moralistic fashion. These are real dangers, and it would be unwise to minimize them.

On the other hand, family policy could emerge as one of several constructive criteria in the evolution of social policy. Social planning should be aimed at social justice, equality, and environmental protection. Perhaps it will also be possible to formulate a criterion related to the well-being of families and other primary groups. It is this latter fundamental criterion that family policy could come to represent.

References

1. *American Families: Trends and Pressures, hearing before the Subcommittee on Children and Youth of the Committee on Labor and Public Welfare, United States Senate, September 24, 25, and 26, 1973* (Washington, D.C.: U.S. Government Printing Office, 1974).

2. President Richard M. Nixon, veto message on the Comprehensive Child Development Bill, December 10, 1971.

3. In March 1974, 55 percent of the mothers of children aged 6 to 17 were working, 39 percent of the mothers of children under 6, and 34 percent of the mothers of children under 3. This data all relates to mothers who worked at some time during the year. See *Children of Working Mothers, 1974,* Special Labor Force Report 174 (Washington, D.C.: U.S. Bureau of Labor Statistics, 1975).

4. See Heather L. Ross and Isabel V. Sawhill, with the assistance of Anita R. MacIntosh, *Time of Transition: The Growth of Families Headed by Women* (Washington, D.C.: Urban Institute, 1975).

5. Of the works available in English see, for example, William Henry Beveridge, *Social Insurance and Allied Services* (London: Her Majesty's Stationery Office, 1942), Morris Finer, Chairman *The Report of the Committee on One-Parent Families* (2 vols. London: Her Majesty's Stationery Office, Commons Document 5629, 1974); Henning Friis "Issues in Social Security Policy in Denmark," in Shirley Jenkins, ed., *Social Security in International Perspective* (New York: Columbia University Press, 1969), pp. 129–150; Audrey Hunt, *Families and Their Needs* (London: Her Majesty's Stationery Office, 1973); Viola Klein, *Britain's Married Women Workers* (London: Routledge and Kegan Paul, 1965); Pekka Kuusi, *Social Policy for the Sixties* (Helsinki: Finnish Social Policy Association, 1964); Eleanor Rathbone, *Family Allowances* (rev. ed., London: George Allen and Unwin, 1949); and Ethel Shanas et al., *Old People in Three Industrial Societies* (New York: Atherton Press, 1968).

6. Daniel Patrick Moynihan, Foreword to the paperback edition of *Nation and Family* by Alva Myrdal (Cambridge, Mass.: M.I.T. Press, 1968), pp. vi, vii, and x.

7. Margaret Wynn, *Family Policy* (London: Michael Joseph, 1970).

8. Barbara N. Rodgers, "Family Policy in France," *Journal of Social Policy*, 4 (April 1975), p. 113.

9. Alva Myrdal, *Towards Equality*, translated by Roger Lind (Stockholm: Prisma Paperback, 1971).

10. Eveline N. Burns, *Social Security and Public Policy* (New York: McGraw-Hill Book Co., 1956).

11. Alvin L. Schorr, *Explanations in Social Policy* (New York: Basic Books, 1968), pp. 143–164. See also, Schorr, *Poor Kids* (New York: Basic Books, 1966) and *Slums and Social Insecurity* (Washington, D.C.: U.S. Government Printing Office, 1966).

12. Ellen Winston, "A National Policy on the Family," *Public Welfare*, 27 (January 1969), pp. 54–58.

13. Of the reports of the Joint Economic Committee, Subcommittee on Fiscal Policy, see especially *The Family, Poverty and Welfare Programs: Factors Influencing Family Instability*, Paper No. 12, Parts I and II (Washington, D.C.: U.S. Government Printing Office, November 1974); and James Morgan, *Five Thousand American Families* (Ann Arbor: University of Michigan, Institute of Survey Research, 1974).

14. See, for example, Urie Bronfenbrenner, "The Origins of Alienation," *Scientific American*, 231 (August 1974), pp. 53–61. Edward Zigler has also discussed family policy in the context of improving conditions for children; for his testimony before the Subcommittee on Children and Youth, see *American Families*, op. cit.

15. Alfred J. Kahn and Sheila B. Kamerman, *Not For the Poor Alone* (Philadelphia: Temple University Press, 1975).

16. Michael Fogarty, Rhona Rapoport and Robert Rapoport, *Sex, Career and Family: Including an International Review of Women's Roles* (London: Political Economic Planning, 1971); Alice Cook, *The Working Mother* (Ithaca, N.Y.: Cornell University School of International and Labor Relations, 1975); Rapoport and Rapoport, *Dual Career Families* (Middlesex, England: Penguin Books, 1971); Hilda Scott, *Can Socialism Liberate Women?* (Boston: Beacon Press, 1974); Ross and Sawhill, *op. cit.* For an earlier example, see Alva Myrdal and Viola Klein, *Women's Two Roles: Home and Work*, (2nd ed., London: Routledge and Kegan Paul, 1968).

17. Sidney Webb and Beatrice Webb, *English Poor Law History*, Part I, in *English Local Government* (London: Longmans' Green, 1927); and Frances Fox Piven and Richard A. Cloward, *Regulating the Poor* (New York: Pantheon Books, 1971).

18. For an examination of this subject in connection with the frail elderly and the mentally retarded in England, see Robert Maroney, *The Family and the State: Considerations for Social Policy*. To be published in London, 1976.

19. Moynihan, op. cit., p. xvii, referring to Nathan E. Cohen and Maurice F. Connery, "Government Policy and the Family," *Journal of Marriage and the Family*, 29 (February 1967), pp. 16–17.

3

Public Social Policy and Families

Catherine S. Chilman

In the 1960s, official concern about public social policies rose to new heights. There was less public concern about families as families during this period, although much attention was given to individuals and families who were victims of racism and poverty.

Today, the United States appears to have become almost a different country. Official interest in public social policy, in terms of positive development of a high quality of life for all people, has dwindled to a small flicker, and concern for the poor the non-white, and the Spanish-speaking has been all but extinguished under the deluge of cries for law and order and lower taxes. It is even claimed that families no longer have a function. Attempts to defuse the population bomb plus other contemporary forces of social change have undermined long-cherished beliefs about the values of family life.

The high hopes of the early 1960s that the country was again mobilizing itself to reduce its numerous social problems through enlightened rational action have been all but destroyed by the tragic events of the last ten years. And many American families, lacerated by these tragedies and the stresses of a supertechnological society, have found their marriages faltering under the impact of contemporary conditions. Many parents who earnestly strove in the past several decades to create healthy, happy children are stricken by troubled youngsters who have been battered by the pressures of a society grown increasingly hostile and uncaring of its young. Along with the current

Source: From Social Casework 54 (December 1973), pp. 575–585. Copyright © 1973 by the Family Service Association of America. Reprinted by permission.

disillusionment with public social policy, with the potential contributions of the family, with the legitimate rights of the poor and excluded goes another dangerous trend: a disbelief in the importance and power of rational planning to deal with the problems of our society. We can not afford these disillusionments and disbeliefs. We can not permit our nation to drift on a tide of disengagement, fear, weariness, and pessimism. Despite the agonies of the past decade, it is imperative to try again.

Public social policy can and must be developed in a far more knowledgeable and effective way than in the past. Although it may take many different forms in the coming years, the family does have a future. People will continue to need to belong to small, intimate groups based on love, commitment, interdependence, and shared activities. The need for close, supporting human relationships is probably more crucial than at earlier times in our history because the larger society has become so impersonal and complex. Although most families in the future will be smaller, the majority will probably have children—and children will always need parents to whom they uniquely belong, even though child care centers may increasingly share the task of child-rearing.

To a considerable extent, the well-being of society is intertwined with the well-being of its families, and the reverse is also true. Although families at all socioeconomic levels are suffering from contemporary stresses, the poor and excluded suffer the most. If we do not improve on the efforts of the recent past to bring them into full, secure membership in our communities, we will have neither the right nor the power to continue as a modern, industrialized, largely urban nation.

The problems that confront us are enormous. We should take heart from the knowledge that some of them have been partially reduced by public policies evolved over the years. However, progress has been slow and partial; at almost no time have these policies been purposefully addressed to the well-being of families, even though families have often benefited from them. It is time to press for more rapid and extensive development of public social policies that take into account both individual and family welfare.

By family welfare, the writer does not mean that family unity should take precedence over all considerations of individual welfare. In fact, we have often sacrificed the needs of individuals to the value of family stability. We have often asked the well members of the family to sacrifice themselves for the sick ones and, quite typically, have expected that wives and mothers should put aside their own needs and interests for those of children and husbands. Policies and programs that support family well-being should support the developmental needs of all family members and, simultaneously, take into account the importance and sensitivities of family relationships. These policies and programs need to be related to broad public social policies.

Rising Interest in Public Social Policy

Social policy is frequently written and talked about, but much less frequently defined. An often encountered view is that social policy consists of statements of principles emanating from some vague place in Washington, such as "Every child shall have free access to high quality education," "The family is America's most sacred institution and we shall move in all ways to protect and strengthen it," or "No family shall know hunger." Much can lie between such stated principles and their development and implementation; if policy is to mean anything, it must be translated into action.

Many social scientists with a special interest in the family emphasize a national family policy as distinct from an overall national social policy. Some call for a bureau or department of family development operating at federal and state levels. They take their lead from such countries as France and Belgium, where strong family organization movements push for national policy devoted primarily to the economic well-being of the family.

A variety of family assistance programs tied to a national family policy has developed in these countries over the past forty years. However, in most of the Scandinavian countries and in England and Holland, there is considerable confusion as to whether family policy is a distinct entity that might be clearly differentiated from social policy. Alva Myrdal makes a strong case for national social policies, implemented by rational social planning, which support the total needs of individuals and families—health, housing, employment, education, economics, and recreation. She describes the Swedish system to illustrate her arguments.

This writer agrees with Myrdal's position. There is much to be lost and little to be gained by arguing that public policy in the United States should be subdivided into various segments, with one of the segments being family policy. Since virtually all public policies affect families, it is more realistic to promote sound social, economic, and political policies that offer promise of aiding the people of the country, nearly all of whom belong to families, in one way or another. As these policies are developed, the needs and characteristics of a diversity of families and family members should be taken into account.

In the past, it has proven virtually impossible to build sufficient support for comprehensive government family policies in this country.[2] Persistent American values are involved: The American tradition of individualism, rather than familialism, affords little basis for this support. The historical division of church and state in the United States appears to have the same effect, concern with the family being traditionally allocated to church rather than to state. Political power groups are generally organized along occupational, rather than family-oriented lines; strongly held cultural values regard the family as being uniquely private—the last refuge of the individual against overpowering and huge public and private bureaucracies.

A More Comprehensive Approach

Public social policy should be based on an understanding that social problems and their solutions are intricately related to each other and to the much larger system of which society is a part—the economic, political, and social subsystems of the societal universe. The concepts of physical ecology are becoming increasingly clear to policy-makers, planners, and at least part of the citizenry; a greater conceptual clarity about what might be termed social ecology is also needed. The concept of social ecology means that all the subsystems of society are intricately interrelated. A change in the economy, for instance, affects both governmental and social operations; changes in the government affect economic, as well as social, functioning.

For this reason, public social policy needs to be linked to economic and political policies in knowledgeable and planful ways. This concept might well call for a highly centralized, authoritarian superstate, although the experience of nations that have taken this route warn of the many dangers and problems involved. Can we not somehow muster the enlightened good sense and popular commitment to a common cause that seeks to accomplish a sophisticated, comprehensive planning approach within a democratic framework?

It is appropriate for those who decry increases in governmental powers to consider the presence of enormous private corporate power in the United States today. The capacity of the business-industrial-communications complex to control and manipulate our lives is only dimly recognized. Many of our apparent freedoms are illusory; many of our opportunities for individual decision-making are sharply restricted. Partly because families have no special lobby, they are particularly weak in the face of organized corporate interests. The average citizen can have almost no impact on private power, but, through his vote and other forms of political activity, he has a far greater chance to affect the operations of public power.

If a family is to enjoy a state of well-being in today's society, it must have sufficient income; adequate housing; opportunities for health care, education, employment, and recreation; ready access to transportation; effective community services; and a chance to participate in decision-making in both the private and public sectors of the society. When only some of these factors are present, families and their members are likely to be in trouble.

In general, we have tended to try to resolve "people problems" by partial methods aimed at changing individuals rather than the larger society.

We have pushed the schools—and the children and their parents—to educate all youngsters so that they could eventually become self-supporting,
well-behaved, knowledgeable citizens. When this operation fails to produce
such paragons in great numbers, the schools—or the parents—are blamed.
But education, alone, can not solve the problems of human growth and
development and adaption to a complex, frequently inhumane society. Nor
can the families who send their children to school.

All systems of society must operate effectively together to make it
possible for children to develop adequately and to have a chance to use their
developed talents as youths and adults. All systems of society must operate
together effectively if families are to establish and maintain a climate that
supports the continuing growth and development of both children and
adults. But this kind of operation alone is not sufficient.

These systems of society need to take into account the dynamics of the
family which is a small ecological system interacting with the rest of society.
Society's systems tend to make strenuous and frequently conflicting demands on the family. For example, the school may ask working parents
without a car to participate in a conference with the teacher about one of
their children; these same parents may have another child with a serious
physical ailment requiring distant and expensive medical services; the
mother may need to work overtime to avoid endangering her job; the children may belong to youth organizations that complain because neither of the
parents contributes leadership or extra donations; money may be a constant
problem to this family, partly because housing is expensive in the "good"
neighborhood where they want their children to grow up. Such parents feel
overwhelmed with the demands and inadequacies of the many systems with
which they must interact; they rightfully feel that the family has little power
to counteract the situation.

Pressures reverberate throughout a family, affecting the marriage and
parent-child relationships, and the resultant hostilities and anxieties affect
the behavior of both children and parents in their interactions with society.
Insensitive feedback from the various social systems then affects each family
member and intensifies internal disturbances. And society is apt to proclaim
that the family has "failed"; socialized in today's culture, the members may
well accept this diagnosis, which makes their problems worse.

What is needed is better policy-making that includes awareness of the
needs of families as dynamic interaction units linked to all the social systems.
These more powerful systems need to protect and support the family as a
complex unit, rather than demanding that families be strained and fragmented in an attempt to cope with an inadequately organized and only
partially adequate society. These systems, moreover, as suggested above,
need to be updated, modified, and coordinated through enlightened public
policies, planning, and programs if society and its families are to weather the
stresses of the years ahead. Thus, staffs and advisory councils of government

agencies engaged in social policy and planning should include specialists in family functioning. And persons concerned about the well-being of society and its families need to add to their skills some knowledge of the public social policy processes so that they can affect the political and other governmental processes that both create public policy and put it into operation.

Public Social Policy and Its Processes

Social policy is a process, rather than a mere statement of principles. Public policy is constantly in flux and, therefore, is most appropriately studied and discussed within the framework of the policy-making process. This process is a species of decision-making activities involving large numbers of individuals and groups.

Public policy might be seen as consisting of three related parts: the development of a set of guiding principles; ongoing decision-making through legislative, judicial and administrative processes; and policy implementation through governmental arrangements.

Factors Affecting Public Policy-Making

Although rational public social policy processes directed toward comprehensive planning for the well-being of society and its people are both desirable and necessary, the question remains as to whether they are likely to occur. There are a number of constraints that are apt to inhibit the rational, overall approaches that are needed. These constraints include the nature and structure of federal, state, and local governments; the operation of special interest or power groups; the processes by which legislation is developed and adopted, budgets are constructed, appropriations passed, and programs are administered; the inadequate development and input of scientific knowledge; the impace of group attitudes and values; and the resources and situation of the nation.

OPERATION OF THE FEDERAL GOVERNMENT

One might call the government of the United States a nongovernment government. It is no wonder that our symbol is Uncle Sam—an uncle with only indirect and vague powers over his nephews and nieces, the states. Domestic policy, as distinct from foreign policy, is only partially developed at national levels. With a few exceptions, Washington proposes but the states make the actual decision as to whether they will or will not accept the proposals. The federal government has had at its disposal federal aid for various social purposes such as public housing, community mental health centers, welfare services, family planning programs, and to acquire these benefits the states are asked to contribute some of their own funds and live up to certain standards. To varying degrees, states have cooperated with Washington, but the resulting alliances have been generally fraught with continual bickering and nagging incompatibilities. At present, action by the president to impound much of the funding for these constitutes a grave threat both to the programs and to the democratic process.

Another problem—or perhaps salvation—resides in the so-called balance of powers at the federal level. No one person or group of persons has final power in the development and passage of legislation, the formation and passage of appropriations, the development and implementation of policy, or even settling the question of whether or not legislation is constitutional. The miracle is that legislation passed by Congress ever becomes operative at state and local levels. That it does so is a tribute to the vitality, intelligence, and awareness of citizen groups at all levels of government. Here, again, there is current concern for the erosion of Congressional powers most vividly seen in the frequent use of the presidential veto, as well as impoundment of appropriations.

THE POWER OF SPECIAL INTEREST GROUPS

It is well known that the federal government is strongly influenced by special interest groups: business and industry, the military, labor, organized medicine, and education. These interest groups are mostly occupational and a central interest is the economic well-being of their memberships. Such lobbies, by their very nature, are not particularly interested in supporting public social policies directed toward the well-being of people in general or families in particular. Their focus is largely on the economic security and advancement of the individuals who belong to these groups, making it difficult to mobilize support for social policy that includes family needs.

Social policy, in fact, differs from other types of policy, and these differences are of a character to make the discovery of who formulates it most difficult. Policies in such fields as agriculture, business regulation, and the like, are pointed to a specific, easily defined group. Social policy, in contrast, is more like urban policy. The clients are diffuse, normally unorganized, and, even more significant, the policies are designed for people primarily in their consuming roles, rather than their producing roles. Yet, society to the extent that it is organized into interest groups tends to organize around production roles rather than consumption roles. Consumer groups (including, importantly, the family), those for whom most social policy is designed, tend to be the most unorganized, and therefore, politically the weakest. . . .

The great periods of economic reform in American life were from 1870 to 1914 and the New Deal years. . . . It seems unlikely that a politically powerful majority coalition made up of a number of minority groups pressing for social change is possible today. It is somehow difficult to imagine that a working political coalition of civil rights groups, college students, clergymen and the poor can replace the familiar triad of organized farmers, organized labor and small businessmen.[3]

The fact that a national social policy is far less specific, readily amendable to quantitative measurements, and less clearly concerned with nationwide problems than a national economic policy makes it more difficult to mobilize public support for it. It took the severe economic depression of the 1930s to convince the people of this nation that a national economic policy was needed. The current social depression should, however, provide impetus for support of a national social policy, although it may be difficult to achieve. Among other things, in support of such a policy, we need further development of social indicators and a social advisory council to the president and Congress.

PROCESS OF DEVELOPING LEGISLATION

Although legislation may be proposed by the executive branch of government, it is disposed through the actions of the House of Representatives and the Senate and their various committees; adoption obviously depends on political factors. Public policy, as shaped through the legislative process, can be significantly affected by an extremely small group of senators or representatives, many of whom have gained powerful committee positions by mere seniority. Attempts to reform this system have been notably feeble; greater public pressure on this score is surely called for. A closely related problem is that congressmen are immensely and necessarily concerned with gaining widespread recognition for their political leadership in relation to specific problems of intense concern to the electorate—not only the electorate of their own state or district but of the nations as a whole.

An appeal to congressmen to press for a broader, more comprehensive approach to social legislation is apt to have little acceptance, because such an approach cuts across committee structures, diffuses lobby supports, and detracts from the congressman's special significance. Therefore, problem-specific leadership in such a field as mental illness, mental retardation, family-planning, public assistance, or drug addiction has a far greater appeal to a legislator than leadership in such a field as comprehensive social planning; social planning is a concept that is difficult for voters to grasp, involves an approach that is extremely expensive, and gives little or no recognition to special interest groups.

Once legislation has been passed and its administration delegated, programs spread across the states and tend to become institutionalized. New weaknesses are added to old ones. Thus, a plethora of projects and programs ensue at various stages of infancy, maturity, and senility.

Increased public understanding of the necessity for reordering our policies and programs and for taking a broader approach to problem solution together with support of congressmen and presidents who take such a stance should help bring about the kinds of more comprehensive legislative programs that are needed. The task is huge, partly because the United States, itself, is so vast, so complicated, and so heterogeneous. Yet these very factors have their assets. This is also a nation with vast resources of all kinds and a tradition of creative problem-solving.

Unfortunately the vast majority of citizens are naive in governmental matters. Many apparently believe that once legislation is passed, they can relax their concerned vigilance. Legislation means little unless money is appropriated for its implementation and unless it is competently administered.

THE FUNDING OF PROGRAMS

The appropriation process has a number of complex components, including the budget estimates made by the department which is to implement the policy, the recommendations of the office of budget and management, the actions of the Congress and of the president. Whether an adequate appropriation is made depends on the political pressures brought to bear on the Congress and the president, the state of the national economy, tax revenues, other federal budgetary commitments, and the like. As noted earlier, the office of the president has powers to release, reduce, or withhold actual expenditures. Concerned citizens need to be alert to developments and make themselves heard on the matter of program financing.

The sharing of federal revenue with the states has become a policy of the Nixon administration, the plan being to reduce the cumbersome grant-in-aid mechanisms that became impossibly complicated with the numerous programs of the 1960s. While the time has certainly come to simplify and coordinate these many programs, a simple return of federal income to the states, with almost no standards set, threatens existing and future social programs.

For instance, many problems need national or regional, rather than state or local, approaches; numerous state and local governments see federal revenue-sharing as a way to reduce taxes through cutting back on social programs formerly required by the grant-in-aid systems; there is apt to be a more narrowly political approach to program development and administration when federal standards are reduced; and the actual amount of money currently being returned to the states is minuscule in relation to the social needs of the people. However, one positive aspect of revenue-sharing is that this freer system gives the more progressive states a larger opportunity to forge ahead in their social programs, relatively independent of today's generally backward-looking domestic policies at federal executive levels.

A word is in order here regarding the way in which taxation policy affects social policy, over and above the total amount of revenue produced by taxes. One of the fundamental functions of taxation, besides the raising of revenue, is to redistribute the wealth of the country in an effort to promote a higher level of social and economic justice. Thus, taxation policy is closely related to overall social policy goals. Taxation policy is also related to the well-being of families both because it heavily affects family income and because it provides the funding resources for public programs essential to family well-being.

At the present time, many serious inequities exist in the tax system, among them the antiquated taxing methods of localities (relying heavily on regressive property and sales taxes), tax loopholes and shelters available mostly to the affluent, and the recent easing of business and corporation taxes. As public expenses mount, far more equitable, simplified, and planful ways of taxation need to be found—not an easy task, considering the complexity of the problem and the many politically powerful special interest groups involved. Increased public understanding is seriously needed, together with a far greater recognition that tax dollars are not gifts to governments but payments for public services that would otherwise be inaccessible to the vast majority of people.

ADMINISTRATION RESOURCES AND METHODS

In order to implement public policy, an effective administrative staff is needed, a fact frequently not appreciated by the public. One of the weaknesses in the implementation of the vast amount of social legislation passed during the Johnson administration was that very little provision was made for an administrative staff to carry it out. It was not uncommon to find one staff member with half of a small office and a half-time secretary attempting to administer a whole national program, if not two or three national programs at once. This responsibility included not only mastering the related legislation, its implementing guidelines, and its attendant appropriations but also a great deal about the subject itself. It also meant establishing cordial relationships with administrative and professional personnel throughout the country and learning as much as possible about the attitudes, resources, and situations of various localities. The "race to implement" grew more and more frantic during the mid-1960s as more and more innovative social legislation was passed, some of which called for new approaches.

Attempts are currently being made to further cut the staffs in the federal executive branch. In addition, the major thrust has been to politicize the system, to reduce the number of people on civil service appointments, to subject the whole operation to business management techniques, and to make the entire bureaucracy responsive to presidential decision-making. This situation is particularly true of the Department of Health, Education, and Welfare. Although the size of its staff seems large, it is small compared to the size of the nation and the number and importance of programs involved. Further staff reductions will probably further reduce the ability of staff personnel to implement the vast array of programs so important to the well-being of the nation and its people. The work of this department calls for a high caliber of professional personnel, motivated largely by conviction about the worth of the programs, rather than by political opportunism. The attempt to administer the Department of Health, Education, and Welfare as if it were a business corporation represents a serious misunderstanding of the complex professional and scientific nature of its programs—and of the public, rather than the profit-making, nature of its missions.

The concept of making federal departments totally responsive to presidential decision-making strongly suggests both a repudiation of democratic values and a miscomprehension about the inherent nature of administration of large complex organizations. One central administrator, or even a group of central administrators, can not possibly have the requisite knowledge and informed judgment to make all the important decisions about an enterprise so vast as a federal department.

General policy-making should be the joint prerogative of the president and the Congress, with frequent inputs from the Supreme Court. Policy administration is a series of decision-making processes, both overt and covert, making their way down from top levels into numerous federal bureaus and branches and, thence, to regional, state, and local administrative units. The practices and views of the current administration seem likely to further undermine the public's belief in, and respect for, the federal government, a condition that is apt to have severe consequences throughout our society.

IMPACT OF KNOWLEDGE AND RESEARCH ON
SOCIAL POLICY

The push during the 1960s for new directions in social policy was occasioned, in part by the rapid increase in knowledge generated by the biological, social, and behavioral sciences and by the great fact-gathering and research operations of the government. Although social and economic problems within the country were becoming aggravated, knowledge about these problems and information about how they might be prevented or mitigated

raised the popular level of awareness about the need for appropriate programs. To know that problems exist, to know that they might be reduced or
prevented, and to know that many of the needed resources are at hand or can
be developed to reduce the load of human misery virtually requires men of
goodwill to act. Knowledge available in the biological, social, and behavioral
sciences that offers promise for a "better society for all" is still rather primitive. Some believe that much more research is needed before direct action
can be taken. Yet the imperatives of the times seem to demand that the
nation push ahead with what knowledge is available and that simultaneous
provision be made to continue to gather more knowledge.

Such an action-now approach has numerous difficulties, many of which
have been demonstrated in the past decade. A large number of programs
were launched more on the basis of speculative social science theory than of
firm knowledge. Examples included the 1961–1965 programs of the Office of
Juvenile Deliquency, chiefly based on theories that delinquency is primarily
caused by the denial to poor youths of access to the opportunity system of
good jobs, high quality education, social status, and the like.[4] Many of the
so-called antipoverty programs were also based on the same theory. The crux
of the matter is that a single plausible theory among the many available was
applied to large national programs before there were sufficient time and
funds to test its applicability in pilot projects. It could also be remarked that
the theory, itself, was never given much of a chance. The various social
systems were never importantly modified. The major thrust was, and still is,
to change people rather than the systems that so unfairly and so adversely
affect them. Then, too, the crucial factor—lack of adequate income for individuals and families—remained untouched.

Unrealistic promises were made about the presumed effectiveness of
many action programs, resulting in the current disillusionment that most
programs did not live up to their claims. These exaggerated claims, however,
should not be attributed to the social scientists who provided many of the
concepts for them but, rather, to those who had the job of selling the programs to the president, the Congress, and the people.

Although there is currently a widespread disenchantment regarding
the contributions that research and scientific knowledge can make to public
social policy, our greatest hope for more effectively tackling social problems
is to develop programs that derive their fundamental rationale from the
available, related research and from survey data such as those supplied from
such sources as the Census, and from the Bureau of Vital Statistics and the
Bureau of Labor Statistics. Simultaneously, it is essential that there continue
to be both public and private support for social and behavioral research, both
basic and applied. Although there are many promising leads from this research at present, we are a long way from learning what we might about how
public social policies could best contribute to the healthy development and
functioning of people, their families, and society. There is a particular need

for additional sophisticated program research to test the impact and effectiveness of various intervention strategies.[5]

VALUES, ATTITUDES, AND TRADITIONS

Much in our culture is against national public social policies and comprehensive, rational social planning addressed to the well-being of individuals and families. Much in our culture is against costly, comprehensive programs as a substitute for relatively cheap, fragmented, problem-specific services.

Pervasive cultural changes are called for, including a shift from the highly individualistic values cherished by so many—values holding that each person should be able to "make it on his own." If a person needs help from the community, his image as an adequate person is somehow undermined. Conversely, it is held that the community should give as little help to its citizens as possible for fear that such help might make them weak and dependent.

Such concepts derive from a now-fading small farm agricultural society and from earlier stages of industrial development in which entrepreneurship and a strong bent toward productive activity was needed and frequently rewarded. The economy, the expanding frontier, and the relatively open opportunity system fostered strong values of competitiveness. Although the conditions that fostered them have changed, the values have survived. "Healthy competition in a free enterprise society" is a phrase so frequently used that it has almost taken on an aura of religiously sanctified natural law, despite the fact that the competition is often spurious, and individual enterprise has lost its freedom to big corporations that evade the puny efforts of government to restrain them.

If the United States is to adapt effectively to the crises that are crowding upon it, new values and attitudes must emerge that are favorable to public social planning: a sense of national and international community; an acceptance of government activity as being of equal integrity and importance to that of activity in the private sector; an appreciation of complexity in problem-solution; and a readiness to change social, political, and economic institutions which are no longer adaptive to the present situation.

There is hope that these values and attitudes will emerge. Typically, neither individuals nor nations face up to their problems until the crises are upon them. The crucial factor then becomes whether the individuals or nations have the strength to face up to the problem and the resources to handle it. The key word here is *handle*, not *solve*. If we ask that our problems be solved, we are asking the impossible. Human problems are not solved. The very essence of being human involves conflict with one's self and others as well as fulfillment through one's self and with others, failure as well as success, deprivation as well as enrichment, suffering as well as pleasure, and conformity to others as well as individual expression. We should look for ways of coping with our problems better, not for abolishing them. Part of the problems of the 1970s lies in the oversimplifications of the 1960s. There will be a longer and more difficult haul than many were led to anticipate.

Do We Have the Economic Resources?

The needed social policies and programs are expensive. Unless we cut back military commitments radically, current domestic needs can not be met without raising taxes. Economies in government may be sought, but they will not be sufficient. Tax loopholes may be plugged, but even this step would not yield sufficient revenue. It is said that the people of this country can not, and will not, stand for higher taxes. Yet our people have higher average earnings and retain a substantially larger proportion of their personal incomes than do the peoples of most modern nations. Many citizens, especially those in the upper income brackets, could readily afford to pay higher taxes. The question is not so much "can they?" as "will they?"

The quest for economic security drives individuals and families to acquire larger and larger incomes so that they can be ready to meet such expenses as those of health care, higher education, unemployment, and transportation. If costs of health care and higher education were more adequately met through public funds, if unemployment benefits were sufficiently high and long-lasting, if low-cost and efficient public transportation were available, then individual and familial anxiety for a high personal income would be sharply reduced. Better public transportation, better paths for bicycles and walking, and better community planning would drastically lower the need for car ownership

The quest for the good life drives individuals and families to seek higher and higher incomes so that they will have a margin for attractive and adequate housing in a pleasant community, enjoyable recreation, and a chance to attend cultural events. If adequate and attractive housing and related public community services were reduced in price through better government planning and support, the push for large sums of money for homes in well-organized communities would be far less. If public recreation facilities were expanded and if the arts were further subsidized from public funds, it would become far less necessary to create the good life out of personal earnings.

During the 1960s, the nation slowly moved in the directions sketched here. There is need for all to renew the concern for a high quality of life for all the people and the commitment to more public programs planned for public purposes. The concept of social insurance, spreading the risks of unemployment and old age through wide participation in a taxation program, needs to be expanded to sharing the risks of poor health, educational deficits, poor housing, transportation crises, community disorganization, and recreational and cultural deprivation.

The people of this nation have the resources to provide a good life for themselves and others if they are ready to understand and accept that the good life can be more nearly achieved by a greater pooling of resources to meet many of the physical, social, and psychological needs of all people and of all its families. Our society already has a mixed public-private economy; we need to go further in the public direction.

Summary

Public social policy, to be effective, should be seen as a process, rather than a mere statement of principles. It is a process that develops and implements public social programs. This implementation requires administrative action at all levels of government and the financing of these actions and programs. It also requires popular understanding and support.

It seems essential that the people of this nation move toward the adoption of social policies based on comprehensive, rational social planning because all aspects of the political, social, and economic systems are intricately interrelated and pervasively affect the well-being of all individuals and their families. Partial, inexpensive programs, especially those addressed to primarily changing people rather than systems, can not possibly meet the human problems—or positive human potentialities—created by a supertechnological society.

If we are to move in the directions indicated and retain democratic values and methods, it seems likely that needed social programs will be developed rather slowly and piecemeal. The disadvantages inherent in a piecemeal approach will be reduced if the overall requirements and basic comprehensive pattern can be understood and kept in mind by policymakers and the general citizenry. An alternative approach, movement toward an authoritarian state and central decision-making by a small group, runs counter to our most fundamental values and experience, while another alternative, a return to the principles of official laissez faire, would probably plunge our entire society into chaos.

Public social policy should include, but not be separate from, public family policy. Just as it should recognize the complexity and interactional dynamics of social, economic, and political systems, so it should recognize the complex interactional dynamics of that much smaller and weaker system—the family.

There are at least six major factors that constitute potential obstacles to the making and implementation of rational, comprehensive, public social policies on a nationwide basis. These are: the antiquated nature and structure of government at all levels; pressures induced by selfish special interest or power groups; the complicated processes by which legislation is developed, funded, and administered; limitations in the formation and input of scientific knowledge; the impact of outworn cultural attitudes and values; and the poor uses of national resources. Although there are important obstacles inherent in these six factors, we should be able to reduce their effects by a positive, knowledgeable approach to their origins and nature.

At the present time, there is a tendency to pessimism, disengagement, and distrust of knowledgeable attacks on human and social problems. The enormous societal changes, overexpectations, and tragedies of the decade of the 1960s have created a mood of retreat and despair. The problems that press upon us, that threaten all our families, are more intricate and difficult of solution than many of us thought. Since they are largely human problems, they can not be solved, but they probably can be modified through a reinvestment of popular intelligence, money, and concerned effort.

References

1.   Alva Myrdal, *Nation and Family* (Cambridge: The M.I.T. Press, 1968).

2.   The only specific national, public family policies that we have at present come close to being anti-family policies. They include family planning programs addressed primarily to reductions in the birth rate and AFDC programs that, in over twenty states, exclude families when an able-bodied male is in the home, provide miserly public assistance, and particularly emphasize getting mothers off welfare and into the work force.

3.   Alan K. Campbell, Who Makes Social Policy. Speech given at National Conference of Social Welfare, June 3, 1970 (Mimeographed), Maxwell Graduate School of Citizenship, Syracuse University, Syracuse, New York.

4.   Richard Cloward and Lloyd Ohlin, *Delinquency and Opportunity* (New York: The Free Press, 1960).

5.   Donald Campbell, Reforms as Experiments, *American Psychologist*, 24:409–29 (April 1969); see also, Donald Campbell, *Methods for the Experimenting Society*. Paper presented at the 1971 meeting of the American Psychological Association, Washington, D.C.

4

Congress and the Family: Reflections of Social Processes and Values in Benefits in OASDI

Ellen Elizabeth Guillot

Social welfare programs take their form in relation to other parts of the society and as a deeply-rooted part of the whole. They reflect the values, processes, and behavior patterns of the society they serve. Thus, an analysis of the changes in any continuing program of welfare legislation of the United States should produce a significant and pertinent reflection of changes in values, processes, and behavior patterns of American society.[1] This paper deals with one aspect of one social welfare program—family benefits in old age, survivors', and disability insurance in the United States. As changes have occurred in the values, processes, and patterns associated with the American family, provisions for family benefits in OASDI have changed correspondingly, if slowly. What the successive amendments to this program have revealed most strikingly, perhaps, is the constant tension between tradition and change which has influenced Congress and which it in its way has had to resolve. On the whole, the trend throughout the course of the many amendments has been toward liberalization of the requirements for entitlement to family benefits.*

As passed in 1935, Title II of the Social Security Act provided benefits only for the insured worker retired because of age. It required only four years, however, for Congress to respond to the pressure of the tradition that holds the breadwinner responsible for the maintenance of his family. In

Source: From Social Service Review 45 (June 1971), pp. 173–183. Copyright © 1971 by the University of Chicago Press. Reprinted by permission.

*The legislation is easily available in Laws Relating to Social Security and Unemployment Compensation (8: secs. 202–216).

1939, therefore, when family members were included as beneficiaries, Congress necessarily prescribed the specifications that would entitle them to benefits. The way in which these specifications have changed and have thus reflected the changes in the American attitude toward the family is the subject of this paper.

In prescribing specifications for entitlement Congress doubtless acted practically rather than theoretically. Nevertheless, its actions resulted in the separation of the family system into its subsystems and the development of criteria through which each family member, according to his position in the subsystem, could claim from the insured worker responsibility for maintenance. The subsystems within the family are those of (a) husband and wife, (b) parent and child, and (c) adult son or daughter and parent. Within the subsystems Congress has used as categories for entitlement to benefits: (i) the degree of financial dependency of the family member on the insured worker, (ii) the legal relationship of the family member to the insured worker, (iii) the duration of the relationship, and (iv) the residence of those in the subsystem within the same household. From the changes in the nature of these criteria, the influence of the changing values, processes, and behavior patterns of the American family can be inferred.

The Husband-Wife Subsystem

FINANCIAL DEPENDENCY OF THE SPOUSE ON THE WAGE-EARNER

The financial dependency of married women on their husbands is a deeply rooted American tradition. Congress, reflecting this tradition, provided in 1939 that wives and widows could be entitled to benefits from the husband's insurance. Regardless of age, wives and widows may receive benefits if they have one or more dependent children of the insured worker in their care. They are not entitled to benefits without some limitations. The value of work, strong in American culture, outweighs the tradition of the wife's financial dependence upon the husband. Thus, to receive benefits wives and widows without dependent children must have reached retirement age.* In these ways Congress has put its stamp of approval on the older tradition that a mother remains at home and cares for children, but it has also accepted the newer practice that women work outside the home. It has even gone so far as to implement its belief that they should take employment if they are young enough and able to do so.

---

*Reduced in 1956 from 65 to 62 and for widows in 1965 to 60; also, from 1967 on widows could qualify for survivors' benefits if aged fifty and disabled, regardless of children in their care.

On the other hand, changes in this family tradition have occurred as a result of the industrialization process, urbanization, the trend toward the smaller and nuclear family and the increasing number of women wage-earners. Recognizing that the wife in the contemporary family may be the responsible breadwinner, in 1950 Congress added benefits for the dependent husband and the dependent widower. Yet Congress has continued to presume that the man is the principle breadwinner of the family and has resisted giving the wife a similar function. Husbands and widowers applying for benefits on the basis of their wives' earnings must present evidence that they have been receiving their support from the insured wife during the year before application. This determination of degree of dependency involves an exact calculation of income and evidence that expenditures for food and other household items had been charged to the wife. Thus, husbands and widowers must prove dependency on the wife, while dependency of the wife or widow on the husband is assumed. Furthermore, a husband or widower, regardless of proof of dependency, must have reached retirement age,* and there is no provision for benefits at an earlier age if he assumes the role of caring for children when the wife retires or dies.

Despite the fact that the law has recognized these relationships of financial dependency within the family, Congress does not give full freedom of choice to individuals to exercise this dependency when work and wage-earning are possible alternatives to accepting support from public funds. Congress has seemed to reflect that aspect of the Protestant ethic—which will be noted more fully in later sections—that stresses reluctance to depend on charity rather than on one's own earning capacity.

THE LEGAL RELATIONSHIP OF THE SPOUSE TO THE INSURED WORKER

In response to the accepted view of sexual morality, the legal validity of the marriage always has required proof in order for a spouse to be entitled to OASDI benefits. Congress has tied the basis for proof to the law concerning devolution of intestate personal property in the state in which the insured individual was domiciled at the time of application or at the time of his death. There was a liberalization in the 1960 amendments, which assured that a purported marriage may be accepted when it can be established that the applicant in good faith went through a marriage ceremony that would have been valid but for a legal impediment not known to the applicant at the time, such as the lack of dissolution of a previous marriage or defects in the procedure followed in the purported marriage. Although allowance has been made here for variations in family law among the states and for the possibility

*Now reduced from 65 to 62 or for widowers to age fifty if disabled.

that accidental circumstances may affect the legal validity of the marriage, it is obvious that Congress has preferred the legally constituted marriage.

Furthermore, it clearly is evident that Congress has placed significant value on the marriage pattern of one husband—one wife, even throughout a lifetime. From 1939 until 1965, a wife, to be entitled to benefits, must have been the current wife of the insured worker, and she became ineligible if a divorce occurred. Until 1958 a widow, to be entitled to benefits, not only must have been the legal wife of the insured worker at the time of his death, but she was deprived of benefits if she remarried. This rather Puritan support of the single marriage was seen in the late 1950s to clash with another tradition—that unrelated persons of opposite sexes should not live together unless legally joined in marriage. Senior citizens managed to persuade Congress that it should not assume responsibility for blocking the formation of legally established unions by cutting off social security benefits when couples, free to marry, wished and had the right to do so. Congress, they insisted, was forcing many of them to live in "sin." Accordingly, the amendments of 1958 provided that the widow could continue to receive her usual benefits if she remarried an individual who also was receiving benefits from the program. In 1965 the widow after the age of sixty could remarry without loss of benefits, regardless of the new spouse's status as a beneficiary. Evidently the one-spouse marital structure becomes less imperative as age advances and the ability of the older husband to provide for his wife is less assured.

It was not until the amendments of 1965 that divorced wives and "surviving divorced wives" could receive benefits, and then only under restricted circumstances. A rather long married life with the insured former husband is required—a period of twenty years before the divorce became effective. In addition, divorced women must have been receiving substantial contributions from the former husband, pursuant to a written agreement or court order. As with wives and widows, they must be of retirement age or have children dependent on the insured worker in their care, and they may not retain their benefits if they remarry, although there are the two exceptions to this restriction, the same as those for widows. Congress has reluctantly recognized that divorces do occur in a significant number of marriages and that the divorced wife may have a claim on the former husband for support.*

In contrast to the provisions for wives and widows, husbands and widowers are not so privileged when they present their claims on the insured wage-earning wife. They must continue to meet the terms of the

---

*There was the provision, enacted in 1950, for a "former wife divorced" to receive a "mother's insurance benefit," if she had in her care children of a deceased insured worker who were entitled to benefits, provided that she had not remarried and had been receiving from the insured individual at the time of his death at least one-half or a substantial amount of her support from him, pursuant to a court order.

earlier legislation. The husband must be the current husband of the insured wife. A divorce deprives him of benefits. The widower must have been the current husband of the insured wife at the time of her death. A remarriage deprives him of benefits, with the same exceptions as for the widow and divorce, although he must wait until he reaches the age of sixty-two, rather than sixty, before he may remarry anyone outside the program without loss of benefits. In this case, too, Congress is not ready to admit complete equality of the sexes in connection with breadwinning and responsibility for support. It is quite likely that this legislation conforms to public opinion that women have greater claim to be taken care of than men, regardless of their marital status.

THE LENGTH OF MARRIAGE

The trend has been toward relaxation in the requirement of length of marriage. At the beginning of the program, in order to share in the benefits, a wife must have been married to the insured worker twelve months before he attained the age of sixty. The amendments of 1946 specified the length of marriage as "not less than thirty-six months preceding application," but this time was shortened in 1960 to "not less than one year." In 1939 a widow must have been married to the insured worker for twelve months preceding his death. Not until 1967 was this period reduced to nine months, or to three months if death of the worker was accidental or if it occurred while he was on active duty in the uniformed services.

When dependent husbands were brought into the program in 1950, they were required to have been married to the insured wife for not less than three years preceding application, the same requirement as for wives at that date. The reduced duration of marriage allowed for wives in 1960 applied also to husbands; but widowers, unlike widows, do not receive special consideration if the wife dies accidentally or while serving in the armed forces, circumstances which are both quite possible.

RESIDENCE IN THE SAME HOUSEHOLD

According to the 1939 amendments, a wife must have been living with the insured worker at the time of application, and the widow must have been living with him at the time of his death. The same requirement held for dependent husbands and widowers when they came into the program. This requirement for all—wives, widows, husbands, and widowers—was struck out entirely in 1957, except when there is a question concerning the validity of the marriage, in which case the requirement of residence in the same household still applies. It is quite likely that this requirement was eliminated in order to simplify the administrative procedure of determining entitlement. Nevertheless, it marks a departure from the most approved family pattern—that of husband and wife living together.

POSSIBLE FUTURE CHANGES IN PATTERNS OF DEPENDENCY

Behavior patterns may change in the future to the extent that dependency may no longer be a pertinent consideration.

The upswing in the employment of women is entitling more and more women to benefits in their own right. However, reports from the Social Security Administration reveal that, although more women are accumulating quarters of coverage, their average earnings remain below those of men, and consequently their average benefits are lower. The average benefit payment for retired women wage-earners at the end of 1967 was 76 percent of the amount paid to retired men.[2] Before the provision for entitlement of the married woman based on the husband's insurance can be removed from the program, it is likely that women not only must join the labor force in greater numbers but also must earn more equal wages in order to bring their benefits up to the same standards. If ever there is no longer need for dependents' and survivors' benefits for wives because all women will be entitled in their own right as insured wage-earners, the question comes to mind: What will be happening to the husband and his dependency status? If some degree of financial dependency is to remain for husbands, it is quite likely that wives must achieve equal earning capacity before Congress will give to the dependent man the same advantages in entitlement that it now gives to the woman. So long as women have less to award in amount of benefits, men are less likely to press their own claims as beneficiaries.

The Parent-Child Subsystem

The presumption that the legal parent is responsible for the maintenance of children is unqualified; the legislation gives no indication that this responsibility may or ever should be placed elsewhere. In its approval of this responsibility, the program has been comparatively generous in offering help to the parent. Furthermore, it has recognized from the beginning that families may be broken and that not all children are taken care of in their original households. The child's need to be cared for has therefore taken precedence over moralistic questions involving parents.*

---

*It was not until the 1967 amendments that maternal orphans became eligible to receive benefits based on their mother's earnings under the same conditions that paternal and full orphans qualify for benefits based on the earnings of their father (1:17).

Not only the natural children of a legal marriage, but also adoptive children and stepchildren have been entitled to benefits ever since children first came into the program in 1939. The early amendments excluded illegitimate children, but the 1950 amendments, permitting use of the law on devolution of intestate personal property current in the state in which the retired or deceased worker resided, included illegitimate children to whom such laws applied. The 1965 amendments spell out the conditions by which an illegitimate child may be accepted through his insured father.*

Although benefits originally ceased when children reached the age of eighteen, exceptions were added in 1956 to permit benefits for children disabled before that age and for as long as the disability lasts, and in 1965 to extend benefits to students up to age twenty-two. These exceptions reflect sympathy for the disabled, desire to help the parent take care of the disabled child, the value attached to education—all of which have been constant in American tradition—and the need of the new generation for a longer period in school.

Supporting the value of the nuclear family, the statute disqualifies children when they marry, with the exception (enacted in 1958) of a child who marries an individual already entitled to benefits. Thus the law presumes that when a new family is formed it should provide for itself independently.

For adoptive children, the specified length of time of the parent-child relationship has gradually been liberalized.† Stepchildren have likewise become eligible for dependents'‡ and survivors' benefits§ under increasingly liberal terms. In somewhat the same tolerant vein Congress has not emphasized the question of whether the child has been living with the parent. The program has not seen its function as the promotion of relationships between parent and child, not even to the extent that they should be living in the same household. Although the criterion of living with the parent has

---

*Conditions for such eligibility are: (a) the insured individual has acknowledged in writing that the child is his son or daughter; (b) he has been decreed by the court to be the father; (c) he has been ordered by the court to contribute to the support of the child because he is the father; or (d) he is shown by satisfactory evidence to be the father and was living with or contributing to the support of the child at the time the child became entitled to benefits.

†The following changes were made in dependents' benefits in the years specified: the insured individual must have legally adopted the child before age sixty (1939); the child must have been adopted 36 months before application for benefits (1946); time spent as stepchild may be included in period required (1950); adoption period was reduced to 24 months before application (1960); for entitlement under disability insurance, adoption proceedings must have been initiated before the parent became disabled (1967). In addition to these specifications, the child must have been supported by or living with the insured one year before application. For survivors' benefits: the child must have been adopted for a year before the insured died (1939); the surviving wife might claim benefits for the child adopted within two years of the insured's death, if the child had been living with the insured (1958).

‡For benefits of stepchildren: insured must have married stepchild's parent before age 60 (1939), 36 months before application (1946), one year before application (1960).

§In 1939, marriage of the parents was required 12 months before the insured's death; in 1967, 9 months.

been used to determine dependency, it has been an alternative to another criterion, "contributing to the support" of the child.* Even these rather vague proofs of dependency were dropped in 1960, and the law now states merely that the child must be dependent upon the parent, a phrase so lacking in specificity that dependency of the child upon the parent is apparently presumed to be self-evident.

In the case of stepchildren the law makes sure that the program does not take responsibility for support away from the biological parent; yet it makes it possible for the stepchild to qualify through his stepparent. The law thus fosters the newly formed family.†

Adult Child-Parent Subsystem

Benefits for parents based on claims from an adult child as insured worker have followed a direction different from those for other members of the family. The trend from the beginning has been to provide for the oldest generation apart from the younger. The legislation has responded to contemporary patterns of separate living arrangements‡ and to the desire of old people to be independent of their children. Indeed, to provide this independence has been a major purpose of the program. With the extension of the life span and the supposedly greater difficulty of the elderly in meeting the demands of fast-moving industrial machinery, provision had to be made to assure the dignity and self-respect of older citizens. In addition, the nuclear family requires that the couple with growing children be left free to direct its own affairs without encumbrance of dependent old people. While responsive to these changes in work and in family patterns, the legislation has still had to accommodate to two deeply ingrained values of American society, the Protestant ethic and filial responsibility. Although the Protestant ethic, with its emphasis on work, thrift, and savings for the future, has been preserved in the criteria dealing with the entitlement of spouses, its manifestation in relationships between parent and adult children has almost disappeared. It is

---

*Reference to "living with parent" has been retained since 1960 only for exceptional circumstances, such as the provisions for a surviving wife to adopt children within two years of the insured's death, which required that the child must have been living with the insured at the time of his death. Also, for the entitlement of illegitimate children, the fact of "living with the father" may be accepted as evidence of dependency in addition to other supporting evidence of paternity.

†Since 1950, an amendment has specified that the stepchild must be living with or receiving at least one-half of his support from his stepparent.

‡Of the total aged population in 1952, 26 percent of couples, 31 percent of nonmarried men, and 45 percent of nonmarried women were living with children. In 1957, 23 percent of couples, 27 percent of nonmarried men, and 37 percent of nonmarried women were living with children (4:102).

retained, however, through the administrative operation of the program, which levies a special tax to finance it. The old people have worked and saved from their earnings through the payroll deductions credited to their accounts, and they feel that they are thereby entitled to benefits. At the same time, the old value of filial responsibility expressed in the Fifth Commandment has almost been rejected. Indeed, the operation of the program is such that it relieves the younger generation of feelings of guilt over their neglect in honoring this responsibility to their parents. Because payments are made from current contributions to the trust funds, the younger generation is paying the benefits.[3] Both the older and the younger generation can therefore rationalize away any possible violations of the older values.

It is clear that the program has not fostered the entitlement of parents through their adult children. From 1939 to the present, parents have been entitled only to survivors' benefits; they have never been entitled to dependents' benefits based on the insured son's or daughter's retirement or disability. Furthermore, in order to receive survivors' benefits, they must have reached retirement age and they themselves must not have earned eligibility in the social security program.

That parents may qualify only at the death of their insured adult child seems discriminatory when one looks at the extensive provisions for dependents in the other two family subsystems. Certainly the lack of provision for parents while their insured children are still alive denies assistance to a family pattern which includes the oldest generation. Actuarial considerations may explain this discrimination and omission in that survivors' benefits to parents simply replace the benefits of their deceased children and do not increase significantly the demands on the trust funds as another category of beneficiaries would do. But, of course, this lack is further evidence that the program has not been designed for the extended family or for those who did not work in covered employment.

With coverage persistently extended to almost all occupations, it has been expected that all old people will be eligible for benefits either in their own right or as dependents or survivors of their spouses, rather than as dependents of their adult children. That this expectation has been fulfilled is shown by the fact that the category of surviving parents as beneficiaries is much smaller than any other category based on position within the family. The increase in the number of persons in this category has been much less rapid than that in other categories. The number of awards made to parents in 1941 was 1,272 and in 1967 it was 2,658.[4] Only 90,253 persons have received parents' benefits from 1940 to 1967. This small number showed that some people were remaining outside the program. To compensate for this lack of entitlement, the amendments of 1965 provided small benefits for certain uninsured individuals aged seventy-two or over who are not eligible through their own attachment to the labor force. This provision was made for them without regard to a relationship with a family member.

DEGREE OF DEPENDENCY

The criteria for entitlement in the category of relationships based on dependency have been restrictive. According to the amendments of 1939, the parent must have been wholly dependent upon and supported by the insured wage-earning child at the time of his death. The word "wholly" was changed in 1946 to "chiefly." A further relaxation in 1950 required only that the parent be receiving at least one-half of his support from his insured son or daughter. In 1958, benefits were extended to surviving parents who had been dependent on an adult child at the time the child became disabled if the child had been receiving disability insurance before his death. A provision early in the program disqualified parents if the deceased worker had a surviving wife or child who was entitled to benefits—a decided indication of the subordinate position in which parents were held. However, this provision was struck out in 1957, and surviving parents may receive benefits, even if there are other survivors. One wonders whether this change showed a reviving respect for parents or merely a greater willingness to appropriate money for the aged.

LEGAL STATUS AND RESIDENCE OF THE PARENT

The parent may be the parent, the stepparent, or the adoptive parent of the insured individual. He may not retain benefits if he remarries, except that, since the amendments of 1958, he may marry an individual who is also entitled to benefits.

The stepparent must be one by a marriage contracted before the insured attained the age of sixteen. An adoptive parent must be one by whom the insured child was adopted before the age of sixteen. These requirements have not changed since the beginning of the program.

The legislation has never included mention of a requirement that the parent and adult child be living together—another recognition that the tradition of the extended family was declining and that, in fact, this trend was already established by 1939.

Discussion

To a degree Congress, in providing for family benefits through Old-Age, Survivors', and Disability Insurance, has taken account of the changes that the social system of the family has been undergoing. In the husband-wife subsystem it allocated in the beginning benefits only for a stable marital relationship, one which continued with the same spouse throughout a lifetime, but it has come to recognize that divorce does occur among a significant number of couples. It has recognized the increasing participation of the married woman in the labor force and even the fact that sometimes she may be the principal breadwinner. But that Congress has valued the older patterns is shown by the slow and ponderous way in which it has made these accommodations. When it did made the change of permitting benefits to divorced wives, it held the first marriage to a length of time that would almost have precluded a second one in generations not long past, when life expectancy was low. It has restricted benefits for husbands more than those for wives, apparently in the expectation that the man would have a more dominant family position and would be the chief, if not the only, breadwinner. It has resisted admitting that a man might properly be dependent upon a woman.

The legislation has been more liberal with the parent-child than with the husband-wife subsystem. It has recognized tha families may be broken, that some children continue with one parent, and that others are transferred into new nuclear families. From the beginning of the program it has provided not only for natural children of a legal marriage, but also for adoptive children and stepchildren. Slowly it has made it easier for children of any legal status to qualify for benefits. The legislation seems to encourage the formation of adoptive relationships, provided the adoption conforms to acceptable legal and social practices.* Children have been provided for despite changes in marital partners. Yet, in this concern for children, the claim for entitlement to benefits rests in the responsibility of the legal parent. The state is not taking away parental responsibility for the care of children.

Congress has responded most directly to societal changes in the adult child-parent subsystem. It accepts the small nuclear family which excludes grandparents. It has almost denied the responsibility of sons and daughters for their parents. Indeed, the insurance program has assumed a significant share of the financial responsibility for older people, and in the course of so doing it has not dallied. When one examines the legislation one detects no feeling of doubt or guilt on the part of the framers for their support of the value of independence for senior citizens from the younger generation.

OASDI is a program which is well accepted by the American public; there has been little adverse criticism of it. Perhaps its acceptance has been due to its responsiveness to changing social conditions. Some may suggest that its acceptance has been due to considerations outside the subject of this paper, for example, its funding through a special tax represented as savings

---

*Amendments of 1968 specify that the adoption take place under the supervision of a public or private child-placement agency and as decreed by a court or competent jurisdiction. Federal regulations of 1970 provide that the investigation by the child-placement agency and its report to the court having jurisdiction of adoption proceedings are mandatory. No waiver or lack of such requirements under applicable state law is accepted.

by workers for the future, the fact that the amount of benefits is related to the amount of wages the individual has earned as his achievement, and the fact that the middle and lower classes pay the tax and thus provide for their own future without a contribution from the rich. Yet, in regard to family benefits, most will probably agree that the legal and nuclear family should be the norm, that adult children should not be financially responsible for their parents and that old people should not have to face the guilt of such dependency. When children marry and form new families, they should lose their claim to dependency on their parents, and even marriage at a young age while the child is still attending school should not justify extension of this dependence. Stable family relationships should have priority, and death-bed marriages should not be accepted. Wives, widows, and children should be entitled to benefits, but husbands and widowers should not be offered quite the same advantages. Nor should wives and widows, if they are young enough and able to work, be included unless they are caring for children. Others may question why this program has been as value-laden as it has been and why an income-maintenance program should be encumbered with family values. Why should this program act as a supporter and even as a controller of social values and behavior patterns? Cannot other forces in society assume the functions of setting family standards?

This examination has not dealt with the impact in the opposite direction—the effect of this legislation on the American family. Wilensky and Lebeaux state that "while social welfare helps to shape the larger society, it reflects more than it determines the nature of the whole."[5] Despite this absorption by social legislation of the cultural setting in which it lives, it is obvious that change agents, such as Congress, should take account of the possible effects of the policies advocated and prescribed. Does Congress know what its policies on family benefits in OASDI are doing to the American family?

The data on the social security program are impressive in scope and accuracy. In connection with the family, the number participating in the program according to position in the family is known. The possible effect of some of the legislative provisions has been studied. For example, it has been ascertained that the percentage of aged people receiving OASDI benefits and living with their children was lower in 1952 and in 1957 than the percentage for the total aged population and that the rate of increase in independent living arrangements was greater for OASDI beneficiaries between 1951 and 1957 than for the total aged population.[6] Thus, the receiving of OASDI benefits may well have been a factor in the choice by old people to live apart from their children. Additional studies of this sort would be helpful.

Among questions that might profitably be answered are: Have the provisions for dependents' and survivors' benefits for adoptive children been a factor in the number of adoptions? Have the benefits for stepchildren lessened responsibility of the biological parent and increased the assumption of responsibility by the stepparent? Have these provisions provided more stable and solid relationships for these children within the second family? Has the prospect of the woman's becoming entitled to benefits in her own right influenced her decision to work outside the home? Known is the number of dependent and surviving children who are receiving benefits extended from age eighteen to twenty-two because they are in school. What percentage of this number would be able to continue in school if these extended benefits were not available? What percentage of children who marry at a young age and surrender their benefits continue or discontinue their education? Of those who continue their education, does the husband set his occupational goals too low in order to support his family quickly, and does the wife who supports her husband sacrifice her own development to his? In regard to parents, two out of five applications for parent support were denied in 1957, the majority for failure to establish "one-half support" from the deceased insured son or daughter.[7] What alternate arrangements were made for these old people? When benefits are increased, how does the change affect family choices and patterns?

Do the provisions actually have the effect the Congress believes that they should and will have and do they achieve the goals that Congress had in mind? What goals for the family have been formulated? In a democracy the legislative body may not have the prerogative of determining family goals; its function may be confined to that of responding to the changes and values of the nation it represents.

It is unlikely that social legislation can ever be devoid of reflections of social values. Of course, it is within the realm of possibility that a highly scientifically oriented society can define its problems within circumscribed limits and design its remedies with objectivity and directness. Still, the determination of which conditions constitute problems and which do not are social-value judgments.

Social welfare programs are linked inevitably to the society of which they are a part, and the ties between them must be understood if changes in programs are to be acceptable. Pumphrey has remarked: "Getting people to change values, or to recognize disparity between conditions and ideas, is the work of the reformer. Organization and provision of services is the job of social welfare. But each alone can be sterile; they must work together for maximum achievement."[8]

References

1.   Harold L. Wilensky, and Charles Lebeaux, *Industrial Society and Social Welfare*. New York: Free Press, 1958, pp. 13–14.

2.   Ella J. Polinsky, "The Position of Women in the Social Security System." *Social Security Bulletin* 32 (July 1969): p. 15.

3.   Alvin L. Schorr, *Explorations in Social Policy.* New York: Basic Books, 1968, pp. 101–31.

4.   *Social Security Bulletin.* Annual Statistical Supplement, 1967, p. 58.

5.   Wilensky and Lebeaux, *op. cit.*, p. 13.

6.   Schorr, *op. cit.*, p. 102; Charles I. Schottland, "Government Economic Programs and Family Life." *Journal of Marriage and the Family* 29 (February 1967): pp. 71–123.

7.   Schorr, *op. cit.*, p. 104.

8.   Ralph E. Pumphrey, "Social Welfare in the United States." In *Encyclopedia of Social Work*, pp. 19–36. New York: National Association of Social Workers, 1965, p. 35.

5
The Implications of Changing Sex Roles for Family Structure

Jean Lipman-Blumen

Changing sex roles are a sound barometer of more pervasive changes within any society. In this article, the author will be concerned first with the shifts in sex roles as an index of more general societal changes. An underlying assumption of this article is that sex roles, generational roles, racial roles, and occupational roles are created by society. Second, that there is nothing sacred in regard to specific role configurations—at least not in the long run. Third, that roles are useful means by which individuals deal with one another in a large-scale, pluralistic society, where encounters are multitudinous, infrequent, and often superficial. Although roles offer helpful clues about meeting and dealing with strangers, there is a fourth assumption that suggests that roles tend to impede long-term, intimate relationships. They act as theatrical masks behind which it is easy to hide our own feelings. They often make the needs and desires of others impenetrable. Thus, when we talk of changing roles we need to remember that there is nothing intrinsically negative about changing roles.

Recently, much has been written about changing sex roles, partly in response to the emergence of the feminist movement. Unfortunately, much that has been written is highly impressionistic, or based on very small samples. Thus, the author will examine demographic trends, to provide a more realistic framework within which to make assessments and predictions about new directions in sex roles.

Source: From Social Casework 57 (February 1976), pp. 67–79. Copyright © 1976 by the Family Service Association of America. Reprinted by permission.

Demographic Trends

Changes in trends in women's lives will be explored first, because in most instances, the rates of change are greater for women than for men; many national statistics are given for the more stable female segment of the population; and they reflect, as well as forecast, growing and imminent changes in males' roles as well.

As a brief overview, women are living longer,* marrying later and less often, remarrying less frequently, having and expecting to have fewer children,† and more often than previously planning to have no children. According to the latest United States Census figures, first marriage rates and remarriage rates have declined. Not so surprisingly, the remarriage rate is down more among women of high educational and occupational levels. The divorce rate, we are constantly reminded, continues to increase.

Female-Headed Households

Increasingly, both young and older women are living alone,‡ they also are heading families more often. In the last decade, there has been an impressive increase in the number of female-headed families, which partly reflects a rising divorce rate. In 1972, 14 percent of all families with children had a female head, representing a 40 percent increase since 1960.[1] This increase occurred in both white and black families, among the poor and

---

*Women's longevity has increased dramatically since the turn of the century. A female child born in 1966 can expect to live, on the average, approximately 74 years, compared to a female born in 1900 whose life expectancy was 48 years. U.S. Department of Labor, Women's Bureau, *Handbook of Women Workers* (Washington, D.C.: U.S. Government Printing Office, 1969).

†This drop in the fertility rate of women eighteen to twenty-nine years of age is partly related to an increase in the age at first marriage; however, it also is linked to increased educational attainment, labor force participation, and metropolitan residence. (*Current Population Report, Population Characteristics*, Series P-20, No. 240, September 1972.)

‡In 1973, there were approximately 13.5 million U.S. households headed by an individual sixty-five years old or older. Of the white households, 8 percent were headed by females; of the black households, 19 percent had female family heads. In addition, approximately 80 percent of all white primary individuals (individuals who maintained their own households while living alone or with persons not related to them) sixty-five years old or over were female. (*Current Population Report, Population Characteristics*, Series P-20, No. 258, December 1973.) Since 1968, the number of female primary individuals has increased by 26 percent to a high of 8.9 million. The median age of primary females remained at sixty-five during this period. This represents a growing portion of the adult female population who are living alone or with non-relatives in the later stages of life. *Current Population Report, Population Characteristics*, Series P-20, No. 240, September 1972; Abbott L. Ferriss, *Indicators of Trends in Status of American Women* (New York: Russell Sage Foundation, 1971).

not-so-poor. The median annual income for female-headed families with children under eighteen was $4,000, compared to the $11,600 median income for all families with children under eighteen. While the number of poor people dropped from 40 million to 24.5 million between 1970 and 1972, the number of poor people in female-headed families rose by 867,000.

Educational Trends

Education is a potential contributor to changing sex roles. But so far, it has not made serious inroads on the traditional female role. Rather, it has served to keep women channeled within a very narrow range of educational options.

The educational system offers only limited options for women. In 1971, women earned only 14 percent of the doctoral degrees granted, reflecting a greater attrition rate of women from higher education. While boys and girls enter primary school in approximately equal numbers, by the time they enter college, there is a drop in the number of female students, despite the fact that in the earlier years girls tend to get better grades, are more likely to be enrolled in a grade above the mode at age thirteen, and are less likely to be underachievers until they enter puberty.

The drop-off of female students beginning in early adolescence is reflected in the U.S. Department of Commerce, Bureau of the Census report which indicates that the proportion of females enrolled in school at each age level from fourteen to twenty-four is less than that of males.[2] The Carnegie Commission.[3] reports that since 1900, women have been less likely to enter college, despite the fact that they are more likely than men to complete secondary school. Women's access to higher education—an important link to occupational opportunity—is apparently limited.

Labor Force Participation

While the educational patterns of women are not noticeably or dramatically changing, women's labor force participation is undergoing some transformation. Women are entering the labor force in increasingly greater numbers and proportions. They are joining and remaining in the labor force after marriage and even during the childbearing and child-raising years of twenty-four to thirty-five. They also are remaining and even entering the labor force during the more mature period marked by ages forty-five to sixty-four.

As of February 1975, 36,198,000 women were in the labor force and constituted 39.8 percent of all workers (U.S. Department of Labor, Women's Bureau). By that time, 45.6 percent of all women sixteen years and over were in the labor force.[4]

The change can be seen most vividly if we recall that in 1940 close to half of the women who worked were single, and approximately 30 percent were married. By 1970, the picture was reversed: approximately one-fifth were single, and 60 percent were married. From 1940 to 1970, the labor force participation rate of married women rose from 15 to 41 percent and the rate of working mothers with children under age six rose from 9 to 30 percent.[5]

By 1973, 42 percent of married women with husbands present worked, and almost 39 percent of widowed, divorced, or separated women were in the labor force.[6] At that time, working wives numbered 19.2 million, amounting to nearly 60 percent of all women workers. Working wives were the group which contributed most to the 72 percent increase in employed women between 1950 and 1971.[7]

By March 1974, the percentage of married women, with husbands present, who worked had risen another whole percentage point to 43 percent, a sizeable gain for such a short time period. In the four-year period from 1970 to 1974 the percentage of working mothers with children under age six had risen from 30 to 36.6 percent, again an impressive jump. Projections for 1980 (made in 1973) suggested that the labor force would expand to 100 million workers, 40 percent of whom would be women.[8] In view of the current growth of female labor force participation, most labor analysts ackknowledge that these projections will be surpassed.

As we have noted previously, more children than ever before have two employed parents. Although the total population of children in the United States has declined since 1970, the population of children whose mothers are employed or who are seeking employment has risen.[9] More specifically, by March 1973, there were 1.5 million fewer children in families, but 650,000 more had working mothers. Of the 64.3 million children under age eighteen, 26.2 million had mothers in the labor force. This included six million under age six.[10]

Despite these increases in labor force participation among women of all marital and maternal statuses, there has been relatively little change in the distribution of women in the labor force over the twenty-year span from 1950–1970. The greatest number of women remained in the three traditionally "feminine" roles of teacher, nurse, and secretary.[11] As late as 1968, over one-third of all employed women were clerical workers, including 3.3 million stenographers, typists, and secretaries. Sixteen percent were service workers, and another 15 percent were operatives, mostly in factories. Approximately 15 percent were professional and technical workers. This group included 1.7 million teachers, many of whom now face reduced occupational opportunities in the field of education.

We gain a somewhat better perspective if we look at changes over the 1940–1970 period. During this period, women's occupational pattern changed from "half blue, half white collar to one that is decidedly white collar."[12] In both the earlier and later periods, women in nonagricultural fields were concentrated in three major occupational groups: service, blue-collar operative, and white-collar clerical and sales. In 1970, however, the service and operative percentages had decreased, the professional and technical had increased slightly, and the clerical-sales percentages had gone up markedly. Some of these shifts represent changes for special sub-groups. For example, the decline in service jobs, such as those for domestics, has been experienced largely by minority women who have moved into white-collar sales and clerical jobs.

Women are still underrepresented in the traditional professions and higher status occupations. By 1970, only 28.2 percent of those individuals employed as college presidents, professors, and instructors were women. In the legal profession, only 4.9 percent of the lawyers and judges were women. Similarly, in the field of engineering, only 1.5 percent of the engineers were women. Additionally, in all of these fields women are disproportionately concentrated in the low-level positions.

It is important to remember, however, that there have been some changes in isolated roles during this time period. Women bus drivers, scarcely enumerable in 1940, now represent 37 percent of the bus driving occupation (although many of them are restricted to school bus driving). There has been a virtual boom in women bartenders, moving from a low of 2.5 percent in 1940 to 30 percent in 1970. Women real estate agents and brokers rose from 9 percent in 1940 to 36 percent in 1970. In the higher status and higher paying professions there have been some slight changes. For example, women numbered one-twentieth of all physicians in 1940, but rose to one-eighth by 1973.[13]

Another change may be seen among self-employed women, where women represented only 17 percent of the total self-employed group in 1940, but 26 percent in 1973. By 1973 1.4 million women were self-employed in nonagricultural fields, an increase of approximately 600,000 beyond the 1940 level. The increase for men among the ranks of the self-employed in nonagricultural industries during this same period was minimal. Most of these self-employed women ran service and retail trade businesses in 1973. Among those in the service category, more than 60 percent operated businesses involved in providing personal services such as beauty salons, dressmaking shops, laundries, and child care services. In the professional services field, 30 percent of the self-employed women within this field ran nursing homes and other medical businesses and conducted educational enterprises.

In terms of their occupations, women who are self-employed differ from women who are wage and salary earners. Twenty-four percent of the self-employed were managers or proprietors compared to 4 percent of salary or wage earners, and 18 percent of the self-employed were in clerical-sales compared to 43 percent of the salary or wage earners. Further, of the 18 percent of the self-employed found in clerical-sales enterprises, most tended to cluster in such fields as real estate sales and court stenography.[14]

Fertility Rate

Technology, legislation, attitudinal, and behavioral changes all have conjoined to help depress the birth rate in more recent years. More women are choosing to remain childless, and legal abortions allegedly are depressing the overall, and particularly the nonmarital, fertility rate.[15] The fertility rate of women continued to decline in 1974, but at a somewhat slower pace than the decline registered between 1970 and 1973.

In 1974, there were 68.4 births per 1,000 women ages fifteen to forty-four, a rate 1 percent below the 1973 rate. The average annual decline between 1970 and 1973 was 7 percent. Despite the slight decline in the fertility rate in 1974, the number of births nonetheless was a little higher than in 1973. In 1974, 3,166,000 births occurred, representing an increase of 29,000 over the 1973 figure. (This increase in births is accounted for by the increase in the number of women of child-bearing age, which offsets the declining fertility rate.)[16]

The development of the contraceptive pill, abortion legislation, the zero population growth movement, the conservationist movement, and the declining marriage rate, coupled with more lenient attitudes toward unmarried people living together, have all contributed to the declining birth rate. As a result, we can expect in the next twenty-five years to witness an increase in the older groups and a decrease in the younger groups within our population.

Marriage, Divorce, and Remarriage

Marriage, divorce, and remarriage trends are contributing to the changes that we likely shall see in family structure. Following a peaking of all three trends after World War II,[17] the first marriage rate began a steady decline that continued through the 1960s and the 1970s.[18] The divorce and remarriage rates began to rise around 1960 and surged dramatically during the following decade.

By 1970, the divorce and remarriage rates were the highest ever recorded in the United States.[19] But things have begun to change since 1970: while the divorce rate has continued to climb steeply, the remarriage rate has leveled off and appears to be on the decline, and remarriage is more often delayed and avoided by women with high educational, occupational, and economic levels. Liberalization of divorce laws, as well as changes in attitudes and sex roles have contributed to the divorce boom. In 1974, the number of divorces totaled 970,000. This figure represented 57,000 (or 6.2 percent) more than the comparable figure for 1973. The divorce rate in 1974 was 4.6 per 1,000 people, amounting to a 4.5 percent jump since 1973.[20]

Overall, low-income groups continue to be most affected by divorce. For men, in 1970, lower income was associated with divorce, while the reverse was true for women. Women with high income levels more often postponed or rejected marriage, while lower income women were more likely to remarry within a short time period. Although a smaller proportion of upper income level men are divorced, their rate of increase in the proportion divorced rose more rapidly than that of lower income men in the 1960–1970 decade. Upper income divorced men remarry more often than lower income men, which is the reverse of the female pattern.

Among all women thirty-five to forty-four years of age during the 1960s, the proportion of those divorced rose by close to one-half. Among the upper income women, however, the proportion of those divorced had a slower rate of increase than among lower income women. Arthur J. Norton and Paul C. Glick suggest that a general trend toward convergence of the proportion divorced among status levels could be seen in the 1960–1970 period.[21] They conclude that part of the leveling of socio-economic differences was attributable to the fact that the percent of upper income divorced men was increasing more rapidly than that of lower income men, while the reverse was true for women: the percent of upper income divorced women was increasing more slowly than the percent of lower income women. Thus, the overall increase in divorce has affected all socioeconomic groups, but the differences between upper and lower income groups are diminishing.

Early age at first marriage has been a steady predictor of divorce, particularly among Caucasians. In the past, low educational attainment and low income were two of the primary factors associated with divorce, but age at first marriage has been seen as stronger than both.[22] Thus the discernible changes in age at first marriage among both male and female groups has influenced marriage and divorce trends.

From 1900 to the mid-1950s, there was a fairly systematic decline in age at first marriage for both women and men. In 1956, the lowest median age at first marriage was recorded for both sexes. Since 1956, the picture has begun to reverse, so that both men and women are marrying later than in previous decades. The increase in median age at first marriage for men leveled off in 1967 and has shown no appreciable change since that time; however, the age at first marriage for women continues to rise. As a result, women are marrying at increasingly later ages, while men are maintaining their age-at-marriage level. What this suggests is that the age difference between husbands and wives is diminishing, and, in fact, we should begin to see some increase in the numbers of women marrying men younger than themselves.[23]

The delay in marriage that first began in the mid-1960s has continued and increased, and is particularly true among young women. Marriage delay is reflected in the increase of single women twenty to twenty-four years old from 28 percent in 1960 to 40 percent in 1970.[24] As age at first marriage increases, and first marriage rates decrease, divorce rates eventually should reflect this, in at least a slight rate decrease.

Norton and Glick[25] tell us that "among both men and women who had ever married the highest proportion who were known to have been divorced after their first or last marriage (or both) was for those with an incomplete high school education." However, the educational levels of women and men, black and white, are rising, so that about 75 percent of the young people today finish high school and about 43 percent of them (or some 58 percent of the high school graduates) can be expected to enter a degree-credit program in a college or university. As the educational level and age at first marriage rise, the divorce trend should feel the impact.

As divorce has become more widespread, it necessarily has involved children. Despite the fact that the "number of children involved in all divorces has been increasing steadily . . . the average per decree has been declining in recent years; in 1969 the average was 1.31 children per decree."[26] Thus, among couples who seek divorce, we may continue to see smaller families.

Sexual Behavior

Improved and widely available contraceptive methods have led to different patterns of sexual behavior. Coupled with earlier physiological maturation of females and males, "the pill" has contributed to the initiation of sexual activity at an earlier age.

In some subgroups within our culture, partly because there are no clearly marked *rites de passage* for adolescents, unwed parenthood becomes such a mark of adulthood. Extramarital sexual activity is much talked about, yet not yet systematically documented in any Kinsey-like national study.

Nonetheless, the signs all point in the direction of increased sexual activity both within and outside of marriage, for younger, as well as older, age groups. Recent medical research suggests that regular sexual activity is possible much later in life than previously had been supposed, and with predominantly positive results for mental and physical health. Simultaneously, attitudes toward sexuality have begun to change, with greater acceptance of sexual relationships between unmarried individuals. This changing norm contributes to shifting attitudes toward the need for sexual exclusivity within marriage.

Energy and Other Resources

Factors beyond changing sociological trends need to be taken into account. Increasing concern about the conservaion of energy and other resources, such as land and air, have begun to make inroads into our life styles. Potential oil shortages already have altered commuting patterns, car-buying behavior, and real estate purchases. Smaller cars, urban housing, more communal or sharing patterns of driving, living, consuming, and working emerge from such concerns. Suburban living, with its necessary commuting and wasteful land use, is being subjected to reevaluation. It is becoming clear that the costs involved in single unit dwellings on private parcels of land, requiring individual sewage and power connections, are too great.

Inflation, which is rising beyond cost of living increases and set incomes is already forcing drastic changes in life styles. Individuals who previously would have been financially independent find that they are squeezed to maintain evan a semblance of their usual existence.

Socioeconomic Factors

Welfare programs have imposed certain life patterns on individuals, or at least created incentives for certain life styles—often negative and self-perpetuating life styles. Cut-backs in funding for welfare programs may very well force us to think in terms of alternative ways of supporting fatherless children, the unemployed, the elderly, and the sick.

Economic pressure, among other factors, is leading toward the four-day work week. Simultaneously, the flexitime work scheduling, already occuring in some European countries, whereby people put in a certain number of work hours, but in any pattern acceptable to themselves, will join with part-time work to produce very different work patterns. The nine-to-five work life, and the day and night shift, as we now know them, eventually will not longer be the standard. As the availability of jobs diminishes, "moonlighting" on second regular jobs will decrease.

Mass Media

The pervasive presence of television is reflected in U.S. Census data that reveal that 96 percent of American homes have one or more television sets which are in use twenty-six hours and fifteen minutes per week. The average set is in operation more than six hours per day. Approximately 25 percent of all children watch television more than five hours each day.[27]

The average American adult male watches television approximately three hours per day, and the average American housewife passes thirty hours and twenty-two minutes in viewing time per week.[28] Surprisingly, adolescents spend the least amount of time per week in front of the television, perhaps as a reaction to the fact that the peak for viewing is around age twelve.

Television both portrays and creates the images we take as real. If viewing continues to escalate as it has over the years, we can anticipate a growth in television's influence on our lives. It is a resource that can be used or abused in terms of sex role images. In the past, it has been a mixed blessing, often portraying images of housewives born with mops in their hands and husbands who are congenitally unfit for any family decision beyond a choice between hot or cold shaving cream.

Television and other mass media have exaggerated the most sensational and least central changes in sex roles. Bra-burning, apocryphal as it probably is, has had more coverage than serious rethinking of sex roles. Occasionally, programs on exemplary dynamic women intersperse the more usual portrayals of women as sex symbols or drudges. But the balance somehow is missing, and the true chronicle of changing sex roles is yet to become what we see on the screen.

Projections for the Next Two Decades

These are some of the demographic changes that we have witnessed and will continue to experience during the next two decades. But where does this leave us, and what can we say about the impact of these changes on family structure? Some of the changes are implicit in the very shifts that have been described, others require some speculation. But one fact is apparent: families soon will not look very much like the nuclear family we have taken as the standard.

New Family Structures

There will be far fewer families that consist of a male and female parent and one or more children. There are and will continue to be more single-parent families, some headed by females and others by males. Fewer families in which one spouse is absent will be reconstituted by remarriage. More single-parent families will join with one or more others to combine food, shelter, childcare, and companionship. Some of these groups will be constituted by adults of the same sex, others will have both sexes. With time, there will be proportionately fewer children in single-parent, as well as two-parent families. The decline of domestic workers will contribute to communal patterns and commercial services for housework and childcare.

As the shortened work week allows fathers to spend more time at home, the paternal role will begin to emerge as more than a shadowy, symbolic role. Families will have to make more real—less ceremonial—room for fathers. Fathers may begin to be more involved in the emotional care of children and wives, as well as of the older generation. Wives and mothers, who will be working more, will share household tasks less guiltily with husbands and children. These new families will have to experiment and explore new ways of developing expectations for one another, new ways of interacting.

New Housing Patterns

A vital change in family living can easily come about from new attitudes and social policies with regard to land use. As land becomes more scarce and more expensive, and as energy supplies are threatened, it is most likely that multiunit dwellings will begin to replace single unit dwellings situated on individual plots of land. In the wake of fuel conservation measures, the development of multiunit dwellings undoubtedly will need to be centered near work places and commuting will cease to be the momentous daily ritual that we now know. This trend means both more urban dwellings and more suburban work places.

These multiunit dwellings will offer an opportunity for less segregated living. At the present time, we live in a totally segregated society. Not only do we segregate by race, but also by ethnicity, age, marital status, and parental status. The elderly live separately in retirement communities, their lives uninterrupted by the sounds or sights of youth. Married couples with children are not allowed in many apartment complexes where only the childfree may live. Even singles are segregated in their own lush ghettos, replete with a multitude of recreational facilities. The affluent isolate themselves in penthouses or tree-lined estates in costly neighborhoods, and the poor and not-so-poor live in their own equally segregated enclaves.

This kind of segregation in homogeneous areas flattens the tone of living, dulls the quality of life, and depletes the richness of existence. When we live and interact only with people exactly like ourselves, we do not grow. Limits are set on our learning and developing because the models that we learn from are limited. New neighborhoods, more heterogeneous in terms of race, ethnicity, age, marital status, and parental status will reintroduce the young to the elderly, the married to the unmarried, the parents to the non-parents, and white to black.

Fragmentation of Roles

Heterogeneous neighborhoods (which we recognize may still be homogeneous for some time to come by economic level and thus by race) offer new opportunities for behavior. Traditional roles of parent, child, grandparent, worker, wife, and husband are becoming fragmented. The old rules will no longer be applicable. When we no longer can expect to have a father play the role of tired worker who must relax and be undisturbed during his two-day weekend, we have to begin to understand a new set of behaviors more appropriate for a less-tired father who works only four days. As roles change, behavior becomes somewhat less predictable, less routinized, more creative, and more complicated. When roles change, we can no longer depend on people to act in stereotyped "traditional" ways. Role change is always beset with opportunities and difficulties.

The fragmentation and reconfiguration of roles have much to recommend them. Roles often are used as escape hatches to keep people from having to confront themselves and each other as individuals. When we step outside of those roles, we give up our protective coloration; our outer shells are gone, and we emerge as vulnerable human beings. Without our shells we are subject to special hurt, but we also face the possibility of new growth—sometimes a danger in itself.

When we can confront our children simply as "impossible adolescents," we do not have to think about the complexities of our very special relationships with them. when our children can relegate us in their thinking to the roles of "square parents," they do not have to deal with us as distinct people with needs, motives, and sometimes deviant desires.

As roles become fragmented, there is much overlap and sometimes dissonance among the multiple roles that we are able to enter. By living in heterogeneous settings we compound the situation. We force ourselves to confront people in other fragmented roles, roles which in their stable state we knew little about in a segregated society. From this situation, new types of social and psychological options emerge.

All of these new options sound vague and perhaps idealistic. How, in fact, would we operationalize this? By way of example let us look at adolescent roles as they are now and how they could become more authentic.

New Roles for Adolescents

In the last decade, many adolescents have sought to bring meaning to their lives through drugs for expanding consciousness; sex; dropping out; and violence. Adolescents sense correctly that they have inauthentic lives, contrived and artificial, lacking few real responsibilities, or even functions, other than school attendance. They have no responsibility for themselves or for others.

Society makes it clear that they are unable to be trusted with anything but learning, and even sets strict parameters on the kinds and uses of that learning. So what one learns is strictly limited, and its application is similarly troubled. No wonder there was the great concern with "relevance" in the sixties which continues to exist today. No wonder adolescents and young adults have a sense of anomie, of meaninglessness, isolation, and futility. It is a totally clearsighted view of their lives that leads them to this rather inevitable conclusion. It is not surprising that "suicide ranks third among the leading killers in the nineteen to twenty-five-year-old age group."[29]

However, if the traditional adolescent role, or that which we have artificially made traditional, begins to undergo fragmentation and change, what will become of it? Adolescents, living in a more heterogeneous society, where parents, grandparents, teachers, and friends are undergoing similar role fragmentation, have the opportunity to forge new relationships. If the work week moves forward to become four days, so presumably will the school week. During the work week, while parents are in offices and factories, adolescents and the aging could develop mutually supportive roles. They could care for and help each other, each according to his or her own abilities and needs. The aging could provide the advice and wisdom that come from experience, the emotional supervision of a loving eye. Adolescents could provide the physical and emotional care that the aging need.

Communication often is easier across a double generation than between contiguous generations. The tensions that exist between parent and child are felt less often between child and grandparent. This communication would provide authentic roles in which both youth and the elderly could develop meaningful functions and *raisons d'être*. In this way, youth and the elderly could reestablish authentic lives.

There are still, however, other ways for adolescents and youth to develop authentic roles, and these can be coupled with expanding and authentic roles for adults as well. With the paid work week and the school week eventually contracting, there will be more time for adults and youth to pass together. It is entirely feasible, and probably desirable, for adults to work with younger people in legitimate apprenticeship relationships, whereby youth can learn and perform in a real, rewarding, and rewarded manner. Community projects can be undertaken first by adult and youth teams in master-apprentice teams, later by youth working alone and even teaching more of the young.

At the present time, there already exist youth programs for peer counseling and for emotional and occupational problems.[30] Teenagers can teach or tutor other students, both young and old. Teenagers, working with others, can develop businesses that service the community. There is no real necessity to relegate young people to menial, non-growth jobs, such as newspaper delivery and lawn tending. Expertise in auto mechanics, woodworking, electrical, carpentry, and similar areas, should be developed into authentic roles for all youth—in non-school hours—and not merely for those young ieople who plan to use these skills in lifetime careers. Driving skills can be used to transport the sick and the elderly to medical appointments, to shopping centers, and to social events. Day care centers can be run by adolescents with adult cooperation. Academic skills can be used in industrial, educational, and social policy decisions.

New Adult Roles and Neo-Families

Adult roles, too, can change in ways that will add dimension and zest to living. Adults who long for more free time to engage in non-occupational activities can look forward to developing their avocations in more meaningful and serious ways. Some may even develop enough expertise and confidence in their expanded avocational roles to exchange them for their present occupations. Apprenticeship relationships, mentioned above, could lead to new business enterprises. Non-family relationships with the young could offer adults opportunities for understanding youth, often denied in their limited roles as parents.

Neo-families could exist, in which non-blood kin could assume the generational roles. Thus, the elderly woman living three units away would be a quasi-grandmother, playing a real and desirable role within the family. The continuation of these non-blood relationships would require as much effort as the non-married relationships of young people who live together. In the case where these relationships break down, individuals could withdraw from them and recreate similar alliances with other individuals.

As women continue to enter the labor market, their roles within and outside the family will change. So will the related roles of husband, child, employer, and employee. Women gradually will enter higher-paying occupations involving roles of greater responsibility. Women entrepreneurs are on the increase, and their ability to develop important resources will grow. Women are beginning to develop the resources of education, occupations, and money, and these resources eventually can be negotiated into political and legal assets. As women's control over important societal resources grows, we will begin to have a less male-dominated society. When women are perceived as controlling important resources, both women and men will turn to them for help and support. These actions will, in turn, increase their power and credit in the world outside of the family. The homosocial world which men have created for themselves[31] soon will be replicated by women who can develop powerful social, economic, political, and legal networks.

When women's work roles begin to assume comparable importance to men's, and particularly when their contributions to the family's economic situation begin to match men's, their roles within the family will undergo change. It no longer will be taken for granted that the husband's economic role dominates the family's life, in terms of its time schedule, its geographic mobility, and its leisure activities. When both adults have equally compelling work roles, we may expect to see more intercity commuting by at least one of the pair. This may, in fact, lead to double residences for such couples. Family decision-making is influenced by the earning power of the adult members, and women's increasing contribution to the family income will strengthen their decision-making roles within the family. In sum, new attitudes and relationships will have to be worked out for these new types of families.

As non-employed women become a scarcity, their value as homemakers and wives may increase. For those men who continue to prefer wives who do not participate in the labor market, the conditions of marriage that they will have to offer to this decreasing group of women may require severe alteration. Allocation of tasks within the home will change for both those women who do and those who do not work outside the home.

The participation of women in the labor force on a more nearly equal level will require a restructuring of work relationships between the sexes. Eventually, it no longer will be feasible for men to expect service and support from women workers, whom they still consider their social and intellectual subordinates. Restructuring of work relationships between women and men will lead to restructuring of social relationships as well. More egalitarian relationships probably will result in more financial expenditures for women, who now expect men to bear the economic costs of companionship and courtship.

As women contribute economically to the costs of social life, however, they will feel more independent in responding to the social, psychological, and sexual demands made upon them by their partners. Women will feel a diminishing need to reciprocate by sexual means, and sexual relationships more likely will reflect mutual desire and control. Women will be more able to approach men as social equals, initiating relationships rather than waiting passively to be asked. Even now, we can see the beginnings of these changes.

While these shifts may be discomforting to some, they will force most women and men to give up their dependence upon the traditional sex roles, which no longer will offer adequate or appropriate guidance for behavior. As a result, the sexes will meet more often in authentic relationships, unencumbered by the often destructive games we all have been taught to play. There is no doubt that these evolving changes will uncover a new host of interpersonal problems between the sexes; but growth rarely comes without difficulty.

Emerging New Patterns

All of these trends will foster still other new patterns. The growing recognition that romantic attachments may not be permanent may be looked at more realistically within the light of multiple relationships. Extramarital relationships may begin to be viewed within a more sympathetic or realistic light, either as temporary or permanent arrangements that fill certain needs in the lives of some individuals. The notion of sexual exclusivity already has undergone serious change and probably will continue to lose support.

The future influence of television and other mass media is certain in one major respect: it will continue to grow, although its use may vary in different segments of the population. We know that educational level influences television viewing, with more highly educated people tending to spend somewhat less time in front of the set.[32] The inability to process the informational deluge to which viewers are exposed may inhibit somewhat television's impact on the very young as well as the very old.[33] The educational potential of television continues to be explored and expanded by educators who hope to make it more sensitive to the needs of an increasingly educated audience.

The influence of religion on social life has shifted somewhat in recent years. More young people have moved away from the religions of their childhood to other, less traditional, religious positions. Traditional religions, with their positions on marriage, divorce, family, sexuality, and other aspects of life, have begun to take our changing life styles into account. While traditional religion still offers support and strength for large segments of the population, nontraditional religious and philosophical movements are capturing the imagination and minds of many followers. As a result, the need for the integration and mutual acceptance of these different religious positions is felt, not only in formal ecumenical tribunals, but in the broader secular society as well.

More leisure time will bring increased time for study, for hobbies, and for exploring other ways of life. Travel time will become more available with reduced work weeks. As more people begin to travel, per capita transportation costs should decrease, thereby offereing more opportunities to more people. Certain industries have adopted the idea of executive sabbaticals, time in which the individuals work not for the company, but for the community. Sabbaticals traditionally have been reserved for élite workers; however, their utility for workers at all levels is being re-examined. Sabbaticals from the entire range of work roles could be an avenue whereby people would be forced out of their occupational ruts for six months or a year. During this time living in a different community, perhaps even in a different country, could become a way of broadening one's life perspectives.

Structural Supports During Role Change

Admittedly, much of this is pure speculation; however, we can be sure that a significant portion of this speculation will become a reality. Society and the subunits within it—roles—are in transition. Transitions, particularly role changes, require structural supports; otherwise they are likely to result in total chaos and crisis.[34]

Structural supports may take a variety of forms. For example, legislative changes in the welfare system could be made to promote more realistic and constructive financial arrangements for single parents. Legislation of all types could act as an impetus to upgrading the occupational lives of women and other minorities. Mary Lou Randour,[35] for example, has suggested that we reconceptualize the role of housewife and mother as a patriotic service role, comparable to military service, and provide a G.I. Bill for mothers. Legislation affecting work, family, health, and so forth, will lead to changes in behavior and ultimately changes in attitudes.

The development of new types of therapy to deal with the range of problems sparked by role transformations is another structural support that will be needed. It offers a serious challenge for therapists. Reevaluation of the assumptions underlying present therapy and the development of a multiplicity of therapies each tailored to different socioeconomic and emotional conditions would be useful. The active recruitment of individuals from a broader set of backgrounds into the role of therapist would enlarge the horizons of the field and its usefulness to clients. New institutional settings, such as halfway houses for families who are experiencing serious problems, must be developed.

Industry and education could begin to create new ways of dealing with the demands of family living. More opportunities for bringing the family into the work setting* would lessen the tensions between family and work, and foster a more realistic understanding of work demands among family members. Bringing the family into the work setting—not for exploitative purposes, as has sometimes been the case—could open the door for different work schedules and work hours. The parent who can bring her or his preschool child to a daycare or visiting program at work will be able to work more steadily and with less conflict and anxiety. Such parents can choose from a wider range of work roles and work settings. The child who watches his or her parent work develops a more meaningful idea of the outside world, while simultaneously learning its realistic requirements. The child also develops an enlarged view of the parent as an individual.

Different types of symbolism, akin to *rites de passage,* may be necessary to mark the transition to new roles. More communal celebration of these changes in life status would bring greater ligitimacy and more emotional tranquility to the changes that we all shall surely undergo.

The next two decades will witness many changes in our society and the individuals who compose it. Families will look and act differently from the way they do now. Neighborhoods will be altered, and work settings will move closer, if not into, the home. Some roles will become obsolete, others fragmented. New ones will emerge.

As traditional roles begin to crumble, authentic, if not totally carefree, individuals will emerge. We shall have to confront and begin to understand our real selves and the real selves of others. Life will be more unpredictable, but also more challenging. Old tensions will become diffused; new ones will occur. There will be more opportunity for growth, also for trauma. This will be a time for new creativity, strength, patience, adaptability, and knowledge.

References

1. Urban Institute, *Search,* November-December 1973.

2. James S. Coleman et al., *Equality of Educational Opportunity* (Washington, D.C.: U.S. Government Printing Office, 1966). James S. Coleman (Chairman), *Youth: Transition to Adulthood,* Report of the Panel on Youth of the President's Science Advisory Committee (Washington, D.C.: U.S. Government Printing Office, 1973).

3. Carnegie Commission on Higher Education, *Opportunities for Women in Higher Education* (New York: McGraw-Hill, 1973).

4. U. S. Department of Labor, Women's Bureau, *Handbook of Women Workers.*

*I am indebted to Ann Tickamyer for this suggestion.

5. Elizabeth Waldman and Beverly J. McEaddy, Where Women Work—An Analysis by Industry and Occupation. *Monthly Labor Review*, 97:3-13 (May 1974).

6. Jean Lipman-Blumen and Ann R. Tickamyer, Sex Roles in Transition: A Ten-year Perspective, *Annual Review of Sociology* 1:297-337 (May 1975).

7. U.S. Department of Labor, Employment Standards Administration, *Equal Pay* (Washington, D.C.: U.S. Government Printing Office, 1973).

8. Ibid., p. 3.

9. Elizabeth Waldman and Robert Whitmore, Children of Working Mothers, *Monthly Labor Review*, 97:50-58 (March 1973).

10. Ibid., p. 50.

11. Richard M. Nixon, *Economic Report of the President*, Transmitted to Congress January 1973 (Washington, D.C.: U.S. Government Printing Office, 1973).

12. Waldman and McEaddy, Where Women Work, p. 9.

13. Ibid.

14. Ibid., p. 10.

15. Lipman-Blumen and Tickamyer, Sex Roles in Transition, p. 2.

16. *Washington Post*, February 28, 1975.

17. Lipman-Blumen, A Crisis Framework Applied to Macrosociological Family Changes: Marriage, Divorce, and Occupational Trends Associated with World War II, forthcoming in *Journal of Marriage and the Family*.

18. Arthur J. Norton and Paul C. Glick, *Marital Instability: Past, Present, and Future*, forthcoming in *Journal of Social Issues*.

19. Ibid.

20. *Washington Post*, February 28, 1975.

21. Norton and Glick, *Marital Instability*.

22. Larry L. Bumpass and James A. Sweet, Differentials in Marital Instability: 1970, *American Sociological Review*, 37:754-66 (December 1972).

23. The marriage squeeze of the mid-60s which contributed to this trend occurred because more eighteen- and nineteen-year-old women were looking for marriage partners than were men twenty and twenty-one years old (who were their traditional age-graded potential partners). The overabundance of eligible females was due to the baby boom following World War II and the smaller pool of eligible men was attributable to lower birth rates during the war period. The pool of eligible men was diminished further by the manpower demands of the Vietnamese War and the increased college enrollments among men. Norton and Glick, *Marital Instability*, 1975.

24. Ibid.

25. Ibid.

26. Ibid.

27. *Washington Post*, May 5, 1957.

28. Jack Lyle, The People Look at Public Television, unpublished ms., 1974.

29. *Washington Post*, April 28, 1975.

30. National Commission Resources for Youth, *New Roles for Youth* (New York: Citation Press, 1974).

31. Lipman-Blumen, The Sex Segregation of Social Institutions: Toward a Homosexual Theory of Sex Roles, forthcoming in *Signs*.

32. Lyle, The People Look at Public Television.

33. Frederick Duhl, Changing sex roles—concepts, values and tasks; and Bunny Duhl, Changing sex roles—information without process. *Social Casework* 57 (February 1976).

34. Lipman-Blumen, Role De-differentiation as a System Response to Crisis: Occupational and Political Roles of Women, *Sociological Inquiry*, 43:105–29 (February 1973).

35. Mary Lou Randour, A Modest Proposal, paper presented to American Personnel and Guidance Association, New York, New York, March 1975.

6
Mexican-American Interaction with Social Systems

Marta Sotomayor

It has been assumed that if we know the cultural elements that determine the structure of the Mexican-American family, we could be effective in the problem-solving process in this particular aspect of the life experience of the Mexican American. A number of descriptive articles have been written that summarily dismiss the issue of the Mexican-American family by presenting the structure of the so-called traditional patriarchal family with an authoritarian father, a submissive mother, and children lost somewhere between these two opposing forces.

This simplistic, descriptive approach is acceptable in scientific research literature. The rationale is that by applying this approach the major characteristics of the sample can be determined, thus enabling us to judge the extent to which the sample is representative of the entire population, and that "by utilizing some elementary techniques of empirical social research one learns to pose a hypothesis and second, how to organize the data necessary to test that hypothesis."[1]

If the prevalent hypothesis has been that all Mexican-American families follow the patriarchal model, then the data can be organized and manipulated to prove this hypothesis. This writer questions such methodology, the exclusive use of one hypothesis that predetermines a definition of all Mexican-American families, as well as the selection for study of a few familial issues isolated from a total view of these families.

Not only is the description of the patriarchal model of the Mexican-American families in the existing literature inaccurate, but the assumption that such structural patterns alone determine the value orientation of its individual members is also misleading. A recent article by Miguel Montiel

Source: From *Social Casework* 52 (May 1971), pp. 316–322. Copyright © 1971 by the Family Service Association of America. Reprinted by permission.

clearly explains how such assumptions have influenced the method of studying the Mexican-American family in a variety of relationships.[2] Montiel also
points out how the psychoanalytic model has been used exclusively in the
definition of the Mexican-American family, emphasizing the themes of "inferiority and machismo."[3]

Issues to Be Considered

The issues under question here are (1) the hypothesis that Mexican-
American families follow only the patriarchal model, one that is frowned
upon by a democratic society that accords equal power to both spouses
(possibly another myth); (2) the methodology of study that manipulates data
to prove this hypothesis; (3) the sole use of the psychoanalytical model based
on a concept of pathology that is unable to tolerate "differentness" and thus
values conformity; and (4) the selectivity for study of such issues as inferiority
and machismo, elements that are certainly not valued in this society.

There exist in the status arrangements of the members of the
Mexican-American family the same variations that exist in any other ethnic
group, and many factors can cause these structures to vary and change.
Although it is important to understand the arrangements of roles in order to
understand the specific functions of the family unit and its individual members, it is more important to understand the depth, subtlety, and complexity
of familial relationships and the economic, political, social, and cultural variations that determine the Mexican-American family experiences.

Social work practice certainly has considered these factors; however, in
working with Mexican Americans and other minorities, the profession has
been ineffective. It is therefore, necessary to analyze critically and systematically those factors that have been ignored in attempts to understand the life
conditions of minorities in this country and other countries, in which members of the majority society have been intolerant of those who are different in
their actions, speech, and skin color.

In practically all cultures, considerable importance is attached to the
family as a social unit regulated by law and custom. Different approaches
have been used in trying to acquire workable knowledge of all the forces that
affect the family as a unit and its individual members. As many divergent
conclusions have been made by studies as there are studies available.

SOCIAL SYSTEMS CONCEPT AND THE FAMILY

The social systems concept is one that is applicable to an understanding
of the Mexican-American family. *Webster's Third New International Dictio-*

nary defines system as "an aggregation or assemblage of objects joined in regular interaction or interdependence."[4] The Mexican-American family, as any other family, should be an open system, sustaining relationships with other systems in the total transactional field.[5]

This concept recognizes the psychological unit of the family with its functional interaction in a variety of combinations and meanings. It also gives due importance to the variety and meanings of the family's functions in relating to the multiplicity of systems and subsystems outside itself, and it acknowledges the effects that the outside structures can have on the family unit's ability to function.

SOCIALIZATION PROCESS

It is generally agreed that one of the family's primary functions is the socialization of the children, which is generally regarded as a process of transmitting and conserving sociocultural traditions from generation to generation. It is also agreed that the values, beliefs, roles, and functions of individuals and the manner in which they promote socialization of their children depend in large measure on variations in social conditions.

In this highly technological society with its history of extreme contrasts—a society firmly embedded in a competitive economic system and characterized by constant and sharp changes—the socialization process has become one in which the child acquires skills, not always effective, to deal with abrupt and contradictory change rather than one in which the child is encouraged to promote tradition. As a result, emphasis has been placed on the development of individualistic, personalistic, and polarized values rather than on the traditional kinship and group values.

This historical perspective of the American identity provides the base for Erik H. Erikson's formulation of an American national character within a psychosocial framework. This formulation begins to explain this country's inability to tolerate "differentness," which is often expressed in institutionalized racism. He says that "the patient, as a baby, was not made to feel at home in this world except under the condition that he behave himself in certain definite ways, which were inconsistent with the timetable of an infant's needs and potentialities and contradictory in themselves."[6] Erikson also says that the mother "stands for the superior values of tradition, yet she herself does not want to become 'old.' "[7]

This socialization process, once a purview of the extended family, has been delegated to outside structures—or institutions—of society. This societal machinery is necessary to maintain the social system as a system, in order to prevent society from being torn by the forces of individual self-interest; institutions, therefore, are essential in maintaining the internal harmony of society and in harnessing the individual to community action.

Within this context, human society can be viewed as a system of organization in which the individual and his range of needs, at all phases and levels, are both satisfied and held in check. These needs can be met only by man in a social interaction system. This social interaction system is conducted through institutions that are established to meet, repress, or oppress the needs of those individuals that compose them or through those that permit the fulfillment of the potentiality of its members.[8]

PARTICIPATION WITHIN SOCIETY

The second function of the family is to participate within society. Through its participation in community life and through the support it receives from the community, a family is motivated to adhere to the norms of the community, including norms regarding its own stability.[9] It is the norms of the community that ascribe status to specific families. It is that status, with all its implications, that becomes the focus of reference for the family and that determines the types of relationships it will have with the community as a whole and with its parts. It is this ascribed status that determines not only the economic, political, and educational aspirations of the family but also its relationship with society's institutions.

The institutions designed to meet the needs of society and to allow, with their systems of checks and balances, for the maximum development of individual potentiality have failed the Mexican-American family. Existing institutions are color blind; they endorse policies that exclude those who are different, that bar admission to educational systems, and that adhere to merit systems ("merit" defined from a narrow point of view without consideration of the total perspective of the Mexican American). These institutions support the "melting pot" concept with its racist core; they value individualistic, competitive achievement that systematically and consistently excludes the Mexican American from participation.

A COLONIZED PEOPLE

If the Mexican-American family is to be understood, it has to be within the historical perspective of a colonized people in its native country and in this country. In this perspective the Mexican Americans have many of the characteristics of other colonized people, with the majority society relating to them as outsiders. The inferior status of the colonized people results in damage to self-esteem, destruction of native cultural traits and adoption of foreign cultural traits, disintegration of the family unit with particular disparagement of the male, and, finally, loss of social cohesion among so-called inferior groups because of their inability to retain their own culture.[10]

All of these symptoms have been identified to some degree in a considerable number of Mexican-American families. There is sufficient evidence of the damage that institutional policies and procedures have inflicted upon Mexican Americans. In an article in the *Los Angeles Times*, Ruben Salazer summarized the plight of Mexican Americans.

> The Mexican American has an average of 8 years of schooling, [and] a significant number of farm workers who are excluded from the National Labor Relations Act, unlike any other group of workers. Mexican Americans often have to compete for low wages with their Mexican brothers below the border, with limited skills in a highly technological, competitive society. Mexican Americans have to live with the stinging fact that the word "Mexican" is the synonym for inferior in many parts of the southwest. Mexican Americans through their large population, are so politically impotent that in Los Angeles, where the country's largest single concentration live we have not one representative in the City Council.[11]

Ordinarily the family participates in community activities in exchange for the support of the community. One functional interchange consists of mutual give and take on a daily interaction basis. The extent and quality of the interaction determines the solidarity of bonds between society and the family unit. This daily interaction with the external system has been blocked for many Mexican-American families, and, as a result, they have withdrawn from participation in community affairs. The merits of withdrawal from or involvement with a hostile environment are open for discussion.

The external community has given the Mexican-American family as inferior status and has defined that status as one with inferior standards of behaviors and rewards. In a functional society the community gives the family a significant status and identity by means of support and acceptance. The present societal structure denies the Mexican-American family a positive status and identity, excludes it from community activities, and gives it the feeling of alienation, marginality, and anomie.

INTERCHANGES WITH SOCIAL SYSTEMS

The type and quality of the interchanges between the family and the external social system determine to a considerable extent the internal family activities and its integration. The Mexican-American head of the household often has been unemployed, or underemployed in menial tasks that constantly remind him of his inferior status. He has practically no access to the decision-making process that could change his situation, and he has no effective means of making those vital institutions respond to his needs. This damaging, limiting process invariably affects the internal functioning and the role arrangement within his family. It has an adverse effect on family leadership, on the maintenance of expected patterns of behavior, and on the integration and solidarity of specific families and their individual members.

Task performance and expected patterns of behavior clearly reflect the family's relationship with external systems. These task performances are regulated in part by the requirements of the interchanges between those systems and the family and the tangible goods obtained from these interchanges. Performance of the expected, assigned tasks in turn affects the quality and integration of the relationships within the family.[12]

The adequate performance of expected tasks is intrinsically related to other goals of the family. When these goals are limited by decision of a system over which the individual family has no control, the equilibrium of relationships within the Mexican-American family suffers, including the degree of closeness of family bonds and the expected familial leadership. These factors affect the Mexican-American father's role as provider, disciplinarian, and protector. His authority, to be effective, has to be couched in strong affective bonds that successfully resolve the problems of the individual's identity.

The patterns of decision making are thwarted and distorted for many Mexican-American families when decisions that involve meeting the basic, essential needs of family members are beyond the control of the expected patterns. These conditions have a circular effect in disrupting the family's equilibrium and in preventing the family from reorganizing and mobilizing its internal resources to deal with a rejecting, destructive external system. The pattern thus is perpetuated.

Other forms of dealing with external systems are attempted with no actual opportunity of testing them to discover effects or alternatives. The interchanges afforded other families and the processes learned in the successful completion of those interchanges are not available for many Mexican Americans because society does not offer them that "testing ground." Can it be possible that the high proportion of inmates of correctional institutions, the number of narcotic addicts, and the high percentage of school dropouts among Mexican Americans can be explained not merely on the basis of individual deviancy but more as a result of attempts to achieve some type of interaction with a destructive external system? In many instances, the only knowledge the Mexican American has of those institutions outside of his barrio is that they repress and oppress him, and the skills he develops to deal with those institutions have to be limited to responding to repression and oppression.

The strong movement for *chicanismo* within prison walls, the recruitment of Mexican-American school dropouts by young Mexican-American students, and the involvement of Mexican-American ex-addicts in the counseling of other Mexican-American addicts—all self-help groups—present the themes typical of an interactional process that mutually affects family and society. The following themes appear repeatedly in the Chicano movement:

open and better employment opportunities, change of policies that have excluded Mexican Americans from the normal activities of society, greater status for Spanish as a spoken language, respect for the Mexican American as an individual of value, cohesion and solidarity of a group united by a cause, pride in the culture and heritage of one's ancestors, and reevaluation of roles and functions of men and women.

Within this perspective, what is the function of the social worker in working with Mexican-American families? This perspective does not totally reject the psychoanalytic model; in fact, there are many Mexican-American families and individuals—particularly those who have achieved considerable mobility within the majority community—who benefit from this traditional counseling approach. The exclusive use of this approach, however, is a narrow one in view of the other factors that dramatically affect the opportunities for Mexican-American families to function adequately.

An attempt has been made to show how a significant number of weaknesses that had been attributed to the internal dynamics of the Mexican-American family can now, through the systems approach, be ascribed to the limitations placed upon the Mexican Americans by external systems. An attempt has also been made to point out how these limitations affect the internal integration of the family unit.

Identifying Supportive Elements

Social workers must be able to identify those elements within the Mexican-American family that have given and promoted group cohesion and individual integration. Having identified these elements, our social workers can then function effectively in encouraging desirable family relationships. The same process applies in working with external systems. Only several elements that have given support to the Mexican-American family will be discussed in this chapter; others have to be identified; all require further elaboration.

EXTENDED FAMILY PATTERN

One element that appears consistently in the Mexican-American family is the extended family pattern. It is a supportive and flexible structure assuming functions in dealing with the environment and with the emotional and psychological aspects of the family unit and individuals. This system is compatible with the present emphasis of the Mexican American on the importance of the group; for example, Movimiento Estudiantil Chicano de Aztlan (MECHA), Mexican American Youth Organization (MAYO), and

Crusade for Justice—all group oriented and having many characteristics of a "tribe."

In the extended family pattern, the members often rescue the head of a household by sharing their goods to meet the daily needs of his family. The head of the household does not lose face, but the extended family pattern couches his feeling of failure. The feeling of isolation of the nuclear family in similar situations is diluted by the support and help of the variety of members of the extended family. Various members of the family assume the physical and effective care of the child when stress from the external system causes self-preoccupation of an individual parent. This prcess is also present at times of internal crisis, such as the birth of a new child, when the extended family gives care to the mother during her convalescence and to the older youngsters. In addition, the extended family provides the daily care that the father expects and continues the routines of family functions within a familiar setting.

The *compadrazgo* relationship has many similar characteristics and functions; relationships assume familial overtones in which the emotional and physical responsibilities for children are also shared. Although it is true that many Mexican Americans who migrated to this country (and others who were in the Southwest before United States expansion into these territories) brought with them the extended family pattern and the phenomenon of *compadrazgo*, with its emphasis on kinship and deep, lasting relationships, the changes experienced in this society have greatly diluted, if not modified, such structures and their accompanying relationships.

RESPECT FOR THE AGED

The aged are greatly respected among Mexican Americans; positions of authority are assigned to them regardless of their sex. Through the continued participation of the elderly in the decision-making process, the issue of authority is diluted among extended family relationships. This practice is in contradiction to the patriachal model, in which it is assumed that the father is the only source of authority. Mexican Americans have strong convictions that commit them to taking care of aged parents and grandparents.

FAMILY ROLE PATTERNS

The mother is given a significant position within the family. Respect for the mother is expressed symbolically by her children's using her family name in conjunction with that of the father. This custom is prevalent in Latin America but is totally overlooked in the United States with the usage of only the father's last name.

The function of the oldest son and oldest daughter to participate actively in the parental function in relation to the younger siblings continues to exist. This pattern is often interpreted by social workers as overdependency, and great efforts are made to "emancipate" such family members from their "unfair" burdens of family responsibilities.

With the exclusive use of the patriarchal model we have overlooked additional role patterns, quality and levels of relationships, sharing of parental functions, and meanings of sibling relationships. A multiplicity of variations exist in these relationships and arrangements, just as they exist in any other ethnic group.

THE BARRIO

The barrio, like the ghetto, has become a negative concept, often destroyed by urban renewal projects that methodically appear to disperse the barrio residents by the intricate construction of freeways. For a group of people who have been consistently rejected by the environment and who value the group and tend to cluster in familial and neighborhood arrangements, the barrio has offered a feeling of belonging and cohesion.

The negative aspect of the barrio is not the clustering of Mexican Americans but the almost total lack of resources coming into the confined community to meet the needs of its residents. With opportunities to reach out of the barrio also limited, there are relatively few alternatives for the expression and development of the potentiality of the Mexican American.

USE OF SPANISH

The persistent use of Spanish, a descriptive language suitable to promoting intensive relationships in a ranking order (that is, use of *tu* and *usted*), has served to maintain and emphasize satisfying, close human relationships that have helped to provide emotional stability for many Mexican Americans.

Certainly there are many reasons for the persistence to continue to speak Spanish in the home and in the barrio. The type of interchanges between the individual and a hostile, rejecting external system raises the question of whether the language is also utilized as protection from outside threatening forces. If a person does not understand English, he does not understand the negative messages coming in, although verbal communication is certainly not the only type of communication available in the interaction with external systems. Institutions, including social service delivery systems, have misunderstood, minimized, and often participated in the destruction of many positive factors presented by the Mexican-American sociocultural framework.

Social Work Function

Social work traditionally has accepted its function of involvement in the process of change; its function to preserve is often overlooked or overemphasized. Effective social work intervention requires careful assessment of areas that require change and areas that should be preserved, encouraged, or supported. The sociocultural strengths of the Mexican-American family, therefore, need to be closely identified, evaluated, and supported. More often than not, the positive factors of the (Mexican-American) family have provided the only strengths available in the life experiences of the Mexican-American people. We do not have to minimize the internal functioning of the family as a system; however, in understanding the degree of negative effect of the external system upon the integration of the family unit, the profession's first priority is to intervene and change those destructive external forces.

In open forum discussions of the consequences of racism, there has been a tendency to assume that if only the laws of this country could be changed or enforced, all its problems would be resolved. This position assumes that many institutions as they exist today are valid and viable. If social work is to be effective in giving service to the disadvantaged Mexican-American families, intervention has to take place at many levels and in many areas requiring institutional change.

New models of decision making have to be supported—specifically, the decentralization of the functions of government and the delivery of services. Accompanying rearrangements of power will bring about "community control," which will not only strengthen the barrios but will bring the decision making to the individuals who are directly affected by the policies of such structures and who hopefully are more responsive to the needs of the Mexican American. This decentralization will affect primarily the educational and service delivery systems.

These local community organizations should have direct access to the central authority. Mexican Americans, therefore, should be supported in their politization process to make this access possible and to begin to influence the political system—an opportunity that until now has been denied them.

The self-help process characteristic of the Chicano movement should be recognized and encouraged. It is only through the careful assessment of internal and external forces and their effects upon each other than internal resources can be mobilized, tested, and refined in the transactional field of families, individuals, and society.

References

1.   Murray A. Straus, *Family Analysis: Readings and Replication of Selected Studies* (Chicago: Rand McNally & Co., 1969), p. 38.

2.   Miguel Montiel, The Social Science Myth of the Mexican American Family, *El Grito*, 3:56 (Summer 1970).

3.   Ibid.

4.   See *Webster's Third New International Dictionary*, s.v. "system."

5.   John P. Spiegel, A Model for Relationships Among Systems, in *Toward a Unified Theory of Human Behavior,* ed. Roy R. Grinker (New York: Basic Books, 1956), pp. 22–27.

6.   Erik H. Erikson, *Childhood and Society* (New York: W. W. Norton & Co., 1959), p. 247.

7.   Ibid., p. 249.

8.   See Walter Goldschmidt, *Comparative Functionalism, An Essay in Anthropological Theory* (Berkeley-Los Angeles: University of California Press, 1966), pp. 58–59.

9.   See Norman W. Bell and Ezra F. Vogel, Toward a Framework for Functional Analysis of Family Behavior, in *A Modern Introduction to the Family,* ed. Bell and Vogel (New York: Free Press, 1968), pp. 1–34.

10.   See A. Kardiner and L. Ovesey, *The Mark of Oppression: Explorations in the Personality of the American Negro* (New York: Meridian Books, 1962), p. 47.

11.   *Los Angeles Times,* February 6, 1970.

12.   See Bell and Vogel, Functional Analysis of Family Behavior, pp. 1–34.

7
Family Functioning in the Low-Income Black Community

Andrew Billingsley

No task of the social worker and social planner is more imperative today than the development of a sensitive appreciation of the structure and functioning of black families. For despite the rapid and sometimes cataclysmic social changes now taking place, the family remains the basic unit of society and the most important social institution for the welfare and the healthful development of children. Elsewhere I have outlined a theoretical framework within which to view the structure and the functioning of family life in the black community.[1] According to that formulation the black family should be looked at as a social system imbedded in the black community; in turn, the black community is surrounded by the largely white community and its institutions. The structure of family life in the black community is a product of forces in the wider white society, though it is to some extent shaped by the conditions of life to which black people have been subjected. In my view, the extent to which black families are able to meet the needs of their members and the requirements society places on all families depends heavily on the extent to which the institutions of the wider society meet the needs of black people in general and black families in particular.

In a very real sense, all black families live in Michael Harrington's "other America," apart from the mainstream of what Kenneth Galbraith has termed *the affluent society,* in which two-thirds of all families in this nation dwell. In this society it is a curse to be poor, and it is a double curse to be poor and black. Being black but not poor is no picnic! For in every facet of American life, black families fare worse at the hands of society than do their white counterparts.

Families may be described according to their capacities for carrying out instrumental and expressive functions. Instrumental functions are those

Source: From *Social Casework* 50 (December 1969), pp. 563–572. Copyright © 1969 by the Family Service Association of America. Reprinted by permission.

functions concerned with the provision of the basic necessities of life, such as food, clothing, shelter, health care, and the acquisition of occupatonal skills. Falling within the realm of expressive functions are the establishment of relationships with relatives; the structuring of the patterns of love, friendship, and affection; and the subtle determination of the intimate but intricate ways in which family members relate to each other, teach each other, and or deflate each other's dignity and sense of worth. The family does not function well or poorly as a whole. Rather, it performs its functions well or poorly in certain specific realms of life. For example, child rearing is only one realm in which the family functions either well or poorly. It is also one area in which the literature about the dysfunctioning of black families is inaccurate and the views are expressly distorted.

The Tangle of Pathology

It is nearly five years since a governmental report concluded that family life in the black community constitutes a "tangle of pathology . . . capable of perpetuating itself without assistance from the white world,"[2] and that "at the heart of the deterioration of the fabric of Negro society is the deterioration of the Negro family. It is the fundamental *source* [italics mine] of the weakness of the Negro community at the present time."[3] I believe that this is an incorrect analysis of the relationship between black families and white society. Weakness in the family does not cause poverty, nor does black racism constitute the source of the pathology that afflicts black people. Quite to the contrary: the family is a creature of the society, and the greatest problems facing black families are problems that emanate from our *white* racist, militaristic, and materialistic society. Ours is a society that places higher priority on putting white men on the moon than putting black men on their feet on this earth. But Daniel Moynihan's analysis, which placed the responsibility for the difficulties faced by black people on the family unit, was eagerly received by the American reading public as a key to understanding black people. Although Moynihan has subsequently modified his position in some respects, one of the unfortunate consequences of his report is that it has given rise to similar analyses by other white students of the black family.

Now, nearly five years later, two white social scientists who call themselves "militant integrationists" have written a book based on their observations during a nine-month sojourn in a black community.[4] It includes a chapter entitled "The Negro Ghetto Nonfamily," which perpetuates the incorrect analysis made so famous by Moynihan but which has been thoroughly discredited by more careful social analyses.[5] Harry Etzkowitz and Gerald Schaflander state candidly their view of black people:

It is our own belief that there are practically no plusses in Negro ghetto culture. We see nothing but bitterness and despair, nihilism, hopelessness, rootlessness, and all the symptoms of social disintegration in the poor speech, poor hygiene, poor education, and the lack of security resulting from a nonfamily background in which the stabilizing paternal factor is absent and where there is no stable institution to substitute for the family.[6]

They go considerably beyond the Moynihan thesis of disintegrating family life in asserting without qualification "that love, warmth, hygiene, education and family stability are absent for most Negroes."[7] They add that "booze, gambling, drugs, and prostitution are the inevitable result of the absence of a stable family institution."[8]

These men are as insensitive and arrogant as they are incorrect in their analysis. They insist that the line of causation runs from the family to the society. After describing in extremely negative terms what they consider "momism"—represented by the harassed, cranky, frustrated, church-going, overworked mothers who dominate their nonfamilies by "driving young children into fierce competition"—these white liberal social scientists conclude that "the damage *resulting* [italics added] from this *typical* nonfamily life often leads to young dropouts and unwed mothers, and to crime, violence, alcoholism and drug addiction."[9]

Despite the incorrectness of their analysis of the relationship between black family life and the white society, their views are similar to those held by many persons, including some members of the social work profession. The authentication of such views by social science scholarship supported by generous foundation grants serves to perpetuate this erroneous thinking. As a consequence enlightened people are stopped from getting on with the task of analyzing and helping to remove the crippling consequences of institutionalized racism that the *Report of the National Advisory Commission on Civil Disorders* so correctly identifies as the most important cause of the difficulties black people face in this country and the most important cause of their outrage against oppression.

For scholars and students trying to understand family functioning in the black community, the chief faults of the type of analysis described above lie in the reversal of the cause and effect relationship between the black family and society and in the ignoring of the forces of institutionalized racism. For social work practitioners and social planners, an additional problem is that this type of analysis ignores the variety and complexity of black family and black community life while concentrating on its negative features. Analyses of this kind are made from the narrow perspective of white-Anglo conformity by which black people are judged outside the context of their unique anchor in history, their treatment in this country, and their contemporary social conditions. More important, such analyses ignore both the existence of a black subculture and the strengths of the black community and the black family that have enabled black people to survive in a hostile environment for more than three hundred years.

Unfortunately, analyses of black families by well-educated, well-meaning white liberal integrationists are based more on their own perspectives and prejudices than on the realities and complexities of life in the black community. The continuation of the white-middle-class-outsider perspective—born out of a combination of ignorance and arrogance—not only obscures the realities of black family and black community life but performs a downright disservice to the understanding the wider society so desperately needs.

The truth of the matter is that most black families in most communities of any size meet the American test of stability. Contrary to the impression generally circulated by white students of the black family, most black families, even those who live in the ghetto, are headed by men. And most of the men are still married to their first wives. Furthermore, most of them, and many black women, too, are employed full time but are still unable to lift their families out of poverty. What we need to know more about is how these families manage. How do they function? How do they meet the needs of their children? My own research, as well as an increasing number of other studies, suggests that black family life—even that of the lower-class ghetto family—is much more varied than is generally recognized.

A Bundle of Complexity

I have discovered, for example, that the lower class consists of at least three groups rather than one.[10] Some lower-class black families are managing well both economically and socially; these are the *working nonpoor*. The vast majority of the black lower class form a middle layer I have termed the *working poor*. The third segment is composed of the relatively large number of families who are economically dependent, termed the *under class* or *nonworking poor*. The latter two groups of poor families account for nearly half of all black families and nearly one-quarter of all poor families in the United States.

The complexity of family life in the black community has been emphasized by Ralph Ellison.[11] When asked by a group of young black writers to comment on how they might more truly reflect the complexity of the human condition, using their own experience as a theme, he replied:

> If [the Negro writer] accepts the clichés to the effect that the Negro family is usually a broken family, that it is matriarchal in form and that the mother dominates and castrates the males, if he believes that Negro males are having all of these alleged troubles with their sexuality, or that Harlem is a "Negro ghetto" . . . —well, he'll never see the people of whom he wishes to write. . . .[12]

Ellison's observations are not confined to fictional descriptions of black family life. He continues:

> I don't deny that these sociological formulas are drawn from life, but I do deny that they define the complexity of Harlem. . . . I simply don't recognize Harlem in them. And I certainly don't recognize the people of Harlem whom I know. Which is by no means to deny the ruggedness of life there, nor the hardship, the poverty, the sordidness, the filth. But there is something else in Harlem, something subjective, willful, and complexly and compellingly human. It is "that something else" that challenges the sociologists who ignore it, and the society which would deny its existence. It is that "something else" which makes for our strength, which makes for our endurance and our promise.[13]

Josephine Carson, a highly sensitive white female writer who went into the South to study the role of black women today, came to a similar conclusion.[14] She found a strong attachment to familism in black communities.

> They are together, the link is not broken. Black is intimate. Whatever the broken family is, one feels unbrokenness here more than brokenness: *My sister . . . My cousin . . . My mother keeps him while I work . . . This is a picture of my son . . . My daddy was a preacher . . . My granddaddy bought my grandma . . . Listen, with a man you has to put up with a heap o' thangs to stay, like you said you would, till death . . . The chillrun stops by my aunt's place till I comes home . . . . .*[15]

"There is," she concludes, "a chain of black being."[16] Her description of the black women among whom she lived is quite in contrast to that of Etzkowitz and Schaflander:

> The impression left is of a formidable woman: a worker, a believer; one who is patient, enduring, full of wit. A fortress. A matriarch by default. Someone had to mother that estranged white South and try to bind the sundered black family. Negro society is no more matriarchal, no more addicted to her healing power than the South itself.[17]

And the black woman of her acquaintance "rarely fails to describe her mother with love and admiration," "a woman who is loved, needed; who is sometimes sacrosanct' often exploited; who endures."[18]

It may be that Josephine Carson's analysis is more sensitive, and therefore more correct, in part at least because of who she is and how she behaved in the presence of black people. She is a woman who got very close to the subjects of her study. More important, perhaps, she was not inhibited by some of the strictures of the more professional and scholarly social scientists who rely so heavily on their own intelligence, their instruments, their tape recorders, and their white faculty advisors. Miss Carson seemed to be aware of her limitations as a white person living among black people. She rode the bus with black domestics returning from a long day's work in the white part of town and commented: "The presence of Miss Ann on this bus at this hour is enough to stop the seriousness, if there is any, of the exchanges. Miss Ann manages to break the domestic barricade, nothing more. *Mr. Charley would do even less* [italics added]."[19]

Rather than considering black families to be the cause of the poverty they experience, Josephine Carson observes and remarks on the amazing ability of black families to survive and maintain stability in the face of poverty and other overwhelming odds: "Love and family solidarity sometimes survive the siege [of poverty]. In this neighborhood, with all its bitter poverty, the statistics show that only one-third are broken homes. Hard to believe."[20] Nor is she confused about the relationship among family structure, poverty, and racism. It is not the female family head, but racism, that causes the poverty. For although it is true that black families headed by women are more likely to be in poverty than black families headed by men, it is also true, and even more relevant, that black female family heads who work earn considerably less than white female heads who work and therefore are even more likely to be living in poverty. Josephine Carson observes this interrelated complex of forces and comments: "When the black family was headed by a woman [in 1966], 61.8 percent were living in poverty," which is "more than twice the percentage of white families headed by women and living in poverty!"[21] Obviously, then, it is not the family structure that *causes* poverty!

At another point she notes some of the positive attributes of the black experience. "A family," she observes, "is not two parents with children in a housing tract, in a housing project. . . . A family is kin. All kin. The black woman's milieu is among kin."[22] And she writes, "When one speaks of poverty and dejection and misery, one forgets to say that the most humor and affection for life, the most sheer creature vitality to be found in this country are surely in the young black face."[23] This fact has escaped the notice of many white experts on black people.

Josephine Carson's sophisticated analysis of the relationship between poverty and family life in the black community has benefited from her ability to listen to the voices and the spirits of her subjects, including the voice and the spirit of that amazing black woman in the Southern Liberation Movement, Mrs. Charity Simmons, who could well have been the co-author of *Silent Voices*, sharing in its rewards as she did in its labors.

I have referred at some length to Josephine Carson's work in part because it is a more correct analysis than the ones referred to earlier and in part because it demonstrates that not all white people are completely insensitive or unable to learn about the complexities of the black experience. Fortunately, her views are not idiosyncratic but are supported by a growing body of careful research.

The Care and Protection of Children

The extent to which a black family functions adequately in protecting its children depends chiefly on the social supports it is given by society and on its position in the social-class structure. Thus, the working-class family, the middle-class family, and the upper-class family in the black community each provides a higher level of instrumental protection than does the lower-class or the under-class family, owing not so much to the family structure as to the nature of the resources available. A husband and father is an important figure, but his presence in the family is neither necessary nor sufficient to insure the instrumental well-being of children. Particularly in the black community other family members, relatives, friends, neighbors, and other role models provide the screens of opportunity that enable some families to function better than others.

Even among the lowest social classes in the black community, families give the children better care than is generally recognized, and often the care is better than that given by white families in similar social circumstances. Black people are not nearly as alienated from their families, from their children, or from themselves as white people are. They have not become as victimized by the debilitating forces of American-style "success," which requires utter lack of regard for others unless they happen to be powerful. Perhaps this is why black families still consider children important and why they go to such great lengths to protect their children and try to meet their basic economic, social, physical, and psychological needs.

It is not generally appreciated, for example, that child neglect and abuse are much more common in white families than in black families. Child neglect is much more common among lower-class white families than among lower-class black families. Child abuse is much more likely to occur in white families than in black families who live in similar, or even worse, economic circumstances. In a study of physical neglect and abuse of young children in low-income families in New York State, Leontine Young found that even though black families were overrepresented in the population she sampled [public welfare clients], neglect and abuse were much more prevalent among white families. She found a similar phenomenon in a series of studies she conducted in various cities across the nation.[24]

A second set of data comes from the 1960 United States census. Although black children were overrepresented in institutions for delinquents, they were underrepresented in institutions for neglected and dependent children; only 8.4 percent of all children in institutions for the dependent and neglected were black, considerably less than their proportion in the population.[25]

It is possible, of course, that some of the underrepresentation of black children in institutions for neglected children is due to the nature of the system itself and how it operates. Since, in general, institutions for neglected and dependent children are a shade superior to institutions for delinquents, there may be a tendency for black children to be more readily categorized as delinquent rather than neglected as compared with white children. There is no doubt, however, that there is something about black culture that is also operative and is in part responsible for this phenomenon. For in the black community a child's or a youth's striking out at society in ways considered antisocial is not only justified but is an exceedingly healthy expression of his reaction against the constraints placed upon him by an uncaring society. It is quite another thing, however, for parents to deliberately mistreat their children or to refuse to feed, clothe, and shelter them when they have these resources available.

A third study was part of my own research. In a randomly selected sample of 40 white and 40 black low-income families headed by women, the researchers found that the physical abuse of children was over twice as common among white mothers as among black mothers; 38 percent of the white mothers but only 13 percent of the black mothers abused their children.[26] And in a study of 206 white and 239 black families in public welfare caseloads, it was found that 63 percent of the white families as compared with 43 percent of the black families were found to neglect or abuse their children.[27]

Finally, in a study of 371 low-income mothers who delivered babies at San Francisco General Hospital between September and December 1966, it was found that black families were more likely to have taken advantage of prenatal care than were low-income white families.[28] Thus, 26 percent of the black mothers as compared with 5 percent of the white mothers were in the group that had received the most adequate care.

These data are not to be viewed as evidence that all black families function well in meeting the instrumental needs of their children. Rather, the point to be made is that there is what Robert Coles terms *sinew* in the black family; many unrecognized positive attributes and coping patterns have been generated in order to provide a measure of protection to children, although the coping behavior varies greatly. Many black families function very well indeed, all things considered. For these families, a little bit more money would solve whatever problems they have. Other families do not manage quite so well, and the care they give their children is marginal. Still others seem to be in a constant state of chronic dysfunction, and their children are likely to be grossly neglected.

Patterns of Child Care

When Hylan Lewis and his associates analyzed the attitudes and behavior of forty-one parental figures in thirty-nine households in Washington,

D.C., they found a high degree of conformity to middle-class norms of child rearing among very-low-income black mothers.[29] They also found, however, a high degree of vulnerability to "unguided, unplanned influences outside the family,"[30] which play an inordinately important role in the socialization of children.

These researchers identified three patterns of family functioning with respect to the adequacy of child-rearing behavior in these low-income families. One group of parents not only showed great concern for their children's health, education, and welfare but also behaved in such a manner as to assure the care and protection of their children. They were adequate parents. Lewis writes, "Working with what they have, [these adequate parents] show high 'copability,' self-reliance, and self-respect."[31]

A second group of parents also had great concern for the welfare of their children, but they seemed unable to behave appropriately; their verbalized concern was accompanied by behavior that was inconsistent with their stated goals. These parents tended to be highly self-centered and demanding; they seemed to love their children, but they could not view them as individuals in their own right. The children were in constant danger of being neglected.

A third groups of parents seemed unconcerned for the welfare of their children, and their patterns of behavior toward and on behalf of the children were dysfunctional. The result was the classic picture of child neglect; the children were undernourished, their physical ailments were untreated, and they were exposed to violence, harsh treatment, and arbitrary punishment. The parents tended to use their children as scapegoats for the frustrations they experienced in their own lives. Dependent and lacking in self-confidence, self-reliance, or self-esteem, these parents seemed to resent their children's dependence on them.

A study made by Joan Gordon and her associates of low-income black families in central Harlem also supports the view that some of these families function amazingly well, others function marginally well, and others are characterized by inadequate social functioning.[32] This study also suggests some of the factors that make the difference: when the forces of the larger society fail these families, many of them are able to call upon the resources of their neighbors and their relatives to support the expressive functions of family life and to enable them to meet the needs of the children. These are rich resources for the very survival of many poor black families in a hostile society.

In her study Dr. Gorodon used black interviewers to conduct intensive interviews with forty-six black mothers, most of whom were recipients of Aid to Families with Dependent Children. Although a great deal of attention has been focused on the presumed disorganization, estrangement, and alienation to be found in low-income black families in the ghetto, this study did not find these phenomena but rather several levels of social integration. Sixteen of the forty-six mothers were considered to be highly integrated into the neighborhood system. Their behavior included helping each other in time of trouble, helping each other in time of illness, minding each other's children, and lending and borrowing food, money, and clothes. These highly integrated mothers also exchanged information with each other about the best place to shop, how to raise children, problems on the block, and problems with the public welfare department. Twelve of the mothers were considered to be moderately well integrated; they were involved in at least two of the four areas of mutual aid and at least two of the four areas of information exchange. Thus, almost two-thirds of the mothers were involved in a network of informal relations with their neighbors. The authors found a similar patterning with respect to kinship ties.

The researchers had not expected to find such a high level of group cohesion. "It is remarkable," they concluded, ". . . that given how little they have in the way of income or material resources and how beset they are with problems, so many, nevertheless, share what they have and try to help in critical times."[33] Fifteen of the forty-six mothers did, however, reveal the classical picture of isolation and estrangement; they gave and received no aid or information.

In the area of child rearing, the researchers examined three dimensions of attitude and behavior: (1) the mothers' behavior, knowledge, and standards with respect to the education of their children; (2) the mothers' attitudes about selected child-rearing items; and (3) the mothers' preferences for child care arrangements. Again, the research found no support for the claim of universal ignorance, apathy, and absence of standards in the area of child rearing.

Both the Lewis and the Gordon studies have shown that family functioning, even among those attenuated nuclear families with the lowest incomes in the urban black ghetto, is far from uniform. Many families are given by their immediate society, their neighbors, and their relatives the resources that enable them to do an amazingly good job in caring for their children. Others are given fewer of these resources. And still other families seem to have been utterly deserted, so that both the families and the wider society suffer the consequences.

Man in the House

Surely one of the more important resources for the care and protection of children is the presence of "a man in the house." Most studies of low-income black families are focused almost exclusively on the mother as a source of data and also as an object of analysis, in spite of the fact that most black families are headed by men. In 1966 R. C. Stone and F. T. Schlamp reported to the California State Department of Social Welfare on their study of 1,200 intact low-income families, 316 of which were black.[34] The study comprised families supported by AFDC and other low-income families who were self-supporting. The men in the families were the major source of data. The comments that follow are based on the findings concerning the role relations in the 316 black families.

Role relationships in the black family are highly affected by the family's level of economic functioning and the pattern of its participation in the world of work. The division of labor for selected household and child-rearing tasks in the black families studied by Stone and Schlamp is shown in Table 1.

It is obvious from this table that the family division of labor falls into a variety of patterns, and that husbands are more likely to help their wives with child care tasks than with household chores. It is of special interest that in more than two-thirds of these families the husband and wife are jointly active in disciplining the children and taking them on outings. And in two-fifths of the families there is joint participation in basic care and in helping the children with schoolwork. Among these low-income black families, the dominant pattern of controlling the use of money is equalitarian; nearly 48 percent of these married couples report that the husband and wife make decisions jointly.

But having a man in the house is not always an unmixed blessing for the children who need care and the other family members who must provide that care. David Schulz, in a study of five families in a public housing project, found three different patterns of relationships the fathers maintained to meet the instrumental needs of their families and children.[35] One

TABLE 1.   Family Division of Labor

	USUAL PERFORMERS (IN PERCENT)			
KIND OF TASK	Wife Only	Husband Only	Husband-Wife Jointly	Husband-Wife Plus Others
Household				
Laundry	59.8	3.4	18.4	18.4
Cooking	59.5	0.0	22.6	17.9
Dishes	38.6	1.2	14.5	45.7
Cleaning	33.7	2.4	20.9	43.0
Shopping	27.7	7.3	57.8	7.2
Child care				
Child care	37.0	0.0	40.7	22.3
Child discipline	22.6	3.6	67.8	6.0
Child outings	18.8	2.5	68.7	10.0
Help with schoolwork	34.9	12.7	39.7	12.7
Control over spending money	36.9	14.3	47.6	1.2

pattern he termed the *indiscreet free man*, a pattern in which the father shared openly his personal, financial, and other resources with one or more families outside his main household. He observed: "Such a father's interests reverberate upon his children, creating an intensified kind of sibling rivalry with his 'outside' children, who, in some instances, are known personally by his legitimate children. Life within such families is thus one of constant conflict and bickering."[36] The second pattern, the *discreet free man*, is a relationship in which the father also has outside family responsibilities, but they are secondary and are not used to antagonize his wife and children. The third pattern is the *traditional monogamous* one in which the man's "home and family are his major concerns and receive his constant attention."[37] Since the study sample consisted of only five families, it is difficult to be sure that these three patterns are the only ones that characterize black fathers' relationships with their families.

Study of Family Life

Camille Jeffers spent fifteen months studying child rearing and family life in a low-income housing project composed primarily of black families.[38] Her study provides further examples of patterns in family functioning and in child rearing in the black community. Her overall findings were much more positive than those of many observers who have spent briefer periods of time making their studies and have used more formal techniques of observation. "My impressions after 15 months," she observes, "were that the overwhelming majority of parents cared deeply about, and were concerned about, the welfare of their children. Their concern took many forms and had many dimensions. Concern about children might be focused on attempting to obtain the basic necessities of life for them.... There was seldom total absence of concern about a child or children on the part of parents."[39]

The three major patterns of family life she found were reflected in the well-being of the children. One group of families held themselves aloof from the other families in the housing project. Their reference group was made up of people who lived outside the project, and they aspired to be upwardly mobile. Usually, the husband had a secure job. They were more likely than other families to control the size of the family, and the children were generally well cared for. A second group consisted of families not unlike the first group in their orientation toward the children, but they were more interdependent with other families in the project. In these families the husband's employment ranged from very stable to very unstable. Life was a bit more precarious for these families, but they maintained a considerable degree of control over the children. A third group of families included, but was not confined to, one-parent families. Income was uncertain and jobs unstable;

money was constantly in short supply. These parents spent most of their time in the housing project; yet the children had more freedom of movement than those in other families and were less closely supervised. "As early as their second or third years, children from this third group of parents could be seen outside playing alone without adult supervision but, supposedly, under the watchful eye of a brother or a sister not much older than themselves."[40]

This research also underscored the importance of mutual-aid relations with friends, relatives, and neighbors as a resource for child care. "It was impressive to see how quickly some mothers could parcel out their children and just as impressive to see the way some neighbors would rise to the occasion when such demands were made.... Some mothers had three or four persons upon whom they could call in an emergency" to care for their children.[41]

Summary

A series of careful and sensitive studies of family life in the low-income black community lends support to the theoretical perspective advanced at the beginning of this chapter. Even in the black under class, family life is considerably more varied than many of the negative generalizations made by well-meaning social scientists would suggest. Furthermore, these studies lift the veil from the mystery of why some families function better than others. Three patterns of family functioning have been identified. Some families manage well to hold themselves together and to meet the children's needs. Others function marginally, and the children are constantly on the verge of difficulty. Still other families are involved in an almost perpetual state of dysfunctioning. And it is the children of these families who are most likely to suffer the scars of racism, poverty, and family disruption.

Several clues emerge from these studies about the factors that are likely to enhance family functioning. Economic viability is, of course, the most crucial element. Education of the family head is another, and it helps if there is a man in the house. Some families manage to hold themselves together by a network of intimate interrelationships of mutual aid and social integration with their neighbors and kin. These are the "screens of opportunity" available to some families and denied to others that help to account for the various kinds of functioning in black families. Rather than relying on the gross generalizations that have emanated from limited studies, social workers should take leadership in creating intervention strategies and building programs based on the resourcefulness and strengths of black communities and black families.

References

1. Andrew Billingsley, *Black Families in White America* (Prentice-Hall, Englewood Cliffs, New Jersey, 1968).

2. *The Negro Family: The Case for National Action* ... , Office of Policy Planning and Research, U.S. Department of Labor (U.S. Government Printing Office, Washington, D.C., 1965), 47.

3. *The Negro Family*, 5.

4. Henry Etzkowitz and Gerald M. Schaflander, *Ghetto Crisis: Riots or Reconciliation?* (Little, Brown and Company, Boston, 1969).

5. See, for example, Elizabeth Herzog, *About the Poor: Some Facts and Some Fictions*, Children's Bureau Publication No. 451 (U.S. Government Printing Office, Washington, D.C., 1967).

6. Etzkowitz and Schaflander, *Ghetto Crisis*, 15.

7. Ibid., 14.

8. Ibid.

9. Ibid., 16.

10. Billingsley, *Black Families in White America*, 136–42.

11. "A Very Stern Discipline," interview with Ralph Ellison, *Harper's Magazine* (March 1967), 76–95.

12. Ibid., 76.

13. Ibid.

14. Josephine Carson, *Silent Voices: The Southern Negro Woman Today* (Delacorte Press, New York, 1969).

15. Ibid., 7–8.

16. Ibid.

17. Ibid., 263.

18. Ibid., 265.

19. Ibid., 11.

20. Ibid., 51.

21. Ibid., 266.

22. Ibid., 8.

23. Ibid., 53.

24. Leontine R. Young, The Behavior Syndromes of Parents Who Neglect and Abuse Their Children, doctoral dissertation (Columbia University School of Social Work, 1963).

25. U.S. 1960 Census of Population, *Inmates of Institutions*, P.C. (2) 3A, table 31, p. 44.

26. Barbara Griswold and Andrew Billingsley, Personality and Social Characteristics of Low-Income Mothers Who Neglect or Abuse Their Children (unpublished manuscript, 1967).

27. Andrew Billingsley, A Study of Child Neglect and Abuse (unpublished, School of Social Welfare, University of California, Berkeley, 1967).

28. Jeanne Giovannoni and Andrew Billingsley, Social Determinants Affecting Prenatal and Well Baby Care, paper presented to Western Society for Pediatric Research, Los Angeles, California, 1967.

29. Hylan Lewis, Culture, Class and Poverty, three papers from the Child Rearing Study of Low Income District of Columbia Families (CROSSTELL), sponsored by the Health and Welfare Council of the National Capital Area, Washington, D.C., February 1967.

30. Ibid., 3.

31. Ibid., 6.

32. Joan Gordon, The Poor of Harlem: Social Functioning in the Underclass, A Report to the Welfare Administration (Office of the Mayor, Interdepartmental Neighborhood Service Center, New York, 1965).

33. Ibid., 42.

34. R. C. Stone and F. T. Schlamp, Family Life Styles Below the Poverty Line, Report to the State Social Welfare Board for Social Science Research (San Francisco State College, San Francisco, California, 1966).

35. David A. Schulz, Coming Up Black: Patterns of Ghetto Socialization (Prentice-Hall, Englewood Cliffs, New Jersey, 1969).

36. Ibid., 127.

37. Ibid., 128.

38. Camille Jeffers, Living Poor: A Participant Observer Study of Choices and Priorities (Ann Arbor Publishers, Ann Arbor, Michigan, 1967).

39. Ibid., 53.

40. Ibid., 19.

41. Ibid., 21.

8
Family Advocacy: From Case to Cause

Robert Sunley

The gap between the individual case of social injustice and broad-scale social action has been a continual source of frustration for the family worker and the family agency alike. The family worker struggles time after time to rectify wrongs suffered by clients. Sometimes he succeeds, often through some personal contact with a counterpart in the offending social institution, but he is only too aware of and further frustrated by the fact that ten or a hundred other people continue to suffer for lack of such influential intervention. His work on behalf of one client will bring about no change in the institution. The sheer immovability and unresponsiveness of the bureaucracy to his individual effort will tend to dull his enthusiasm and dedication as it does with many workers, who drift toward "adjustment" rather than attempt to change the organizations. The client may also be directly or subtly encouraged to come to terms with "reality"—the reality of formidable arrays of laws, rules, regulations, and practices.

For the agency, the gap has also posed a difficult problem. Though aware of the need for social action, most agencies—the board and administration— have had no agencywide structure within which to operate. Isolated efforts by the board, such as passing resolutions or writing letters to legislators, hardly meet the need. There is little or no linkage between client, staff, board, and the needed action. At best, staff and board are linked by the traditional role of the caseworker in social action as set out by Mary Richmond, Charlotte Towle, Gordon Hamilton, and most recently by Harry Specht, which may be summed up in Towle's brief description:

> ... the caseworker [would] be responsible for initiating or instigating social action by making known unmet needs and social ills as revealed in his practice.

Source: From *Social Casework* 51 (June 1970), pp. 347–357. Copyright © 1970 by the Family Service Association. Reprinted by permission.

He would contribute his findings, through agency channels, to those writing social policy, conducting publicity campaigns, drafting legislation. . . .[1]

According to this point of view the family agency also has a limited function. Worker and agency together are only too likely to see themselves as small and rather inactive members of a large-scale process, limited to polite and long-range efforts at legislation, examples perhaps of that sense of powerlessness and of that disjunction between goals and structure fitting under the general catchword "anomie."[2]

Quite a few family agencies have recently made efforts to bridge this gap. Perhaps most notable was Project ENABLE, a national program which brought agencies into direct touch with the poor, those suffering daily from social injustices. This project, like other special programs, was not integral to the regular agency function; separately funded through the Office of Economic Opportunity, the programs for the most part ended with the termination of the special funding.[3] The regular agency programs remained as before, though the awareness of the need for something comparable was undoubtedly heightened. The prospect of large-scale ongoing funding for projects such as ENABLE appear quite dim for the near future whatever agencies do must be done within the fairly narrow margins of regular budget allocations.

Family advocacy is a move toward bridging the gap, but within the regular agency functioning. It delineates a basic function of the caseworker and assures a continuing link with the action program. It recognizes the professional obligation (not option) of the worker for social action, for fighting through to the finish for clients' rights and needs.[4] The concept of family advocacy also embraces the vital principle of involving the client in the action, of helping the client to help himself in this area as well as in that of individual and family functioning.

As will be seen, family advocacy requires more than good intentions; in effect, it is a discipline in itself, as yet only partially developed. A body of knowledge, principles, and methods exists in part. Even interviewing, the specialty of the family worker, must take on an additional focus and objective. A new commitment by the agency is necessary to back up the family worker. It must be expressed in new structuring as well as in new distribution of staff time and emphasis.

Several of the important aspects of a family advocacy program—interviewing, case study, interventions and objectives, and agency structuring—are discussed here. Examples are given from one agency, the Family Service Association of Nassau County, which recently established a Department of Family Advocacy, headed by a full-time social worker, which embraces the work of the family workers, administration, and board.

Interviewing for Family Advocacy

By training and practice many family caseworkers focus on individual and family dysfunction or pathology. The material elicited from the client tends to bear upon this focus. Thus, when a child is referred as a slow learner, not achieving his potential, a family caseworker may accept the basic premise of the referral which is usually buttressed by evidence from the school. This evidence might include poor grades, I.Q. and other psychological tests, or examples of poor behavior. The caseworker does not usually make as careful a study of the school, the educational approach and philosophy, and the teacher as he does of the child and parents in his effort to determine the cause of the learning or behavior problem evidenced by the child.

Interviewing for advocacy introduces a range of new factors into the sessions with the client and "collateral" sources. Some of these perhaps sound obvious, but all reach much further than appears at first sight. Clients may not, for various reasons, give complete information, and the caseworker's skill is needed to develop a relationship of trust and confidence. In contacting public and private organizations on behalf of clients, workers have frequently been baffled in trying to find out precisely the relevant regulations, practices, requirements, or entitlements. The difficulties may be attributed to bureaucratic timidity or fearfulness, or as Charles Grosser points out, some institutions are "overtly negative and hostile, often concealing or distorting information. . . ."[5] Reconciling conflicting stories of clients and professional colleagues in other organizations can be as difficult as reconciling those of husbands and wives in marital conflict.

Caseworkers themselves are often lax in facing or establishing facts, although their sympathies and actions may be in the right direction. For example, Daniel Thursz cites the example of a group of social workers who were called upon to document with cases the "man-in-the-house" rule; they "did not have one bit of supporting evidence."[6] Or, more serious yet, David Wineman and Adrienne James charged in a recent article that students are "systematically taught to abandon reality," describing the many abuses they encounter and the many "cop-outs" used by supervisors and administrators (and eventually by the students and caseworkers as well).[7]

Difficulties Facing the Worker

In addition to the problems centered around obtaining accurate information, the caseworker may well encounter his own difficulties stemming more directly from the "medical" model of pathology. For example, the assessment of pathology in a client may well affect the worker's perception and evaluation of an injustice the client is undergoing. Paranoid tendencies in the client may lead a worker to discount reality problems. The worker may see a sullen welfare recipient only as withdrawn, depressed, and distorting reality—the pathological view—instead of as a person who is suspicious out of experience and seeks to protect himself against further attack.

Also, value judgements enter in. For example, the client's mismanagement of money or time or role may offend the caseworker. In one situation, caseworkers from several agencies were in accord that a certain client was an unfit mother, leaving young children unattended on many occasions; yet her lawyer entered a suit against the department of welfare alleging that it had failed to make provision for sitters while she did necessary shopping and errands. Regardless of the merits of this situation, it is notable that caseworkers had not taken any advocacy position for their client, nor since then for clients in comparable difficulties. Perhaps as a result of interagency sanfus and frustrating experiences in dealing with governmental bureaucracies, many caseworkers have tended to fall back onto the "adjustment" solution to environmental problems: the client adjusts, that is, if he or she possesses the "ego strengths" to do so. In fairness, the individual workers may well be aware of better solutions and approaches, but they have had within their job no channels or groups through which to exert pressure.

The caseworker may also be subject to other internal stresses. The nature of the issues involved may subtly "turn him off"; the fact that the client does not come into the situation with "clean hands" may keep him from seeing that legal or human rights have been violated; his own fear of authority may also induce him to hold back; or his identification with authority may predispose him to side with the world of rules and established practices, perhaps rationalized as a conviction that the authorities may make mistakes, but that they mean well. Yet another extreme may be that of the caseworker whose own rebellious feelings cause him to secretly provoke a client into arbitrary rebellion.

All these examples may be termed "countertransference" in a general way. Workers may have mastered such reactions in relation to individual and family relationship problems but be less able to recognize them in advocacy situations. The result may merge not only in misjudgments or failure to elicit information, but more importantly in an inability to develop that outlook and commitment necessary for advocacy for the client.

A situation reported recently illustrates the possibilities and pitfalls. Three children in a family receiving public assistance were sent home the first day of school because of inadequate clothing. A recent New York state law eliminated all special grants, including clothing, for such families. In responding to the situation, the caseworker could see to it that the family received a donation of the necessary clothing, could help the mother with budgeting, or could try to help the mother with a presumed depression that kept her from managing her funds—possible solutions, but not advocacy. Or, the caseworker could ask such questions as: Are these and other children being denied their right to an education by the new welfare law? Is a mother being forced to put herself in risk of a charge of child neglect because of the new state law? The caseworker now has made the large first step in advocacy—a commitment to the client rather than to the existing system involved. The caseworker should then have recourse to a lawyer to determine whether there is a basis for a court case to test the constitutionality of the new law, or to a welfare rights group to determine if a public issue should be made of the situation. These alternatives, it sould be noted, will involve the client acting on her own behalf.

Where does family counseling enter in? Its place is clear with clients who come for family problems and subsequently reveal social problems calling for advocacy, although the worker must as with any client be alert to the possibility that the actual injustice may also become a focal point in the client's defensive system to resist any internal change. On the other hand, clients who come essentially for redress of wrongs cannot be treated as if they are indirectly asking for personal counseling. Although this assumption has been made by many workers in the past, it may well run counter to the reality seen by the client. Low-income families (and others as well) tend to view such interviewing activity by the worker as prying into their personal lives, and from that may make a reasonable deduction that there is something behind the scenes they do not understand and do not trust. Also, the worker's eagerness to get to the family problems (as if this were the only justification for his job) may seriously disrupt the client's sense of priorities in his personal life, leaving the client overwhelmed and the worker helpless by premature exposure of all problems.

Case Study

Just as casework treatment is based on a study of background material, current situation, and related factors, a case for advocacy should rest upon a comparable study. More specifically, in advocacy the worker needs to familiarize himself not only with the specific client, problem, and situation but also with such factors as the institutions involved and the legal implications.

Broadly speaking, situations are presented to the caseworker either directly as situations for advocacy—the client comes seeking help for a problem in which rights are apparently being violated—or the client comes for some other difficulty but the caseworker elicits the advocacy need. As a first step, as already noted, the caseworker must be alert and committed to the client's position in relation to social institutions. Perhaps a good working method is to see every problem the client "has" as a possible problem that the social institution "has"; this is not to negate the client's possible internal problem but to ensure that we carefully examine in what ways this is a shared problem and whether solutions may not lie outside the client, either partly or wholly.

Many grievances relate to possible legal rights of the client. The caseworker has a responsibility to uncover such possibilities, to obtain necessary facts, and to consult a lawyer or legal service for the poor to ascertain whether a legal case exists. The caseworker is also responsible for helping the client understand that there may be possible publicity, delays, and other strains involved in pursuing a court case. He must inform him of possible alternative solutions. He must determine whether the client is assured of financial support and other needs during the trial period, if this enters into the situation. And he must help the client reach a decision, which may mean going into motivations, conflicts, and fears. Looking further ahead, the caseworker must plan to be available throughout and even after a case is settled, for it can happen that a client may win a court case but meet further delays and appeals. Thus, in the area of legal rights, caseworkers need not only some knowledge of law in those areas often involved in client problems, but also a working relationship with a legal service or lawyer who handles advocacy cases, to understand the practical workings of the legal system and to be able to obtain opinions quickly and informally.

For various reasons, however, legal recourse may not be sought even though rights have been violated. This may be the choice of the client or test cases may already be pending; nevertheless, other immediate action may be desired. In addition, in cases where legal rights have not been violated but other "human" rights are involved, resulting from institutional insensitivity to the needs of the poor and elderly, there may also be cause for further action. Interventions suitable in such cases will be described later.

Familiarity with pertinent law is but one of a number of areas of knowledge the caseworker needs. Credit practices, school policies and practices, family court, handling of alcoholics and drug addicts, probationary methods, psychiatric facilities, and systems theories are others. In short, the caseworker as advocate needs to develop knowledge and understanding of the institutions and systems with which clients are most often in contact. This refers not only to general knowledge but also to specific institutions in the community. While caseworkers perforce develop a working knowledge of local institutions, this is usually developed piecemeal and not fully shared and pooled with other staff to develop a full picture. The caseworker—not in isolation but with other staff—needs in effect an outline with which to study a given organization, just as he explicity or implicitly follows such an outline in developing his study of an individual or family, however imperfect such an outline may be in its ultimate explanations.

An institution or organization is first characterized by the fact that it has an entity (usually a legal base for its existence), its own structure, regulations, premises, staff; it is set off from other organizations by its clientele— it serves certain people for certain specified purposes only. There is a hierarchy of command and accountability. The worker should become familiar with these aspects of each important organization in the community. Beyond the formal structure, however, and perhaps more important, is the informal structure of the organization and its relationship to the community. The caseworker needs to ask the following questions: What is the orientation of the organization toward the people it serves? What is its tone and morale? How does one evaluate the discrepancy between clients' complaints and agency position? What efforts have been made to change policies, by whom and how, and with what results? What is the response of the organization to criticism or attack? Does it have vulnerabilities (adverse publicity, for example)? At what level, within or above the organization, is there discretionary power to make changes?

On a practical level the caseworker needs to know the following: procedural structure in relation to clients, to whom grievances are first addressed and what further steps are specified, such as appeals or review boards; in what ways retaliation against the client may be resorted to, and what protection can be found for the client; and whether or not other clients of the agency encounter the same difficulty. He will also want to know if clients of other agencies have encountered similar difficulties and what if anything they have tried.

It becomes clear that an institution must be viewed more as an "adversary" in advocacy, rather than as a cooperating or allied agency (even though in other situations this may be true). "Adversary" does not perforce mean "enemy," but does require a different approach than the "consensus" approach to which caseworkers are accustomed.[8] Even from this brief description, it can be seen that the full ongoing assessment of an advocacy case may require case conferences or outside consultation—or both—just as in an evaluation of a family treatment case.

Interventions

In casework, the worker (and other staff at times) selects the methods and modes of treatment for each client, based on the initial case evaluation. In family advocacy, similar steps seem necessary, from the initial interviews, through the study and diagnostic thinking, to the selection of interventions; the necessary participation of the client or client group is, obviously, on a different level in this process.

Family agencies have traditionally used only a small number of the many kinds of interventions available for an advocacy program. The selection of which interventions to use in a given issue is a complex one, involving the nature of the problem, the objective, the nature of the adversary, the degree of militancy to which the agency will go, and the effectiveness of the method, generally and in relation to certain kinds of situations. All of these factors suggest the desirability of expert consultation for many agencies in an ongoing advocacy program. More than one method is usually included in an action program, with the result that the staff and the agency as a whole will become involved in various ways.

In advocacy programs it is important for the agency not to get caught in dilatory tactics so common in bureaucratic procedures; an overconcern for the niceties and politeness of "due process" may dishearten staff and cause suffering for the clients. Yet failure to study the situation carefully may result in a quick action being dismissed because a necessary step was omitted. For example, a case brought against a school system was dismissed after a period of months because the court ruled that the plaintiff had failed to exhaust other remedies first, namely, an appeal to the board of education. By this time, the school year was almost over, the complaint no longer had any validity, and the child had been subjected to adverse conditions.

The following methods of intervention hardly exhaust the possibilities or the many variations used by groups (mainly nonsocial work) but suggest the wide range and the many types suitable for a family advocacy program.

1. *Studies and surveys.* These often form the groundwork for further action, both for the advocacy program itself and for educational and publicity purposes. Whatever the sources of the material, staff and board must be prepared to answer penetrating or hostile questions, and material should in effect be subjected to such an approach before it is used. Otherwise embarrassing loopholes may be exposed and the effort weakened.

2. *Expert testimony.* Social workers may be called upon to testify as professionals or agency representatives, with or without the backing of studies and surveys. While this method may not have great effect upon legislators or public officials, the absence of the social work voice may be noted adversely.

3. *Case conferences with other agencies.* This has traditionally been one important way in which the agency tries to effect change; by presenting the conditions and results of certain practices and regulations in given cases, one hopes to induce the other agency to change. This method may be of value in early stages of an advocacy effort, especially if it can involve higher officials of the other agency. It also elicits much about the potential adversary organization and may help to clarify just where the crux of the problem lies—at the level of staff practice, supervision, middle or top administration, board, or beyond the agency. Such conferences held with clients present can have other values as well and may be the first step in developing a client group determined to go further in action on its own behalf.

4. *Interagency committees.* Such committees, which often have proven to be splendid time-wasters, can offer the advantages of case conferences mentioned above. They can also be developed into types of permanent bodies which can represent yet another method of action in a given locality. In large suburban areas, encompassing several small communities, various agencies may provide services within each small community but obviously cannot have a local base in each. An interagency committee can be developed involving local community agencies and the wider-based agencies to handle local issues. For example, Family Service Association of Nassau County along with another agency started such a committee in one community, originally around overlapping case concerns. Over a five-year period, the committee has developed into a kind of local welfare council, though without separate corporate existence. It takes up local issues and is called upon by other organizations to help in certain situations. This type of committee, for example, can be used by a local agency which may have complaints against the school system but hesitates to take action alone. It also provides a vehicle for the interagency sharing of grass-roots problems arising from specific cases, which councils embracing large areas and many agencies cannot do.

5. *Educational methods.* This refers to activities such as informational meetings, panels, exhibits, pamphlets, and press coverage, all aimed at educating segments of the population. These may include also public appeals on specific issues made through the press, radio, and television. Legislators and public officials may be somewhat influenced by these methods.

6. *Position taking.* The agency formally takes a position on an issue, making it known publicly through the press, as well as to officials, legislators, and others directly. This goes beyond an educational effort in an attempt to put the weight of the agency onto a specific position. Generally, the agency's position will be newsworthy only if it is among the first to take the stand, or if board members represent an influence with important segments of the community. The taking of a formal position may be often of greatest value internally, that is, in conveying to staff and clientele that the agency is committed and moving.

7. *Administrative redress.* Governmental bodies usually provide for various steps to appeal decisions at the practice level. While such steps may appear to delay action, they may nonetheless be necessary preludes to further action (such as court suits) or desirable in that they will call the attention of higher officials within or without the agency to conditions. Also, where the imperfect working of a system has resulted in an injustice to one client, grievance procedures through an ombudsman often result in a correction for that one client. Taking such moves may be necessary although the advocacy program need not stop there in fighting a larger battle.

8. *Demonstration projects.* Even though focused directly on problems of the poor, demonstration projects are generally long-term methods of ad-

vocacy. They may be necessary in order to elicit the specific material needed for advocacy, and to help a group or community develop the awareness, leadership, and determination to embark upon a course of action. Further advocacy is usually needed to carry the message of the demonstration project into a larger scale service or institutional change affecting the total population involved in a problem.

9. *Direct contacts with officials and legislators.* The agency may approach them formally to make positions known, give relevant information, or protest actions carried out or contemplated. Informal meetings, individually or with groups of legislators, may be similarly used and may enable the legislator to reveal ignorance, ask questions, and listen to more specific material. The agency might attempt to set up some type of regular contact, which in time may result in greater impact as agency personnel and views become known.

10. *Coalition groups.* These can be described as ad hoc groupings of organizations around a specific objective. The advantages lie not only in the combination of forces, but in the fact that agencies do not have to bear the burden and risk separately. The coalition concept also points to the involvement of disparate types of organizations and groups, which maintain autonomy while pursuing a common goal. Each organization usually has a circle of adherents who in turn may be more willing to work in concert than alone. Drawbacks involve the danger of setting too general goals and methods, and a proliferation of meetings and committees seeking to "clarify" and "cooperate."

11. *Client groups.* The wide-scale development of the potential of client groups has occurred only recently, and has revealed that this is a major instrument of social change. By client groups is meant any local group or grouping of individuals sharing a problem; while they are not the traditional agency "clients," they are so termed in the sense that they are in some way helped through an agency service. This service may be limited to giving some impetus to the forming of the group, but may continue in the form of consultation to the group, supportive efforts in such ways as helping the group obtain information or gain access to certain people, or mounting collaborative efforts with other community groups. At the outset the advocate may assist in helping the group role-play contemplated action, help solve problems with the group, or suggest ways of augmenting the group. Through community contacts the advocate may help in bringing several groups together to develop coalitions; he may also suggest various methods of action for the group's consideration. Some family agencies have already had valuable experience with such groups in Project ENABLE, which by its very name indicates the primary role of the advocate in relation to such groups.

There is already considerable literature on client groups that covers many aspects of this method of social change. There are, however, two dangers to which the caseworker-advocate should be alert from the start:

one, being too verbal, directive, not remaining where the group is, or directly or indirectly using the group as a means to ends other than what the group develops; second, the failure to develop other sources of support toward the same general objectives and to help the group relate to other support in a meaningful but autonomous manner.

12. *Petitions.* While petitions appear to have little direct effect upon officials and legislators, they are valuable in calling attention to an issue. Getting petitions signed is also a valuable activity for a new group in that it mobilizes members around an action and gives them an opportunity to talk to people about the issue, develop their abilities in making public contacts, and formulate points and rebuttals. It may also provide a way of reaching other interested people who might join or support the group.

13. *Persistent demands.* This method in effect means bombardment of officials and legislators, going beyond the usual channels of appeal. Thus a welfare group protesting welfare cuts directed one effort against the local board of education, in an attempt to get the board to join in action to influence the state legislature. This method represents a kind of escalation of a campaign, and may be directed against figures inaccessible or unwilling to submit to personal contacts. While within lawful limits, it may be the precursor to "harassment" or other extra-legal means.

14. *Demonstrations and protests.* These include marches, street dramas, vigils, picketing, sit-ins, and other public demonstrations. The family advocate should become familiar with these methods, although organizing and conducting them may lie beyond his competence and role. To what extent an agency as such will organize and participate in these methods will have to determined within the agency. An agency will have to consider carefully, however, whether its other forms of action are not being conducted from too far behind the firing line, and whether commitment may not require some such firing line activity at times.

Selecting the Method of Intervention

The objectives of any plan of intervention are closely tied in with the methods selected and the nature of the issue and of the adversary organizations. An effort to challenge a state law usually will require a massive effort, on many levels and with various methods, whereas challenging a practice of a local organization may be accomplished through such means as meetings, pressures, client groups, and administrative redress. A demonstration project may represent a fresh and optimistic approach to a problem that has eluded solution for years; it cuts through a problem in a different way and represents a long-term investment toward an objective. For example, the very early childhood experimental programs now in progress in several places in the country, such as one being conducted by Family Service Association of Nassau County, represent a new approach to one goal of reformers and advocates—that of forcing the school systems to provide vast remedial and enrichment programs for the many low-income children who suffer cognitive deficiencies. The objective of these new programs is to foster early development in the child so that the need for later remedial efforts is minimized or even eliminated. The program conducted by Family Service Association of Nassau County has the additional objective of enhancing the role of mothers and fathers in low-income families, an objective pursued in the past through various other methods.

The family advocate and the agency must consider the order of priority of their objectives, leaving room for sharpening or shifting of focus as practice reveals more clearly the nature of the issues involved and points to new approaches, such as those mentioned in relation to demonstration projects. The family advocate should also be alert to the many seemingly minor petty harassments, indignities, and omissions he will suffer—these are often the only part of the Establishment iceberg that is visible to the poor. Ultimately they may become larger issues than the clear-cut injustices which are amenable to lawsuits or other definable actions. Behind the small indignities lie the encrusted attitudes and structures which are far more impervious to change than a given rule or regulation. As William Blake wrote in 1804, "He who would do good to another, must do it in Minute Particulars/General Good is the plea of the scoundrel hpyocrite & flatterer."[9]

Agency Structure

The commitment of the agency to action on behalf of families is obviously the cornerstone of an advocacy program. But commitment can rather quickly be dissipated unless a workable structure for advocacy is established. The structure must be one which can and does involve the entire agency, including staff, board, and volunteers in an ongoing activity. Commitment must also be represented by a commitment of time; if advocacy is to be the second major function of a family agency, it must receive the time, attention, and thought that have gone into the counseling program. For example, does the staff time committed to advocacy equal that committed to recording interviews? The staff can tell by such allotments what the agency really means to emphasize. The board, with overall responsibility for the agency, will probably need to delegate to a committee the charge for advocacy. Such a committee, already existing in a number of agencies under such names as Public Issues or Social Concerns, should probably be separate from a committee focused on legislation per se, as the latter would be dealing primarily with bills introduced into legislative bodies. At times, of course, the two committees may be concerned with the same issue and even the same legislation.

The advocacy committee has several important functions. One is to become and keep informed on local problems and issues in order to make continuous assessments of priorities for action and give guidelines to staff involved in advocacy; staff in turn will inform the committee on the pressing concerns of the people. Also essential to advocacy is the potential for quick action. The committee consequently must establish methods by which the advocacy staff can move quickly and still be assured of its backing. This can be done only through an ongoing process in which the committee learns to set guidelines by considering the methods, successes, and failures of the staff and others involved in advocacy. A close and continuing contact between staff and committee is necessary.

The committee has a key responsibility in thinking through the implications of any course of action giving particular thought to follow-through so that client groups are not stirred up and then disappointed by an action that is abandoned. It must also consider the risks involved for the agency in taking action and in making alignments with various groups. Finally, the committee itself becomes involved in action. Members may attend public meetings and hearings or call upon officials and legislators. For example, the Public Issues Committee of the Family Service Association of Nassau County took up the transportation problem in the county as it affects the poor. The committee met with the County Planning Commission and with a representative of the bus companies, obtained much background material, and then, with staff, attended public hearings to present the agency position. Usually board members carry more weight in efforts to influence officials and legislators than do social workers; they may speak not only as residents of a community but may also be able to mobilize other local groups unaffiliated with the agency.

Agency staff also needs to be involved, so that advocacy is not an isolated, specialized function. While historically the caseworker has been seen as one who relays case material to administrators and board, it is evident that staff is for the most part not content with this role, which has no follow-through and which may only occassionally involve any given worker. On the other hand, not all caseworkers can be closely involved in every advocacy action, and there are aspects to advocacy which call for the development of expertise and knowledge to be exercised more centrally in an agency.

Different patterns for staff advocacy are possible, depending on agency size, funding, staff interests, and other considerations. The following are four examples:

1. An agency may have a full-time staff position of Family Advocate, or a Department of Advocacy headed by the Family Advocate. This position, as recently established at Family Service Association of Nassau County through

a foundation grant, is initially projected to include two main functions: first, to work with staff, providing consultation on action on behalf of individual clients, or handling certain situations directly and compiling case material on problems for the Public Issues Committee. In addition, the Family Advocate will be working to involve the staff in further action, such as the formation of client groups concerned with specific problems, and participation in committees and hearings. It should be noted that clerical staff may also be involved in such actions; most clerical staff in social agencies have or develop a commitment to the purposes of social work, and should have opportunity to ally themselves in their capacity as agency personnel as well as private citizens.

The second major responsibility of the Family Advocate is to act as the staff person to the Public Issues Committee. He helps the members define priority problems through case material and background information and by bringing in officials and others who are involved in the problems; he works with them to set guidelines and steps for action, to think through implications, to review what has been done, and to evaluate methods. The Family Advocate may act as agency spokesman, and as liaison to officials and legislators; he may act as agency representative with coalition groups and community groups, and as consultant to client groups; or he may act as advisor to staff or board people who carry out these functions.

One example will illustrate how guidelines and priorities are established, and how the Family Advocate can take action accordingly. The Public Issues Committee defined several priority problem areas before adjourning for the summer; one involved what appeared to be the inequitable distribution and possible poor use of federal education funds siphoned through the state (Title I funds of the Elementary and Secondary Education Act provide added services for children of low-income families). The Committee had no specific cases with which to document this possible problem; it had been suggested by agency staff whose contacts with schools on behalf of clients have them good reason to believe this was an area to explore further and possibly act upon. Shortly afterwards, the Family Advocate spoke with the superintendent of a school district which was rapidly becoming a ghetto and needed massive governmental funding to cope with educational needs. The superintendent, failing to obtain funds anywhere, was ready to explore this area.

The Family Advocate, acting as consultant and organizer, helped prepare factual material which documented the inequitable distribution of funds and helped assemble a group of other superintendents in similar situations. State education officials came to meetings, and one school district instituted a court suit to force redistribution. Throughout, the Advocate worked cooperatively with the Title I Director of the County Economic Opportunity Council. All this activity took place in line with the priorities set down by the Public Issues Committee, which had not anticipated that this particular problem would suddenly come alive—this rested upon the work of the Advocate and the decision of the executive director.

2. Variation on the establishment of a full-time Family Advocate might include creating a part-time position instead. Or, an "indigenous" worker might fill the position. This pattern might require the investment of more staff and consultation time but bring about other advantages such as better contact with local poverty groups.

3. A present staff member might be assigned in agencies where the budget does not permit expansion of staff at present. Or, a part-time assignment could be made, as an expedient only, since the conflict between the demands of a caseload and of the advocacy function would be frequent and onerous for the worker.

4. A staff committee might be formed, with a chairman bearing responsibility for the advocacy function, but delegating pieces of work to committee members. This method has the advantages of involving more staff directly, keeping the advocacy function related to the casework, and keeping the staff in direct contact with the board committee. Obviously it could present difficulties in carrying out actions, as well as in the kinds of demands upon the worker's attention and time mentioned above.

It may be possible in the context of the four patterns that have been described for the agency to obtain graduate social work students for the program. This would provide needed manpower. Students can, for example, do much of the background work which is time consuming for the caseworker but essential to the advocacy function. Some schools of social work, in preparing "generic" workers, may find this a highly desirable type of placement, since it can provide the student with selected cases related to advocacy, client groups with which to work, again in connection with advocacy, and community organization and action experience.

In agencies where a separate position of Family Advocate cannot be established, staff members carrying the functions in one of the patterns suggested should have direct access to the responsible board committee and work with that committee. Otherwise the resulting delays in cross-communication and lack of clarity may impede any action. An agency may find it needs the advice of one or more specialists in the areas of agency structuring and functioning for advocacy, orientation to clientele, assisting client groups, and defining areas of action and strategies.

Conclusion

Family advocacy offers a way for agencies and staffs to bridge the gap between the many cases of individual grievances against social institutions and the broader-scale actions needed to bring about institutional change. The caseworker's intimate knowledge of individual families provides a grassroots basis for social action, and his concern for families becomes an integral and vital part of the advocacy process.

The defining of the function of family advocacy points to the need for special knowledge and skills, to support the caseworker's activity and to promote social change. A meaningful commitment by the agency is essential to carrying out the second major function of the family agency—improving the social environment of families.

References

1.   Charlotte Towle, Social Work: Cause and Function, *Social Casework*, 42: 394 (October 1961); see also Harry Specht, Casework Practice and Social Policy Formulation, *Social Work*, 13:42–52 (January 1968); and Gordon Hamilton, The Role of Social Casework in Social Policy, *Social Casework*, 33:315–24 (October 1952).

2.   Ann Hartman, Anomie and Social Casework, *Social Casework*, 50:131–37 (March 1969).

3.   Ellen P. Manser, *Project ENABLE: What Happened* (New York: Family Service Association of America, 1968).

4.   NASW Ad Hoc Committee on Advocacy, The Social Worker as Advocate: Champion of Social Victims, *Social Work*, 14:16–22 (April 1969).

5.   Charles F. Grosser, Community Development Programs Serving the Urban Poor, *Social Work*, 10:18 (July 1965).

6.   Daniel Thursz, Social Action As a Professional Responsibility, *Social Work*, 11:17 (July 1966).

7.   David Wineman and Adrienne James, The Advocacy Challenge to Schools of Social Work, *Social Work*, 14:26 (April 1969).

8.   Irwin Epstein, Social Workers and Social Action: Attitudes Toward Social Action Strategies, *Social Work*, 13:101–8 (April 1968).

9.   *Jerusalem*, Ch. 3, lines 60–61.

PART III
The
Group-Interactional Facet

Introduction

The group-interactional facet deals with the internal functioning of the family, the relationship of members of a family to one another. The article by Ackerman helps to make a transition from the previous section on the institutional approach to the group-interactional focus of this section by asking what takes priority—the person, the family, or the state? According to Ackerman, the world surrounding the family is in such disarray that this question is impossible to answer. Rather, he dwells on how the family can become an instrument of protection, sheltering its members from the devastating impact of modern society. He then asks the question: "Is the unique flexibility of the human family failing?" It is Ackerman's view that the answer must be negative as long as the family helps man to conquer his fear of the unknown, which is a paramount problem of a rapidly changing society. People must move from an orientation toward power, acquisition, and exploitation to more humanistic values. In this context family therapy is a social movement rather than a treatment modality.

The article by Krill focuses specifically on the initial family interview as a diagnostic method. Krill's study of 20 families treated in a clinic that served Anglo-Americans, Spanish-Americans, and blacks produced six areas important to the diagnostic process: assessment of the core problem, discovery of roles and coalitions in the family interaction pattern, direct knowledge of

162

nonverbal communication, knowledge of the family's cultural mores, objective reports from healthier family members, and family confrontation.

Devis offers an interaction-based diagnostic and treatment scheme for the caseworker who embarks on family therapy, focusing on four concepts: value orientation, scapegoating, role differentiation, and transmission of behavioral defects. These concepts are used to help the caseworker understand the family's conflict and living processes by looking beyond individual-psychological to group-interactional phenomena.

On the basis of a large sample of cases from various agencies, Voiland and Buell have developed a classification of disordered families as perfectionistic, inadequate, egocentric, or unsocial. The article explains these four categories as well as the diagnostic format used to develop them and offers a prognosis for each type. This classification system is a good general scheme that can be used by practitioners with various degrees of education and experience, and in a variety of practice settings.

Because of the rising divorce rate in the United States and the increase in the number of troubled couples seeking treatment, Nadelson et al. believe that it has become necessary to develop evaluative procedures that can result in the use of more comprehensive and flexible treatment techniques. They point out that when marital stress develops, both partners undergo disturbance, but wives appear to manifest more disturbance than husbands because of the culturally induced expectations of performance in marriage. Given this complex mix and variation of disturbance, the authors identify situations when conjoint treatment is appropriate and when it is contraindicated.

Bardill presents an approach to marital problems based on the view that the husband-wife relationship can be treated as a subsystem within the total family system. Distinguishing between relationship dynamics and individual-psychological dynamics, the author identifies principles that can be used in selecting couples that can benefit from this type of intervention as well as pinpointing the characteristics of couples for which such a focus is contraindicated. He explains the worker tasks in this approach and appropriate use of separate and joint interviews.

Hallowitz draws a distinction between process material and family dynamics and the problem-solving content in family treatment. The problem-solving component is portrayed as the vehicle through which many of the other dynamics flow. The role of the therapist in this perspective is explored. All of the theoretical material is applied directly to case material.

Brown explains a specific technique of providing feedback in family interviews which he refers to as "ascription." He relates the concept of feedback to current theories of practice and then provides detailed discussion of the major types of ascriptive statements used by workers in giving feedback to clients.

Golner explains the technique of in-the-home family counseling for children with school-related problems. The emphasis is on treating the child and his entire family in the home setting through the use of a counseling team. The article outlines home-family counseling goals, assignment of a key person to coordinate the intervention, counseling-team seminars, the inclusion of professionals and nonprofessionals in the counseling, the focus of the sessions, and seating arrangements. Evaluation research on the use of this approach is summarized.

Scherz explores in detail the maturational crises that impact on parent-child interactions as the family moves through the family life cycle. She begins by documenting universal family tasks and familial conflicts and crises. Then she identifies the crucial maturational points in the family life cycle—establishing a new marriage, birth of the first child, separation points, adolescence, achieving adult status, and problems of old age.

Epstein describes techniques of brief therapy to be used with children and their parents when crisis occurs. The goals and process of brief therapy are explained as are methods of conducting parent groups, interviewing children, and using combined parent-child groups.

Laughlin and Bressler describe a program developed in a family agency to help heavily indebted families. The authors cover the process of becoming indebted, problems that parallel indebtedness, and common coping efforts. Also discussed is the worker's response to discussing money matters. The authors give detailed coverage of an innovative program combining short-term therapy and debt counseling conducted by professional social workers and nonprofessional volunteers. Training of the volunteers is explained as well as the actual counseling process.

Hallowitz argues that although clinical services for poor black families have never been highly regarded, there is a need and a place for such services. The article delineates a range of potentially effective counseling and treatment modalities and methods and presents some of the substance of such clinical practice.

Social workers have generally become involved with marital partners after problems occur, but increasingly they are being called upon to provide premarital counseling as people become more concerned about the growing divorce rate. The article by Freeman offers guidance to the worker in providing this form of counseling in groups. The author covers aims of the group, screening procedures, appropriate techniques, appropriate content at various stages of the counseling process, and evaluation procedures.

9
Family Healing in a Troubled World

Nathan W. Ackerman

In a world transformed by despair, alienation, drugs, violence, and war, what happens to the healing function of society? What is the impact, in particular, on family healing?

Human adaptation is characterized by a dynamic balance of change and continuity, change within continuity, and continuity within change. Today the forces of change race far ahead of the forces of continuity. The vertical vector, tradition and authority, is reduced; the horizontal vector, current events and peer culture, is overweening.

Our whole way of life has become irrevocably altered; the transformation is little short of staggering. People and families are experiencing cataclysmic upheaval. They tend to lose their bearings. In effect, they navigate without a compass. Can man, remarkably resilient as he is, adapt to this tidal wave of change? If he can, how great will be the cost in relation to the wreckage of human lives? Or, to rephrase the question, how far can the new society be expected to accommodate to the basic needs of man and the family of man? Which comes first—the person, the family, or the state? There is much talk these days about the dangers of pollution of the physical environment. What about the dangers of pollution of the social environment? There seems, in fact, to be an insidious poisoning of the social atmosphere.

The disorders of our society, resulting from radical change, invade and infect our daily family and community life. These disorders include the combined impact of technology, a state of continuous war, racial conflict, crowding, violence, the invasion of personal freedom, the decline of humanistic and spiritual values, and the loss of human connectedness.

Source: From *Social Casework* 52 (April 1971), pp. 200–205. Copyright © 1971 by the Family Service Association of America. Reprinted by permission.

Effects of Society's Disorders

From these influences emerge the "mass man," the orientation to power, manipulation, acquisition, and a trend toward depersonalization and weakening of moral fiber. People are being mechanized, dehumanized, brutalized, and rendered numb to the suffering of others; and they no longer seem to care. Whereas fifty years ago the problem was too much conscience, today it is not enough conscience.

> The malady of the modern family shows itself in several ways: 1. A form of family anomie, reflected in a lack of consensus on values, a disturbance in identity relations and a pervasive sense of powerlessness; 2. Chronic immaturity, the inability to assume effective responsibility, and an impaired potential for viable family growth; 3. Discontinuity and incongruity in the relations between family and society.[1]

Family relationships are off kilter. Following an upset, the family is less able to right itself, less able to restore balance. Parents today are confused, frightened, and helpless. They try the impossible. They try to barricade the family against the disorders of the community. Parents act phobic; youth turns counterphobic. The young refuse to admit fright. The failure of leadership in a family brings a vacuum. Nature, however, abhors a vacuum and youth rises to fill that vacuum. The traditional role of youth has been characterized as "his majesty's loyal opposition," which is the responsibility of son to father. Today there is an inversion of this relationship. It is almost as if the role of the father in our time is to be his son's loyal opposition. Father and son do, in fact, have a common ground; they hold the power to enhance one another's strength, dignity, and wisdom.

The pollution of the social environment magnifies the forces of fragmentation and alienation in family relationships. The work pressures of contemporary society remove the man from his family. The conflicts of the community divide husband and wife, parent and child, parent and grandparent, parent and teacher, parent and community leader. There are rising complaints of feelings of emptiness, meaninglessness, loneliness, despair, and deadness. In alienated persons, the incidence of delinquency, addiction, mental illness, violence, and suicide is conspicuously high.

"Alienation has two meanings, estrangement or detachment and a trend toward depersonalization, toward a state of mind approaching madness."[2] The dual aspect of this experience, the cutting off of feelings from self and others and the dread of loss of mind, is a malignant threat.

Conflict of Social Forces

The social patterns of the modern community are in an acute state of flux. There are clashes of social forms and ideals everywhere about us. It is, to say the least, an unstable shifting of forces that maintain health and forces that induce breakdown and sickness. On the gloomy side, we might, for example, consider the statement of Charles Peguy: "The modern world debases. It debases the state, it debases man, it debases love, it debases the family. It even debases a particular kind of dignity, the dignity of death."[3] On the more optimistic side, we might point to the social participation and protest of our youth. Disregarding the actions of a minority, the socalled crazies, we might look with pride at the dignity, determination, intelligence, and idealism of the major segment of our nonviolent, protesting youth. The youth of our time lives out both sides—the healthy and the pathogenic elements of our patterns of family, society, and culture. In the main, youth does not want to adapt to a sick society. It wants to change it.

The forces of revolution are changing our perspectives about the problems of mental health. The human condition today is in crisis. Conflict is all-pervasive. It spreads by contagion to every level of the human experience and to all relationships. It is nowhere contained. The issue becomes one of sheer survival.

W. Hanson says, "In a few short years the world of order has become transformed into a nightmare of uncertainty."[4] With the crumbling of social forms, the models and guidelines for adaptive behavior fade away. The sense of danger spreads. The perception of real danger becomes fused indistinguishably with fantasy threats. There is a loss of belongingness of individual to family and of family to community. The fragmentation and alienation of relationships become progressively severe, conflict becomes externalized. People armor themselves to carry the fight to the environment. The atmosphere of the community becomes permeated with a contagion of anxiety and violence and takes on a paranoid tinge. Under these conditions the spontaneous healing forces of family and community are rendered less effective.

Lines of Defense

Conflict and coping are the head and tail of a single process. Conflict, coping, and healing are functions of social change. In the human struggle with conflict within a psychosocial framework, the first line of defense is to perceive the conflict correctly and to search for a realistic solution. Assuming that the perception is correct, the second line of defense is to contain the conflict while a solution is sought. If this line of defense is breached, conflict and coping move to a third level. The conflict is misperceived, can no longer be contained, and erupts into an acting-out pattern. Finally, the fourth line of defense is a progressive retreat leading ultimately to a contagion of panic, disorganization, violence, social madness, and even genocide.

What is involved here is a progressive shift from the rational to the irrational, from the appropriate to the inappropriate, in the coping with danger. When the equilibrium of man and society falters and fails, there is a forced movement toward deeper levels of irrationality and more destructive patterns of action. In our social fabric we are in danger of moving into the third and fourth lines of defense.

Healing Processes

The healing of a rift in family life is often incomplete and pathogenic, and it brings secondary complications. What are the potentials for restitution and healing in our time? An analogy from the field of surgery might be applicable in approaching this question. In the healing of wounded body tissue, the surgeon draws a distinction between health and pathogenic healing. Pathogenic healing often brings unfortunate complications, such as deficient blood supply, pallor, discoloration of the skin, scarring, and finally, deformation and disabled functioning. Applying this analogy to the processes of family healing, we can speculate that such healing may be healthy and relatively complete with no permanent residues of damage to structure and function; the healing may be partial although of adequate healthy quality; or the healing may be incomplete and pathogenic causing deformation and crippled functioning. It may be pertinent here to list some of these self-healing family trends.

1. A shared search for suitable solutions to conflict in family relationships.

2. A strengthening of family unity, integrity and functional competence through an enhancement of the bond of love and loyalty, and with this a consolidation of sound family values.

3. Mobilization of external support for family unity, stability and growth through community and social service [religious guidance, psychotherapy, and so forth].

4. Reintegration of family role relationships through tightening of the family organization; rigidification of authority, sharper division of labor, constriction and compartmentalization of roles.

5. Reintegration of family role relationships through a loosening of the family organization; dilution of the family bond, distancing, alienation, role segregation; thinning of the border between family and community and displacement of family functions from inside to outside.

6. Realignment of family relationships through splitting of the group and scapegoating of a part of the family.

7. Reduction of conflict and danger through avoidance, denial and isolation.

8. Reduction of conflict and danger through compromise, compensation and escape, i.e. sexual escapades, delinquency, alcohol, drugs [and so forth].[5]

A fleeting survey of these processes instantly discloses that they constitute a hierarchical series, moving from the more healthy to the more pathogenic level of coping and healing. When these operations veer toward the unreal and inappropriate side, they tend to decompensate and thereby release additional symptoms and signs of a disabled or crippled family; these are the secondary complications of incomplete and pathogenic healing.

In our time, the capacity to find effective solutions to family conflict with consolidation of sound family values is sharply reduced. There seems instead to be a shift from a first effort to hold a family together by tightening and rigidifying the family organization to a trend toward the loosening of family bonds. There is a conspicuous movement toward family splits, alienation, and scapegoating. In a parallel trend, the instability and degradation of family relationships seem to erode our social and emotional health.

For many years we have been trying to understand the processes by which man adapts to society; now, we must be concerned also with the other side of the question: how society must adapt to the needs of man and the family of man. The healing function does not emerge in a social vacuum. Just as disordered behavior can be understood only in the social context, so, too, healing can be understood only in a social context. The healing of an emotionally pained individual occurs optimally in a relatively dependable and predictable family environment. The healing of a pained family also has its best chance in a relatively dependable and predictable society. A dependable and predictable society, however, is exactly what we do not have today. In order for people and families to grow and keep healthy, they must determine how they can either find or create a healthy environment.

Family healing encompasses a wide range of restitutive, regenerative forces in family life as these occur in nature. In essence, these forces are spontaneous self-healing processes. There is a significant healing potential in such events as family gatherings, religious observances, rituals of confession and atonement, feasts, festivals, games, music and dance, initiation ceremonies, weddings, and deaths and the rituals of mourning. The healing potential in these events pertains to the family within the community and to some version of the extended family integrated into the community but not to the nuclear family in isolation. Family therapy, on the other hand, refers to a systematic method of professional intervention on the multiple, interlocking emotional disorders of a family group. As a professional procedure, it is challenged, among other things, to catalyze an optimal expression of the natural self-healing processes of family life.

The ecological perspective has relevance for the contemporary problems of mental science and mental healing. Surely we cannot trust our observations of disturbed persons if we study them in an artificial setting, separating them from their usual human habitat. In the past we examined disease in an isolated way as part processes in a living organism. Learning that this procedure was often wrong and misleading, we began to study the whole person's way of coping with disease. We then moved a step further; we evaluated the person's struggle with the seeds of sickness within the family group and community. Now, perhaps we have made a further advance to the examination of the pathogenic potential of the social environment.

Man's Dread of Change

The trouble surely is not with that remarkable organism, man, nor with that extraordinary invention, the human family. The trouble is to be sought rather in the chaos of the system of social relationships. The forces of disintegration derive perhaps less from the swift pace of change and more from the unpredictability of change. It is the not-knowing, the sheer incomprehensibility of change, that evokes the deepest dread. It is the panic of the unknown, man's fear of the dark, that impels the cry for sameness and certainty; it is panic, also, that unleashes the forces of violence and destruction. Is man's capacity to adapt to almost any living conditions, his extraordinary resiliency, reaching the breaking point? Is the unique flexibility of the human family failing? That is the question. The fear of change is the fear of life itself. There is but one choice: to go forward, not backward.

We do not know, however, to what one goes forward. Who can say what lies ahead? Our vision is blurred, sometimes even skewed. Concerning the big issues of war, racial relations, problems of economy, welfare, and education, the lines of allegiance among the people are fluid, rapidly shifting, unstable. There is mounting agitation in group relations. The pattern of alignments and splits continuously change. New social forms are emerging, but they are still relatively amorphous and only dimly outlined.

Bombarded by these social issues, the family is hard put to stay in one piece. Its function as a protective envelope is diminished, it has a kind of "rubber fence" that expands and contracts but one that seems vulnerable and easily penetrated.

The family is surely here to stay but must find a creative rebirth. It cannot return to an outworn, outmoded version of fifty years ago but must have a new design for family living, a bond of husband and wife, parent and child fitting the new future. This change in family living can happen only within a larger change, a creative rebirth of the entire social community.

Beneath the turmoil, one senses potentials for healing on several levels: group action for social reform, the striving to build a better community, the involvement of youth in social change, a new kind of joining of whole families in the struggle with social problems.

Particularly valid is the youth movement. Youth says, "Build bridges, not walls." They want an open, honest, and warm human connectedness, not exile from society. In the main, they exhibit a remarkable moral commitment and courage and increasing maturity and sophistication. They are rebels with a cause. This writer believes there is a spontaneous healing value in group interaction among the young people. Yet, wherever they go and whatever they do, they must take the core of their being with them, or else they become lost. To make the start, it is the family that must provide the core.

In the last analysis, the only real test of a healthy family within a healthy community is its orientation to the problem of values. The major question, of course, is how to move away from an orientation to power, acquisition, and a master-slave pattern of exploitation to a humanistic set of values; for life, not against life; for peace, not for death and destruction; for respecting the dignity and worth of all persons, regardless of race, color, or creed; for sharing and cooperation, not destructive competition; for openness, honesty, and intimateness in human relations, not isolation and alienation; for recognizing the creative values of difference, not fostering prejudice and violence; for a meaningful place and function for youth and for senior citizens in society; and for a relevant educational program that promotes growth and fulfillment in the new world. Within the superhuman universe, we must try to create human cells, teams, groups, and neighborhood groups, which join people through common goals and activities. Within such groups we must nurse a new kind of connectedness and mutual caring.

Relevance to Mental Health

Now, finally, what is the relevance of these thoughts for the family approach to mental health? Amid the turbulence of the times, we grope for a few answers. During the past thirty-five years, this writer has extended his conceptual orientation toward the problems of behavior, step by step, from the inner life of the person, to the person within family, to the family within community, and now to the social community itself.

As the Family Institute in New York works to develop the principles of family therapy, the staff members become increasingly concerned with the problems at the interface of family and community. More home visits are being made, and a special study called "Family House" is being conducted. This project provides for a family therapy team in a welfare housing unit in order to integrate help for the emotional problems of a family receiving public assistance with its total living situation. Furthermore, it is planned to have a get-together of all our families in the Institute home, four times yearly for a day or a weekend, to enjoy each other, to give and take comfort, and to discuss the problems of all families in our time. We are considering also how we may stimulate the growth of a real community on our street. We hope, thereby, to learn more about the real issues in the relations of family and community. In so doing, we expect that our therapy of the inner life of the family will become more potent in energizing the spontaneous healing forces of the social environment.

Moving along this path we are interested in the model of the "social doctor" in Denmark, who leads a team of helpers trained in domestic science. These people knock on doors and ask the woman of the house, "Do you have trouble, can we help you?" These workers give immediate help in the form of action, not just talk. These family helpers, guided by the "social doctor," move inward from outside. First they take care of the immediate reality problems; then they attend to the emotional problems within the family.

Family therapy is not just a treatment modality. It is a social movement. In rapid succession a series of Family Institutes have been born in the largest cities in this country: New York, Philadelphia, Boston, Los Angeles, San Francisco, Chicago, and Palo Alto. The Family Institute in New York set the precedent; others have followed. This movement is a clear sign of the need for a force in the community that can give the family new life.

References

1.   Nathan W. Ackerman, What Happened to the Family?, *Mental Hygiene*, 54:459 (July 1970).

2.   Ibid., p. 461.

3.   Charles Peguy, *Man Alone*, ed. Eric Josephson and Mary Josephson (New York: Dell Books, 1962), p. 43.

4.   W. Hansen, Environment and Design, *ETCETERA* (Autumn 1955), p. 19.

5.   Ackerman, What Happened to the Family?, pp. 462–63.

10
Family Interviewing as an Intake Diagnostic Method

Donald F. Krill

Even in the most traditional psychiatric settings an understanding of family dynamics has always been considered essential to an adequate assessment of a child's problems and intrapsychic conflicts. Yet too frequently, only the social worker sees the parents and even he only *hears about* family interaction. The only relationship he directly observes is the one between the parents themselves. And this, too, is lacking in many clinics in which workers choose to see parents separately, groups of parents, or only one parent. Other members of the psychiatric team rarely interview the parents and their orientation is focused primarily on the identified child.

Too often social workers prefer to maintain their professional comfort by using the old style of divided evaluations in which their primary function is viewed as service to the intake team: reporting what the parents say and maintaining liaison with community agencies involved. Today the social worker can take the lead in demonstrating the importance of the family operation as a crucial pathological system that often needs to be seen to be well understood.

Presented in this paper are a description and assessment of the use of the family interview as an intake diagnostic tool. The work was conducted in a medical school—the University of Colorado Medical Center, Denver—by a staff social worker and the diagnostic team, which sometimes included medical and social work students, pediatric residents, and postdoctorate psychologists in addition to residents in child psychiatry. Team members were invited to sit in on the family interview conducted by the social worker.

The total family interview changes the traditional picture, for now there is the possibility of observing the whole family interacting as individu-

Source: From *Social Work* 13:2 (April 1968), pp. 56–63. Copyright © 1968 by the National Association of Social Workers, Inc. Reprinted by permission.

als in a time of stress. The parents' description and story of the problem need not be taken as total reality; now the live reality of the family interaction is also seen and discrepancies between what is and what is said to be are often flagrant. Another valuable result of the family session is that the child's problem is often revealed through his current family relationships. The family interaction frequently displays the nature of the past and early traumata from which a child's problem arose and their elements often remain operative in present relationships.[1]

The variety of families seen in this study was considerable owing to the nature of the clinic itself. The Children's Diagnostic Center was established by the State of Colorado but attached to the University of Colorado Medical Center to provide psychiatric evaluations for children referred primarily by welfare agencies and courts throughout Colorado. Some children are referred because there are no other mental health resources in their local areas. Others come because of an emergent need or complex organic-emotional problems that the center is better able to handle than a local clinic with diagnostic limitations.

Client Population

The clinic's patients are Anglo-American, Spanish-American, and Negro, the majority being Anglo- and Spanish-American. Families are frequently poverty stricken or in the low-income range with few in the middle class. The maximum age treated is 16; a large proportion of the patients are teenagers. There is no minimum age requirement, but preschool children are rarely seen. The diagnoses are usually neurotic behavior disorders, character disorders, psychotic disorders, and ego deviations. Occasionally, a neurotic child or one whose problem seems to be primarily an adjustment reaction is referred.

One characteristic of the clinic population had some influence on the decision to see families together. Even though the service is statewide, there have frequently been referrals of children whose sibling previously had been evaluated. And with welfare departments becoming increasingly family-service minded, simultaneous referrals of children from the same family have increased. Because some families have far to travel on limited travel budgets, it seemed practical to see a family together on each referral. After an evaluation, when the case was reviewed in conference with the referring agency, it would be possible to plan together an agency or community approach for helping the family as a whole when such a procedure was indicated.

In setting up this new procedure it was decided that nearly any family would qualify for a family interview. A few exceptions occurred in which it was obvious that the family was already broken and living apart, and there seemed no real likelihood of its reuniting. Such an exception might occur when a child had been in an institution (which had referred him) or when the parents lived apart but were both available for evaluative contact. When there were broken homes and only one parent was available, then one-parent families were seen. The participation of all children living in the home and over age 7 was requested. Occasionally younger children were seen if they were already identified as problems or the parents simply preferred to bring all the children.

This study comprised twenty cases that were evaluated in order as they were referred to the clinic. This order was broken a few times (in the cases described previously as exceptions) when a family unit no longer existed.

It was decided to do the traditional intake work-up with all parents, obtaining the usual social history information apart from what was revealed in the one-hour family interview. This meant that an extra hour was added to the social worker's intake schedule. However, it decreased the strain of using the family interview to get a description of the history of the identified patient's problem. The primary interest could then be strictly interpersonal and the worker could comfortably develop and use any techniques to help this process come alive in the family.

Team members were invited to attend and participate in the family interview if they wished. The families seemed to accept meeting the other members of a team who would be seeing their child (the family session was nearly always the family's first contact with the clinic). No special parental permission was sought for this procedure and the referring agency had already briefed the parents that the whole family would be interviewed.

In a breakdown of the twenty evaluations, the family constellations interviewed included the following: thirteen complete families (young children sometimes excepted), four families without fathers, two with a mother and one child, and one with a father and one child. In only one complete family was the patient an only child. In six cases it was found useful, after a family interview, to see one or two of the siblings separately for further clarification of the family problem.

The method of interview, as already indicated, was to focus on the manner in which the family members communicated with one another and to learn how they viewed each other as individuals. Following some of Satir's ideas, the worker would commonly seek a response to the following types of questions: Why was the family here and what did the members expect might happen? What differences did the parents see in each of their children, and how did each of the children view their parents? How were various feelings—usually anger and hurt—expressed by each family member, and how were their expressions similar or different? What kinds of occurrences did the children think made the parents unhappy? What would each member like to see changed or different in the way the family lived or functioned?[2]

What is easily apparent from this focus is that the primary concern is not with the nature or history of the identified patient's problems, but rather the process of family interaction. The effort is toward developing a picture of the family power structure, the varying roles of its members, and their ways of communicating.

As might be expected, the families' capacity to respond to these questions and ways of thinking about interrelationships varied considerably. The differences seemed related to cultural background, levels of intelligence, the family members' severity of pathology, and the amount of privacy and isolation from others a family seemed determined to maintain. There is no doubt that the worker's experience and skill in family interviewing was an important factor as well. A creative, freely open, experimental attitude is frequently necessary to help a family become interpersonally alive. This often means that the worker must find a language of mutual understanding to increase trust and openness.

Was the information obtained in the interviews valuable? Was it worth the time and added effort? Aside from the worker's gained experience in family interviewing and the team's observation, how much new data could be learned about families with this approach? The experience showed that while interviews varied in the nature of productive verbal revelations, there was a variety of benefits that resulted and the family intake interview did seem to be significant for acquiring more valid knowledge of the family.

Six positive findings will be illustrated in this paper. These include the following: (1) the revelation of the core problem between parents and child, (2) discovery of roles and coalitions by observing the communication and interaction patterns, (3) direct acquaintance with other family members with information sometimes communicated nonverbally, (4) knowledge of the family's cultural mores, (5) acquisition of more objective reports from psychologically healthier siblings, and (6) bringing about a family confrontation.

Assessing the Core Problem

It is directly observable in some families that the nature of the child's problem is clearly connected with the family's tensions and conflicts as they are manifest in the interview situation. The issue can be brought out and looked at directly by all and some consideration may be given to how conflicts might be eased or the relationships changed. There are cases in which it is soon apparent that the child is brought in as a means of requesting help for the entire family. In such situations it is often necessary to help the family redefine the problem rather than accept the way one family member wishes to present it.

In one family, a 15-year-old, attractive blonde girl, an only child, was referred by a welfare department for rebellious behavior and running away. The three family members soon delved into the father's alcoholism and the mother's withdrawal from family life that accompanied her effort to earn the family living outside the home. They then talked of the girl's fear of her father and his drunken male friends and her despair at the loss of her mother's former interest and emotional support. The session was so productive that it continued through the two and one-half hours set aside for the complete social history. The final recommendations for change made by the staff, following the completed evaluation consisting of individual psychiatric interviews, psychological testing, and a pediatric examination, were the same as those proposed by the family in the initial family session. No serious emotional disturbance was found in the girl. The parents had discussed a plan by which the father would come to Denver, find a job, and work until he could send for his wife and daughter (who would remain at home). Alcoholism services were found in Denver that were not available in the family's small community.

Communication and Interaction

More often, the problem is not so clear-cut and apparent to the family even after discussion. However, in the majority of families interviewed, it was still considered useful to see the family members' interaction patterns in action. Coalitions, seductions, rivalries, both authoritative and subtle controls of one another, children used as scapegoats, children acting in parental roles, and a variety of forms of nonverbal communication could be observed. Relationships with parents and siblings were not just talked about but often acted out, which made later discussion all the more vivid for team members. There were cases in which the child referred by the agency was not the child the parents were most alarmed about and for whom they wanted help. Each family seems to have its own way of revealing what problems it needs help with.

A 16-year-old girl from a small, distant mining town had been referred for blackout spells and underachievement in school. She was a tall, spindly, unattractive girl, quite rigid, righteous, and proper, but obviously immature and operating at what appeared to be a latency-age level. Her 14-year-old sister was also asked to participate in the session. The younger sister's rhythmically swinging legs and ever shifting torso revealed considerable energy she was unsuccessfully trying to control. It was soon apparent that the parents were more worried about when and how she might run off with a boy than they were about their older daughter—the identified patient. The stepfather's friendly, subtle seductions of the younger girl were as obvious as his concern for her. The mother's masochism and low-key demands for someone to help her seemed clearly related to the older girl's stifled emotional growth and compliant behavior.

The older girl's resentment of her sister was often put into direct, challenging words. However, the younger sister was unruffled and seemed too intent on managing her own restless feelings to pay any attention to her sister. An interesting speculation made by the staff was that the mother identified with her older daughter and therefore stressed that daughter's problems as a means of revealing her own unhappiness and desire for change. If this were true, her worry over her younger daughter's potential sexual acting out would be primarily her husband's concern and she would simply be going along with his view. The older daughter's hostility toward her younger sister may have reflected jealousy over her relationship with the stepfather. Here again, the mother and older daughter shared feelings of being left out of the relationship between the stepfather and younger girl. This particular evaluation was followed by a visit of two team members to the mining community in which the family lived. Recommendations for both girls were discussed with staff of the local welfare department and school and the family doctor, all of whom participated in a planning conference. The conclusion was that little could be done for the older girl other than to support her present adjustment, including her tie to her mother. To attempt any other approach would probably lead to rapid upheaval and decompensation of her personality. Therefore, attention was focused on the younger daughter, and plans were made to provide her with a local counselor who could become an identity figure and encourage improved peer relationships and gradual emotional separation from her sister. The welfare department's work with the parents was considered an important means of helping the younger sister gradually emancipate herself from the family. This treatment plan undoubtedly had a different emphasis as a result of seeing the entire family in action. Furthermore, it is obvious that these plans were geared to handle the most urgent problem first. However, in retrospect, it is possible that more emphasis might have been placed on supportive help to the mother and older daughter.

Direct Knowledge

In a few families, productive interactions in response to questions simply never happened. Yet even in these cases, merely to see another family member could be useful. During the course of an hour, there is always some kind of apparent behavioral response, even when there is no verbal communication. People cannot avoid some reaction in a situation. Slips of the tongue, muddled answers, and misinterpretations of what is said to them are at times revealing. Body movement itself conveys nonverbal messages. The extreme variance between what is said and what is meant is apparent in the following example.

In the case of a fatherless family of which two sons, ages 13 and 6, were referred by the welfare department of a small crossroads prairie town, it was soon apparent by the collective silence that no one wanted to be there or felt they should be there. The mother haltingly said the appropriate things and agreed that the boys had some problems and it probably was a good idea to "go along with the welfare lady's suggestion" that the boys stay in Denver for a week and be evaluated. She tended to avoid any detail about the soiling, rebellion, stealing, fire-setting, and lack of peer relationships that had been the list of complaints furnished by the welfare department. At the end of the interview both boys put on a crying, squawking display and physically resisted any notion of staying in Denver. The mother's ambivalent message-bearing behavior was apparent among her hardly audible comments that said, "You must stay here, they want you to stay here." She would hold the boys close to her by putting her arms around them, look pleadingly at the staff, and shake her head as if to say silently: "They're not staying."

This interview revealed not only the mother's hidden "antievaluation" messages to her children, but also another useful fact. The local community had been viewing the family as a blight to the town for some time. The children's problems were the concern of the community rather than the mother who seemed perfectly satisfied with their maladjustments.

Cultural Mores

Another valuable result of the family intake session can be the revelation of family cultural mores that shed new light on the described pathology. The following case illustrates a characteristic that is not completely generalized in the Spanish-American culture but applies more to the specific family and their community.

A 14-year-old girl and her 9-year-old brother were referred from another fatherless family, which might best be described as "primitively Spanish-American." A 10-year-old sister and 13-year-old brother were also asked to participate. The welfare department thought the 9-year-old boy might be psychotic. Three years before he claimed to have seen a woman without a head, after which he had been fearful, plagued by sleeping problems, and sometimes heard and saw strange things at night. In the family session the boy began to tell of his frightening experience. Soon the other siblings spoke up. A whole gang of them had recently seen a strange woman in black walk across a nearby field. The question of her having a face or head was obviously still of considerable doubt. A next door neighbor had also seen the "woman without a head" in his garage and shot at her with his rifle. The grandfather, with whom the boy slept, had told the children that a hand had grasped him by the shoulder, a hand he suspected of being his dead wife's. The family washing machine had been placed over the trap door leading to the cellar because of unexplainable phenomena occuring there in the past—strange sounds and doors opening and closing by themselves. There was even a story in their little community about how the "woman without a head" had been decapitated. All of these stories came from the siblings. The social worker questioned the 9-year-old boy in more detail: "What did she have where her head should have been?" He replied quickly, "Just a black thing, like cloth." He was then asked: "And what did you think was under that black cloth?" His eyes widened and he said, "A sort of skeleton head." The final inquiry: "How did you know that; could you see it?" He said he did not really see it but some boys told him about it. The worker reflected that boys sometimes like to tease and scare other boys with such stories. He was able to consider this possibility. It was found that the boy was not psychotic; he was only a bit slow and gullible and had received little help with reality-testing from his superstition-loving family.

Objectivity

Frequently the strongest, healthiest family member is a sibling who has escaped close, neurotic involvement with the parents' pathology and has managed to find supportive relationships outside the family. The most honest, direct, objective report of what occurs in the family may often come from him. Once he speaks up, the family must somehow respond to what he has revealed.

In a middle-class family (the father was a rancher), the 15-year-old son was referred to the clinic for attempting to molest an 8-year-old girl. The welfare department described the family as wholesome, comfortable, and loving. In this instance, an exception was made and the parents were seen first; then the patient and his 17-year-old brother were brought in to complete the family. The 15-year-old boy—the labeled patient—was quiet and agreed with his parents' picture of a pleasant family life. However, the 17-year-old boy supplied a new and revealing view with his description of a cold distance preserved among the family members, so that they consistently avoided expression of any feelings because they were all worried about the father's lack of patience with anyone who disagreed with him. This revelation was followed by some hesitant agreement by the mother about her husband's attitude and how it affected her way of handling conflict in the family.

Family Confrontation

The nature of the family interview sometimes produces confrontations between family members that are otherwise avoided. When these occur, they can be used both diagnostically and therapeutically because they often open up areas for discussion that are crucial and seldom revealed.

In another middle-class family, one from a small prairie town, the oldest child was referred because of difficulties both at home and school. He was 13 and experienced conflict with peers, teachers, and his mother, and was repeating seventh grade. Fears and hypochondriac complaints were also involved. There were six younger children in the family and all were included along with the parents in the family session. The interview began with some concern by both parents about the problems of the identified patient. Soon it shifted to the mother's general concern about conflict and arguments between the other siblings as well. Several of the children then commented about their mother; she differed from their father in her impatience, irritability, and headaches and these made her difficult to deal with. The father could settle their arguments but when the mother was involved she seemed to stir up more arguments and actually extended the conflict. The mother was interviewed alone after this session and she began by confessing that she probably needed help more than the child. The focus shifted to her despair about her own problems and her struggles to manage them over the years. In the final interpretive hour, in which both parents participated, the planning emphasized the necessity of the mother's getting psychotherapeutic help, even if this meant that the family must move to a community in which such a resource were available. The boy needed therapy as well, but the point of urgent emphasis was the mother. It is questionable whether this information about the mother would have been revealed if several of her children had not confronted her.

The effect of family confrontation seems to frighten some workers away from using family interviewing. In the staff's experience, it appears that families have much more tolerance for stress than social workers often credit them with. There seems to be some expectation of discomfort and pain when they seek outside help for a problem they have not been able to manage themselves.

Conclusion

There were other apparent values found in the family interview. For example, when the family was included with the child in the initial interview, some of the burden was lifted from the child and he did not have to see himself as the only problem in the family. At the same time, the interview conveyed to the family the clinic's feeling that the problem was not isolated in the child but was rather a part of the family's functioning. When a second child from a family that had already been evaluated was referred several months after the first evaluation had been completed, the staff, because of its previous knowledge of this child as well as its clear picture of the way the family functioned, was able to do a much abbreviated, yet effective evaluation of the second child. Another value was that when other staff members were present in the family interview, the entire team was better able to assess whether a family could respond to family therapy as a method of treatment because each member had seen how the family members communicated or behaved with each other.

It is well to mention that no adverse effects on any of the families or on the identified problem children's ability to respond to subsequent evaluation procedures were encountered. The family intake interview broadened the social worker's own experience in the varieties of family interviewing techniques and furnished direct, vivid diagnostic knowledge to team members. The positive results of these family sessions varied, but in every case they added to the knowledge of what really happened in the family and how this was related to the child's particular emotional disturbance.

An interesting sidelight to this study was the learning experience made available to other team members. Psychiatric residents find that their supervisors talk about the importance of the family in understanding the child's problem, yet evaluation procedures are structured to discourage them from seeing the parents and they seldom have an opportunity to see the entire family interact. An obvious learning opportunity is bypassed. At a time of hesitancy and uncertainty on the part of many to explore and experiment with concepts of pathological family interaction, the family intake interview can provide a valuable teaching as well as learning procedure. Better than any lecture series or bibliography is the presence of and involvement with a live family. While such a direct approach also arouses interest in the use of family therapy, this is quite a secondary issue to the obvious and primary one of its being a significantly valuable diagnostic tool.

References

1.   This view is descriptively elaborated on in Virginia Satir, *Conjoint Family Therapy* (Palo Alto: Science and Behavior Books, 1964).

2.   Satir, *op. cit.*, chaps. 12 and 13.

11
Four Useful Concepts for Family Diagnosis and Treatment

Donald A. Devis

When a caseworker wants to add family therapy to his repertoire of techniques he finds that a new frame of reference to view and analyze data and a new model for his participation in the helping process are needed. No matter how knowledgeable he is about personality growth and development and the therapeutic processes of casework, he needs additional concepts to deal with the family group of three or more persons. In the family group the primary focus and the intent of treatment shift from the individual with his intrapsychic conflicts and their interpersonal manifestations to a family that is treated as a unit. Since most of the caseworker's experience is with dyadic relationships, his efforts to help individual family members break away from the group and establish rapport with him may be complex and difficult. He is confronted not with a symptom, attitude, or problem to be solved by an individual but by a family social system that is ineffective in achieving one of its major goals—adjustment or the self-realization of at least one of its members. Bell in his discussion of family group therapy indicates this.

Consciously, the therapist seeks to improve the means by which interaction may take place within the family. This is at least a two-fold process: first, of releasing the respective members of the family from inhibitions about the expression of feelings, wishes, ideals, goals and values; and second, of developing new forms of expression to channel the interpersonal communication. To increase spontaneity is only one side of the picture; the other is to pattern the more spontaneous activities so that the perpetuation of activities that are helpful to the family's purposes is facilitated and the change of interactions that may

Source: From Social Work 12:3 (July 1967), pp. 18–27. Copyright © 1967 by the National Association of Social Workers, Inc. Reprinted by permission.

retard the needed growth for the family life is accomplished. We can say, then, that both release and discipline are the goals of therapy.[1]

In another sense Pollak has theorized that the family is

> . . . a social organization representing a working system of living and development among people of different sex and different stages of physical and mental maturity. . . . [Such families] . . . must submit to norms in order to gain the benefits of maturation and development and mutual protection.[2]

He suggests that the clients who represent the greatest challenge to social work, especially in the field of family therapy, are those who lead a life of normlessness and, therefore, are not responsive to psychoanalytically oriented helping efforts. He believes:

> Social work and psychiatry are without appropriate armamentarium because the helping professions have learned essentially only how to liberate people who have become the prisoners rather than the beneficiaries of a norm-directed life. Social work is here faced with the challenge of becoming a rearing, binding, superego-demanding profession rather than a liberating one.[3]

The caseworker may be encouraged further by the language of the Galveston group that talks of "the intrusion of the worker into the family" and by Satir who uses the phrase, "putting right things in right places."[4] Bell asserts that a "determinative focus for family casework is to deal with the problems which primarily concern the family as a whole."[5] However, other authors such as Grinker, MacGregor, and Perlman, to name a few, have further enlarged the field by including communication and information theory, field theory, and such newly created concepts as transactional theory.[6] New journals such as *Family Process* and the investigations of the Mental Research Institute in Palo Alto into the possible treatment of the schizophrenic's whole family further compound the learning problem for the caseworker who wants to practice family therapy with a reasonable investment in study and training.[7]

Diagnostic and Treatment Approach

The following material is presented as a useful set of concepts and guidelines for the caseworker who wishes to undertake family therapy. Inasmuch as it is a distillate, it does not constitute a unified theory of family dynamics or a model technique for family therapy. However, in a system as complex as the family, it is apparent that a selective attention to variables and their reduction to a manageable number are essential. Therefore, the caseworker undertaking family group therapy needs a priority system to deal with family interaction as well as some basic determinants for his role as participant.

As a beginning, it is important to consider Bell's notion that no matter who is identified as the "sick one,"

> the symptom is thought of as a part of disruption in family interaction, most usually a breakdown in intrafamily communication and not as a product of intrapsychic conflict. From this point of view, conflicts within the individual become the end result rather than the causes of disturbance. The normal interpretation of what is symptomatic is thus modified.[8]

The caseworker then is in the position of "functioning as an interpreter of family interactions and the roles played by family members but not as an arbiter passing upon the values of the roles."[9] Also, it is important for the caseworker to deal not only with hurts, disappointments, expectations, and disequilibrium, but also to "demonstrate to the family its essential unity and thus the mutual interdependence of each with the other and with the family as a whole."[10]

Another helpful idea is found in Grunebaum's discussion of her approach to families in which children manifest learning problems. She has labeled her technique "providing an intellectual framework," and indicates reasonable success in sharing information with families as follows:

> I told them that many parents had had experiences that they considered bad and often they try to protect their children from knowledge of these events or they try to keep this knowledge strictly within the family. We had also observed, I noted, that although their actions were understandable, parents inadvertently communicated something to the child which gave him a feeling that knowledge is dangerous. The parents listened intently and then discussed areas of their own experiences that will be central in our future work with them but which had not emerged in previous diagnostic interviews.[11]

Ackerman clarifies this approach further by stating:

> ... in the interview process, he [the caseworker] moves immediately into the arena of the family's living as it struggles with its current problems. The emphasis is on the immediate distress of the group, the tensions of family relations, the conflicts and the functional disablements here and now.[12]

Granting the apparent efficacy of this route, what landmarks are there? When is the "system" in working order? Where does one look if it seems to be malfunctioning? In this search some concepts that have been found to have high pragmatic value as diagnostic and dynamic frames to discover and deal with the central conflicts of families in treatment are those related to the family's functions and internal processes. Four such concepts that will be discussed in this article are (1) cultural value orientations, (2) scapegoating, (3) role differentiation, and (4) transmission of behavioral defects.

Cultural Value Orientations

Cultural value orientation is a most useful concept in understanding role disturbance conflicts at a number of levels in any given family. It is most strikingly apparent in military social work, when the marked differences in cultural and family backgrounds of soldiers with foreign-born wives are seen. Differences in definition of roles, child-rearing practices, and models available in the life experiences of adult family members are demonstrated vividly when one or more of the family members have been reared in such divergent cultures as those of Japan, Germany, Mexico, and the Philippines. However, there are more subtle and less easily observed value orientations that tend to cause family conflict and disequilibrium. One study of families whose disturbed children were treated in a child guidance clinic found "one of the main sources of tension was conflict in cultural value orientations."[13] Most of these conflicts arose because the marriage partners had been socialized in different patterns and were working on different assumptions. Some were trying to

> ... shift too quickly to a set of orientations that they had not thoroughly internalized and without having neutralized previous orientations. Others were trying to live by conflicting orientations.[14]

Caseworkers who work with family groups continually need to sharpen their perceptions of the family's myriad variables that derive from their families of origin. Although some of the more gross variations in orientation have been delineated in the literature, more refined differentials often escape the practitioner. It is only when the caseworker can ask the adult member of the family group, "How did that go in your family?" or "How were such things settled when you were a child?" that he will be able to discern the many subtle roots of conflict that operate to restrict family cooperation.

One such example is found in parental role performance and the meaning of achievement in American society. While most caseworkers are familiar with ideas of self-concept, identity, introjection, and the parent as a model for the child, it has been much more difficult to integrate the concept of variations in value orientation as a meaningful formulation in understanding family dynamics. How can the classification of relational orientations as lineal, collateral, or individualistic be used in a meaningful way to diagnose and treat the defection of a father from his paternal responsibilities?[15] Does it add to his or his wife's understanding of their difficulties? Will it reduce her complaint or her appeals to various legal or social institutions to coerce him into "better" behavior? It seems very likely that this can be helpful simply because these are areas for investigation that can provide leads in looking at the conflict areas that were not previously considered. Therefore, one will not simply ask, "How did you get along with your father?" but will take a broader view of the laterally extended family group, the autonomy afforded children in the family of origin, and the ordinal and sex distribution of siblings as well as other similar significant determinants of the male's functioning as father, uncle, grandfather, and in other roles.[16]

Whether the family is viewed as a collection of individuals, a small group, or a specific kind of social organization, there is a need for clarity about the family's method of dealing with problems by both the caseworker and the family in treatment. Methods of communication become crucial in this area of exploration and treatment. The mere fact that one spouse's family orientation is rooted in a setting in which action and unilateral decision-making were valued highly and the other is oriented to discussion ("hashing it out") generates tremendous difficulties in the nuclear family's attempt to arrive at an operational system for itself.

Fantl's exploration of assertive casework among lower-income groups is highly useful in this area.[17] Her succinct statement that "differences in social conditions may give rise to differences in expressions of anxiety" is sufficient to provide a strong suggestion that such differentials may well be crucial to the diagnosis and treatment of the family's internal alienation. In the conjoint family interview there is no question that

> multiplicity of standards, norms, and values, differences in the use of language or other symbolic behavior are apt to multiply misunderstandings and conflicts. They cause tension and errors in judgment; they may even lead to crime.[18]

In summary, it is important to realize that the impact of the family of origin of both adult members of a nuclear family (and of the caseworker himself) is a behavior determinant for diagnosis and treatment that demands respect and attention. Both individual and family values are strongly influenced by the adult members' life experiences. What was expected of the marital partners in their families of origin may be as crucial to family integration as the satisfaction of neurotic needs of the partners currently in treatment. When one of the family members strains to attain individualistic goals at the cost of his obligation to other members of the family and this is viewed as "selfish," an imponderable conflict may occur. *How love is demonstrated* may be as crucial to family solidarity as whether it exists. Added to this is a wide variation in basic values of the family system itself so that compromise alone will not provide a systematic reorganization of the nuclear family. Perhaps the real quest is to find a key for joining together the elements of family experience in other family groups, that is, in amalgamating family systems learned in childhood.

Scapegoating

Group workers long have been aware of a tendency for groups to isolate and victimize one or more of their members. It is important that the group leader attend to the needs and integration of excluded or "abused" group members. Although the continuity of the group as an entity is of primary concern, the individual's welfare and his integration in the group are also important. Scapegoating seems to be a characteristic maneuver within families also. Bell and Vogel established a hypothesis relating to the family's use of certain members—particularly children—as the family scapegoat.[19] In the field of delinquency, too, this concept has been used to indicate that the delinquent is often the family's representative in attacking the school or the community. New research in the etiology of schizophrenia suggests that the mentally ill patient may be the "labeled member" or the "mark" who serves in some way to enhance the family's integration through his disturbed behavior or illness.

Some useful findings come from Bell and Vogel's research on disturbed families and the role of the child as a scapegoat.[20] They found that a particular child becomes involved in the conflicts existing between his parents and that scapegoating arises from tensions between parents that have not been resolved satisfactorily in other ways. The tensions are so severe that they cannot be contained without some discharge. One member is then designated as the family scapegoat, whose primary function seems to be the maintenance of family solidarity. The child or labeled family member is the symbol of the family's pathology. "Just as a dream condenses a variety of past and present experiences, the scapegoat condenses a variety of social and psychological problems impinging upon the family."[21]

The scapegoated child serves as an escape valve for the parents and their conflicts that stem from opposing orientations. And unquestionably, although many possible sources of tension are in the personality problems of parents as individuals, there are other areas of exploration that stem from group determinants of such tension. The value orientations discussed previously, the relationship of the family to the larger community, alliances with and antagonisms toward families of origin, and a multitude of other factors give rise to these tensions. The selection of the child to serve as a scapegoat, his induction into the role, and the functions and dysfunctions that accompany this process have implications for the dynamics of family disturbance and the resulting delinquency, personality disorders, and mental illness.

The caseworker in the child guidance clinic is, unfortunately, too familiar with the family's propensity toward scapegoating, which has been viewed variously as the parents' resistance to treatment, the family's defection or early discontinuance, or, conversely, the child is considered a "ticket of admission." Durkin, in the group therapy she conducts for mothers of disturbed children, has devised a set of techniques that are aimed at helping the mother to stop using the child as a rationale for the family's difficulties and enter into therapy herself.[22] The family therapist has some advantage over the group worker with a heterogeneous group because he may work with the family group around its faulty problem-solving method that uses the scapegoat to resolve conflict. If he applies the concept of providing an intellectual framework that Grunebaum uses in dealing with the learning disabilities of children, he may influence the family members to drop the scapegoat as a tool of the family process and involve themselves in healthier means of solving their problems. If the family is permitted to retain the scapegoat, it loses its efficacy for bringing about growth and change in its members because they become involved in an endless process of splits and alignments. All the family's energies are then dissipated in various maneuvers to maintain, change, or restore the structure and solidarity that is based on the presence of the scapegoat.[23]

Role Differentiation

Perlman has presented a comprehensive review of the role concept and its relation to social casework.[24] One of the most useful facets of this for the family therapist in both diagnosis and treatment is role differentiation, which relates to the internal processes of the family and its adaptive functions. In applying this concept to family organization, the family is viewed as a special case in the general class of social systems. But as a social system it will, if successful, differentiate roles so that the system's instrumental leadership and expressive leadership are discriminated. Social scientists have stated that the American middle-class family is a prime example of an equivocal case in which there is equal allocation or no allocation of such activities. Social workers, especially those who work with military families (because of the "exigencies of the service"), are aware of multiple shifts and alterations in these roles. The father is frequently absent in the military family because of overseas commitments and other special requirements. Therefore, the family is required to adapt not only to the ambiguous general nature of this differentiation but to move temporarily from one allocation to another. Contrast, for example, the adult male role of the soldier on duty as a training instructor, living in quarters on a permanent army post, with his role if he is on a year's assignment in Vietnam. Intensity of contact and daily performance of roles shift to no contact with or performance in the family; consequently the female role must adjust to such shifts and demands.

John P. Spiegel and Florence Kluckhohn have spelled out the significance of role theory in understanding integration and conflict within the family.[25] Ideas such as role complementarity and impairment, disappoint-

ment of expectations, and family equilibrium-disequilibrium aid the observation and analysis of family dysfunction.

> Analysis of social roles is a method of conceptualizing behavioral processes of
> transaction between individuals from the point of view of the social system. It
> is only by looking at the whole system that one can segregate parental roles
> from occupational and recreational roles. Looked at from the point of view of
> the individual, however, these same roles now appear related to inner needs
> and drives.[26]

It is in the consideration of these "inner needs and drives" that most
caseworkers can do diagnostic and treatment work more comfortably. It is
more difficult to move on into the family diagnostic arena and inspect roles
for "incompatibility and conflict both as an internal system and in relation to
the integration of the family with other parts of the social system."[27]

Pollak provides another fruitful area for exploration beyond the parents' role differentiation in his suggestion that the sibling system of families
merits more study than has been devoted to it.[28] He proposes that it is the
area in which aspects of rivalry and competition may be viewed. The typical
middle-class American family is a small nuclear family largely isolated from
lateral kinship relationships. The children have little exposure to adult
models of aunts and uncles or to the family systems of grandparents and
cousins. Relationships between children and parents are, therefore, intensive and supportive and the family expects that the siblings, too, will share in
this pattern. One major area of family disintegration is adult chagrin and
outright anger at the siblings' antagonisms. Because parents often think they
have strong affectional bonds with their children, they expect that their
children, in turn, will develop similar supportive and affectionate interchanges. The siblings' competitive bickering is considered to be evidence of
family discord and frequently is dealt with sternly by parents to whom Pollak
refers as "compulsive peacemakers."

Toman and Gray report research findings indicating that sibling ordinal
and sex distributions have important bearing on the middle-class American's
preparation for future marriage roles.[29] A parallel was found between successful marriages and the positions the spouses held in their nuclear
families. For example, a man who was an older sibling with younger sisters
married to a woman who had older brothers had a more compatible marital
experience than couples without similar sibling distribution.

Another important aspect of role differentiation is the inappropriate
assumption of roles when there is a deficit in the family structure. The ideal
family seems to be one in which there are *both* parents and two children,
one boy and one girl. Serious problems in role differentiation seem to arise
when one parent is absent on an extended or permanent basis. Pollak
hypothesizes that the deficit in structure produces a stimulus to inappropriate role assumption when, for example, the mother dies or leaves home

and the daughter takes on a wifelike housekeeping role.[30] He states further that the experimentation within this inappropriate role and the performance of some of its major tasks lead to the reawakening of repressed feelings. This may become a vital concept for the family therapist in dealing with the truncated family in which such homely, commonsense admonitions as "You are now the man of the family" or "Take care of your sister" may be at the root of the difficulty and it suggests that the social worker should alert himself and his clients to the problems that may occur if the oldest child assumes the absent parent's roles.

Transmission of Behavioral Defects

Giffin, Johnson, and Litin's provocative contributions on acting out and Grunebaum's on the learning problems of children have considerable utility for the family therapist.[31] These investigators provide not only a more rational concept of the etiology of some of the puzzling behavior of individuals or families but also point up specific techniques in reducing the influence of such factors. Also they stress attention to the family's communication system and invite a review of Reusch and Bateson's findings, whose conclusions that communication functions as a carrier of information that elicits the style of adaptive responses within any social system are essential to the understanding of adaptive and role expectation responses in the family.[32] Communication includes not only the verbal messages and the context in which they take place, vocal and linguistic patterns, and bodily movements, but also interpersonal assumptions and relationships. All of these must be a part of the worker's observational field if he is to understand individual behavior that stems from communication from one or more of the family members. The study of such communication systems is a science in itself but it is necessary for the caseworker entering family therapy to be aware of the many levels of communication. The two most apparent types of messages are the open circuit and closed circuit. The open circuit is the verbal message that is understandable to all and the closed circuit is one that has specific meaning only to those members who have been indoctrinated into the family's communication system. Between these there exist all sorts of innuendoes and sanctions that help determine the family members' behavior.

There are many open ways in which parents direct the behavior of their children and the worker in child guidance or family counseling looks for the particular way that an incident is handled within the family structure. For example, if a child runs away from home, it may be a result of a clearly stated invitation from one of the parents: "If you don't like it around here, why don't you take off?" Similarly, a parent's reaction to his child's account of hostility toward a teacher or schoolmates may convey clearly to the child that aggressive behavior is an acceptable way of dealing with hostility. This is particularly apparent in military social work when a child is referred by the school because of aggressive and restless behavior and is brought in by his father who is a soldier. More often than not the father had dropped out of school, left his family, and enlisted in the army during World War II. His aggressive, vigorous behavior was rewarded in combat or in similar situations and he somehow worked through his aggressive feelings with social approval. Later, he was able to channel these feelings into such socially acceptable activities as sports. However, his son's school behavior, in which he manifests negative attitudes toward the principal and teacher and aggression toward his peers, is familiar to him and he may convey to his son that he approves of it.

Grunebaum delineates the problem areas of families who have children with learning problems and provides insight into the relevance of the parents' unconscious motivations and negative childhood experiences. She reports that from the developmental histories of children with severe learning problems it is not they but their parents who have undergone pathological parental management or life experiences.

> It is they and not their children who have suffered basic losses and deprivations in early life. A striking proportion of them have been deprived of parents early in life through death or other serious illness. They have been thrust into a too early assumption of responsibility.[33]

Her work further reveals that while these parents developed a variety of defenses to deal with their feelings of loss and subsequent anger,

> still, most of their behavior and thinking has an infantile cast, the echoes of their unmet needs and their anger can still be heard, particularly in their communication to their children.[34]

These parents tend to set up family communication systems that limit or repress the verbal expression of feelings and, like Pollak's "compulsive peacemakers," they find it necessary to set up taboos against their children's expressing various emotions. A home environment is created that is marked by a sense of precariousness for the infant, and a sibling position is then assigned in which love is given only when the child assumes a nonthreatening role. It is further hypothesized that such a nonthreatening role makes it difficult for the child to enter vigorously into a learning situation because learning implies independence, which is seen as a threat to parental controls.

Giffin, Johnson, and Litin, in their discussion of the specific factors determining acting out, indicate:

> . . . antisocial acting-out is seen as a superego defect which stems from unconscious parental initiation and fostering because of poorly integrated forbidden impulses in the parents. These impulses and their permission to be acted upon

are communicated usually unconsciously to the child. In his acting-out, the child affords the parents vicarious gratification for their own forbidden impulses and concomitantly satisfies parental destructive feelings toward the child. Such behavior is destructive toward both the child's and the parent's ego organization as well as toward society unless adequate collaborative therapy is initiated. [35]

On the basis of this thesis, the investigators raise two basic questions: (1) How is sanctioning communicated to the child? and (2) Why is one child implicated in the family when the other children are conforming? This is an important concept for the caseworker who is interviewing a family in which communications are devious and complex and may form an inscrutable barrier in understanding the family's dynamics.

The "double bind"[36] and Wynne's "pseudomutuality"[37] are necessary concepts for the family interviewer, although too complex to be included in this discussion. However, if the concept of superego defect is to be useful to the family therapist, at least two aspects of this formulation should be considered: (1) the idea that the defects are in specific areas while other parts of the superego may develop appropriately and remain intact and (2) that at least two generations are always involved in the behavioral disturbance, whether it is in acting-out or learning difficulties. If these basic concepts are valid, then a consideration of etiological factors and the development of an adequate diagnostic study must necessarily approach not only the nuclear family but also the parents' families of origin. All investigators seem to agree that the identified member or the scapegoat represents the family's distress signal, which shows its internal difficulties or its inability to integrate itself successfully into a larger social system. For therapeutic intervention one would need to label and treat (1) the conflicts that remain unresolved in the adult family members, (2) how they "reverberate" in family transactions to cue others to behave in certain ways, and (3) why some family members pick up and act on the coded messages and others do not. Since the observable behavior—a maladjustment of the child in a sense—mirrors the internalized defect of the parent, it becomes a "roentgen" finding that can be used in aiding the parent to modify his own disorder and the infection he is transmitting to the child. Even though the goal is not personality reconstruction of the adult family members, it is important to know what their defenses are and why and how the child is used in this maneuvering that usually produces unwanted but tragic consequences.

Summary

The social worker's approach to family therapy presents new demands for technique and a set of dynamic frames for observation and analysis of the basic data. To understand the family's conflict and living processes it is necessary to look beyond the concepts of individual psychology and find explanations for group and interactional phenomena. This chapter suggests both a positional stance for the family therapist as an agent of change and four useful frames for observation of family process, diagnosis, and intervention. These frames relate to the family's functions and internal processes in the general areas of (1) cultural value orientation, (2) scapegoating, (3) role differentiation, and (4) the transmission of behavioral defects. Detailed knowledge of these approaches and constructs is essential to a disciplined intrusion of the caseworker into the family to be treated.

References

1. John E. Bell, *Family Group Therapy*, Public Health Monograph No. 64 (Washington, D.C.: U. S. Department of Health, Education, and Welfare, 1961), p. 5.

2. Otto Pollak, "Social Determinants of Family Behavior," *Social Work*, Vol. 8, No. 3 (July 1963), p. 98.

3. *Ibid.*, pp. 98–99.

4. Robert MacGregor *et al.*, *Multiple Impact Therapy with Families* (New York: McGraw-Hill Book Co., 1964); and Virginia M. Satir, *Conjoint Family Therapy* (Palo Alto: Science and Behavior Books, 1964).

5. Bell, *op. cit.*, p. 4.

6. *See*, for example, Roy R. Grinker *et al.*, *Psychiatric Social Work* (New York: Basic Books, 1961).

7. *Family Process* is published semiannually by the Mental Research Institute, Palo Alto, California, and the Family Institute, New York.

8. Bell, *op. cit.*, pp. 4–6.

9. *Ibid.*, p. 5.

10. *Ibid.*, p. 6.

11. Margaret G. Grunebaum, "A Study of Learning Problems of Children—Casework Implications," *Social Casework*, Vol. 42, No. 9 (November 1961), p. 46.

12. Nathan W. Ackerman, "Dynamic Frame for the Clinical Approach," in Ackerman, Frances L. Beatman, and Sanford N. Sherman, eds., *Exploring the Base for Family Therapy* (New York: Family Service Association of America, 1961), p. 63.

13. Norman W. Bell and Ezra F. Vogel, eds., *A Modern Introduction to the Family* (Glencoe, Ill.: Free Press, 1960).

14. *Ibid.*, p. 384.

15. *Integration and Conflict in Family Behavior*, Report No. 27 (New York: Group for the Advancement of Psychiatry, August 1954), p. 11.

16. Walter Toman and Bernard Gray, "Family Constellations of 'Normal' and 'Disturbed' Marriages," *Journal of Individual Psychology*, Vol. 17, No. 1 (May 1961), pp. 93–95.

17. Berta Fantl, "Integrating Psychological, Social and Cultural Factors in Assertive Casework," *Smith College Studies in Social Work*, Vol. 34, No. 3 (June 1964), pp. 188–200.

18. *Ibid.*, p. 197.

19. Bell and Vogel, *op. cit.*, pp. 382–397.

20. *Ibid.*, p. 384.

21. *Ibid.*, p. 386.

22. Helen E. Durkin, *Group Therapy for Mothers of Disturbed Children* (Springfield, Ill.: Charles C. Thomas, 1954).

23. Bell and Vogel, *op. cit.*, p. 395.

24. Helen Harris Perlman, "The Role Concept and Social Casework: Some Explorations. I. The 'Social' in Social Casework; II. What is Social Diagnosis?" *Social Service Review*, Vol. 35, No. 4 (December 1961) pp. 370–381; and Vol. 36, No. 1 (March 1962), pp. 17–31.

25. In *Integration and Conflict in Family Behavior*, p. 7.

26. *Ibid.*, p. 6.

27. *Ibid.*, p. 7.

28. Otto Pollak, "Analysis of Social Structures," lecture presented at lecture series, "Current Trends in Army Social Work," Walter Reed Army Medical Center, November 1962.

29. Toman and Gray, *op. cit.*, p. 95.

30. Otto Pollak, "Analysis of Social Structures."

31. Mary E. Giffin, Adelaide M. Johnson, and Edward M. Litin, "Specific Factors Determining Antisocial Acting-Out," *American Journal of Orthopsychiatry*, Vol. 24 (October 1954), pp. 668–684; and Grunebaum, *op. cit.*

32. Juergen Reusch and Gregory Bateson, *Communication, The Social Matrix of Psychiatry* (New York: W. W. Norton & Co. 1951).

33. Grunebaum, *op. cit.* p. 462.

34. *Ibid.*, p. 463.

35. Giffin, Johnson, and Litin, *op. cit.*, p. 670.

36. Gregory Bateson, Don D. Jackson, Jay Haley, and John H. Weakland, "Toward a Theory of Schizophrenia," *Behavioral Science*, Vol. 1, No. 4 (January 1956), pp. 251–264.

37. Lyman C. Wynne *et al.*, "Pseudomutuality in the Family Relationships of Schizophrenics," *Psychiatry*, Vol. 21, No. 2 (April 1958), pp. 205–220.

12
A Classification of Disordered Family Types

Alice L. Voiland
Bradley Buell

A classification of four types of functionally disordered families de-scribed in this article was developed as one aspect of an integrated series of research and experimental projects which Community Research Associates has been conducting since 1947. Materials from the original St. Paul study had documented the heavy concentration of all community-supported wel-fare and health services in a relatively small group of seriously disorganized "multiproblem" families. This term was drawn from statistical facts, the program implications of which were presented in CRA's first published book.[1] As then defined, these were families presenting two or more of the three basic problems of dependency, ill health, or maladjustment. This evi-dent clustering both of numerous problems and numerous services in certain families was of important epidemiological significance for the planners and administrators of many welfare and health agencies. It underscored the need to co-ordinate and integrate the various services rendered to the same family by separate agencies. In essence it called for the use of the total family as the primary unit and base for community planning.

Increasingly the term "multiproblem family" gained prominence. It is now in common usage. However, its program-planning implications are fre-quently overlooked or unknown. Moreover, it is often used as if the multi-problem family were presumed to be a clinical or diagnostic entity in itself. As here defined, it is not. Structurally, the families of the original St. Paul study ranged all the way from those in which both parents and children were present to an aged person living alone. While the social functioning of all was

Source: From *Social Work* 6:4 (October 1961), pp. 3–11. Copyright © 1961 by the National Association of Social Workers, Inc. Reprinted by permission.

disordered in some area, the precise area and the degree of pathological dysfunction varied greatly.

The significance of these variations moved CRA in 1952 to explore the possibility of developing a classification of disordered family types that would have clinical and diagnostic utility in the practice of social casework. A pilot study was developed to see whether profitable hypotheses might be developed as a companion piece of research to supplement three experimental projects[2] (in Winona County, Minnesota; Washington County, Maryland; and San Mateo, California) in the prevention and control of psychosocial disorders. A random sample of 100 cases of "multiproblem" families identified in the original 1948 St. Paul study and known to Family Service, Inc., of St. Paul was selected for exploratory analysis.

The preliminary findings were highly provocative and suggestive. They indicated that it *should* be possible to develop a classification of disordered family types that *would* be useful in family casework diagnosis. At the same time, however, early experiences in CRA's experimental projects clearly pointed to the presence of considerable confusion about what did and did not constitute a "family diagnosis."

A second study was therefore planned in 1953 with a broader purpose.[3] Its intent was to explore the whole subject of family diagnosis, including the classification of disordered family types and testing of the hypotheses suggested by the findings of the pilot study. Beginning in January 1954, new and well-structured case materials were assembled over a period of eighteen months with the co-operation of seven voluntary family service agencies.

The co-operating agencies are the Family Service of St. Paul, St. Paul, Minn.; the Brooklyn Bureau of Social Services and Children's Aid Society, Brooklyn, N. Y.; the Family Service of Cincinnati and Hamilton County, Cincinnati, Ohio; the Family and Children's Bureau, Columbus, Ohio; the Family Service of Milwaukee, Wis.; Family and Children's Service, St. Louis, Mo.; and Family and Child Service, Washington, D.C. Data on a total of 888 selected continued-service cases accepted by the agencies during this period were recorded on a forty-page schedule and in the case record. By plan all cases had marital partners under 65 years of age. Approximately 93 percent were families in which both parents and children were present. Statistical analysis of the total sample was followed by an intensive clinical and statistical analysis of a representative sample of 100.

Two Basic Elements

It became apparent in the early testing of the preliminary hypotheses of the pilot study that classification of distinctive disordered family types could not be developed with any degree of validity without two other elements. First, a classification of social problems or psychosocial disorders, the presence or absence of which could be compared from family to family; second, a systematic framework for family casework diagnosis which could be consistently used in the clinical analysis of all data, and which might throw light on the causal factors underlying the problems presented. As indicated, the development and use of a framework for family casework diagnosis had become a necessity to the successful operation of CRA's three experimental projects previously mentioned.

Thus the diagnostic framework and the psychosocial disorder classifications as a part of its basic structure were developed simultaneously along with the process of identifying disordered family types, each influencing the other. Because of space limitations, the essence of these two elements can only be suggested here to indicate the foundation on which the classification of the four family types rests.

The proposed framework for family diagnosis consists of five basic areas related to family and individual functioning. The following outlines the basic structural elements:

PROPOSED FRAMEWORK FOR FAMILY DIAGNOSIS

I.   FAMILY COMPOSITION

II.   PSYCHOSOCIAL DISORDERS
      Level A and Level B disorder classifications
      External stress precipitating identification of disorder

III. FAMILY SOCIAL FUNCTIONING
CHILD-REARING FUNCTIONING
Parental Functioning
Events and circumstances influencing parenthood
Physical care provided child
Love relationships encouraged in child
Self-identity development encouraged in child
Socialization measures and standards
Child Development
Events and circumstances influencing child development
Early childhood behavior—under sixth year
    Love relationships to parents
    Self-identity development
    Socialization
Latency and adolescent child behavior (6 through 12 years, 13 through 20 years)
    Love relationships to parents
    Love relationships to siblings
    Self-identity as manifested
        in home
        in school
        in sexual behavior

Socialization:
  friends
  social conformance in community
MARITAL FUNCTIONING
Events and circumstances
Love relationship in marriage
Self-identity maintained in marriage
Socialization in marriage:
  helpful concern
  problem-solving
FINANCIAL FUNCTIONING
Events and circumstances
Division of labor
Income production—self-identity
  Work situation:
    (a) skill and efficiency
    (b) cooperativeness
    (c) achievement incentive
  Income management—socialization:
    (a) emotional acceptance of provider role
    (b) financial support undertaken
    (c) planfulness and spending of income

IV. INDIVIDUAL CHARACTERISTICS OF FAMILY MEMBERS
ADULTS
  Intelligence
  Physical condition
  Preferred ego defenses
  Emotional stability
CHILD
  Physical condition
  Intelligence
  Emotional stability—latency child
  Emotional stability—adolescent

V. FAMILY OF ORIGIN HISTORY
Events and circumstances
Continuity of contact between adults and own parent or parental substitutes
Adequacy of financial support within adults' families of origin
Emotional ties to own parents or parental substitutes
Self-identity and identifications
Standards of socialization

The major factors that bring each of the *three family functions* into focus are generally designated as (1) events and circumstances, or the happenings in the life of the family that shape patterns of social adjustment; (2) love relationships, or the basic qualities and strengths of genuine emotion the family members have for giving and receiving affection, including genital sexuality for adults; (3) self-identity, or the developed self-concepts and feelings of personal worth of family members and their readiness to exercise initiative in use of natural talents and acquired skills; (4) socialization, or the developed moral, ethical, and social values of family members. The choice of love relationships, self-identity, and socialization represent the attempt to introduce selected aspects of human motivation into definitions of the social tasks intrinsic to child-rearing and to marital and financial functioning responsibilities.

Both conceptually and structurally the disordered family types identified derive from the fundamental principles of family casework diagnosis intrinsic to this diagnostic scheme. Essentially this means that all factors encompassed by this framework, when identified and evaluated in the aggregate, are seen as influences contributing or not contributing to family dysfunction.

The working utility of this approach to family diagnosis independent of the disordered family types is already being demonstrated in a series of public welfare operations in the states of Minnesota and Pennsylvania and in the cities of San Francisco and Omaha.

The framework embraces both the normal and the pathological. Its nucleus is the area of "Family Social Functioning." The remaining four areas would be interpreted for diagnostic purposes in terms of their relevance to family functioning, namely, the child-rearing, marital, and financial functioning patterns of the family.

The psychosocial disorder classification identifies disorders in five basic categories: child-rearing, marital, financial, adult, and child. Two levels—A and B—are defined within each. Level A psychosocial disorders consist of conditions or behavior of primary concern to the community. Their presence is established by the action of official legal and administrative processes. For this reason they are sometimes referred to as "official disorders." Child neglect, desertion, dependency, crime, and delinquency are examples of Level A disorders typical of each of the categories. These social problems are generally understood and communities have accepted responsibility for doing something about them. They can be defined precisely for purposes of statistical comparability. In CRA's three experimental projects, 75 percent of *all* families known to *all* community-supported public and private welfare and health agencies presented one or more problems in this classified list.

Level B disorders consist of behavior or conditions that represent failures in social role expectations which will not invoke official action by a legal or social agency, but which may have the potentiality for so doing. They are identified by any health or welfare agency with which the family member has contact, voluntarily or involuntarily. Examples are stubborn resistance to responsibility, irrational fears, continued defiance of authority, distorted affectional responses, questionable child care practices, faulty or defective judgment in dealing with socially incompatible behavior of family members, and so on.

A Classification of Disordered Families

It should be clear that the criteria for selection of families for this particular research did not require that they be "multiproblem" as defined in the St. Paul study. Some do fall within the major official categories of dependency, ill-health, and maladjustment. Others do not. Thus, the proposed classification of disordered family types is neither based upon nor is it restricted to the multiproblem family. Of greater importance is statistical evidence that empirically supports conclusions that the psychosocial disorders identified in the 888 cases and the 100-case sample are in fact representative of the continued service loads of a large number of family agencies reporting annually to the Family Service Association of America.

It also should be clear that only families with children (93 percent) or childless married couples under 65 were selected. Even with these basic limitations, the disordered family types were used with considerable success by the casework staff in classifying cases of *varying* family structural types in CRA's three experimental projects. Further experimentation is definitely indicated in this regard.

The intention here is to present a condensation of the salient features of the family types: the *perfectionistic* family, the *inadequate* family, the *egocentric* family, and the *unsocial* family. They represent a beginning attempt to classify pathology in family social functioning that is clinically useful as a supplementary aid in family casework diagnosis. They are not presumed to be the only possible groupings. It is, however, a classification system with its own integrity; its validity has been empirically established by statistical methods.

Clinically speaking, each of the four types is differentiated from the other by characteristic syndrome groupings of psychosocial pathology. That is to say, when taken collectively, the psychosocial disorders typically present; the predominant patterns characteristic of child-rearing, including child development and marital and financial functioning; the nature of the intrinsic physical, intellectual, and emotional characteristics of adult and child, and family-of-origin history—all form psychosocial constellations that are generally distinctive for each family type.

The particular titles of each reflect the dominant individual characteristics and social functioning patterns of the family heads, which definitely color the clinical picture of total family functioning. As such, they are suggestive of the nature, degree, and extent of family pathology likely to be present.

Finally, it may be said that the four family types in order of arrangement represent a continuum in the direction of the family's decreasing capacities for mastering social tasks and allaying psychic tensions. It will be noted that it has not been possible in this article to give a full clinical description of the family pathology. Particularly in the child development areas is this true.

The Perfectionistic Family

The perfectionistic family's underlying characteristics derive from the tendency of one partner, and frequently both, to overemphasize expectations for "good" social conduct in themselves and in their children in order to be without fault and to avoid friction. Its goals are most clearly identified with cultural values accepted as "typically American," such as achievement, the importance of planning, responsibility for one's acts, and "good" social adjustment.

What labels its social functioning as pathological is the *overemphasis* placed on perfectionism in the attainment of these goals. Herein lies the defect in this family's approach to life: the quest for perfection itself.

Such self-imposed demands for good behavior leave no margin for human error. For these reasons marital relationship, child-rearing practices, and child development will bear this hallmark of distorted objectives for personal and family living.

Early in marriage at least one partner has a beginning awareness that there is something within himself or about his partner that causes anxiety in the relationship. As a result, social relationships, work, and happiness suffer. With success the supreme ideal, and failure the greatest sin, typical behavior and neurotic symptoms appear in the children. If not treated, such symptoms are known clinically to result in crippling adult neuroses which ill prepare such individuals for responsibilities of parenthood.

In sharp contrast to the other three family types, there is apt to be a general absence of Level A psychosocial disorders in the perfectionistic family. Divorce, a marital disorder, is one of two exceptions. The other is psychotic illness of an adult partner who has to be hospitalized. In this latter respect this family type ranks next to the unsocial family.

Level B psychosocial disorders, however, typically cover all family functional areas except the financial, where these families are generally self-sufficient. Most prominent in order of frequency are symptoms of maladjusted behavior manifested in marital functioning, child-rearing, and individual (child and adult) disorders. These may have the potentiality for developing into Level A disorders of official concern to the community, particularly as noted.

Prognosis for the perfectionistic family is generally favorable as compared with the other family types, when correctly diagnosed. The predominance of Level B psychosocial disorders as contrasted with Level A is one important influence. This positive outlook is further accounted for by the following combination of factors: (1) the adult partners' tendency to seek corrective measures early in the history of the disorders, and (2) most important, there is greater awareness and assumption of responsibility for the development of the problem. Treatment of the current difficulty is thus more effective and the prevention of more serious problems more likely.

The Inadequate Family

The inadequacy of this family type arises from the customary reliance of one partner, and usually both, upon others for encouragement, continued support, guidance, and help in resolving problems of social living which are ordinarily handled independently by the average family. The social motives of the adult partners rarely run counter to cultural ideas for family behavior. The unique character of the family's social dysfunction lies in their attempt to build a stable family without the ability to perceive accurately the practical and emotional issues involved in marital living, rearing of children, and providing for a family as a self-contained unit. Problems in adjustment are not typically traceable to personality tendencies of a deviant or antisocial nature. It is a matter of missing the mark for two basic reasons: (1) they hope for the best without anticipating the rewards and sacrifices of family living; (2) they tend to rely too readily upon others under conditions of stress.

The psychosocial disorders most prominent in this family reflect this characteristic symptom picture. Level A disorders most frequently occur in three functional areas: child-rearing, child development, and financial. These families are susceptible to the entire range of Level B disorders in the functional areas of child-rearing, marital, financial, and individual disorders.

Two main external stresses cause trouble for this family type: money and child-rearing—precisely the fact of pregnancy, in the latter case. As precipitants, the two become fused. The partners themselves, however, invariably focus on the financial disorders. Marital, child-rearing, and individual adult disorders come to the fore only if there are "money troubles," also. When this is the case there may be some recognition that the total symptom picture is related to the causes of their problems. Crises directly accounting for lack of money will reflect limited planning and meager foresignt in connection with such realistic situations as "unanticipated" reductions in overtime and pay, layoffs, discontinuance of unemployment compensation, threatened eviction, withdrawal of relatives' or separated husband's support, and so on. Crises in child-rearing are immediately associated with insufficient income, precipitated by the second, third, fourth, fifth, and successive pregnancies of the wife. Occasionally the physical disability of the wife or child will act as a codeterminant in this regard. These partners are not apt to have antisocial tendencies.

Prognosis for the inadequate family is relatively good, provided (1) it is accurately diagnosed and *not* confused with the unsocial family, and (2) the agency caseworker has the time, patience, and teaching ability needed for the required rehabilitation process. To educate these parents, particularly the mothers, in many practical matters pertaining to running a household, planning expenditures, attending to health needs, and training children will constitute a large part of the therapeutic job. The first objective is to gain the confidence of the family. Once accomplished, the relationship with the social caseworker will assume importance and will seem to the family worth trying to keep, because of the dependent satisfaction and the boost to their self-esteem that this affords. This then can be used to stimulate more grown-up behavior by making gradual demands for self-sufficiency in the various functional areas, and by systematic follow-up.

The Egocentric Family

Self-seeking motives mark the social conduct and the interpersonal relationships of the egocentric family members. In many respects this family type is a social contradiction, since the family unit functions capably within certain of the rules of social behavior which society upholds. Achievement in work is usually an accomplished fact, of importance to the male head. Undoubtedly the marital partners will be competent financial managers and self-sufficient in the administration of practical affairs. Both are apt to be keen and logical in their thinking.

The pathology of this family's social functioning lies in the fact that these accomplishments result from an excess of self-interest, an overstress on the importance of some form of social status or personal prestige. This pattern dominates all interpersonal relationships. In consequence, members of the egocentric family achieve value and importance in the eyes of one another only as they offer to each the opportunity for gratification of some self-seeking intention—namely, giving, receiving, or withholding love, affection, consideration, possessions, or money in accordance with the dictates of their own impulses. People are thus important, not as individuals, but as objects to be used personally or socially for some selfish purpose. Overbearance and self-opinionated attitudes characterize the egocentric family. For these reasons the intimacy of heterosexual living creates an emotional hazard for these family heads. From the beginning the marriage is intermittently fraught with friction, hostilities, and antagonisms, because this is a "partial" relationship. Each partner relates to the other as though he were a thing; he may like only a particular trait; or for example, use him only as a sexual object or a means to an end.

This orientation to life not only endangers the stability of the marriage itself but results in child-rearing practices which imperil the developmental progress of children. If children are avowedly desired, the mother's wish invariably stems from the need to prove fertility; the father's from the self-gratification gained in impregnating a woman, having "produced" an off-spring, or both. For this reason the child generally becomes a subject of controversy between the parents, not out of concern for his welfare, but to perpetuate the pathological opportunistic aims of the marriage.

This family is susceptible to Level A psychosocial disorders mainly in the areas of marital functioning and the child development aspect of child-rearing, and occasionally the parental aspect. They rarely become involved in major or minor crimes. The behavior of the parents may be antisocial in nature, but is usually confined to the home setting. Level B disorders, however, are glaringly present in all categories, even the financial, where egocentricities in regard to money become displaced points of controversy in the marital relationship.

The types of marital stresses that characteristically upset the partner and prompt him to seek redress usually involve a misfire in the hostile-controlling pattern of the partnership: an ultimatum to "get out," issued for the *first time* by the wife; "twisting" the wife's arm, also for the first time; persistent refusal of spouse to talk, replacing former verbal aggression; and so on. Sexual experimentation and a fascination with deviant forms of sexuality are basic characteristics of these partners.

These family heads incline strongly toward initiating contact with professional guidance agencies or other experts in regard to their marital relations. Almost without exception this will be undertaken as a hostile retaliatory gesture.

The precipitant in the social situation which brings to light Level A child disorders usually will be an *event* involving the larger community, such as the child's suspension or expulsion from school, third or fourth truancy from home, or physical attack upon another child requiring police action. In the majority of egocentric families, community intervention originates from school teachers, principals, doctors, or friends with some kind of professional background. Other symptoms that reflect the basic nature of child development and parental functioning of child-rearing disorders, whether Level A or B, are (1) the parents' interpreting a child's independent strivings, belligerency, and negativism as "just being mean," and (2) use of the child as a substitute for adult love.

Prognosis for the egocentric family is guarded. Histories of this family type will reveal that the wife has probably initiated a variety of professional contacts. Moreover, the need for guidance may often be intellectually recognized by husband and wife. However, they both like and dislike the prospect of receiving advice from "experts." This is because they prefer to influence the adviser to take up the cudgels in their own behalf rather than emotionally involve themselves in a therapeutic relationship for purposes of resolving the problem. For these reasons treatment is difficult and results are open to question.

Ideally for the child, treatment of the parents should be undertaken when his behavior is in the reactive stage, *i.e.*, when he is young. Foster home placement may be effective at this time in order to lessen current conflicts and thus help the child to regain his capacity for emotional growth.

However, this seldom happens, because of the particular egocentric emotional needs which the adults seek to gratify through their children when the child is young. With older children the chances are better. However, manipulation of the environment *alone* is unsuitable to the therapeutic needs of most older children in this family class. Residential psychiatric treatment is required for the child who "acts out" his conflicts in severe antisocial forms. Certain older adolescents, however, can be treated through psychotherapy alone, either by a social caseworker or by a psychiatrist, if the boy or girl is becoming emancipated and the parents no longer assume personal responsibility for his behavior.

The Unsocial Family

The unsocial family attains its basic characteristics by reason of both partners' lack of social rapport with other people and their social environment. These derive from their strong tendencies toward acting-out behavior, delinquent conduct, and/or regression into psychosis as a pattern of life adjustment. These adults face the responsibilities of family functioning without benefit of two essential qualities: a capacity for meaningful personal relationships and a normally functioning conscience that guides and stimulates socialized behavior. Such pervading deficiencies adversely affect male and female relationships, parent-child relationships, work habits, and relationships to the community at large. The multiplicity of the problems as well as their severity distinguishes this family type.

Marriages are likely to take place as a result of impulsive action, often without a genuine interest in the partner or in fulfilling marital obligations. Attitudes toward parenthood include outright acknowledgment of never having wanted children; an effort to sell or give them "away"; a demand for abortion; a desire for children only for the provocative value they have in controlling or depreciating a marital partner; a desire for a child in order to allay fears of marital unfaithfulness.

Earning a living and providing for the family are adversely influenced by a combination of mental illness and acting-out behavior in one or both heads. A poor work record and/or illegal methods of obtaining money will characterize the male partner; management of income is typically unplanned or poorly budgeted by both.

Almost without exception Level A disorders appear across the board in these families. Adult disorders include hospitalization for mental illness and/or apprehension for antisocial acts. Children in this family type as well as in the egocentric tend strongly toward truancy, delinquency, and hospitalization for mental illness. This family type is distinguished by the number of female partners who have had one or more previous marriages dissolved by divorce. Physical and emotional neglect charges against parents, with state guardianship, occur with frequency because of the children's delinquent activity. Level A financial disorders of dependency are centered in the unsocial and inadequate family types.

The external stresses that stimulate voluntary application to social agencies mainly concern financial and marital problems. The need for money heads the list somewhat as in the inadequate family. However, the basic distinction between the two lies in the nature of the stresses that immediately precipitate the problem, their duration, and the partner's ideas as to solution. In the unsocial family all the following events may bring about financial crises: quitting or inability to hold a job, dismissal for cause, withdrawal of relatives' support, legal action for antisocial acts which interrupts or limits income. The precipitants of marital disorders not associated with financial problems will be events that threaten physical dependency status or sexual adequacy of a partner, such as learning of a spouse's long-standing sexual infidelity, an extramarital pregnancy, the threat of divorce because of refusal of sexual relations, or a divorced husband trying to force remarriage. The external stresses which bring to light a child or child-rearing disorder will usually arise from the environment, such as apprehension of children for delinquent acts, a child's bizarre behavior noticed by the school, truancy, and so on.

Prognosis for the unsocial family, the average casework practitioner would probably concede, is poor or at best only fair. Nevertheless, CRA's experience in the disordered behavior project in San Mateo County, California, did show that in certain families classified as unsocial, therapeutic results were better than anticipated.[5] Continuity and responsibility in keeping track of these families and a measure of supervision and support warded off at least some of the eruptive and more destructive types of psychosocial disorders.

From the community's standpoint, these families comprise a substantial proportion of its public health and welfare agency case loads. Little is known about treatment goals and methods suitable to this family's particular problems. Yet the manifest forms of maladjustment cannot escape recognition by society at large—the high susceptibility to delinquent conduct, the hospitalization for mental illness, often combined with financial dependency.

Based upon CRA's findings and those of other experimental projects, a fair or poor prognosis for the unsocial family type is largely a matter of the willingness of social agencies to see the importance of systematic identification and classification of this family type, and then to invest the time necessary to find out what more can and should be done. Underlying all else is the necessity for understanding the psychosocial dynamics that produce the symptom picture and the utilization of treatment methods consistent with these dynamics. Therapeutic goals will of necessity be modest and aimed at better self-management, not involving drastic personality changes in adult members. Experimentation and research with this most pathological of all family types is badly needed. The very identification of these families as a distinct, recognizable group should prove a stimulus in this direction.

Finally, it is perhaps unnecessary to repeat that the proposed disordered family types are not presumed to provide all the answers to the problems of classifying psychosocial pathology. Nor do they represent the only classification potentially useful in family casework diagnosis. However, there are increasing indications that their use can further the systematic identification of family pathology, as witnessed in the operation of CRA's three experimental projects as well as in a recent study of a mental hygiene clinic.[6] Their reliability in clinical practice is still to be tested. CRA is shortly initiating plans to undertake this professional responsibility.

References

1.   Bradley Buell and Associates, *Community Planning for Human Services* (New York: Columbia University Press, 1952).

2.   For accounts of these projects *see*, respectively: Donald B. Glabe, Leo J. Feider, and Harry O. Page, *Reorientation for Treatment and Control: An Experiment in Public Welfare Administration*, special supplement to *Public Welfare*, Vol. 16, No. 2 (April 1958); Community Research Associates, Inc., "Health and Welfare Issues in Community Planning for the Problem of Indigent Disability," *Journal of Public Health*, Vol. 48, No. 11 (November 1958); Bradley Buell, Paul T. Beisser, John M. Wedemeyer, "Reorganizing To Prevent and Control Disordered Behavior," *Mental Hygiene*, Vol. 42, No. 2 (April 1958).

3.   Funds for the pilot study in 1952 and this second study were provided by the Louis W. and Maud Hill Family Foundation of St. Paul.

5.   Buell, Beisser, and Wedemeyer, *op. cit.*, pp. 155–194.

6.   *A Study of the Hartley Salmon Child Guidance Clinic* (New York: Community Research Associates, Inc., 1961).

13
Evaluation Procedures for Conjoint Marital Psychotherapy

Carol C. Nadelson
Ellen L. Bassuk
Christopher R. Hopps
William E. Boutelle, Jr.

The marital relationship requires that the partners bring together preexisting psychological and cultural histories which are often quite disparate. The expectations of the couple and society are that love is sufficient for the development of a partnership. The partners often expect to share goals, understand and accept each other, and be satisfied and happy simultaneously. These expectations occur in a society where there is increasing stress and temptation and where permission for divorce tacitly exists because religious and other social pressures against divorce are diminishing and its stigma has lessened. Rather than attempting to work out a resolution of conflict, divorce may appear to be the solution.

Values regarding marriage have undergone a radical change in the past century, shifting from an emphasis on survival and security to a focus on companionship, love, and communication. With this shift in marital expectations, increasing attention must be paid to individual developmental changes. As goals, values, and expectations change, a marital interaction may cease to be gratifying or rewarding. It is also possible that the individual adaptive changes that disturb the balance of the relationship may occur in only one partner. The marital relationship itself may cease to be functional if complementary shifts are not possible or if they are not strongly desired by the other partner.

An understanding of the development of conflict and the modes of conflict resolution is crucial for the success of marital therapy.[1] Marital con-

Source: From Social Casework 56 (February 1975), pp. 91–96. Copyright © 1975 by the Family Service Association of America. Reprinted by permission.

flict arises from many sources, including differences in information, beliefs, interests, desires, and values, and from competition between the partners. One can distinguish between productive and destructive conflicts. Productive conflict may be characterized by mutual recognition of different interests, open and honest communication, and trusting attitudes that allow both partners the possibility of finding creative solutions to conflict. Destructive conflicts are characterized by tendencies to rely on strategies of power and tactics of threat, coercion, and deception, leading to mutual suspicion and lack of communication.

With a dysfunctional marriage, the therapist must elucidate the patterns that result in the predominance of destructive conflicts in the marital interaction. Because of the growing divorce rate in the United States and the increase in the number of couples seeking treatment, it has become necessary to develop evaluative procedures that can result in the use of more comprehensive and flexible treatment techniques. To facilitate successful resolution of conflicts, both partners must be involved in the therapeutic process.

Although Crago reported that the incidence of mental disorders is lower in married than in single people,[2] when mental disorders do occur among the married, both partners are likely to manifest some degree of disturbance. A spouse is affected not only by the partner's disorder, but also by the partner's treatment and hospitalization.

The rates of diagnosed neurosis and of hospitalization tend to be higher for wives than for husbands. Crago hypothesized that fulfillment of a marital role causes greater emotional stress for the wife. She described the wife's roles as "accommodating, expressive, and integrative" in contrast to the husband's "rigid, instrumental role."[3] She concluded from these differences that the wife must make greater adjustment in a marriage and that the resultant strain may increase the probability of an emotional disorder. In the writers' experience, it is usually the wife who requests psychotherapy. This request may reflect the wife's role in the relationship, rather than a greater degree of intrapsychic disturbance.

Indications for Conjoint Therapy

Jay Haley suggests that marriage therapy is specifically indicated when techniques of individual psychotherapy have failed or can not be used, when a patient has a sudden onset of symptoms related to marital conflict, when a couple requests it because of conflict and stress they are unable to resolve, or when it appears that improvement in a patient involved in individual psychotherapy will change the equilibrium of the marriage and cause increased conflict.[4]

Andrew S. Watson recommends conjoint therapy for couples when family relationship distortions are gross and disruptive of reality and when speed in halting family disintegration is a critical factor. He feels that conjoint therapy is also indicated with couples when the problems involve acting-out and are of characterological nature. It can also be useful when the partners are poorly motivated and unprepared for individual treatment.[5]

A number of other authors stress the importance of including both partners in a program when one of them is severely disturbed.[6]

A relationship in which equilibrium is based on one partner's mental illness is often unstable because as the "sick" partner improves, the "healthy" one may develop symptoms.

Sylvia Brody suggests that conjoint sessions may be indicated at different times in the individual treatment process and recommends such sessions to make definite any gains made in other forms of therapy.[7] She considers the patient's ability to utilize conjoint sessions as an indicator of progress toward the achievement of treatment goals.

Contraindications to Therapy

Stated contraindications for conjoint couple therapy include: inadequate tolerance of anxiety by one or both partners; inability to control hostility within a therapy session by one partner; an active psychosis; fragility of defenses of one partner; severe character disorders; paranoid reactions; excessive sibling rivalry or attitudes that preclude the sharing of a therapist; and one partner's acting-out behavior, such as infidelity or homosexuality, of which the other partner is unaware. Other negative considerations include the possibility of a severe psychoneurotic reaction by the patient which might develop if the homeostatic balance of neurotic marital transaction is disturbed and the persistent use by patients of the therapeutic situation to manipulate their spouses.

Other professionals, including Clifford J. Sager, disagree; they feel that severe disturbance of one partner is not a contraindication to conjoint therapy.[8] Sager believes that the most important contraindication is the therapist's inability to prevent a spouse from utilizing the session for destructive purposes against his mate.

In view of the differences of opinion on when to use conjoint marital psychotherapy, it may be productive to consider a spectrum of treatability, with flexible treatment techniques that can be adapted to each couple. It is apparent that goals differ and that during the course of assessing the presenting problems and working in therapy the couple continuously reevaluates the goals of the therapy; for example, for some couples, an agreed-upon divorce may be the goal. Measures of treatment success are best determined by the couple after they have negotiated their goals and worked together with a therapist.

In order to approach the problem of evaluation, the writers studied the presenting problems of twenty-five heterosexual married couples who were evaluated and treated at the Beth Israel Hospital in Boston, Massachusetts, over a two-year period. A preliminary study attempted to assess which evaluative approach was most productive in leading to an optimal recommendation for treatment and which factors were most critical in treatment success.

As a result of the initial work, further refinement of the procedures is being attempted. Questionnaires have been developed to be filled out by the couple and by the therapist at the time of evaluation, in the middle of treatment, at termination, and six months after termination of treatment.

Couples entered therapy in several ways. Some couples who recognized mutual difficulties made a direct request for joint treatment. Sometimes one partner was presented as the sick one. This partner often had had individual treatment and was identified by himself and the partner as the "patient." In the evaluation, it became apparent that both partners felt the marital stress was caused by the psychological difficulties of the disturbed partner. This partner had fewer adaptive patterns and fewer ego strengths, but both partners contributed to the problems in the relationship by maintaining this equilibrium.

> Mrs. R was a twenty-eight-year-old secretary, initially seen five years before her marriage when she decompensated following the death of her mother. Immediately after her marriage, she lost interest in sex and became increasingly anxious, preoccupied, and hostile as the couple made plans to move to a distant city. Mr. R, a thirty-three-year-old minister, was supportive, but confused by the intensity of his wife's feelings and her behavior. He felt that she needed treatment. In the course of the evaluation, it became clear that despite Mrs. R's difficulties with separation, Mr. R contributed to the problem between them by becoming too forgiving and passive and by supporting her image of herself as incapable. Sharing these feelings in the joint therapy allowed the couple to develop more adaptive communication and diminished the need to have a bad-sick and good-well partner in this relationship.

In this group of people, it is possible to recognize the partner who is more symptomatic as the major contributor to disharmony; the other partner, who presents fewer ego alien symptoms, is often considered less significant in the etiology of the problems.

For other couples starting joint therapy, one partner was in individual treatment and the other was not. The partner who was not in treatment was unable to allow a shift in the relationship to occur when the other partner improved in treatment.

> Mrs. T, a thirty-eight-year-old mother of four, presented her therapist with a complaint of chronic anxiety with episodes of hyperventilation over a period of

two years. She was referred for short-term individual psychotherapy. Her symptoms improved within twenty sessions. Near termination, she reported that her husband had been demoted at work and that he was exhibiting her hyperventilation symptoms. When he was evaluated, it became apparent that he had been unable to allow a shift in the equilibrium to occur when his wife improved.

Another precipitating factor in entering therapy was the presence of symptomatic distress in one partner. This emotion was not recognized by the other partner until the distressed partner communicated his need by applying to the clinic.

Mrs. V, a forty-three-year-old housewife, was referred by her family physician, to whom she had gone with a history of headaches and loss of interest in sex. On evaluation, she reported that she and her husband had not had sexual relations for eight years and that she was concerned since they were childless and had not decided to remain so. Mr. V was surprised that his wife had sought consultation because he had assumed that there existed a tacit agreement to remain childless and to refrain from sexual relations. In the course of brief joint treatment, the agreement was clarified, and their decision were renegotiated explicitly.

Some partners could not commit themselves separately to individual therapy because they found separation from each other, even in therapy sessions, too threatening.

Mr. G. was a twenty-five-year-old student with a borderline character structure, who became physically abusive when pressured. His wife, a masochistic twenty-five-year-old housewife, was terrified of him. His fear of loss of control and his projection of his anger made it impossible for him to tolerate being seen alone or to have her seen without him. Joint therapy in this situation provided the kind of support that each partner needed and avoided involving them in a potentially threatening separation.

The participation of both partners was considered important because it enabled each to learn to be supportive and tolerant of some of the conflicts of the other partner. Such a change was especially important when communication of mutual needs had not existed previously.

Mrs. F, a twenty-five-year-old mother of two, applied to the outpatient department requesting individual psychotherapy. She complained of boredom, depression, and social isolation. She stayed at home, sleeping and watching television. She left the house only if her husband escorted her. She left her two-year-old child in his crib all day and paid little attention to him. Mrs. F's infantile behavior appeared in part to be in response to Mr. F's increasing distance from her. At the time she began individual treatment, Mr. F had made a commitment to the marriage but was unable to understand or tolerate her regressive behavior or to attend to her more actively. It was felt that Mrs.

F would only become functional with the support of Mr. F, and joint treatment was recommended.

In all of the couples, the motivation to explore marital problems together was considered the primary indication for treatment of couples, and techniques were modified, depending on evaluative findings. Motivation for therapeutic work was considered distinct from the determination to save the relationship, because the latter frequently involved a fantasy of magical cohesiveness brought about by the therapist.

Each couple was seen for a least three evaluation sessions. In the initial interview, the partners were seen individually and in later interviews as a couple. The therapist agreed to respect the confidentiality of each partner because it became clear early in the study that each partner needed the opportunity to confide any information which might be relevant but which that partner felt he could not share with the other. As the therapeutic work proceeded, sharing was sometimes possible, but it was not necessary for successful treatment.

This procedure was used because it permitted the optimal use of professional orientation and skills in work with individuals in order to evaluate and plan a treatment program with a couple. It was possible to assess and understand the dynamics and ego functioning of each partner and to begin the establishment of the transference. In addition, it was considered important to explore individual goals, wishes, and concerns which frequently differed from those stated by the couple together. When differences existed, the final conjoint session provided an opportunity to explore them and to focus early on the communicative issues. This intervention often proved to be a turning point, particularly when motivation for treatment was tenuous.

The writers found that Freud's concept of transference in individual terms did not apply to the couples' situation where the interactional aspects involving both partners and the therapist were of primary importance.[9] When a couple starts treatment, an intense, ongoing transference interaction exists between each partner. Five transference manifestations can be identified: man to woman, woman to man, woman to therapist, man to therapist, and couples as a unit to therapist. There are multiple transference reactions and there are multiple countertransference responses.

The writers attempted to redefine transference in interpersonal or interactional terms in which the therapist and the two individuals are "more than a well polished mirror."[10] They used Janet Rioch's conceptualization of transference as an interpersonal experience.

> The transference is the experiencing of the entire pattern of the original reference frames, which included at every moment the relation of the patient to himself, to the important persons and to others, as he experiences them at that time in the light of his inter-relationships with the important people.[11]

The outline used for evaluation covered the following three areas.

Presentation of the Couples

Information on the start of therapy included how the initial contact with the clinic was made and the sources of recommendation or referral. Other material in the outline involved the factors leading to the request for therapy and the threat to the integrity of the marriage as seen by each partner. A description was given of the motivation of each partner for joint therapy, including stated commitment to marriage, evaluator's opinion of commitment to therapy, reality of treatment expectations, and secondary gain of the problem.

Individual Contribution to the Problem

In the process of obtaining a complete psychological history of each partner, several items were considered important in order to formulate the dynamics of the couple's interaction. They included: ego defenses and patterns of adaptation, including an impression of how the individual manages affect, frustration, and disappointment; self-image; personal values and goals; and role and identity outside the marriage.

Assessment of the Couple

The current marital situation and past phases in the development of the relationship were assessed for the evaluation. Marital identity was explored through discussion of such topics as: the role of individual expectations, values, goals, and conflicts in the relationship; the effect of each partner's adaptive patterns on the other partner; the need for control by one partner or the other, including how control is obtained and maintained; the existence of mutual trust and ability to share; and the importance of individual and mutual dependency issues.

Areas of communication were also assessed. They include emotional affection, empathy, and mutual support; areas of sexual satisfaction and dissatisfaction, daily interaction, including the sharing of activities, flexibility of roles, rivalry and competition, and the balance of power; major conflicts in the relationship, including development, intensity, and means of resolving conflict; and relationships with family, including children and friends.

The primary focus of the evaluation procedure for a couple should be on the interaction between the partners. However, in order to understand the multiple ways in which they affect each other, each partner must be evaluated individually. It is necessary to clarify individual roles and views of the relationship, as well as the personality dynamics which contribute to the problems presented. The evaluator can not underestimate the importance of individual styles of adaptation, use of defenses and resistances, tolerance of stress and ego strengths, and the capacity of each person to be supportive and empathetic to his partner. All of these factors, together with motivation for treatment, are components in formulating therapeutic plans. The model of treatment that evolves is eclectic and flexible, but the framework of understanding derives from a psychodynamic perspective.

References

1.   Martin Deutsche, Conflict: Productive and Destructive, *Journal of Social Issues,* 25:7–41 (January 1969).

2.   Marjorie A. Crago, Psychopathology in Married Couples, *Psychological Bulletin,* 77:114–28 (February 1972).

3.   Ibid.

4.   Jay Haley, Marriage Therapy, *Archives of General Psychiatry,* 8:213–34 (March 1963); and Haley, Marriage Therapy, in *Strategies of Psychotherapy,* ed. Jay Haley (New York: Grune and Stratton, 1963).

5.   Andrew S. Watson, The Conjoint Psychotherapy of Marriage Partners, *American Journal of Orthopsychiatry,* 33:912–22 (November 1963).

6.   Bernard Greene, ed., *The Psychotherapies of Marital Disharmony* (New York: Free Press, 1965); Clifford J. Sager, Transference in the Conjoint Therapy of Married Couples, *Archives of General Psychiatry,* 16:185–93 (March 1967); Sager, The Treatment of Married Couples, in *American Handbook of Psychiatry,* ed. Silvano Arieti (New York: Basic Books, 1966), 3:213–25; Sager, The Conjoint Session in Marriage Therapy, *The American Journal of Psychoanalysis,* 27:139–46 (May 1967); Sager, Marital Psychotherapy, *Current Psychiatric Therapy,* 7:92–102 (1967); Virginia M. Satir, Conjoint Marital Therapy, in *The Psychotherapies of Marital Disharmony,* ed. Greene; P. Kohl, Pathological Reactions of Marital Partners to Improvement of Patients, *American Journal of Psychiatry,* 118:1036–41 (May 1962); and Otto Pollak, Sociological and Psychoanalytic Concepts in Family Diagnosis, in *The Psychotherapies of Marital Disharmony,* ed. Greene.

7.   Sylvia Brody, Simultaneous Psychotherapy of Married Couples, in *Current Psychiatric Therapy,* ed. J. Masserman (New York: Grune and Stratton, 1961).

8.   Sager, Treatment of Married Couples.

9.   Sigmund Freud, *On Beginning the Treatment* (London: Hogarth Press, 1961), 12:121–44.

10.   Alice Balint and Michael Balint, On Transference and Countertransference, *International Journal of Psychoanalysis,* 20:223–30 (July-October 1939).

11.   Janet Rioch, The Transference Phenomenon in Psychoanalytic Therapy, *Psychiatry,* 6:151 (May 1943).

14

A Relationship-Focused Approach to Marital Problems

Donald R. Bardill

The purpose of this article is to discuss some ideas gained from casework experience with couples in marital conflict who were seen at Walter Reed General Hospital and Family and Child Services of Washington, D.C. In the spring of 1961 a program was initiated at the hospital that, basically, approached adolescent problem cases as nuclear family system problems. The conjoint family interview was the method of choice. Casework activity was focused on the family system of interaction.[1]

As experience in this program increased, the following question arose: Can some of the basic ideas used with family groups be used in cases involving marital problems? Several factors seemed to indicate that the husband-wife relationship could be treated as a subsystem within the total family system.

First, similarities between the marital unit and the family group as a whole had been noticed in previous work in this area. Both problem couples and problem families exhibit relationship characteristics that tend toward rigidity and inflexibility, which inhibit freedom of interaction and the expression of feelings in the relationship. Second, communication between marital partners and in families is impoverished both quantitatively and qualitatively. Couples with marital problems tend to communicate progressively less as their conflict deepens. When communication does take place, it is often ambiguous or contradictory. Even simple tasks often result in arguments because of the nature of the ambiguous communications and, on other occasions, there are contradictions between the different levels of communication.

Communication and other interactional difficulties contribute to a situation in which transactions between the husband and wife are in terms of the

Source: From Social Work 11:3 (July 1966), pp. 70–77. Copyright © 1966 by the National Association of Social Workers. Reprinted by permission.

past rather than the present. This adherence to the past often precludes any effort on the part of either partner to bring about a relationship change. Change-inducing behavior in the present is overlooked because of references to the past. An example of this kind of interaction can be found in the "crock of errors" phenomenon observed in studies of alcoholics made at Walter Reed General Hospital. In a large number of cases involving an alcoholic husband, it was found that the wife remembered a "crock full of errors" that the husband had previously committed. When the husband discontinued his drinking for an extended period of time she would dip into this "crock," as it were, and bring up for discussion her husband's past "sins."

Finally, treatment of the husband-wife relationship has been alluded to by various authors. Gomberg said:

> Only recently have we focused attention on the interaction in marriage, recognizing it as a separate factor—something beyond the intrapsychic phenomena of the individual personalities involved.[2]

He went on to say:

> A "good" marriage and a "good" family do not have as a prerequisite two neurosis-free individuals. The constructive and destructive elements and their continuation in the interaction are at least as critical to the ultimate balance or equilibrium attained in the marriage. It is possible to offer treatment for certain discordant marital situations and to achieve substantial improvements in these relations, without working through all the unconscious neurotic complications in each partner.[3]

Ackerman has stated:

> . . . in confronting problems in this particular area we shift our traditional focus of interest from the pathology of the individual personality to the pathology of a human relationship as a social unit.[4]

With support from the professional literature and on-the-spot experience, both with family groups and marital couples, an effort was made to treat selected marital problems using a casework approach that (1) focused more on the husband-wife relationship than the personality systems of each partner and (2) used the conjoint interview with both partners as the interview method of choice. In other words, treatment of the marital problem would be relationship focused.

Selection of Cases

The selection of cases most appropriate for this approach poses a problem in terms of treatment plans. This difficulty is owing to the lack of workable marital system diagnostic categories that adequately would take into consideration the unique aspects of the marital unit. Because of this, marital units are often discussed in terms most appropriate to individual personality systems. Although the lack of usable categories poses some problems, the following are principles found useful in selecting cases that can benefit from marital unit casework:

1. As is true of individual clients, couples who seek help with their marital problems must be committed positively to an exploration of the nature of their marital relationship; both partners should be aware of the necessity for a mutual effort geared toward changing the basic nature of their transactional system.

2. Couples who from the first contact exhibit communication problems can usually benefit from marital unit casework; the conjoint interview is an excellent method of exploring their communication system.

3. When there is a lack of awareness of the role each partner plays in the relationship and little realization of the impact each role has on the other, conjoint interviews may serve to clarify relationships. Interview techniques may be used that force an awareness of the effect one partner has on the other.

4. Couples who experience marital difficulty precipitated by a crisis situation seem to react most positively and quickly to marital unit casework. It is not unusual for a crisis situation to increase the narcissistic needs of each partner, the result being that neither can offer support to the other. In one case, a wife who was having a difficult time during menopause suffered in a very short period of time the death of her father, the psychiatric hospitalization of her brother, and the loss of a maid of long standing. When she sought increased attention and love from her otherwise distant husband he failed to respond. As she pushed for attention he withdrew further. During the course of treatment both partners were able to discuss, with a good degree of objectivity, the present situation and their responses.

5. There are also clients for whom a one-to-one relationship with a worker is too threatening. In cases of marital conflict when one partner is extremely passive and easily threatened, a conjoint interview may serve to diminish the fears and fantasied discomfort of the treatment method. Later, if indicated, either or both partners may be helped to seek individual casework.

6. A marital relationship in which projection is a major element in interaction is especially appropriate for this treatment method. The here-and-now aspect of the interview method facilitates the process of bringing destructive projections of the relationship into the open. Projections in an interview are visible to both. Each partner often recognizes the way a projection is accommodated by the other.

It almost goes without saying that any couple that has inherent relationship strengths will benefit most positively from marital unit casework. As in individual casework, healthy systems—whether personality, family, or marital—offer the best prospect for treatment success.

Inadvisable Cases

The following are characteristics of marital units for which marital unit casework may be contraindicated. However, each situation must be evaluated in terms of its individual problems and strengths.

In a certain number of cases marital conflict is only a manifestation of rather deep personal conflict in one of the partners. Such an indication is frequently found when there is a persistent emergence of transference reactions; when, for example, one partner continues to dwell on past experiences with parents and others. The skill and perceptiveness of the worker in recognizing situations when personality problems transcend the entire marital relationship is of crucial importance.

This method is also contraindicated when the defensive maneuvers are so intense that little order can be brought to the interview situation. In situations of this nature the forces of marital disintegration seem to have pushed the couple beyond commitment to the marriage. Therefore, individual casework may be needed (if the couple desires it) to prepare the way for a conjoint effort.

In the final analysis the decision to attempt marital unit or individual casework lies, to a large degree, with the intuitive feelings of the worker. After a careful consideration of all the factors involved, he must, on the basis of skill, innate ability, experience, and training, decide on the treatment method of choice.

Underlying Assumptions

In providing a frame of reference for a relationship-focused approach to marital problems, it is useful to recognize—and the idea is not new to social workers—that human behavior can be approached from different frames of reference. Community service programs represent a broad social work frame of reference; individual casework represents still another level from which to view behavior. In individual casework the person has been abstracted from his family, society, and so on. Marital unit casework approaches problems from the viewpoint of the marriage relationship.

The theoretical and operational base used in the program is derived from a number of closely related characteristics of the marriage relationship. For instance, every married couple evolves a unique relationship for itself.

> A marital relationship, like a chemical compound, has unique properties of its own, over and above the characteristics of the elements that merge to form the compound.[5]

The exact quality of the relationship depends on many things, such as the partners' personalities, their cultural backgrounds and value systems, the social situation, and the perceived roles and role expectations of each partner. Also, in this society, the marriage relationship is the most intense of all adult interpersonal relations. It provides each partner with more than the usual narcissistic gratifications, as well as threats. The emergence of the isolated nuclear family as the characteristic family in this society indicates that marriage relationships may become even more intense.

Because life situations as well as the needs of each partner change with the passage of time, a relationship must be flexible enough to adapt to change, if needed. For example, a heretofore satisfactory marriage may become disrupted if it cannot adjust to such things as a husband's loss of job or a physical injury to one of the partners. An essential ingredient in the capacity of a marriage relationship to change as needed is an adequate marital communications system. If it does not exist, the partners may be unable to perceive the need for making readjustments in their relationship.

It is common for both marital partners to recognize that a change in the nature of the relationship is indicated, yet still to have an emotional investment in maintaining the status quo. This seems to stem from the common fear of the unknown—a current relationship, as uncomfortable as it may be, is less fearful than one that is unknown. There is also the possibility that the relationship in its present form actually does provide a way of meeting some of each partner's needs. In treatment this means that efforts to explore a couple's interactional system may encounter strong resistance by both.

It is generally recognized that marital problems are seldom, if ever, caused primarily by only one of the marital partners—most often both partners unwittingly contribute to the disrupted relationship. The interactional aspects of marital problems have been recognized by Ackerman, who posed the question:

> Is neurotic conflict in a marital pair to be conceived as having dynamic connotations identical with neurosis of individual personality?

He then answered it by saying:

> Even when we take full cognizance of the principle that neurosis in the individual implies a particular set of propensities in interpersonal adaptation, we must nevertheless draw a distinction between interpersonal conflict, real or neurotic, and conflict within the individual . . . a given individual with a fixed neurosis will interact in significantly different ways with different partners.[6]

From this point of view any marriage conflict may be a result of the distinctive kind of relationship evolved by the two partners.

Operationally, the principles used in marital unit casework primarily will be those that are appropriate to the behavior in a relationship, rather than to individual behavior. This shift of focus makes it necessary to think of change in an interactional system rather than in an individual personality. Therefore, a statement by one partner that he or she is more relaxed will not necessarily be viewed as casework progress unless some concomitant change has been made in the interactional system.

The vehicle of change is derived from a change in the nature of the interactional field. Each spouse increases his competence as a marital partner by becoming more aware of the subtleties of their way of interacting. In one case, the husband had increasingly involved himself in activities outside the home. Prior to treatment the wife had been unable to express her feelings about being left at home all the time. When the subject was discussed in the treatment sessions the husband, in a thoughtful manner, speculated that his wife's complaints were justified, but he also expressed resentment because she had "never expressed herself this way before."

As the nature of the couple's communications system is explored feelings are elicited that help the partners increase their empathetic capacities. In many cases, when their ability to communicate increases, couples find areas of agreement they previously did not know existed. The constant emphasis in the interview sessions on the here and now of interaction helps the partners expand their capacity for self-reflection.

In the individual marital partner this approach is directed toward the healthy, adjustive, and rational processes of the ego—those ego apparatuses that have to do with perception, thinking, language, object comprehension, intention, and so forth.[7] By encouraging transactions that allow his roles and nature of communication to become aligned with subjective experience, each partner is helped to regard his sensual responses as a reliable guide to expectations. By promoting competence in the ability to communicate, each partner is better able to determine what he really means when he is talking—an essential part of normal human transactions. Through an examination of conflict areas each partner is given the opportunity to experience the possibilities of relating to people who differ—an essential element of differentiation and self-identity. In the framework of the therapeutic process each partner is given an opportunity to release feelings and to learn new forms of communication.

Worker's Task

Although the task of the worker is somewhat different than for individual casework, the basic vehicle of change is still the controlled use of relationships. In individual casework the nature of the relationship between the client and the worker is of primary concern. In marital unit casework the relationship of one part of the marriage unit to the other is the focal point.

The worker must, by his relationship to the marital unit, create a treatment atmosphere that encourages the couple in self-examination. He does this by focusing more on the interview process than the interview content and does not allow himself to become entangled in splits or alignments with either partner. By his manner and language he implies a nonjudgmental attitude toward the words and actions of the partners but he assists them to explore areas that may produce the ingredients necessary for a more meaningful relationship. Most of all, however, he relates *to* the marital unit and he does not get involved *in* it.

During the initial stages of therapy the worker must discuss with the couple the nature of the task both he and they are about to undertake; experience has shown that this area should be covered fully with the couple. Structuring the casework sessions helps the couple to understand better what is and is not to be expected. Furthermore, it is the worker's task, from the beginning, to point the couple toward areas of conflict that must be resolved. In other words, he must at all times adequately assess the areas of "real" conflict.

Also he must offer support to each partner when needed. The support given is most often geared toward increasing the communicative abilities of the couple. If one partner has been attacked by the other, the worker might ask the attacked partner to express his feelings about what has just happened. When appropriate, he may ask for clarification of what has just been said. This is especially useful when the nature of the communication seems to be at a different level of understanding for both partners.

The partners must be helped to confront themselves with the nature of an action or communication that has just taken place in the interview. If a certain piece of communication is contradicted by an action the worker may note the contradiction and confront the couple with the apparent nature of their roles toward each other. An overall task is to assist the couple to become more "self-aware" of the many elements that go into the make-up of their unique relationship. As their ability to engage in self-reflection increases, the worker encourages them to use their relationship strengths to bring about any adaptations needed in the marriage system.

Agent of Change

It is felt that the very nature of the worker's relationship to the marital unit enables the worker to be the "agent of change." The worker is outside the marital interactional system but he is an observing, intruding outsider. In essence he places the couple in a situation in which they are forced to interact differently. By the nature of the worker's role, old methods and tactics formerly used by the couple are not allowed to be used again. When one partner shows emotion he is requested to verbalize his feelings. When no feelings are shown but obviously called for the worker encourages their expression. When nonverbal communication takes place verbal clarification is called for. When contradictory or ambiguous messages are transmitted their nature is brought up for discussion. When the partners blame each other they are told that their task is to explore the nature of their relationship. When one partner says he is more anxious or that things are getting worse in the marriage, he may be told that it is part of the treatment process; then expression and clarification of the areas in which things are worse are requested. As one partner begins or is forced to behave differently the other partner is forced to respond to this change in behavior. In the interview these new ways of interacting point up the possibilities for a different kind of relationship. In other words, the worker as the "agent of change" has placed the couple in a situation in which they are both forced to act differently and also has given them the opportunity to examine the nature of their marital relationship.

Initial Separate Interviews

The basic interview method used in marital unit casework is the conjoint interview. Although this is basic to the relationship-focused approach, experience seems to indicate that there are also advantages to separate interviews with each partner at least once in the initial stages of treatment. For one thing, a separate interview gives the worker a chance to compare the actions and reactions of each client both alone and in the presence of the spouse. It also allows each partner to discuss areas of concern that he would find difficult to talk about in a conjoint session. It seems that once having talked about a subject in the individual session it is easier to bring it up in the presence of the partner. Furthermore, each partner, being unsure about just what the other has talked about in the individual sessions, finds it difficult to hide what might be regarded as "family secrets." During these interviews the focus of the discussion is on the marriage and consequently it is beneficial to take a brief marital history during these sessions.

After the individual interviews it is best to see the couple together consistently. This forces both partners to discuss areas of concern in the presence of the other—a procedure that is often therapeutic in and of itself. In addition, insistence on the conjoint interview strengthens the assumption that relations can be improved by focusing on interaction in the marital system.

Tactics

Because of the diversity of situations encountered in any interview and the unique abilities of each caseworker, it is impossible to discuss specific tactics to handle certain phenomena. It is possible, however, to discuss broad ideas gained from the experience of using certain techniques in the treatment of marital problems. In general, any tactic should reflect the unique character of the couple, the worker, and the time, place, and basic assumption under which the treatment effort was undertaken.

During the initial stages of treatment the worker is often silent in order to allow the couple to present their problem but he also poses probing questions that serve to direct the focus of the casework process. He may discuss the treatment structure but he emphasizes that it is flexible to adjust to the couple's needs.

Couples who experience intense conflict frequently begin treatment by attempting to justify their own position to such a degree that little is accomplished during the interview. In a number of such cases the couples were helped to abandon this phase more quickly when the worker discussed in detail the difference between *being* right and *getting* right. The worker's refusal to permit them to blame each other discourages further attacks.

At times when the vituperations are so intense and/or events occur so fast that nothing seems to make sense, the worker may use the "name the game technique."[8] For example, partners who continue to justify their own position and blame the other may be told they are playing the game of "courtroom." The ingredients that go into playing this game, such as blaming others or justifying one's own position, are then discussed. In one case, a couple engaged in arguments that were never settled and jumped from subject to subject with such speed and subtlety that little of a positive nature was accomplished. Toward the end of the interview, however, the worker identified the events of the interview as the "confusion" game. The effects of this game were discussed and they were able to see that the game essentially caused them to maintain a status quo in their relationship. During the next interview they made a conscious effort to avoid confusion and began to explore their relationship more objectively and introspectively.

Taking seemingly unrelated, but recurring phenomena and placing them in a category serves to make the entire course of events more manageable. In addition, experience has shown that couples tend to be less defensive about discussing a "game" even though it refers to them. The names used to label series of events are as numerous as the kind of actions that occur in an interview, but in general the name should express what is going on at the time.

Attempts to entangle the worker in splits or alignments with one of the partners usually appear in the form of a direct value judgment question about the "rightness" or "wrongness" of a certain action. This maneuver can usually be handled by such statements as, "It would probably be best to hear how your wife feels about that" or "Since this is obviously something that concerns *your* relationship it might be best to hear from your wife on that question."

When the partners continue to avoid directing the flow of communication to each other the worker may request that each spouse avoid talking about each other in the third person (he or she). He may then suggest that they refer to each other in the second person (you). This tactic serves to force the partners to confront each other with ideas and feelings rather than present them to the worker. When couples are unable to settle an issue the worker may take a frequently mentioned area of conflict and ask the couple to resolve that issue one way or the other during the interview hour. These problem-solving efforts frequently clarify for everyone present the destructive processes at work.

Another closely related technique is "homework." When couples are unable to resolve an issue during the interview hour they are told to resolve the issue before the next meeting. They are further told that the next interview hour will be used to talk about how they resolved it. Insight can be gained from talking about the manner in which the problem was solved.

Finally, the tactic of "frequent summaries" is useful in almost all cases. At frequent intervals during the interview one of the partners is asked to summarize what has occurred in the preceding ten or fifteen minutes.

Summary

Some ideas for a casework approach that focuses on the relationship of a disrupted marriage have been discussed in this article. While the crucial importance of the individual personality system of each partner is recognized, it is also recognized that the relationship itself can be a focal point for treatment. The intense focus on the functions of what has been called the "conflict-free sphere of the ego" does not deny the importance of working with ego defenses and conflicts. It does however allow for a method of treating a relationship. For it is in the areas of perception, language, judgment, and so on, that access to the treatment of a dysfunctioning relationship can be gained. As each partner increases his reality-based sensitivity to situations, the ego gains in strength and it may be postulated that a strengthened ego is better able to perceive the irrational aspects of earlier life conflicts for which resolution is sought in the present. Just as the healing of a wound is a natural function of the human body, so is the integration of new insights a normal function of the ego.[9] In this sense increased personal adaptability may result: each partner has not only resolved his marital relationship problem but finds himself a more socially competent individual in relationships with other people.

This approach makes use of an understanding of the interactional dimension of the marital relationship—the forces that are affected by the interaction of the marital partners. Such an approach utilizes the increasing awareness of the continuing nature of personality development—the unique needs that must be met at every stage of life—and recognizes the concept that a marriage relationship has stages of development in which crucial needs must be met for the relationship to progress. As we are better able to understand the developmental forces working in a marriage relationship we may be better able to assist the partners in using the ego's adaptive rational functions to bring about a satisfying marriage..

References

1.   Donald R. Bardill and Francis J. Ryan, *Family Group Casework: A Social Work Approach to Family Therapy* (Washington, D.C.: Catholic University of America Press, 1964).

2.   M. Robert Gomberg, "Casework Treatment of Marital Problems," in Victor M. Eisenstein, ed., *Neurotic Interaction in Marriage* (New York: Basic Books, 1961), p. 270.

3.   *Ibid.*

4.   Nathan W. Ackerman, MD, *Psychodynamics of Family Life* (New York: Basic Books, 1958), p. 150.

5.   Ackerman, *op. cit.*, p. 151.

6.   *Ibid.*, p. 151.

7.   Heinz Hartmann, *Ego Psychology and the Problem of Adaptation*, David Rapaport, trans. (New York: International Universities Press, 1958), p. 17.

8.   For a detailed discussion of the methods of game labeling in the analysis of transactions between people *see* Eric Berne, *Transactional Analysis in Psychotherapy* (New York: Grove Press, Evergreen Books, 1961).

9.   Franz Alexander and Thomas M. French, *Psychoanalytic Therapy* (New York: Ronald Press, 1946), p. 27.

15
The Problem-Solving Component in Family Therapy

David Hallowitz

Family therapy usually has a practical and realistic problem-solving component that is embedded in and grows out of deeper-level discussion of breakdowns and conflicts in intrafamilial relationships.[1] Without the problem-solving component, it is doubtful in most instances that significant change would take place in the family relationships and in the functioning and behavior of individual family members. The therapist provides guidance and leadership in helping the family members work out different ways of handling issues that have previously driven them apart.[2] This article will attempt to separate from the process and dynamics of family therapy the problem-solving component so that it can be examined in some detail. Care will be taken, however, to show its integral connections with the family therapy process.

A review of the literature, with concentration upon the past five years, showed that the subject of this article has not received much attention. John Bell notes its significance: "Most frequently one, two, or a few problems are sifted out for discussion as symbols of the full range of problems. They are concrete representations of the areas of tension, ambiguity, indecision, and breakdown of solidarity in the group. . . . The therapist is an agent who works to start and keep alive this problem solving program."[3] Ludwig Geismar and Jane Krisberg comment: ". . . effective communication can be established between social worker and treatment families when the focus is on problem solving."[4] In the family therapy literature generally, the problem-solving component is implicit. It is woven into the continuum of the work with the

Source: From Social Casework 51 (February 1970), pp. 67–75. Copyright © 1970 by the Family Service Association of America. Reprinted by permission.

family members on their relationship with one another. Helen Perlman writes extensively and comprehensively on the theory and dynamics of "the problem-solving process" as part of casework practice.[5] An article by Kurt Spitzer and Betty Welsh is also of interest in this regard.[6]

The problems brought into the therapy situation and the family's efforts to cope with them constitute the medium through which the positive and negative feelings, misunderstandings, and conflicts in the relationships are expressed. The problem-solving component may become predominant at any point in the family therapy process. The point at which it becomes predominant depends upon whether deeper and more complex emotional and psychopathological factors and forces exist that may first have to be worked through or, if possible, encapsulated to permit constructive and practical work on immediate reality problems. Early problem-solving efforts in therapy may be undermined and thwarted by these factors and forces, which often operate on a preconscious or unconscious level. The therapist can use this problem-solving component as a lead-in to the deeper conflicts by pointing out that something is obstructing their efforts and wondering what it might be. On the other hand, it is also possible that a family could have some success with the surface and immediate issues, despite the existence of deeper pathological processes. Dealing with the situation in this way would have therapeutic value because the family members would gain confidence, and their energies would be freed to go into the more central and underlying conflicts. Although there is considerable variability and interrelationship between deeper conflicts and immediate reality problems, the problem-solving component generally emerges into prominence earlier in the treatment process when there is a greater degree of health and strength in the family relationships and in its individual members. It emerges later in the process when these factors are minimal.

The problem-solving component contributes to the development of better understanding and feeling in the family relationships, and this development in turn generates even more productive problem-solving work. Sometimes, as in individual therapy, change for the better in the relationships and the functioning of the family members takes place without explicit discussion of reality problems. Nevertheless, it should be recognized that this change is an outgrowth of the family's relationship with the therapist and the treatment process—that agreements and decisions are being made implicitly with the therapist and with each other. The therapist supportively communicates his understanding and recognition of the progress that the family and its members are making. More often than not, however, the problem-solving component explicitly becomes a vital part of the content of family interviews.

A specific case, with verbatim excerpts from tape-recorded interviews, illustrates this component and shows how work with the family members on their problems is an integral part of building their relationships.

Case Illustration

Tom and Carl D, fifteen and sixteen years of age, and their parents were referred to the clinic by the family court after the boys had been placed on probation. Mr. and Mrs. D had filed a petition stating that the two boys were ungovernable. Moreover, Tom and Carl, as members of a gang, had committed such antisocial acts as stealing and vandalism. They were frequently truant from school and often stayed out until the early hours of the morning. Although they had above-average intelligence, they were failing in schoolwork. The reports from the family court showed that the whole family was in a chronic state of disorganization and turmoil. Mary, thirteen years of age, was evidencing the same behavior as her older brothers; she was beginning to stay out late at night, was a behavior problem in school, and was doing near-failing work. The parents were equally ineffectual in the discipline of the two younger children, Betty, nine years of age, and Eddie, eleven years of age. With the exception of Julie, who was nineteen years old, the children were extremely destructive of the household furniture and furnishings. They would not clean up after themselves, leaving their rooms in constant disorder and causing fires by hiding cigarette butts and matches under the rugs and beds. All the efforts of the parents to control the children had been ineffective for many years, and they had long ago ceased to invite friends to their home.

The mother had a history of mental illness characterized principally by profound depression and inability to function. She had been hospitalized several times over a ten-year period. For the past four years, she has been relatively stable, not requiring psychiatric care or hospitalization. During the ten years that the mother suffered from her mental illness, a housekeeper was employed. The father was involved in his work much longer than the usual workday and workweek. Well-educated and intelligent people, the parents had tried unsuccessfully over the years to reach the children mainly through reason but also through a complicated system of monetary fines and rewards.

Process of Family Therapy

The therapist met weekly with the parents, Tom, Carl, and Mary in a continuous process for six months. Thereafter, interviews were held monthly for the next five months. Julie participated in two interviews when she came home on vacation from college. The children's feelings of being rejected by the parents and the parents' feelings of being rejected by the children were expressed and discussed in the beginning phase of therapy, and these feelings continued to be the theme in the ongoing process. The specific issues dealt with in a problem-solving way were the continual and uncontrolled stealing from each other, the destruction in the household, and the inability of the parents to discipline the children. The therapist's role in the problem-solving work was to stimulate and help the family members develop their own solutions even though some solutions were unconventional according to the stereotyped conception of the ideal family.

In his early diagnostic assessment of the family's problems, the therapist found that Tom, Carl, and Mary were reacting to considerable emotional deprivation and feelings of rejection. Pronounced character disorder traits—narcissism, poor impulse control, poor reality testing, and weak superego development—were already evident in Carl and, to a lesser extent, in Tom and Mary. Dynamically, the stealing represented an attempt to fill the void of emotional deprivation with material things. It also represented the children's accumulated anger and resentment toward the parents for having failed to meet their needs for love, affection, and realistic controls and for having engendered in them the pain of anxiety and insecurity. The parents had comparable feelings of being mistreated and rejected by the children, so that they, in turn, had been feeling very angry and resentful toward them. This destructive vicious cycle in the family relationships had been in force for many years.[7]

The therapist made two important decisions for himslef. First *it would not be advisable to go deeply into and to treat the mother's past mental illness and the currently quiescent pathology.* Rather, he thought it best to have the other members of the family consider the effects of her illness upon them and the parent-child relationships. Most important, the therapist decided to work with the strengths rather than with the pathology and weaknesses in the individuals and the intrafamilial relationships. Second, *the weakness of the parents in the area of discipline should be accepted virtually as an unalterable fact of life; an emphasis upon trying to help them achieve greater competence in this sphere would be unrealistic and probably unproductive.* As an alternative, the therapist chose the approach of supporting the leadership role of the parents and placing upon the children the responsibility for achieving greater self-discipline.

One vital aspect of the therapist's work with the family was his sensing their underlying feelings through verbal and nonverbal communications and expressions, and his eliciting the feelings of an individual family member. The therapist thereby helped each member of the family to enunciate his feelings and to interact with the other family members. Tom and Carl at first tended to be fairly inhibited and guarded, but gradually the therapist succeeded in helping them express themselves freely and spontaneously. For example, in an early interview, the parents were criticizing Tom. The therapist observed that Tom's lips tightened and he looked angry. He asked Tom what was bothering him. Tom replied, "Nothing." The therapist persisted, "I can see that you look very upset. What's the matter?" Tom then blurted out, "They can only say bad things about me." Turning to his parents, he said, "What about all the good things I've done this past week!"

Another important aspect of the therapist's work was his stimulating the family to join him in thinking diagnostically and dynamically—in discovering the "why" of problems and behaviors. In the first interview, after the parents took the lead in describing the chronic problems besetting the family, the therapist encouraged the three adolescent youngsters to discuss their perceptions of the family's difficulties. He asked the family members, "What have some of the causes been that brought these problems into being? What's at the bottom of it all?

The mother talked about her mental illness and how it must have been a major cause of the trouble in the family. She spoke of her awareness of the resultant emotional deprivation. The father talked remorsefully about the emotional strain of his wife's illness upon him, the demands of his work, his inability to handle the total responsibility for the upbringing and control of the children, and his frustrations and sense of defeat and helplessness. Tom, Carl, and Mary reflected upon their diffuse feelings of unhappiness during the years that the mother was afflicted, especially when she was in the hospital for long periods of time. The therapist commented: "Oftentimes, young children feel that when a parent is sick and goes into the hospital, it is because the parent really does not care for them or want to be with them. They are too young to understand that the parent cannot help himself, but that it is a medical and physical necessity to go into a hospital in order to get well. I suspect that you may have had such feelings yourselves when you were young." This comment caused the youngsters to be pensive, but it led to a discussion by all the family members about their feelings of rejection. The parents expressed their guilt and remorse over having sent Tom to a military school when he was eleven years old because of his unmanageable behavior in school and at home. Tom's face was dark and the therapist encouraged him gradually to reveal his feelings. He told his parents that he had felt terrible about being sent away, that he had thought they wanted to get rid of him, and that the military school had been "a rotten place." The parents then spoke with deep sincerity about how they really had not wanted to get rid of Tom; they just had not known what else to do.

Toward the end of this first interview, the therapist discussed with the family his recommendation that they continue to come each week. He introduced the notion of the youngsters' trying to assume responsibility for their own self-discipline rather than expecting the parents to develop the controls for them. The therapist outlined the objectives of the therapy process: the family members were to gain greater understanding of each other and their feelings; they were to come to grips with the problems within the family and try to find solutions to them in very practical ways; and they were to achieve more positive feelings for and better relationships with each other. The therapist had them react to and discuss his proposal. They accepted it.

The ensuing therapy consisted, on the one hand, of an integrated, reciprocal dealing with the relationship conflicts and feelings, and, on the other hand, of helping the family find better ways of cooperating and working together. It became a relationship-building process. The first three months of therapy showed an overall forward trend, but then regression started to set in. The turning point at which the regressive trend was stopped and at which the process as a whole moved more securely and steadily toward the treatment objectives occurred in one critical interview of the fourth month.

The opening remarks of the father and the youngsters were of a light and superficial nature to the effect that "everything was fine." The mother looked haggard and forlorn. The therapist said to her, "You look very upset and unhappy." She found it hard to talk. The therapist waited. Haltingly, and then bursting into tears, she said, "My family just doesn't care for me," and she proceeded to pour out her feelings of rejection by the children. If they cared for her, they would not be making life so miserable for her and they would try to cooperate and help her. Everyone in the room was deeply moved. The youngsters' eyes filled with tears. They talked it all out and then proceeded to discuss what they were going to do about the problem.

The foregoing overview of the family therapy process constitutes the context of the problem-solving component. Two of the specific problems dealt with can be illustrated by tape-recorded verbatim excerpts: (1) stealing within the family and (2) discipline.

STEALING WITHIN THE FAMILY

What follows is taken from the second interview. Julie, home on vacation from college, also participated. The family had decided the week before that she should come because Tom, Carl, and Mary were angry and upset about her "bossing us around." This relationship problem, thrashed out in the first third of the interview, resulted in better understanding and a redefinition of Julie's role in the family. The family went on to consider the problem of the rampant stealing that has been going on within the home.

FATHER: Is this problem of stealing in our home worth working on?
THERAPIST: It certainly is. It's the whole matter of being able to trust each other, to believe each other—a very basic thing.
MOTHER: This is it; there really is a lack of trust in the family. I'm sure all of you will bear this out with me. We can't trust one another. Right, Carl?
CARL: Yeah.
JULIE: If something of yours is taken, do you know who's taken it?
CARL: No.
JULIE: All right, and do you ever find out?
CARL: No.
JULIE: So it just goes on and on, and nothing is done about it.

MOTHER: I can't leave money around the house. You've got to carry your purse around with you no matter where you go. Or your cigarettes, anything valuable, you've got to lock up somewhere. And even the locks are picked. We really have a talented group in that you can't hide anything. And what I said is true. When I go into the house, I have to carry my purse, and this is a terrible way to live.

FATHER: Last night I was thinking about Mary. I never know whether she is telling me the truth or not. Now a year ago Mary was always completely honest, so that this has happened within the course of a year. With Carl, it's been longstanding, and with Tom, it's not so much lying as it is deceptiveness, and this has been longstanding.

THERAPIST: What are some of your ideas as to why this problem exists in your family? How did this get started? What's the basis of it?

FATHER: The price is worth it; it's worth the price.

TOM: That's what I used to think. Whenever I saw something I wanted, I took it.

THERAPIST: Do you think that's what it is? You want something so you take it and don't stop to think about consequences? Or is there something more to it?

TOM: I used to think that I could get away with it.

THERAPIST: What is it with you, Mary?

MARY: I don't know. I just want it and I don't think about it until after it's done. I put my conscience aside.

THERAPIST: What is it with you, Carl?

CARL: The same as her. I wanted it and I didn't think about it until after it was done. I just wanted it and I'd forget about what would happen if I got caught. Feelings about it started to bother me afterwards, but then it started to be a habit.

THERAPIST: Sometimes we find that kids will steal not so much because they want something but because it's a good way of punishing somebody or getting even. You can get rid of your angry feelings that way.

TOM: That's not it; we have better ways, like messing up someone's room.

(Spontaneous narrations of various stealing incidents followed, with a concentration on Carl's smooth operations.)

THERAPIST: Let me get back to Carl for a moment. I just want to check something out. The way it sounds to me, you're describing Carl almost like a con man. Is that what you are? I mean, do you put the charm on to get something?

CARL: Yeah.

THERAPIST: How come you agree so readily?

CARL: Because it's true.

FATHER: We sometimes worship peculiar heroes in our family. I don't understand it. I think Carl wants to be a con man as his vocation. Is that right, Carl?

CARL: No. I may have seen it in a movie or something, but I don't know where I pick up this stuff. It's a habit.

MOTHER: Well, I think you fooled us all once too often. I mean, we've all been taken in. I, probably more than anybody else.

MARY: You keep trusting him and I don't do that any more.

THERAPIST: My next question, Carl, is: Do you really want to continue being this way—the con artist?

CARL: I don't really want to be a con artist. I don't want to grow up to be a con artist. But right now I really don't use my "connery" as much as I used to. If I try to work with my parents better and my brothers and my sisters better, no one will believe me. So how can anyone try and do something right? Because you have the reputation of being a con artist. You can't. It's impossible.

THERAPIST: That's a real problem. Carl wants to change and win your confidence. How can he go about it? How can he overcome the reputation he's built up?

MARY: I think if he would be good for a long period of time, he would gain our trust back.

TOM: If he wouldn't pull any more bets, that would start it off right.

MOTHER: I think Carl has to make a big effort to start telling the truth. I really think he's gotten to the point where sometimes he doesn't know if he's lying or telling the truth. It's become such a habit with him. Certainly his father and I want to be able to trust him, and I think we will be most cooperative with him on any efforts that he does make.

THERAPIST: My next question is: Carl, do you want to make the effort and get over the habit? It would be a rough row to hoe because you do have a reputation and people aren't going to believe you, even when you're telling the truth, unless you keep it up for a long time, as Mary suggested.

. . . . . .

FATHER: We're talking about the instances that are petty or grand thievery. We're really worried about that. We were asked if we can do anything about that. If we decide that this can't go on as a group, then maybe we should all start putting things on the table and trust that it's going to be there. And start trusting each other all the way. I don't know, I think we've all got to express ourselves as to what we think the answer might be.

CARL: I'll never be trusted, so I may as well just keep going on. I'm not going to spend three or four months of my life trying to be trusted. Because why should I? It wouldn't do any good anyway.

JULIE: Why not try it? You spent years being untrustful.

CARL: That's right, because I never had the chance to really be trusted.

JULIE: Have you ever tried it—being good for three or four months?

CARL: No.

MARY: How are we going to know if we can be trusted if we keep our things hidden all the time?

MOTHER: Really trust. Like I'm going to put all my stuff on the table and then go to bed and the next morning find all my stuff gone. I'm not doing that!

MARY: All I'm saying is we don't know when this trust will begin, and you guys just won't know unless we all try together.

THERAPIST: How is this thing going to be tested if you're going to keep on hiding your things?

JULIE: You know, the first time something goes wrong, we're all going to go back to hiding. All it takes is one false move.

CARL: One person can wreck the whole thing.

THERAPIST: Do you feel ready to try leaving your things out, including little things like chewing gum?

TOM: I could leave my cigarettes out now.

MARY: I'll put out my candy.

THERAPIST: It would be worth the try, I think.

THE PROBLEM OF DISCIPLINE

What follows is taken from the fifth interview. The therapist essentially revived an unconventional plan that was tried by Tom, Carl, and Mary in relation to Eddie and Betty and abandoned a few days previously.

THERAPIST: The idea itself—the older kids disciplining the younger ones—may be a good one because it was effective for several days. Yet, your objections [father's] are certainly valid too. Is there a way of overcoming these objections so the plan itself can be reestablished? Tom, you seem to be pretty glum. What's the matter?

TOM: There is no other effective way of going at it, and it was hard enough getting to do it that way. It worked because we could give demerits that cost Eddie and Betty money out of their allowance. They just won't listen no matter what you substitute for money.

FATHER: Well, you set up this system and said there was no room for recourse. Eddie and Betty couldn't say to you, "Well, you get a demerit."

CARL: Nobody said that Eddie and Betty couldn't give us demerits.

TOM: It wouldn't work anyway if they could give us demerits.

THERAPIST: Why wouldn't it work?

TOM: Let's say I went into their rooms and found them a mess and I gave them demerits. Well, they'd just be snooping around and getting under our nerves just trying to find something wrong with our rooms. And then it would be just like a war.

THERAPIST: Well, would it work if your parents took over the demerit system for all of you?

MARY: They do. But let's face it. Mom and Dad, you're just not strict enough.

TOM: You don't stand over the kids the way we do.

FATHER: Oh? Well, we stand over you.

TOM: Yeah, but we're going to a clinic and they're not.

MARY: Let's put it this way, Dad. We're all equal, and you two worry about us and not Eddie and Betty.

FATHER: I've never said we're all equal as far as discipline in the family.

CARL: You said we all make the same amount of mess.

FATHER: Oh, is that what you mean by equal? Well, that could be so. So it doesn't make sense to have a couple of mess-makers put in charge of the other mess-makers.

MOTHER: But these boys did take the responsibility of cleaning after themselves, too, which has been an improvement over the past. Whatever their system was, it seemed to be working well.

THERAPIST: Let me check this out. Your mother said that during these four days the two of you were pretty much on the ball. While checking up on the other kids, you were checking up on yourselves. Is that so from your point of view? If it's working, can we bridge the gap between your objections [father's] and the basic plan? In other words, as Tom suggested before, can some method be found where the two of you [parents] kind of keep an eye on Tom and Carl, delegating the responsibility to them to watch over Eddie and Betty?

CARL: Seeing that you two don't have the time to watch over them as we do.

MOTHER: Well, it was especially helpful last week. It was just very reassuring to me to know that things were being handled in a good way. I really think that if the boys are up to it and they're willing to do it, this can be very helpful to us. It's just too difficult when you're not there, not having anybody in authority.

FATHER: I've always said that I don't think more than one of us could be the fine-maker. But you are now saying that you'd only *recommend* demerits and the decision is mine. Right?

TOM: Yes.

FATHER: OK. That can be done.

(*Mary's role was discussed and argued at length. It was decided that she would come directly under the jurisdiction of the parents. She would be in charge of Eddie and Betty only at breakfast time. All gave her recognition for doing a fine job with the younger ones in that particular sphere.*)

. . . . . .

MOTHER: Remember, let's not try for perfection. Let's just try to keep the house averagely neat.

CARL: I don't feel like being a policeman, but we'll have to for a while. Otherwise, they'll both slip back. If we do it strictly, they won't do such a spotless job, but at least it will be neatness.

FATHER: As mother said, we're not looking for perfection, just ordinary neatness and cleanliness, sanitation if you want. Plus getting away from destruction; we've got to get away from destruction, breakage. OK? Especially the willful breakage.

CARL: I'm talking about perfection for a couple of months.

MARY: We've got to aim for the highest point for a while.

FATHER: You can aim for it, but I think you should be ready to settle for an improvement over what we've got.

TOM: I mean I don't feel like doing this for more than three or four months.

FATHER: By then Eddie and Betty should have the right habits. Oh, we're not talking about forever either.

THE THERAPIST

The therapist here represents in part a parent figure to all the family members, supplementing the role and strengths of the parents. He is also a catalyst by providing the climate and stimulus for the family members to tap their own resources in finding solutions to problems and resolving their relationship conflicts. The therapist uses skills of discussion leadership. He keeps the discussion focused; stimulates participants to think, react, and work together on the problem at hand; gives encouragement and recognition to particular family members for their good points and ideas; and brings the family to the threshold of decision making. With the D family, the therapist purposefully subordinated his discussion leadership role in order to support that of the father. Confrontation can be part of the discussion, as exemplified by the therapist's gently and supportively showing Carl that his family regards him as a con man. The therapist's interpretive comments touching upon deeper dynamics—his comments about the mother's mental illness possibly signifying to the children rejection of them and the stealing possibly representing the children's subconsciously acting out their suppressed anger toward the parents—can also be part of the problem-solving discussion. In other words, the thread of the deeper-level discussions with the family may run through the problem-solving discussions.

The timing of problem-solving work is important. It should coincide with the growth of improved understanding between the family members and the progress in relationship building. Premature problem-solving efforts, which may occur either as technical errors by the therapist or as a result of anxiety and pressure of the parents, need not impede the therapy process but can become pitfalls if the therapist fails to recognize the inappropriate timing and persists with the problem-solving endeavor. An even greater danger would be to overemphasize problem-solving work by making it the totality of the therapy process. It is nothing more than a component that must be integrated with the broader and deeper process of the family therapy. Problem solving in and of itself can have little therapeutic value.

One might wonder if the problem-solving component in family therapy can be used and developed with less sophisticated, less intelligent, less verbal, and less self-examining people than the members of the D family. Can it be productive and effective, for example, with economically, socially, and culturally deprived families? The author has found that the component is applicable with such families as well. Geismar and Krisberg also found it applicable.[8] The level and content of discussion is usually more direct and concrete than with more sophisticated clients.

Summary

The problem-solving component in family therapy has been closely examined using verbatim excerpts from tape-recorded interviews, and its roots in the context of the total treatment process has been shown. Helping a family deal constructively with the reality problems besetting it has direct and indirect therapeutic effects on the deeper, underlying relationship conflicts and pathological forces. As the family members progress in solving their reality problems and their relationships become more emotionally gratifying and fulfilling, family life is strengthened and growth in individual family members also takes place. Attention has been called to possible pitfalls in terms of overemphasis and inappropriate timing in the use and development of the problem-solving component, with consequent insufficient work on the deeper feelings and conflicts in the relationships. The therapist's role as a parent figure, catalyst, and discussion leader has been presented.

References

1.   For the author's philosophy and methodology of family therapy, see David Hallowitz and Albert V. Cutter, The Family Unit Approach in Therapy: Uses, Process, and Dynamics, in *Casework Papers, 1961* (New York: Family Service Association of America, 1961), pp. 44–57; and David Hallowitz, Individual Treatment of the Child in the Context of Family Therapy, *Social Casework*, 47:82–86 (February 1966).

2.   David Hallowitz et al., The Assertive Counseling Component of Therapy, *Social Casework*, 48: 543–48 (November 1967).

3.   John Elderkin Bell, The Theoretical Position for Family Group Therapy, *Family Process*, 2:9 (March 1963).

4.   Ludwig L. Geismar and Jane Krisberg, The Family Life Improvement Project: An Experiment in Preventive Intervention: Part II, *Social Casework*, 47:664 (December 1966).

5.   Helen Harris Perlman, *Social Casework: A Problem-solving Process* (Chicago: University of Chicago Press, 1957).

6.   Kurt Spitzer and Betty Welsh, A Problem Focused Model of Practice, *Social Casework*, 50: 323–29 (June 1969).

7.   David Hallowitz and Burton Stulberg, The Vicious Cycle in Parent-Child Relationship Breakdown, *Social Casework*, 40:268–75 (May 1959).

8.   Geismar and Krisberg, The Family Life Improvement Project, p. 664.

16
Feedback in Family Interviewing

Robert A. Brown

Social work interviews are complex transactions that may provide clues to understanding change in clients. Bartlett, Briar, Greenwood, and Gordon suggest that the interview process should be investigated so that elements of professional practice may be identified.[1] Whereas counseling was once characterized by free association and nondirective techniques, it now includes such constructs as aggressive intervention, confrontation, and feedback. For many years social workers did not provide specific information to clients about themselves. However, this is not characteristic of contemporary practice.

The concept of feedback is not well defined as it applies to interviews. Feedback may be communicated both verbally and nonverbally. In its simplest form, it represents one person's attempt to communicate information to another. Although the information may be provided surreptitiously through questions or inferential statements, its most direct form is the declarative statement. When a social worker uses a declarative statement to communicate information concerning the client with whom he is interacting at the moment, he is using a specialized form of feedback. Because this occurs repeatedly in social work interviews, the process should be more clearly understood.

The author calls this type of feedback "ascription." Because it occurs repeatedly and should therefore be under the conscious control of the interviewer, it should be considered an interviewing technique. With this in mind some important questions are raised: to what extent is feedback sanctioned by current theories of social work practice? What information is provided and how is it received by clients? When does the technique appear to work? In this article the author discusses the various applications of ascription utilized by the major social work theorists and describes a research

Source: From *Social Work* 18:5 (September 1973), pp. 52–59. Copyright © 1973 by the National Association of Social Workers. Reprinted by permission.

project that identified ascriptive statements made by social workers in interviews and their clients' responses. [2]

The author defines "technique" as one of the many specific acts each participant in a relationship uses to accomplish his purposes. "Client system," as he defines it, includes the interfacing of biological, psychological, and social systems within the individual client, as well as the similar interfacings of individuals who are related to the client and each other through a family system. Thus a client system may comprise one or many persons.

"Ascription" is the act attributing or imputing a characteristic to someone. [3] For the purposes of this article, the characteristic ascribed may be anyone that the social worker perceives in the client and communicates to him. It may refer to physical, psychological, or social attributes of an individual or a group, including their relationships. It may have a socially positive or negative meaning and it may refer to the past, present, or future. The only criterion is that the statement clearly impute something to the client with whom the worker is interacting in the interview. For instance, a worker may say to a client "You look depressed" or tell a family "You have been having fun together."

This definition of ascription includes interpretations given to clients but also something more. Whereas interpretations bring "an alternative frame of reference to bear on a set of observations or behaviors with an end in view of making them more amenable to manipulation," ascriptions may also reinforce an existing frame of reference in the client. [4] For example, a simple statement of agreement ("Yes, you are right!") or of support ("You certainly handled that well!") may seek to reinforce the client's own interpretation.

The author defines an "ascriptive episode" as that part of the interview which begins with an ascriptive statement, spoken by a social worker, and ends with a shift away from the ascribed characteristic. In most instances the episode includes a client's responses to the ascription.

Social Work Theories

All the major theorists in social casework, social group work, family treatment, and combined practice include provisions for workers to offer their observations, discoveries, and conclusions to clients.

SOCIAL CASEWORK

In Hollis's framework, the purpose of such statements is to help clients reflect on themselves and their environmental situation (e.g., "I have a feeling that you may be afraid I will criticize you."). [5] Perlman uses ascriptive comments that may reflect the client's feelings and offer interpretations or support to maximize the client's participation in the problem-solving process.[6] Other casework theorists use ascription to interpret the client's behavior in the treatment relationship,[7] to point out recurrent behavioral patterns,[8] or to help clients achieve valid ego identities.[9]

SOCIAL GROUP WORK

Social group work theorists have tended to focus on the social workers' actions and goals that precipitate change in clients. Ascriptions are used by Northen principally to enhance the client's perception of reality by calling attention to an emotion so that an integration of cognitive and affective components within the client may be promoted.[10] However, ascriptions also lend themselves to other aspects of the social worker's role, such as providing support, improving communication, enhancing competence, and modifying the environment.[11] Schwartz uses ascriptions to present the client's problem to him in a new form.[12] Ascriptions may be used in all the worker's tasks (e.g., to detect and challenge the obstacles that obscure and frustrate the client).[13]

Phillips limits ascription to providing information clients could not provide themselves. Her purpose is to enhance the client's sense of his relation to others through a shared experience.[14] The interview itself, which is a shared experience, offers the best perspective for ascriptive statements because it is immediately accessible to all the participants. .

Vinter uses ascription to modify the behavior of group members. In his framework ascriptive statements are made by workers who act as "spokesmen of norms" and "stimulators of potentials."[15] The purpose of Konopka's use of ascription is to individualize and enhance the social functioning of group members as well as the entire group. She would probably stress the worker's dynamic, conscious use of himself while implementing an interview technique and would use only ascriptive statements that have socially positive implications.[16]

FAMILY TREATMENT

Theorists of family treatment, such as Overton and Tinker, utilize ascriptive statements as "shared observations." These observations focus empathically on the behavioral indicators, both positive and negative, that constitute the reason for a professional investment in the family. The purpose of these observations is to bring about a change-oriented partnership of the worker and the family. From this perspective, most ascriptive statements would be directed toward the family-as-a-whole rather than individual family members.[17]

Satir stresses two roles for the worker: a model of communication and a resource person who provides a family with impartial information about itself.[18] Others in family treatment use ascriptive statements to confront clients with their inconsistencies,[19] to challenge individual family members,[20] or to draw attention to transactional family patterns.[21]

COMBINED PRACTICE

Smalley's and Polansky's theories relate to combined practice with individuals and groups. Smalley uses ascription for the purpose of enhancing a client's psychological growth through the worker's frank expression of his own understanding.[22] Polansky notes that a client's willingness to communicate is partially dependent on the worker's skill in receiving a client's communication.[23] Use of ascriptions may be considered one such skill.

Thus one may see that in some form ascription is sanctioned by all major social work theorists. These theorists agree that experiences shared by workers and clients result in self-awareness and changes in behavioral patterns in clients. They differ regarding the worker's role in providing these experiences and the purposes behind his actions. That is, most theoriticians provide for ascriptive statements that vary in their degree of directness, ranging, for instance, from reflective consideration to aggressive intervention.

Although theories of social work are descriptive of practice situations, they do not suggest how ascriptions produce change in clients. Buckley has proposed a systemic model of interaction that emphasizes the client's learning of symbols and the exchange of information in client-system functioning.[24] From Buckley's model it may be concluded that ascriptive statements produce change in two ways: as instruments of communication and as feedback to client systems.

As instruments of communication or statements in a conversation, ascriptions represent an opportunity for social workers and clients to achieve a "common mapping of the environment" or an exchange of information that alters the cognitive organization and hence the concept of self and the environment of both the client and worker.[25] They are not labels with which clients must wrestle, but statements in conversation that generate new understanding for everyone. Consider, for example, what happens when a client rejects an ascription with: "No, in fact I feel rather good."

Research Design

In research conducted by the author between September 1969 and December 1970, tape-recorded interviews with families were used to identify selected statements made by social workers and to note clients' responses. Twenty fieldwork instructors from schools of social work in the Los Angeles metropolitan area agreed to tape-record a one-hour interview with a family. This was both a random sample and a universal survey of instructors conducting family interviews who were willing to participate.

Characteristics of social workers in the sample were compared with characteristics of an NASW membership survey.[26] The sample was biased in favor of interviews conducted by social workers in private practice, in psychiatric services, or in family services other than public services. Characteristics of social workers in the sample and in the NASW survey were not otherwise significantly different.

Characteristics of the clients in the sample did not differ significantly from a Los Angeles County population survey with respect to ethnic backgrounds; however, clients in the sample had greater social position and status than had been assumed. Thus, except for the biasing factors noted, the interviews that were studied were typical of all social work family interviews.

A total of 526 ascriptions were identified in 20 one-hour interviews. Each example was analyzed by the researcher and two other judges through the use of questionnaires, completed by the workers.[27] Descriptive and evaluative data were gathered that related to the purpose for which each statement was made, its content, various factors related to the communication process, and the client's reactions. A linguistic analysis of selected phrases and words used by clients and workers during ascription was done by computer.

All social workers in the sample used ascriptive statements, which indicates that the technique is used extensively. The average number of ascriptive statements used in each interview was 26. However, the frequency of use was subject to great variation among the workers.

Of a total of 526 statements, 85 percent stimulated immediate verbal responses from clients. Thus one may conclude that the ascriptive episode was an experience shared by participants in the interviews and from which a mutual view of the environment could result. What type of experience was it? Apparently it focused on the individual at the time of the interview.

Instruments of Communication

Although these were family interviews, workers tended to focus on individual members instead of the family-as-a-whole or some subgroup. Most ascriptive statements (83 percent) were addressed only to one person and relatively few (17 percent) to subgroups. Therefore, the "shared experiences" were primarily experiences shared by a social worker and one family member while other members observed or shared the experience in a secondary way.

It is the author's impression that few ascriptive statements stimulated an overt dialogue among family members. This finding is in contrast to Overton's and Tinker's concept of the worker's partnership with the family-as-a-whole and suggests that workers may be overlooking one method of increasing family interaction by not addressing ascriptive statements to the entire family. The author believes that if a substantial number of ascriptions were directed to the family-as-a-whole, a sense of relationship would increase among family members. For example, consider the difference between the worker stating: "You missed her message" and "That message got lost between you."

It is also interesting to note that 52 percent of the ascriptive statements related to what had just occurred in the interview (e.g., "You seemed angry just then.") This supports Phillips's belief that the present offers the best perspective for enhancing a sense of relationship through shared experiences. However, if the purpose of an ascription is to provide feedback, clients are more likely to evaluate critically the ascribed characteristic when it is expressed in a universal time reference (e.g., "You spend a great deal of time being angry.")

If the goal is to enhance a sense of relationship or to achieve a common mapping of the environment, the worker should project himself, as a real person, into the interview. Yet, ascriptions contained few statements that specifically included the worker (e.g., "You seem to me... "). In effect, clients were asked to consider ascribed characteristics as characteristics by themselves, not as the perceptions of a worker. The author believes that these statements should be clearly identified as the interviewer's perceptions.

The frequency with which social workers and clients use common symbols is a measure of the extent to which they share a common environment. The workers referred to others by name (noun or pronoun) twice as frequently as they did to themselves ("I, me"), and they referred to themselves in singular form seven times more frequently than in plural form. When a social worker refers to himself and his clients together, calling attention to "us," "our," or "we," he is focusing on their mutual relationship in treatment and, in effect, is mapping a common environment.

The extent to which ascriptive statements lend structure to an interview is another indication of how "shared" the experience really is. Using the number of ideas contained in the statements and clients' responses as a measure, ascriptive episodes were found to be rather simple instruments of communication that provided little overall structure to the interview. Most such statements (69 percent) and most responses of clients (57 percent) contained no more than two distinct ideas.

A client's opportunity to respond is another indication of structure in the interview. Workers gave clients an opportunity to respond to 85 percent of the ascriptive statements. However, when clients were blocked from responding, the worker's activity was the most apparent cause. Generally, this activity consisted of the worker oververbalizing or otherwise diverting the client's attention from the ascribed characteristic.

Feedback To Client Systems

The second major way in which ascriptions produce change is as feedback to systems. In feedback the worker gives clients specific pieces of information about themselves. Feedback produces change because the ascribed characteristic turns experience of the individual or the family group back on itself, producing a symbol of the individual or the family. This "organized self" represents a learned set of attitudes the individual and the family members maintain about themselves and their environment.

Self-consciousness and self-control are mechanisms of feedback that are internal to the client system. Ascriptions represent feedback that is external to the system. If they are understood and accepted by the client, ascriptions become a part of the client's self-consciousness. To be accepted by a client, an ascription must in some way relate to his goals and must meet criteria he sets.[28]

The feedback provided in ascriptive statements reflects the fundamental concern of the social work profession for relationships between people. However, an analysis of selected phrases spoken by social workers and clients during ascriptive episodes indicates that although both workers and clients focused on a discussion behavior, workers expressed relatively more interest in the clients' relationships than did the clients themselves.

A classification of the observed ascriptive statements is presented in Table 1. Relationship statements—the most frequently observed type—included statements such as "You and your mother argue about things" and "You were beginning to say you wished something different from her." Behavior-oriented statements included "You are talking about your mother and she is sitting next to you." and "You said you try not to give way to yelling quite so much." Feeling statements included "You noticed him getting scared" and "I think what you want is for him to feel more cheerful." Value statements included "I think we should keep on working on this last thing" and "I think we will have to think about the good start he has made and not get lost." Other ascriptive statements referred to cognition, environment, agreement, and disagreement.

Although the author recognizes that agreement can be communicated without using words, such as nodding, it was thought that verbal feedback expressing agreement would be used by workers (e.g., "Yes, you are right!"). However, no examples were identified in the data. It is believed that this type of feedback is an important facet of bringing about change in clients. Thus if workers did not use ascription to express agreement, what were their

TABLE 1.   Types of Ascriptive Statements

TYPE OF STATEMENT	NUMBER	PERCENT
Relationship	164	31.2
Behavior	117	22.2
Feeling	105	20.0
Value	72	13.7
Other	68	12.9
Total	526	100.0

motives? As Table 2 shows, the principal reasons for use of ascription were to improve the client's perceptions of reality and to improve communication with the client.

It is of interest to note that the purpose of 90 percent of the ascriptive statements was to produce change and only 10 percent to support clients. Providing supportive information, such as bringing out the client's strengths, is surely a viable facet of producing change. Intuitively, at least, it would seem to warrant proportionally greater use than was revealed in these data.

What evidence is there that clients are involved in the feedback process? Evaluation by the judges indicated that 82 percent of the ascriptive statements were percieved and 80 percent were considered by clients, but only 46 percent were critically evaluated. This suggests that workers may need to redirect their clients' attention to the ascribed characteristic and to ask them to evaluate it. This was rarely done among the sample tested.

TABLE 2.   Social Workers' Judgments of their
Purpose in Making Ascriptive Statements [a]

PURPOSE OF STATEMENT	NUMBER	PERCENT
To improve the client's perception of reality	239	46.05
To improve communication with the client	161	31.02
To help the client achieve competence in his actions	59	11.37
To support the client	54	10.40
To use environmental resources	6	1.16
Total	519 [b]	100.00

[a] Assuming an equal probability of occurrence among the categories, the probability associated with the observed frequencies in each category was beyond the $p = .0000$ level.

[b] The remaining seven statements were not classified in this framework.

In general, clients used profitably those statements they considered but did not evaluate. They used them, for example, as a point of departure to another subject or to be woven into another overriding thought. The judges found that 62 percent of the ascriptions that were evaluated were accepted and only 9 percent were clearly rejected by clients. They further found that children rarely evaluated ascriptions critically, whereas adults, especially men, did. Some questions are raised, therefore, concerning the effect of ascriptions on children. Together, these data indicate that about half the ascriptive statements were used by clients in a meaningful way. To the author's knowledge, there are no other research findings available that indicate whether a 50 percent level is cause for alarm, indifference, or celebration.

The judges agreed that ascriptions were most helpful when they were expressed clearly, simply, and directly and when workers explained that the statements were their perceptions, not objective facts. Ascriptions were helpful when their expression reflected a sensitive awareness of the client, when they were not judgmental, and when they permitted responses from the client. They were also helpful when their content related to the client's feelings, behaviors, or central problem area or to the communication process within the family or the interview.

Conclusion

In this article some facets of the feedback process have been examined as they apply to social work interviews with families. Feedback is sanctioned by theories of practice and is widely used by social workers. The information given to clients reflects the profession's concern with human relationships. However, because its use is undisciplined, many opportunities are missed to use the process more effectively. If the worker considers the feedback process as an interview technique, he might bring its use under conscious control. For instance, before using an ascription, he should know whether his purpose is to increase a sense of relatedness or to provide needed information, or both. Used as a technique, ascriptions can produce changes if they bring the worker and client together in a way that is dynamic and meaningful to both.

References

1. Harriett Bartlett, "The Place and Use of Knowledge in Social Work Practice," *Social Work* 9 (July 1964), p. 40; Scott Briar, "The Casework Predicament," *Social*

Work, 13 (January 1968) p. 10; Ernest Greenwood, "Research on the Clarification of Casework Concepts: A Review of and Commentary on the Nolan Study," p. 67, unpublished manuscript, University of California at Berkeley, 1965; and William Gordon, "A Critique of the Working Definition," *Social Work,* 7 (October 1962), p. 11.

2. Findings are reported in greater detail in Robert A. Brown, "The Technique of Ascription." Unpublished doctoral dissertation, University of Southern California, 1971.

3. C. L. Barnhart, ed. *The American College Dictionary* (New York: Random House, 1964), p. 73.

4. Leon H. Levy, *Psychological Interpretation* (New York: Holt, Rinehart & Winston, 1963), p. 7.

5. Florence Hollis, *Casework: A Psychosocial Therapy* (New York: Random House, 1964), pp. 71–75, 91–93, and 104–106; and Hollis, "Crisis-Focused Casework in a Child Guidance Clinic," *Social Casework,* 49 (January 1968), p. 41.

6. Helen Harris Perlman, *Social Casework: A Problem-Solving Process* (Chicago: University of Chicago Press, 1957), p. 159.

7. Herbert H. Aptekar, *The Dynamics of Casework and Counseling* (New York: Riverside Press, 1955), p. 236.

8. Alice Ullman and Milton Davis, "Assessing the Medical Patient's Motivation and Ability to Work," *Social Casework,* 46 (April 1965), p. 201; and Ann W. Shyne, "An Experimental Study of Casework Methods" *Social Casework,* 46 (November 1965), p. 535–541.

9. Elizabeth Meier, "Interactions Between the Person and His Operational Situation: A Basis for Classification in Casework," *Social Casework,* 46 (November 1965), p. 547; and Herbert S. Strean, "Casework with Ego-Fragmented Parents," *Social Casework,* 49 (April 1968), p. 226.

10. Helen Northen, *Social Work with Groups* (New York: Columbia University Press, 1969), p. 73.

11. Ibid., pp. 52–85.

12. William Schwartz, "Group Work and the Social Scene," *Issues in American Social Work* (New York: Columbia University Press, 1959), pp. 134–135; and Schwartz, "Toward a Strategy of Group Work Practice," *Social Service Review,* 36 (September 1962), pp. 268–279.

13. William Schwartz, "The Social Worker in the Group," *The Social Welfare Forum, 1961* (New York: Columbia University Press, 1961), pp. 157–158.

14. Helen U. Phillips, *Essentials of Social Group Work Skill* (New York: Association Press, 1957), pp. 93, 133–134, and 149–153.

15. Robert D. Vinter, "Approach to Group Work Practice" and "The Essential Components of Social Group Work Practice" in Vinter, ed., *Readings in Group Work Practice* (Ann Arbor, Mich.: Campus Publishers, 1967), pp. 3 and 26 respectively.

16. Gisela Konopka, *Social Group Work: A Helping Process* (Englewood Cliffs, N.J.: Prentice-Hall, 1963), pp. 163–171. This represents a shift in thinking from Konopka's earlier position that only the client may draw interpretations. For further details *see* Konopka, *Group Work in the Institution* (New York: William Morrow & Co., 1954),

p. 123; and Konopka, "Social Group Work: A Social Work Method," *Social Work*, 5 (October 1960), p. 59.

17. Alice Overton and Katherine Tinker, *Casework Notebook* (St. Paul, Minn.: Greater St. Paul Community Chest & Councils, 1957), pp. 39–40.

18. Virginia M. Satir, *Conjoint Family Therapy: A Guide to Theory and Technique* (Palo Alto, Calif.: Science and Behavior Books, 1964), p. 97; and Satir, "Conjoint Family Therapy," in Bernard L. Green, ed., *The Psychotherapies of Marital Disharmony* (New York: Free Press, 1965), pp. 132–133.

19. David Hallowitz, Ralph Bierman et al., "The Assertive Counseling Component of Therapy," *Social Casework*, 48 (November 1967), p. 546.

20. Robert M. Nadal, "Interviewing Style and Foster Parents' Verbal Accessibility," *Child Welfare*, 46 (April 1967), p. 211.

21. Donald R. Bardill, "A Relationship-Focused Approach to Marital Problems," *Social Work*, 11 (July 1966), p. 76; Murray H. Sherman, Nathan Ackerman, Stanford N. Sherman, and Celia Mitchell, "Non-Verbal Cue and Reenactment of Conflict in Family Therapy," *Family Process*, 4 (March 1965), pp. 133–162; Rae B. Weiner, "Adolescent Problems: Symptoms of Family Dysfunctioning," *Social Casework*, 47 (June 1966), pp. 373–377; Frances H. Scherz, "Multiple-Client Interviewing: Treatment Interpretations," *Social Casework*, 43 (March 1962), pp. 234–240; and Arthur Leader, "The Role of Intervention in Family-Group Treatment," *Social Casework*, 45 (June 1964), p. 328.

22. Ruth E. Smalley, *Theory for Social Work Practice* (New York: Columbia University Press, 1967), pp. 130 and 139.

23. Norman A. Polansky, "The Concept of Verbal Accessibility," *Smith College Studies in Social Work*, 36 (October 1956), pp. 4–6.

24. Walter Buckley, *Sociology and the Modern Systems Theory* (Englewood Cliffs, N.J.: Prentice-Hall, 1967).

25. Ibid., p. 124.

26. *See* Alfred M. Stamm, "NASW Membership: Characteristics, Deployment, and Salaries," *Personnel Information*, 12 (May 1969), p. 1.

27. The .05 level of significance was required to reject the null hypothesis. Findings reported here were at or well beyond this level. In many instances, alternative probability models were used to confirm findings. The criterion level of .02 determined reliability of judgments.

28. Buckley, op. cit., p. 174.

17
Home Family Counseling

Joseph H. Golner

Home Family Counseling (HFC) involves counseling the entire family in the home on a regular basis. The counseling team consists of the counselor plus a group of helping persons assigned by community social and education agencies to assist one or more of the family members.

Evolution

The author first carried out HFC as part of a research project sponsored by the Judge Baker Guidance Center and the Newton, Massachusetts, public schools from 1964 through 1966. The objectives were to explore new ways of reaching antisocial children and their families, diagnose needs of both children and families, and refer them to appropriate individuals or agencies in the community. In order to fulfill the threefold requirements of the project—acting as referral agent in accord with the research design, helping improve the children's behavior at the school's demand, and meeting needs of parents who could not keep office appointments—the author introduced the HFC intervention technique whereby all members of the family are interviewd at the same time during regular home visits. This technique was designed to prepare and motivate families for referral and simultaneously bring about some behavior modification in the children.

When school personnel or community agencies were engaged in a helping intervention on behalf of children and their families, HFC was not used. In such cases the HFC counselor's responsibility was to verify that the helping agencies were serving these children and to see that relevant agencies were in touch with each other.

During the next two years the HFC model evolved further under the auspices of the North Reading, Massachusetts, High School in cooperation

Source: From Social Work 16:4 (October 1971), pp. 63–71. Copyright © 1971 by the National Association of Social Workers. Reprinted by permission.

with the Eastern Middlesex Guidance Center. The project was not limited to antisocial children, and the counselor was responsible not only for helping children with a variety of school-related problems, but also for helping school personnel and community agency workers become sensitized to the family's role in the evolution and resolution of the children's problems. Guidance counselors, probation officers, and nurses of the five towns served by the guidance center and staff members of the center were invited to attend HFC meetings. At first they were silent observers; later they were encouraged to become active participants, which enriched the HFC sessions.

From 1968 to the present, HFC has continued to develop, and there has been increased involvement of community helping persons. Responsibility for the child and family members in relation to referral problems has been delegated to a key person, often the professional in the community to whom the family first turned for help. When a professional could not be recruited to assume this responsibility, appropriate nonprofessionals have been invited to take the role of the key person.

Goals

Goals have changed since HFC was started. Its present goals are to (1) modify the behavior of referred children, particularly those from low-income families, (2) modify behavior of other members of the children's families and improve family relationships, (3) refer family members to appropriate school and community services and coordinate these services, and (4) maximize the effectiveness of key persons helping the family.

HFC techniques represent a departure from the clinical-medical model and movement toward an educational model in regard to their focus on (1) the responsibility of key persons, (2) the home setting for treatment and the family group as the target, (3) family interactions in the here and now, (4) active efforts to solve problems, and (5) the family members' strengths.

Key Persons

Primary responsibility for the referred child and his family is assigned to a key person, usually a professional in one of the community's helping servies. This key person may be a physician, nurse, clergyman, lawyer, school principal, teacher, guidance counselor, or other professional or a nonprofessional whom the family trusts and respects—perhaps a housewife or neighborhood leader. The HFC counselor is presented to the family as an informal consultant to the key person and as an additional resource for assisting the family to improve its communication.

On the strength of mutual understanding and good relationships with the family, the key person motivates family members to request and utilize HFC by pointing out it advantages and helping them to see which HFC goals are relevant to the family's requirements and expectations. The key person also has overall responsibility for coordinating the family's needs with appropriate community services. Therefore, he has the option of inviting all relevant helping persons from the school and community to serve as members of the counseling team during home visits. Personal involvement of relevant helpers can make possible a simultaneous interpretation of needs and services. It avoids duplication of time, energy, and services by the community and prevents the feelings of rejection that are prevalent among families seeking help.

The HFC counselor sees the family during the home visit only, but he is available to the key persons at other times as well. He has an obligation to share his understanding of family dynamics with members of the counseling team. They in turn share with him the insights of their respective disciplines. Exchange and integration of understanding takes place during the home visit, which is designed to widen the perspective of both the HFC counselor and team members.

Counseling Team Seminars

To supplement the exchange that occurs during the home visit, an hour-long seminar is held—usually each week—for all helping persons involved in the program. The seminar's objectives are to (1) permit the counseling teams to share their experiences and conceptualizations, (2) evaluate HFC's strengths and weaknesses, and (3) modify procedures to accommodate the changing needs and styles of the client families and their helpers.

The seminar includes both structured and nonstructured agendas. The nonstructured agenda calls for the HFC counselor, key persons, and other counseling team members to simulate a "family" to a limited degree so that they may better perceive their own helping roles. The primary objective of such simulation is to understand the client family; personal therapeutic gain to seminar participants is incidental. This emphasis differentiates the seminar from sensitivity training and psychotherapy groups in which the primary objective is personal therapy for the participants.

The structured agenda calls for discussions in which key persons and other team members take major responsibility for evaluating HFC results. When the families occasionally attend seminars to report their impressions of

HFC, they are explicitly presented to seminar participants as resource persons rather than clients.

Professionals and Nonprofessionals

The assignment of major responsibility to the professional key persons is supported by observations of community mental health studies. Cowen, Gardner, and Zax point up the valuable role of those individuals whose everyday functions in society place them in an influential position vis-à-vis mental health problems.[1] These persons are trusted, authoritative, and influential professionals—other than mental health clinic professionals—who come into frequent contact with people at times when the personality is most modifiable, e.g., during crises and early childhood. A mental health consultant can help these significant persons to maximize their effectiveness. The attractiveness of such cooperation resides in its geometric potential, for the professional key persons have much influence with many people. It is expected that what the consultant contributes to their effectiveness in HFC will carry over to their subsequent everyday work.

There is support also for assigning nonprofessionals to helping roles, especially with low-income families. Cowen, Gardner, and Zax note that nonprofessionals—housewives, neighborhood leaders, and college students are in a "better position" than mental health clinic professionals to help low-income persons for the following reasons:

1. The nonprofessional may have greater energy and enthusiasm and become more involved.

2. Clients see the nonprofessional as a peer, whereas they view the clinic professional as an unapproachable authority with whom they cannot communicate.

3. The nonprofessional is less formal and less rigid. He can do things that the clinic professional by virtue of tradition and role prescription ordinarily cannot or will not do.

4. To cite Rioch, nonprofessionals bring fresh points of view, flexible attitudes, and new methods that professionals would have rejected as unsophisticated, improbable, or foolish.[2]

Thus traditional training in the mental health professions may be neither optimal nor necessary for promoting therapeutic behavioral change in clients. Instead training of nonprofessionals should be used to

> activate systematized and searching reflection about relevant people or situations and to help build confidence and security under relatively nonthreatening circumstances.[3]

The nonprofessionals selected to serve as key persons in HFC should therefore be individuals who—by personality, life experience, or whatever—have much to offer others. "It would be unwise to tamper excessively with their styles and natural reflexes by teaching them the 'right' way to do things."[4]

Home Visits

The setting of HFC is in the home rather than in the office and the target of intervention is the family group rather than the individual. There must be at least one parent and one child in the family unit. Beyond that, the family is encouraged to invite all relevant members whether or not they reside in the home. Friends, neighbors, and pets are also welcome.

The home visit is one hour a week, and the number of visits is determined by the family and counseling team. The visit takes place in the parental home of the "problem" child who was originally considered for referral. The family chooses the room to be used for the visits.

Family members are asked to express their feelings freely without fear of recrimination, yet without obstructing normal parental authority. Freedom of speech implies the obligation to listen to the speaker, as well as the freedom to remain silent. Young children may play quietly, but must not interrupt those speaking. Parents, and other family members as well, are encouraged to accept responsibility for their own feelings and opinions. They are discouraged from "volunteering" others to talk in their behalf or volunteering to talk for others.

Emphasis on the home and the family is supported by Levine. In her home treatment approach all family members were present and the social worker related to all of them. Levine's focus on the family as a group was based on the conviction that psychopathology is an integral part of socioeconomic pathology and cannot be treated in isolation from other problems and other family members who are contaminated by the same set of influences.[5] She concludes that home treatment should prove more economical in the long run because problems are revealed in the living situation, distortions are eliminated, diagnoses are more accurate, the treatment process can be utilized quickly, and progress toward resolving conflict can be more rapid. Because all family members participate, all can benefit and thus do not usually need individual or successive referrals. Above all, time, money, and manpower are conserved, and the effort expended initially to identify the sources of problems for all family members should assure more lasting improvement.[6]

Here-and-Now Focus

The HFC counselor focuses on the family's current interactions rather than the individual's past experiences. Emphasis is placed on the here and now. The here and now involves examination of feelings and reactions to behaviors that occur during the home visit and within the HFC meeting room. Feelings about and reactions to experiences occurring at other times and places and the examination of behavioral motivations are deferred for private reflection by the individual, who is encouraged to seek the assistance of the key person and other appropriate members of the counseling team between HFC meetings.

Although past experiences and behavioral motivations are recognized as highly significant, their use sometimes inadvertently obscures the meaning of the here and now and therefore tends to weaken the impact of immediate feedback on one's behavior. References to past experiences, future expectations, and behavioral motivations are welcomed only when they are used either to recognize competence in family members or to understand better the implications of the here-and-now analysis—not when individual pathology is thereby identified.

This emphasis on the here and now derives its major impetus from a study that the author conducted at the end of the Newton-Baker phase of HFC, in which he attempted to ascertain HFC's effect on certain pathological dimensions characterizing family interaction.[7] From records of HFC sessions with six families over a ten-month period, he identified twelve dimensions. He later discovered that these dimensions were directly related to certain patterns of family interaction, which predictive studies by the Thom Clinic had previously isolated as patterns producing antisocial traits.[8]

The dimensions found most pertinent by a panel of six independent guidance counselors were (1) denial versus acknowledgment of helping person's interest and (2) inability versus ability to express feelings. These two dimensions contain the essence of here-and-now issues and reflect the function of feedback; the other ten contain there-and-then issues and relate primarily to criteria of task achievement.[9] Consequently, a here-and-now emphasis might contribute to HFC's success. In turn, this emphasis might ultimately be responsible for changing family members along there-and-then dimensions.

Seating Arrangement

The HFC counselor takes a problem-engaging, problem-seeking stand and adopts the active role of educator. For this role he uses both demonstrations and intervention, which are carried out through a special seating arrangement and symbolic role-playing.

The family is first asked to "indulge" the HFC counselor in a gamelike seating arrangement. The father is asked to sit to the mother's right. The sons sit to the father's right and the daughters to the mother's left, according to order of birth, with the oldest sibling sitting next to the parent. Maternal grandparents sit to the left of the youngest daughter, paternal grandparents to the right of the youngest son. Others, such as neighbors and friends, are invited to join the family circle, but not to come between family members.

Empty chairs are left for missing family members, irrespective of the reasons for or duration of absence. The empty chair represents both the actual family member and also the ideal qualities desired in that person. It points up the significance of missing family members as well as the increased importance of those present. In some families symbols are used to identify the absent occupant. For example, "God" may be perceived by some families as occupying the absent parent's chair until such time as the original parent returns or a new parent is added to the family.

Young children may sit in their assigned places or move around the room freely. They may sit on empty chairs if they wish only to express warmth and tenderness to the chair's owner, not to take his place or encroach on his rights in any manner.

The seating arrangement is designed to reinforce the parental administration of the family and the legitimate family authority figures, to assign each family member his rightful place in the family circle, and to differentiate family members according to age and sex. Seeing that one may learn clockwise, counterclockwise, and around the circle dramatizes the ability of family members to learn from each other. Thus parents learn from their children and from each other and juniors and seniors learn from one another, as do brothers and sisters.

Symbolic Role-Playing

During the session the key person, the HFC counselor, and other members of the counseling team are encouraged to become symbolic family members. Role assignments, as far as possible, are consistent with sexual, chronological, and professional differences characterizing the counseling team. For example, if the key person is a woman, she becomes the symbolic mother and the HFC counselor the symbolic father. If both key person and HFC counselor are men, the key person becomes the symbolic father, the counselor takes another role, and a symbolic mother is recruited. A role-playing unit of at least two symbolic family members is required. A professional helping person identified primarily with the child takes the role of symbolic son or daughter. A professional person identified primarily with a parent may take a symbolic parent's role. Such assignments of course do not preclude the desirability for symbolic parents to empathize with children and symbolic children to empathize with parents.

The counseling persons do not artificially try to assume and act out family members' feelings. Rather, they try to express honestly their own spontaneous feelings in the roles they are playing—without being inhibited by the usual social or professional restraints. Their feelings and reactions are then ascribed to the respective family members and are interpreted as being similar to those that the family members might experience. The more honest the counseling persons' expressions are, the more honest the family can become and the more meaningful the visit can be. Conversely, family members' reactions during the role-playing are interpreted as being similar to those of the respective counseling persons.

Inherent in symbolic role-playing is the opportunity to teach through example and experience rather than through intellectual formulations. Family members tend to pay more attention to how members of the HFC counseling team behave toward each other than to how they clarify and interpret points of view. Questions like the following are the family's ultimate concern: Can the counseling "parent" express tenderness toward his "spouse," "parents," and "children"? Can he accept similar feelings from them? Does he respect their feelings and opinions? Can he admit his mistakes and atone for them? Can he forgive others' mistakes?

Having both senior-level and junior-level persons on the counseling team—such as a clinic director and a social work student—provides another kind of example that extends dimensions of learning and widens opportunities for growth. For grandparents and children, the presence of counseling persons who are close to their own hierarchical position is a strong stimulus for expressing their feelings and rectifying undesirable attitudes and behavior.

Focus on Strengths and Competence

The HFC counselor does not presume illness in the family and avoids diagnostic labeling. Individual defenses or levels of maturity are not his concern. Rather, he focuses on the strengths of family members and encourages the expression of warm, tender feelings. Such warmth is one of the objectives of symbolic role-playing. Also, because the counseling persons express themselves honestly and freely, the family is challenged to perceive them as real persons rather than as omnipotent beings. This change in perspective permits family members to see themselves as competent.

A special opportunity to reinforce their sense of competence presents itself toward the end of the visit during the evaluation period. At that time everyone is given a chance to express his feelings about the meeting's effectiveness. At first family members may hesitate to voice their gripes because they feel that the HFC counselor is omniscient and cannot make mistakes. Instead their grievances may go underground and lead to premature termination. Therefore, it is important that the key person and other team members openly express any dissatisfaction to the HFC counselor during the visit. In doing so, they demonstrate that acknowledging grievances is legitimate; at the same time they provide the family with a powerful stimulus to perceive its competence.

The family members are best able to clarify the counseling person's perceptions. They alone know whether HFC helped them. However, their judgment regarding HFC's helpfulness is less significant than the sense of competence they achieve in arriving at the judgment.

Case Illustration

The following representative example shows how HFC helped one referred child and his family. It has been summarized from a case illustration prepared by a key person.

The B family was referred for HFC in early May 1968 by the Division of Child Guardianship, Massachusetts Department of Public Welfare, which was serving the mother, and the Somerville Guidance Center, which was serving her and Phil, the problem child. Both agencies felt that the family needed additional help because of the summer gap in the center's activities and the seriousness of the situation.

The atmosphere in the home had grown increasingly tense as Phil had begun to act out more flagrantly and frequently, setting fires and befouling the walls of his sisters' room. He had become a problem at school, although previously was well behaved. The mother felt unable to cope with his behavior and was seriously considering relinquishing him to the authority of the Division of Child Guardianship, which would place him in an institution or foster home. Both parents expressed hopelessness toward Phil and the family situation in general. The father was about to leave on a long army assignment.

HFC seemed appropriate, and the B family readily agreed to it. Participants were the two co-counselors, the father, the mother, and the five children. The father was frequently absent because of army duty. During the first meeting the family was courteous, cautious, nervous, bewildered at the subjects discussed, and distrustful of what they called HFC counselor's "craziness." Visits took place weekly from May through October 1968. Summer termination was attempted in early July because Phil and his brother Bob were going to camp, but family members still at home requested that HFC be continued. Visits ended in October when the family moved out of town to be near Mr. B.

HFC helped the B family in a number of ways. Mrs. B showed increasing confidence in her ability to be a good mother. She was firmer in disciplining the children and began to realize the consequences of not giving them more independence and responsibility. She saw the need to have a life of her own and was considering piano lessons or part-time work. Increase in self-esteem, which had been lacking because of her parents' constant belittling of her, enabled her to differ with them and act independently.

All family members were increasingly able to express their feelings to each other. Phil ceased to be the scapegoat for the family's angry feelings; he began to speak up and did not act out as much. The mother was able to treat him as she did the others, even when he did act out. Both boys did well at camp. Phil was noted as an "outstanding camper in character" and won the best-camper-of-the-year award. The school reported that Phil and his sister Ruth improved in their school work; they also became more assertive and friendly in school, with both teachers and peers.

Results

From April 1968 to July 1969 HFC served 78 adults and 148 children in 39 families; the average number of visits per family was 7. Sixteen nonclinic professionals—representing 9 public and private agencies, public and parochial schools, churches, and courts—served as HFC key persons for 16 families. The director and 8 professional staff members of the Somerville Guidance Center—representing the disciplines of psychiatry, psychology, social work, psychiatric nursing, and nursery school teaching—assumed this role for 18 families. Two nonprofessional staff members, a housewife, and a neighborhood leader served as HFC key persons for the remaining 5 families. There were also 12 observers (students and visitors) representing 12 schools of education and social work, public and private agencies, and the Massachusetts Department of Mental Health.

At the end of the year key persons were asked to give their impressions of the families' degree of improvement. (See Table 1.) They based their assessments on varied criteria that centered around the HFC goal of modifying the referred child's behavior. Even with the simple evaluation procedures used, two factors affecting HFC effectiveness seem to emerge: (1) less improvement is apparent when a clinician is involved as the key person and (2) the more visits made to a family, the greater are the chances of improvement.

The first factor may be related to the clinician's resistance to the physical action properties of HFC. As Riessman and Goldfarb suggest:

> Psychiatrists, social workers, and educators are often resistant to role playing because they fear what they believe to be its sensationalistic, charlatan-like overtones . . . they feel it is an in-group gimmick lacking in dignity [and status]. [10]

TABLE 1. Key Persons' Ratings of Improvement in Families Undergoing Home Family Counseling ($n=39$)

DEGREE OF IMPROVEMENT	RATINGS BY NONCLINICIANS		RATINGS BY CLINICIANS		TOTAL		VISITS (AVERAGE NUMER)
	Number	Percentage	Number	Percentage	Number	Percentage	
Marked improvement	9	23	7	18	16	41	8.4
Limited improvement	3	8	7	18	10	26	6.7
No improvement	4	10	9	23	13	33	5.6

HFC's main thrust is through symbolic role-playing. Its ultimate objective is to establish the family as a medium for changing the various social systems that impinge on its individual members. Not only is the family expected to change its system, but the educational, social, and religious institutions in the community are also expected to change their systems as a result of their representative participation at HFC meetings.

The author hopes that more systematic evaluation procedures and measures of uniform criteria will be devised and applied, not only to the first but also to the other three HFC goals: improving family relations, coordinating community services, and maximizing the effectiveness of key persons. These three pertain primarily to changing social systems and may ultimately be more significant to the referred child and family than the first, more direct, and more traditional goal of modifying the child's behavior.

References

1.   Emory L. Cowen, Elmer A. Gardner, and Melvin Zax, eds., *Emergent Approaches to Mental Health Problems* (New York: Appleton-Century-Crofts, 1967), p. 414.

2.   Margaret J. Rioch, "Changing Concepts in the Training of Psychotherapists," *Journal of Consulting Psychology*, Vol. 30, No. 4 (August 1966), pp. 290–292.

3.   Cowen, Gardner, and Zax, op. cit., p. 425.

4.   Ibid.

5.   Rachel A. Levine, "Treatment in the Home: An Experiment with Low Income, Multi-problem Families," in Frank Riessman, Jerome Cohen, and Arthur Pearl, eds., *Mental Health of the Poor* (New York: Free Press, 1964), p. 330.

6.   Ibid., p. 331.

7.   Preliminary findings suggest that the group of children in HFC improved somewhat more than either the control group receiving only normal assistance from the school or the experimental group receiving comprehensive psychiatric and psychological casework, therapeutic tutoring, vocational counseling, and group work services provided by the staff of the Newton-Baker project. *See* Joseph H. Golner, "An Investigation of the Effect of Conjoint Family Help on Interaction in Antisocial Families," unpublished doctoral dissertation, Boston University, 1969; and Maxwell J. Schleifer, Joseph H. Golner, and Louise Gorman, "A School Social Work Approach to Boys with Antisocial Traits," paper presented at a symposium of the Newton-Baker project at Boston Children's Hospital, Boston, Massachusetts, June 23, 1967.

8.   *See* Eveoleen N. Rexford, "A Developmental Concept of the Problems of Acting Out," *Journal of the American Academy of Child Psychiatry*, Vol. 2, No. 1 (January 1963), pp. 6–21; and Rexford, "Antisocial Young Children and Their Families," in Lucie Jessner and Eleanor Pavenstedt, eds., *Dynamic Psychopathology in Childhood* (New York: Grune & Stratton, 1959), pp. 186–220.

9. The other dimensions were as follows: (1) parental inability versus ability to perceive their own experiences as different from the child's, (2) parental prediction of child's failure rather than success, (3) confusion and inconsistency versus clarity in presenting rules, (4) pressure versus respect in presenting rules, (5) inability versus ability to understand child's feelings, (6) blaming child for family's problems versus acknowledging one's own responsibility, (7) parental abdication versus assumption of responsibility for the child, (8) appreciation versus depreciation of HFC, (9) inability versus ability to concentrate at HFC meetings, and (10) inability versus ability to admit HFC counselor to family setting. Compare with Frances J. Pilecki, "An Investigation of the Predictive Value of Intermittent Feedback and Relay Feedback in Task Accomplishment," p. 29. Unpublished doctoral dissertation, University of Rochester, Rochester, New York, 1966.

10. Frank Riessman and Jean Goldfarb, "Role Playing and the Poor," in Riessman, Cohen, and Pearl, eds., op. cit., p. 344.

18
Maturational Crises and Parent-Child Interaction

Frances H. Scherz

Within recent years there has been increasing interest in understanding the nature of the normal range of family developmental tasks. Investigators such as Reuben Hill, Talcott Parsons, John Spiegel, Rhona and Robert Rapaport, and Theodore Lidz have pursued studies that have yielded knowledge about family tasks.[1] The emergence of family therapy as a treatment approach, with the resultant need to understand the ways in which families usually function, has led to similar interest by social workers. Although knowledge is still in an early state, enough data are available and enough concepts are developing to warrant an attempt at some formulation for present use. Moreover, practice experience in agencies has added to the available data, and it has increased the need to understand—for purposes of assessment and treatment approach—how family and individual developmental tasks interrelate and influence each other.

The complexities of understanding a family in all of its interactions are far beyond this writer's knowledge and the scope of this article. Relatively little information is known at this time about how children in a family influence each other, why children are selected for particular role assignments, how family tasks influence different children, and how family life circumstances affect each child in similar and different ways. Whatever knowledge is available has emerged primarily from study and work with disturbed families. Social workers need and are gradually developing knowledge of normal family interaction. The purpose of this article is to describe some normal psychological life tasks that parents and child have in common and that, in this context, appear to parallel each other. The major emphasis is on universal psychological tasks that become critical during transitional periods in the family's life cycle.

Source: From Social Casework 52 (June 1971), pp. 362–369. Copyright © 1971 by the Family Service Association of America. Reprinted by permission.

The interrelating and influencing of family and individual developmental tasks is presented here as a basic component of the point of view that the family is a system—an interlocking, interdependent network of forces that relate and react as a unified whole. The system develops in order to regulate the interaction of its members toward meeting their growth needs and discharging the tasks of the family. Regulation of interaction provides a dynamic balance between the status quo and the necessities for change. In the family system, the individual's development is conditioned not only by his own biopsychological needs and motives but also by the needs and motives of the other family members and by the needs of the family as a whole. It is understandable, within this context, that the developmental tasks of the individual frequently parallel the tasks of the family.

Universal Family Tasks

There appear to be certain psychological tasks for the family and the individual that parallel each other, interrelate, influence each other's development, and are repetitive at different times during the life cycle. These tasks can be described as universal in the sense that, despite differences in social and family cultures and rapid changes in family lifestyles, every family apparently needs to live through the same tasks. They are repetitive in the sense that the same tasks, although they may be expressed differently, recur at known times during the life cycle according to age-stage individual developmental phases and the family's perception of its task in relation to the particular phase.

These universal psychological tasks for the family that parallel individual tasks are (1) emotional separation versus interdependence or connectedness, (2) closeness or intimacy versus distance, and (3) self-autonomy versus other responsibility. For the individual, these family tasks are often equated as separation, the working out of dependency needs; closeness, the establishment of sexual identity; and autonomy, the development of self-control and self-worth.

Familial Conflicts and Crises

Inherent in the management of these tasks is necessary conflict—conflict that arises from the needs of the family to regulate interaction in order to accomplish its tasks and from the needs of the individual to assert his own developmental wishes. This conflict provides impetus for growth. The successful resolution of this repetitive conflict in various individual developmental phases depends to a great extent on the establishment of a family system that is flexible as well as constructively stable, that can permit individual growth and still keep it within the bounds of the family's tasks and society's demands, and that is not too beset by such situational factors as economic problems or such accidental factors as illness and death.

Of particular importance in the family system is the subsystem of the marital pair. For the management of family tasks and individual growth needs, the marital pair must coalesce for mutual support. The parents have had to work on the universal tasks in their own development and together must again work on them to promote the growth strivings of their children. Because it is assumed that no one ever fully resolves the conflicts inherent in developmental tasks, these conflicts are to some extent aroused in the parents as the children move through developmental phases. The new dimension for the parents is to replace the old, personal conflicts within the perspective of the current family system rather than to view them as fixed on the personal past and, therefore, unamenable to growth.

The conflicts that are engendered by family and individual developmental tasks are dormant or quiescent when work on the tasks proceeds smoothly and constructively; at the same time, paradoxically, it appears that at every stage of development, when change toward the next stage or task is imminent, there is a high point of stress. The stress appears to be brought about by the conflict between the wish to retain the status quo and the wish for change. This high point can be described as a transitional, developmental, or maturational crisis. Each maturational crisis involves repetition of the universal tasks, although one or another task may be in ascendency at a particular stage of development. Each crisis involves the family, and the outcome will affect the family system as well as each of its members. Each crisis also offers potential for growth.

The crisis often is accompanied by temporary regression to earlier modes of expression and behavior on the part of the family as well as on that of the individual. Perhaps the temporary regression can be called regression in the service of the ego because its purpose appears to be the mobilization of energy for the new task. The crisis carries with it a mourning process— mourning for the loss of gratification of the old, for relationship feelings, and for behavior that must be given up if the new task is to be mastered. As in all mourning, there are temporary mixed reactions of sorrow, often mild depression, anger, and a wish to hold on to the old. One has only to witness, for example, the mixed parental expressions of pride and sadness when a child begins to walk. The expressions reflect joy in the child's moving toward autonomy and sadness in the emotional separation. The child struggles with the same normal conflict. The child's success depends on the ability of the parents to mourn and to permit the child to mourn and on the child's ability to move back and forth toward autonomy and to obtain gratification in the new task.

First Family Maturational Crisis

The first family maturational crisis occurs in the establishment of a new marriage. Preliminary work by the couple during courtship includes the conscious tasks of beginning to make decisions about designating and allocating role functions in the use of money, household management, relationships with others, and testing of sexual compatability. An unconscious process of intrapsychic accomodation to each other's needs begins. These tasks are carried into the marriage.

In the early period of the marriage, the partners have a number of major tasks. One is that of separating emotionally from their families of origin and yet remaining connected in a new way. Another is the development of new modes of communication, particularly in learning how to express needs and wishes directly and openly. The honeymoon period frequently resembles the early symbiosis between mother and child in the partners' wish to incorporate each other and their concurrent feat that incorporation will mean the loss of individuation. After the "symbiotic" period is over, there is a normal crisis over separateness and connectedness, closeness and distance, and autonomy and responsibility to each other as the partners gradually, with "good" disillusionment, establish patterns in these tasks. Their unique marital system develops. Mature marriages allow partners not only to be different, to be individuals, but also to give up some of this differentness and individuality in order to accept and give to each other's needs.

Birth of the First Child

The coming of the first child is a critical period of stress as well as of happiness. The marital relationship must alter to accommodate to the new family member and, at the same time, must maintain a distinct husband-wife bond that retains its own identity and unique relationship system, although it includes the parenting roles.

During the pregnancy and after, when mother and child are involved for months in a symbiotic relationship, emotional separation and connectedness between husband and wife in a new form is a major task. The husband often needs the support of his wife against undue regression as she temporarily denies his needs in the intensity of her relationship with the child. Specific parenting roles and new divisions of responsibility, with attendant normal anxieties, have to be learned actively. The parents' ability to trust their continuing love for each other, to deepen their intimacy, and, at the same time, to provide room for distance from each other so that the child's needs can be met is put to a test. The father's support of the mother's competence as a mother enables the child to develop a sense of trust. It is no wonder that, as parents remember this period of pleasurable but anxious time, they express the wish that the second child could have been born first.

First Transitional Family Crisis

A transitional family crisis occurs when the first child develops independent physical motility. There is necessary developmental conflict between the parents and child. The child's autonomous strivings, his need for some emotional separateness from the parents, and the fact that he is no longer totally dependent on them—although he cannot unduly challenge their control over him lest he lose their care—create conflict in him. The parents are torn between the wish for the child to develop and the desire to have him remain emotionally close and dependent on them. They begin to have doubts about their roles as "good" parents as they question how much freedom, how much protection, or how much control they should exercise over the child. It is usual and normal for parents to disagree on the management of these issues. The separation has its painful aspects for each parent as well as for them together. The child, in his own interests, may add to the disagreements now that he is also aware that each of his parents has a different role, although he loves them both. The specific disagreements may not be serious; but there must be basic agreement over permitting the child's autonomous strivings to proceed within bounds, and the parents must support each other against undue regression over feelings of loss.

When the parents can encompass the major tasks of emotional separation and autonomy, the child can develop self-control, self-esteem, and self-responsibility for his actions to others. The biological sphincter development at this stage that leads to toileting and comes at the same time as motility adds to the crisis aspects. The battle of control between parents and child again involves, to a minor degree, the parents' sense of responsibility as opposed to the child's wish to assert responsibility for himself.

The family problems of separation and autonomy are often symbolically displaced on toileting issues. In some families, when the battle is prolonged and intense, the seeds of delays or defects in the child's development are sown. There may be serious regression to earlier stages in both parents and child. The parents may infantilize the child so that he is overly dependent, and later he becomes inhibited or uninterested in school learning tasks. The child may participate actively in the infantilization because the gratification in the parents' love and approval is greater than that derived from autonomous strivings. If the child is innately a fighter, he may "win" at the cost of the loss of some parental love and, in extreme cases, at the cost of parental emotional abandonment. He may develop an undifferentiated, rebellious life stance, a lack of self-control, and insufficient boundaries in relation to self-responsibility and responsibility to others that are often reflected in school learning difficulties as well as in other life tasks.

Separation Tasks

There is a critical repetition of separation tasks when the child enters school and the family must release the child to a greater world. In relation to his biopsychological development, the child is likely at this time to be seriously involved in working through his sexual identity with both parents. Intimacy and distance then become additional tasks with which to cope. All the universal tasks overlap at various developmental phases, but in this phase, the overlapping in the tasks of separation and intimacy is so great and so closely linked that for both family and child there is likely to be confusion and lack of differentiation between the tasks. In the usual family this lack of differentiation does not cause any serious problem although there is a normal degree of anxiety. The family grapples with the joys and conflicts over separation and, in preparing the child for school, is likely to emphasize the difference between the sexes. It can be helpful, however, in the usual family crisis to know what the struggle is about in order to deal with the anxiety.

For families in trouble who seek help at this stage, it is important for the therapist to know whether the separation or sexual aspect of the task creates the greater part of the problem. For example, school phobias, which are common symptoms at this time, are not always indicative of a hostile dependent tie between mother and child. The broader view of the phobia as a family problem of emotional separation that is created by the family and affects all its members enables the therapist to look for a greater variety of causative factors in the family system, to identify the specific task to be worked on, and to plan treatment in differential ways accordingly. If the therapist considers this stage of development as a family transitional crisis in which family and individual members have parallel tasks, he may, for treatment purposes, separate families into two distinct groups: (1) those who may require long and complicated treatment, and (2) those who need brief crisis intervention to assist them over a developmental hurdle.[2]

Problems of Adolescence

Adolescence brings, as Erik H. Erikson describes it, "the identity crisis,"[3] not only for the adolescent but also for the parents.[4] The long period of adolescence is characterized by successive waves of turbulence and quiet and a series of transitional maturational crisis, during which all the universal tasks are heightened for both the family and the adolescent. Old personal conflicts in the parents that may have been quiescent now emerge under the stress of the adolescent's struggles with himself and with them. If the family has not successfully mastered the tasks of earlier stages, the tasks now become more difficult and more irreconcilable. Parents experience normal difficulty in maintaining a supportive coalition under the impact of the adolescent's divisive tactics, frequently not understanding that these tactics are designed unconsciously for the purpose of working out the adolescent's sexual identity. The adolescent's periodic regressive, dependent behavior—appropriate to an earlier phase—frightens and angers the parents who are themselves struggling with their conflict over separating from him. The confusion of the adolescent over self-responsibility and projection of responsibilities onto the parents is duplicated in the confusion of the parents, who are torn between protecting and controlling the adolescent and permitting him to experiment in ways that are alien or repugnant to them.

The threat to integrity and self-esteem felt by the parents because of the attacks by the adolescent, the arousal of residual conflicts of universal tasks, and the need for the family to rework these tasks create situations in which the parents compete with the adolescent. They compete over achievement, over sexual identity and abilities, and over separation. The competition and conflicts, part of the normal transitional crises, are expressed most often in clashes over family values and standards about behavior, school and work achievement, and sexual interests. These clashes—or battles—may intensify if the father's achievement status is either unsatisfying or on a plateau, if the parents' sexuality seems to be waning and they find it difficult to tolerate the adolescent's budding sexuality, or if they have undue fears of separation. The adolescent, in turn, experiences both desires for growth and fears about it in all his tasks, and he fans parental fears and anxieties.

It is not uncommon, during this transitional crisis, to have the emergence of temporary marital disharmony because the arousal of personal conflicts in the parents is eased by projection on each other in which they accuse each other of failures in child rearing. If this conflict is temporary, it is more helpful to the adolescent than the collusion of parents who unite to preserve the marriage by attacking the adolescent. Again, in the usual family there is some temporary collusion and a good deal of coalition in which the parents support each other against more than temporary regression.

Achieving Adult Status

The next transitional crisis occurs when the last child leaves the family home for work, further education, or marriage. To the late adolescent or young adult, this transition seems to be a final leap into adult self-identity, in which the universal tasks merge, the conflicts become quiescent, and he feels himself to be a whole person in his own right but still connected to the family on an equalitarian footing—no longer a child. There may be periods of mild regression under stress, but the major identity crisis is over for him and the parents.

As in all developmental phases, to achieve this state there must be permission by the parents for individual growth. In some ways this transitional crisis is more difficult for the parents. When the last child leaves, they face the need for a marked change in their relationship to each other, particularly in the task of closeness and distance. A different marital equilibrium is required. Temporary marital disharmony may occur as the partners struggle to find new modes of communication, to change the patterns of intimacy that were established during the long child-rearing years, and to effect new divisions of responsibility. There may be temporary regression in their efforts to hold on to children, to involve them in inappropriate mediation between the partners, or to complain to them about the partner. There is gradual resolution of the crisis when the parents settle into a new equilibrium, and a relationship of nonpossessive warmth develops between parents and adult children.

Problems of Old Age

Old age is the last great transitional crisis for the family. It usually brings with it problems in separation for the older and younger members of the family. The older members inevitably suffer losses in work, in health, and in important people. They often become dependent on their children for money, for physical care, and for emotional needs that had been met by spouses or others. It is difficult to maintain integrity and self-esteem in a culture that usually does not highly value the aged person. Adult children often find themselves in the position of having to take care of parents in ways that arouse old conflicts about dependency, achievement, and separation. The inevitability of death exacerbates conflicts and fears over separation. The demands and, at times, the regressive behavior of the older member are frightening and embarrassing to the adult child. Remnants of old anger, old hurts, and guilt over these feelings come to the fore in both the adult child and the aged parent. The usual denial of these feelings by both makes it difficult to work through the critical mourning process of separation that has to take place, for example, when the aged member can no longer sustain himself in his current way of life and a change in living arrangement must be made. Frequently both generations can be helped to manage separation and mourning when they understand the normalcy of their feelings and can place aroused residual feelings within the current context. This process can also help, in a preventive sense, the third youngest generation as they hear parents and grandparents express feelings that all too often are buried or concealed from them.

At each transitional maturational crisis, changes must take place in family tasks that parallel individual developmental tasks in order to permit individual growth and facilitate the management of family tasks. The marital partners should develop and maintain a flexible coalition without giving up their individual differences. This coalition serves to support each partner against undue regression during the crises and enables them to be models of differentiation for the children. Changes in object relationship, identifications, and alliances in the family—between parents and children—need to alter to permit growth. Unconscious accommodation should take place between the marital pair to encompass the various developmental needs of children and to maintain flexible stability in the marriage as new family tasks arise. They are observable in conscious derivatives in changes in role allocations and responsibilities. Mourning for losses sustained in each developmental crisis should be recognized and given expression. Recognition that these tasks are universal and repetitive tasks makes it easier to tolerate the pain of loss, creates awareness of their transitional nature, and provides impetus to change.

During the life cycle, until children become mature adults, it is important that the parents establish and maintain flexible generational boundaries between themselves and their children. These boundaries are necessary for the children to establish their own ego boundaries. The family, therefore, is not seen as a democratic institution or system.[5] Rather it is seen as a hierarchical structure in which parents take responsibility for leadership and authority. Role designations in specific tasks and in decision making are the responsibility of the parents. Children can and should participate in tasks and in decision making, but their participation always should be commensurate with their developmental needs and abilities. Abdication or confusion by the parents of generational boundaries can lead to confusion and diffuseness of ego boundaries in children. Rigid generational boundaries can lead to tight, constricted ego boundaries in children. Adequate, flexible generational boundaries are essential in the management of the universal tasks.

It was not the intent in this article to stress the *content* of the universal tasks at the risk of making them appear to be mechanistic. Although the content is certainly significant if the nature and timing of the tasks are to be understood, it cannot be divorced from the *process*—the family interactional patterns and specific transactions through which the content is transmitted into the daily operations of life. The process is the family communication style and its patterns by which the universal tasks are managed.

Importance of Communication

It is pertinent, then, in this discussion to emphasize the need for open, direct, and honest communication in the family. No family probably ever achieves total communication, especially when it is under stress of crises, including the transitional crises. Messages that convey constructive congruency in verbal and nonverbal communication—in words, meaning, and feeling—are helpful in the management of life tasks. Such negative injunctions as, "I want you to grow up, but remain my baby," or such double-bind messages as, "Do as I say, not as I do," if persistent, pervasive, or emphatic during critical developmental tasks, create confusion, delays, and defects in development.

The management of these universal tasks at any time in the life cycle will depend on how successfully the family has managed previous tasks, on what intrafamilial conditions prevail, and on situational factors. Lack of mastery, however, at one stage in any of the repetitive tasks does not mean, necessarily, failure of the same task at another time. Families are not equally successful or vulnerable to the same tasks at all times in the life cycle. Separation tasks, for example, may be more difficult for a particular family when the child is young than when he is older. Perhaps in that family old memories and conflicts are more reactivated by the young child; this process is sometimes called an anniversary reaction. Or perhaps in that family there is marital strife at that time, and the parents include the child in their battles. Or perhaps the family is experiencing difficulty with money, illness, or death or in moving to a new community. The emergence of any or all of these conflicts may make the family more vulnerable at that time and, therefore, create interferences in the management of the transitional maturational crisis. Entrenched, unresolved past problems in the parents may make the family vulnerable at all stages in development, such as the family in which all the children develop phobic symptoms at critical stages. It is not uncommon to find that at a particular time one family member is more highly vulnerable than others and lacks sufficient energy to participate actively and appropriately in the meeting of a maturational crisis, such as the mother who is depressed over the loss of her mother and who cannot meet a child's needs at a significant point in his development.

The one-parent family is inevitably more vulnerable in the management of the universal tasks. All the normal problems and conflicts are compounded when only one parent is available. Parental coalition is, of course, impossible. Generational boundaries are distorted. Mourning is less often resolved than when parents can support each other. The adequate establishment of the child's identity is difficult unless substitute parental figures can be found in the extended family, in other resources, or, if necessary, in treatment. The one-parent family suffers particularly at the points of transitional crises for lack of support by the marital pair to each other.

It would be important to know, for all families, how the transitional crises affect, not only the first child, but others. Is there diminution of intensity for all? Further exploration should illuminate this question.

A crystal ball that predicts the future might show a time when all families will have available resources for understanding and managing these tasks so that the crises could be minimized in duration and intensity. At the same time, what is already known can be put to use therapeutically. It can help therapists in making quicker and more accurate assessments of family and individual difficulties and can assist them in determining the treatment approach—individual, family, or group—that is likely to be more effective at a given time.

References

1.   Reuben Hill, Sociological Insights Relevant to the Conceptualization of and Interpretation of a Family Development Program in a Family Life Center, Unpublished, 1968; Talcott Parsons et al., *A Family Socialization and Interactional Process* (Glencoe, Ill.: Free Press, 1955); John J. Spiegel, The Resolution of Role Conflict Within the Family, *Psychiatry*, 20:1–16 (February 1957); Rhona Rapaport, Normal Crises, Family Structure and Mental Health, *Family Process*, 2:68–80 (March 1963); Rhona Rapaport and Robert Rapaport, Family Transitions in Contemporary Society, *Journal of Psychosomatic Research*, 12:29–38 (January 1968); Rhona Rapaport, New Light on the Honeymoon, *Human Relations*, 17:33–56 (February 1964); and Theodore Lidz, *The Family and Human Adaptation* (New York: International Universities Press, 1963).

2.   Howard J. Parad, ed., *Crisis Intervention: Selected Readings* (New York: Family Service Association of America, 1965).

3.   Erik H. Erikson, *Identity and The Life Cycle: Selected Papers*, Psychological Issues, vol 1, no. 1 (New York: International Universities Press, 1959).

4.   Frances H. Scherz, The Crisis of Adolescence in Family Life, Social Casework, 48:209–15 (April 1967).

5.   A. C. R. Skynner, A Group Analytic Approach to Conjoint Family Therapy, *Journal of Child Psychology and Psychiatry and Allied Disciplines*, 10:81–106 (October 1969).

19
Techniques of Brief Therapy with Children and Parents

Norman Epstein

The development of the techniques of brief therapy with children and parents can not be discussed without an evaluation of the cultural factors affecting the process of child rearing and child development in the United States. Concomitantly, the role of the child guidance clinic as a depository of the breakdowns in the process is a crucial component that also requires examination. There is a need to focus on the bewildering and often contradictory directions that serve as relationship guidelines for both parent and child, as well as on the role of the clinician as mediator, arbiter, and educator in the complex maze of parent-child conflict.

The clinician is often witness to the results of conflicting messages that victimize parents who constantly seek direction in their perplexing role as child rearers. The mental health profession, in offering alternating and contradictory waves of information with pendulum-like regularity, has ensured perplexities that generate cases for treatment. Periodic variations in styles of child rearing that alternate between permissiveness and structure create different guidelines for each generation. As a result, the experiences of one generation become an imperfect script for the next generation. Rapid changes in the environmental structure further compound the conditions of life confronted by parent and child.

The development of a host of mythologies has further served to increase the confusion. The propagated perception of children as helpless, weak, and frightened beings driven by unseen forces ignores the fact that often children are experts in the area of conscious power manipulation, quite adept in discovering means to outwit and paralyze parental authority, eventually habituating themselves to lifestyles characterized by grandiosity and domineering behavior which may be camouflaged as passivity.

Source: From *Social Casework* 57 (May 1976), pp. 317–323. Copyright © 1976 by the Family Service Association of America. Reprinted by permission.

Another myth that has succeeded in gaining acceptance, and has been responsible for converting child guidance agencies into covert marital counseling clinics, has been the belief that children's problems necessarily reflect and are the result of marital pathology. This belief has resulted in therapists' tampering with marriages and opening Pandora's box because of a failure to respect the delicate balances that are inherent in the marital relationship. Therapists often fail to recognize that many marriages show evidence of deterioration as a consequence of a child's victimization of his parents who, in their helplessness, take out their anger and frustrations on one another. Thus, the result is often mistaken for the cause. This myth has aided those "child therapists" who, unable to develop comfort and ease in treating children, gradually direct their practice toward the more verbal adult, with the concomitant development of a host of family or individual therapies which tend to remove the emphasis from the child and his or her specific problems.

A brief therapy program for children and parents needs to tackle the myth that children (as well as parents) are the victims of compelling unconscious forces and can neither control nor take responsibility for their behavior. In spite of the lack of substantive research, speculation concerning unconscious forces has survived, and has often taken the form of theological disputation. A brief therapy program views the child and the parent as being able to give expression to their beliefs and expectations about themselves and each other, as well as to evaluate the congruence with reality of those beliefs and expectations. The program does not seek to provide cures (another clinical myth), nor is it especially potent in the treatment of chronic personal and familial disturbances.

Role of School and Parent

Appropriate therapy for parent and child requires knowledge of and sensitivity to the predicaments that surround the growing process. Many children are no longer permitted to experience academic failure, and their parents have been enlisted to serve as extensions of the teacher, to the point where the home has become an annex of the school. Such parents feel compelled to prove their competence not only to themselves and to the child, but also to the school. The child is often at a loss to find a haven from the demands imposed by daily living.

A generation of teachers has been trained to be on the alert for evidence of psychological dysfunction and is prompt to interpret misbehavior or academic difficulties as being the product of psychopathological forces. Parents are often urged to seek psychological help for children who, in actuality, require firm teachers or educational remediation services. The parents' oversensitivity to the possible presence of emotional disturbance converts them into acquiescent figures who submit themselves to the mercy of clinicians.

Parents and children are equally subject to the influences of the media that convey the message that one must constantly seek out the devils that lurk below awareness, and that are instrumental in determining behavior. Combined with these communications is the implicit suggestion that insight into one's own feelings and thought processes will be rewarded with improvement and a realization of one's potential. The democratic ideal of our society fosters the belief that there is no limit to the potential for self betterment. This belief has caused the expenditure of endless energies in a fruitless search for self betterment through therapy.

Goals of Brief Therapy

A primary goal of brief therapy (which is limited to one or two sessions weekly for a period of six weeks) with children and parents is the establishing of a focus that is central to the problem for which the primary applicant (the parent) seeks help. Although brief therapy has tended to be identified with crisis intervention, the implications have been somewhat misleading in that the concept of crisis suggests a phenomenon that is a deviation from the normal state of affairs in child rearing. A central tenet of a brief therapy program is that crisis is a recurring situation in the interaction between parents and children, and that the goal of therapy is the development of competence in the areas of relationship and control. For the parent, the goal is development of realistic expectations and greater consistency in their enforcement, including the development of more appropriate strategies for dealing with the child's power ploys.

A basic goal, involving the child, is to help stimulate interest in examining the range of self-defeating, immature behaviors that are mired in misperceptions of the self and others. Central to the therapeutic interventions is the attempt to explore and bring into greater awareness the systems of expectations of both parent and child. This process includes an examination of their respective value systems and the extent to which the elements contribute to or defeat professed desires. In its most elemental thrust, therapy is directed to maximizing parenting abilities in the adult and growth-producing behaviors in the child.

Both parties are helped to accept greater responsibility for their behavior and to seek solutions to difficulties in an understanding of the here and now aspects of their mutual situation. The participants are urged not to seek rationalizations of current behavior through repeated explorations of the past. Utilizing the here and now focus, parent and child are encouraged to view the relationship as being composed of ingredients that are subject to conscious control and manipulation by the participants in the relationship.

Process

Brief therapy by its very nature precludes the use of long and extensive intake procedures and the attendant taking of lengthy social histories. Diagnosis is not separated from the treatment process; rather, it is dependent upon what occurs within therapy. An essential component of brief therapy, and indeed all therapy, is developing and clarifying the facts of the situation, generally a most neglected activity in treatment regimes. Specifically, the basic data relative to developmental history as well as IQ testing (of extreme importance) must be elicited from the parent, or as in the case of the latter, the school. Many a child has been inappropriately placed in treatment for academic problems because the therapist did not know or consider the child's IQ and its possible limitations.

The Children's Psychiatric Center uses a set of printed questionnaires (Family Information, Problem List, and Health) filled out by the parent prior to the first appointment, to elicit direct, concrete information as an alternative to dependence upon the parent's propensity to editorialize in relation to basic data, as well as a means of deriving data that can lend itself to statistical tabulation and correlation.

A technique that is quite potent and revealing involves encouraging parent and child to verbalize their expectations of themselves and each other. Bringing to the discussion both the distorted and the unrealistic expectations can provide a very meaningful service in brief therapy, as it permits examination of the tenets upon which individuals base their behavior toward one another.

Parent Groups

The utilization of parent groups (six weeks' duration) during the brief therapy period is a useful medium for developing an exchange among the participants, and an examination of beliefs and feelings held in common. The process often succeeds in reducing the feelings of emotional isolation of parents who tend to view their problems as unique. The therapist assumes responsibility for maintaining the focus on child management, addressing himself to the technology of child rearing, and does not imply that lack of know-how is evidence of pathology. The therapist encourages the parents to try alternate approaches to problem solving, while discouraging high expectations of success in child rearing or the belief that the child's future emotional health and destiny is solely dependent upon the parent's doing "the right thing." Encouraging greater consistency in response and helping the parent become more knowledgeable about the power ploys that are part of the standard repertoire of all children redistributes the balance of power.

Brief therapy with the child (or adolescent) can employ the medium of the group as a facilitator of discussion. Many therapists tend to prefer the individual treatment modality because they feel that it provides a more intensive situation, although it does not offer the opportunity to witness the child's behavior pattern in a group of peers. The group provides the laboratory for eliciting material that can be utilized in dramatizing the disruptive and immature behavior patterns.

Putting together a group that will function relatively comfortably for a brief period does depend to some extent upon following the criteria that have been developed by experience. The age span of the children is important. The therapist should not attempt to put together a group of parents whose children represent an age span of more than two years. The parents of a fourteen-year-old do not want to listen to the tribulations of the parents of a nine-year-old. A number of seasoned therapists have claimed that the brief therapy groups should be comprised of parents of pre-adolescents, because the problem of adolescent behavior does not seem to lend itself to amelioration within a six-week period. The evidence is not particularly convincing that this claim is valid, but it does reflect the experienced effectiveness of a brief therapy program with parent-child management problems that have not hardened as a result of lengthy duration.

Arrangements with parents who have made application for service are made on the telephone. The therapist informs the parents that a group focused on child management is being formed and an invitation to join is extended. The parent is generally not free to apply for individual therapy unless there is a particularly compelling reason, for example, if a parent is involved in an extra-marital affair that has direct bearing on child rearing. As will be noted even from the example, brief therapy addresses itself to priorities of child rearing, and requests that parents commit themselves, at least initially, to the remediation of the parent-child relationship.

Parents are advised of the fee for the service, a sliding weekly fee, and the fact that the group will meet for six weeks, once a week. Fathers are strongly urged to attend if they are in the home, and meetings are scheduled in the evening to permit fathers' attendance. The parent is told that the child will also be seen regularly during the six-week period. It has been found that these arrangements can be satisfactorily completed on the telephone. Parents are often relieved to hear that the focus is on child management; many of them approach obtaining counseling with the stereotype of the youngster as a victim of the parents' unconscious, and fear that they the parents, require extensive probing therapy, or exorcism, before the child can be helped.

Initial Phase

The group therapy with the parents can be divided into three phases, initial, middle and closing. The initial phase, comprised of the first two sessions, is devoted to encouraging the parents to state their perceptions of the child, the problems, and their projected solutions. The therapist, through questioning and careful listening, attempts to elicit the expectation system of self, the child, and therapy: he also helps the parents to evaluate and become sensitive to the differences between opinions and facts in presenting the situation. The parent is literally taught the process of giving facts in support of statements. As in all therapy, belief based on questionable facts often leads to inappropriate behaviors in the relationship.

The initial sessions of brief therapy are further devoted to an understanding of the client's expectations of the therapist. Unless this system is understood, the client is doomed to feel a gap between expectations and reality. The therapist must correct the client's anticipations that therapy is capable of turning child rearing into an unmitigated joy. Basically, as in all therapy, a primary goal is not to erase struggle but to accept its presence as a condition of life and to increase the client's coping abilities.

Interviewing the Child

By the second session, the therapist will have met the child in order to evaluate whether congruity can be achieved between the therapist's perception of him and that of the parent. As a result, the second session of the parent's group is often the most meaningful and pivotal. The parents are laden with anxiety about what the therapist discovered in meeting with the child, and they usually expect the worst. The therapist will often find that his perceptions are not as extreme as those of the parents, and sharing these differences often results in the lessening of anxiety. In some cases, where the parents are exceedingly repressive, there may be a loosening of restrictions following the therapist's reassurance that the child is not doomed to a life of irresponsible behavior because of a current lack of alacrity in taking out the garbage (a form of testing and rites of initiation parents seem to assume that all children must undergo in order to uncover their talents for independent, responsible living as adults). Essentially, the second interview is devoted to adjusting perceptions and mitigating anxiety in the parent. Only at this point can the parent begin to take in and begin to consider new approaches to the child.

During the initial phase the therapist attempts to gather data and to evaluate the child's functioning. The modality may be the individual interview or the group setting. This author prefers, at this point in therapy, to employ the individual interview with the child, because it permits for a greater intensity of contact and concentration upon the child's preception of why he has come to the clinic. In fact, the answer to this question can serve as a crucial springboard for discussion, including the companion inquiry as to whether the parents prepared the child for the appointment. This latter question seeks to elicit information about the parents' comfort in confronting the child with their reaction to the noxious behavior. It also provides a clue to how they communicate with him.

The therapist, as has been noted, is seeking in a rather limited time to establish some concept of the child's ability to conceptualize ideas. In the final analysis, the most rewarding patients are those who demonstrate a good ability to conceptualize. The therapist, with pencil and paper, should test the child's comprehension of basic arithmetic reasoning in order to assess the youngster's abstraction abilities (can the child grasp the concept of subtracting 29 from 58—namely, how one borrows to pay back)? Very often one can perceive the child's difficulties in life from observing the manner in which difficult words are conquered in the effort to read. Does the child struggle to master or choose to avoid the difficulty by evasion and distortion of the printed word? Concomitantly, the degree of correlation between the child's office performance and school reports is tested. It is not unusual to find a rather low correlation resulting in school conferences and participation in more adequate program planning. Scholastic expectations may be based upon erroneous data or the neglect on the part of school personnel to respect the implications of their own testing results, as for example, in the case of IQ testing.

The next step can involve exploring with the youngster his perception of the difficulties. All therapists (at least in the beginning) dread the non-talker, and much ruminative time has been spent in planning strategies in dealing with this rather common variety of youngster. In most cases, bringing the parent(s) into the room becomes a stimulus for talk, even if it is only to confront the youngster with the parent's complaint. The therapist's primary task is to begin to conceptualize for the child what appears to be the problem, whether the child talks or not. In the vast majority of cases, it can be explained to the child as a problem in development. For example, in basic, simple language, the child is told that he still has at least one foot in babyhood and is fighting growing up. The therapist confronts the child with the reality that he usually prefers not to admit, namely, being defiant is not being strong and powerful. This basic theme, and its variations, are of sufficient import to take up the six weeks of brief therapy. The aim is to motivate the child to move to the next developmental stage by clearly outlining what behaviors are appropriate for the next stage, while the parents are helped to recognize that, probably in ignorance, they have been reinforcing the behavior about which they are complaining. The child is explained as not merely a passive recipient of parental assault or ignorance, but rather as an active force not only resisting the parent but also mounting campaigns against parental authority.

Middle Phase

The middle phase of brief therapy, two to three sessions, is devoted to helping the parent evolve a workable strategem in developing a more balanced relationship with the child. The therapist serves as an educator who offers tentative—pending testing—alternative directions to the parents to increase their coping and relating abilities. The suggestions, although tentative, are quite specific and are offered with the proviso that tactics are not absolutes and must vary from child to child. This is an especially important note for parents who are wedded to the belief that because all the children in a given family come from the same womb they must of necessity be alike. Sensitizing parents to basic constitutional differences among children is no small accomplishment in the brief therapy program. For example, parental demands on the motorically lethargic or uncoordinated child for athletic-like performance can constitute a form of child abuse and torture inflicted upon a helpless victim.

As noted, the middle phase of brief therapy is the testing period for alternate parental behaviors. The child is helped to become increasingly aware of the growth in the parent's abilities and must seek more appropriate means of meeting proper parental expectations. A primary force is identification of the annoying behavior with "babyishness" and noting the self-defeating aspects of the various maneuvers.

As was done with the parents, the therapist attempts to help the child develop more appropriate techniques for coping with a range of situations and people. Direct suggestions may constitute a valid form of procedure. For example, the youngster may not know how to react to teasing—even when he is the provocateur—and needs to be educated that teasers will perpetuate the teasing only if they succeed in bringing forth crying and other temper displays. The child needs to develop a belief in the ability to exert control over behavior, and to some extent over the attitudes and actions of others.

The concept of cause and effect has to be established for the youngster by the therapist. The therapist's most potent ally is often the desire for growth on the part of the youngster.

Combined Groups of Parents and Child

An experimental program that has combined latency children with parents in the same brief therapy group has yielded interesting results, not the least being observable communication patterns between parents and children that allow for direct experience with what transpires in the family. The therapist serves as judge, arbiter, confronter, and teacher, in attempting to effect the development of appropriate roles and techniques for relating. The nuances and subtleties that are missing when meeting only with parent or child are brought into the arena. The children respond to each other's productions and often astound the parents by their astuteness and perceptiveness. The parent develops a healthy respect for the youngster's ability to understand what is going on, and is less inclined to treat the child in an arbitrary fashion. The child's powers to exercise power based on an ability to comprehend parental limitations and weaknesses can often be sharply exhibited in the combined parent-child group. It is incumbent upon the therapist to meet with the parents at least once without the child being present, in order to set ground rules for the meeting with the youngster. For example, it would not be appropriate for the parents to discuss the intimacies of the marriage in front of the child. In the first meeting of the combined group, a basic ground rule that the therapist sets is that no child is to be admonished for anything he says unless it is clearly irrelevant abuse of the parents.

Final Phase

The final two weeks of brief therapy are devoted to an evaluation with the parents and the child of what has been achieved. It is the summation of the question "What has changed and what needs further examination?" At this time, the parents are often encouraged to test the results of brief therapy via a short period of living with the child without therapy. The therapist's immediate availability to see the parents and child should the situation warrant such intervention tends to decrease the anxiety felt by parents who dread the prospect of confronting a waiting list. In this final stage, the focus is on trying out and experimenting with the suggestions supplied by the therapist and other group members. Parent and child are often surprised to discover that they can influence each other's behaviors by exercising a new pattern of controls. The parent is taught how to give verbal rewards for the child's attempts at more mature behavior.

Conclusion

Brief therapy is an appropriate form of intervention for approximately 50 percent of our clinic population. It does not provide a complete service for many cases that are referred and reflect severe problems. It is evidently not the treatment of choice for children or parents who exhibit chronic patterns of severe acting out, depression, and withdrawal. Chronicity is thus an index of anticipated success or failure in brief therapy.

It appears that brief therapy probably lays its greatest claims to success with the pre-adolescent child, although by no means should brief interventions not be attempted with adolescents. The latter, however, tend to bring to therapy problems of longer duration, and their parents can not employ controls that are more readily exerted upon a younger child—confinement to room or forfeiture of viewing television, allowances, and so forth. The desire on the part of the adolescent to conform to the peer group detracts from both parental and therapist influence.

Long-term therapy, with clearly defined goals, is available for the population for whom brief treatment is not adequate. Brief therapy, however, can delineate the goals for long-term treatment and can act as a screen to filter out the population that, because of chronicity and multiplicity of problems, requires the most intensive interventions of professional staff. Brief treatment guards against the dissipation of energies on cases that can respond to vigorous handling, and reserves staff energies for those for whom the success record is meager, namely, the psychotics and the delinquents. In addition, diagnostic thinking evolves from evaluating the results of actual intervention rather than the questionable speculations of conferences that are many degrees removed from the client.

The success of brief therapy often depends upon building in a follow-up procedure that permits the evaluation of results as well as quick access to the therapist should further difficulties arise. The easy availability of the therapist provides security to the clients, who may be reluctant to terminate therapy lest they have to take their place at the bottom of a waiting list should further difficulties arise. The telephone constitutes a crucial link with the therapist, who need not always offer an in-office interview to be effective.

It should be noted that the six-week period of brief therapy is not immutable. In some cases, it is found that the difficulties can be cleared in less time. In other situations, as therapist and client begin to conceptualize the gains of brief therapy, it may be realized that several extra sessions are needed to work out a problem. The extra sessions can be added to the six-week period and will be successful if the therapist clearly delineates the facet of the problem to be worked on. Any secret agenda on the part of the therapist devoted to performing personality reconstruction is obviously not appropriate to a successful brief therapy termination.

20

A Family Agency Program for Heavily Indebted Families

John L. Laughlin
Robert Bressler

Our protean social institutions shape—and are shaped by—the events surrounding them. The social work profession has undergone a gradual metamorphosis from the days of the influence of Freudian theory to its present concern with client advocacy—a change considerably affected by the civil rights movement. The fact that growing concern for personal and civil rights has influenced social work seems natural in retrospect because of the basic moral conviction that propels most social workers into the closest kind of contact with troubled people. In the midst of this shifting focus, however, social workers have, for the most part, remained unaffected by the awesome economic changes overwhelming so many of today's families—changes that have moved many financially minded people to refer to this time in history as the Age of the Consumer. Leonard Schneiderman suggests that we are in a period of history when it is easier to discuss one's sex life than talk about the details of one's financial situation. He says, "The money-life of people with its social and emotional significance in modern urban America may be as significant today in understanding social-psychopathology as was the sex life of people in Freud's day."[1]

Money has always had an influence on values as well as on personality. We are in part a product of the environment to which our financial position exposes us.[2] Economic security, or lack of it, shapes values and tolerance for others of a different class. Despite the country's so-called affluence, far too many blue- and white-collar workers "still live too near 'layoffs,' 'reductions,' 'strikes,' 'plant relocations,' to be personally secure."[3] Although hard-line union demands have reaped higher salaries, other forces including the

Source: From Social Casework 52 (December 1971), pp. 617–626. Copyright © 1971 by the Family Service Association of America. Reprinted by permission.

Vietnam War have reduced buying power. In Nassau and Suffolk counties in New York State, for example, a factory production worker with three dependents who earned $107 a week in 1965 is making $128 today [1971], but his buying power is down $3.31.[4] The letdown experienced by the bulk of middle-class Americans, despite hard work, improved wages and fringe benefits, and aspirations to improve their lot, is expressed in resentments toward ethnic minorities whom they see as beneficiaries of their "victimization."[5]

Accompanying this spiraling economy has been an unprecedented growth in consumer credit. For example, in 1966 the volume of outstanding consumer credit reached $95 billion with installment credit accounting for $75 billion of this amount and interest costs $13 billion.[6] Installment credit and installment debt have become a part of the American way of life, with gains to be made by the borrower as well as the lender. Responsible use of credit allows people the luxury of many commodities they would otherwise not be able or willing to purchase. However, living on credit became a reality before there was a chance to study its disastrous possibilities. This is poignantly evident in the recent rise of credit frauds and personal bankruptcies. In June of 1968, for example, personal bankruptcies, which account for over 50 percent of all bankruptcies, reached 191,729, a 9 percent increase over the previous year, three times what bankruptcies had been ten years earlier, and eighteen times higher than was recorded in 1948.[7] A more recent documentation of mounting family debt reports that out of every $100 of personal income (after federal income taxes) the amount subtracted by debt payments has shot up from $6.40 in 1946 to $22.40 in 1969.[8] These figures reflect the increasing number of families feeling the uneasy pressure of debts. "For every family experiencing bankruptcy, 20 more, it is also believed, are being squeezed in the debt vise."[9] Unfortunately, no one is able to indicate with any reliability when these growing financial problems and their inherent strain on family life will subside. In fact, after a two-year quiescence, personal bankruptcies were again on the upswing in the first four months of 1970.[10]

The central question counseling practitioners must ask is what their response should be to this infectious influence on family life that leads to an impressive number of individuals and families facing marital breakup, job loss, mental illness, and even the eventuality of receiving public assistance because they cannot cope with the factor of easy credit.[11] Before examining how some persons have attempted to solve this problem, it might be relevant to mention a few of the resistances that have influenced our work with those people with money problems and the resistances that have played a role in our reluctance to deal substantially with indebtedness.

In the process of serving any client, we constantly struggle within ourselves to identify and cope with the morass of our own complex feelings that give us both the greatest sense of empathy and the difficulty of remaining objective when these same feelings touch experiences we share with those we wish to help. Perhaps nowhere can we see this problem more clearly than in situations in which the client's money mar.agement brushes uncomfortably close to the social worker's own struggle to "make it" in a money world. If we are sincerely going to assist the debt-troubled individual, we must honestly examine our own feelings about money. How many of us, for example, feel a certain uncomfortable twinge when we discuss fees with a client, especially when he or she does not accept the fees readily? What kind of feelings do we wrestle with when someone inquires about out income? How many of us are uncomfortable, or even resentful, when we face the labyrinth of complexities associated with debtors? How frequently is such an indebted person likely to receive more response to his personality problem than to his financial one? How often do we escape our responsibility by rationalizing that his is a problem of a concrete nature to be handled by the home economist? Nevertheless, all of us at one time or another have had to deal with such conflicts.

If we are to become sensitized to the effect of money problems on families, Schneiderman suggests, "We must learn to be as stimulated and concerned about indebtedness as we are about impotence; as concerned about money management and levels of financial adequacy as we are about frigidity."[12] If we are to provide an answer to the problem of heavy indebtedness, we must develop a new approach that departs from the tenets of strict budget management—a surface, mechanical approach only—and from the doctrines of modern psychoanalytic thought that help us understand the individual but too often ignore the social significance of such a problem.

Evolving Patterns of Credit Counseling

How has debt counseling—or as it is more euphemistically called, credit counseling—been provided in recent years? Although a handful of credit bureaus, credit unions, and even some credit grantors provide some form of credit advice, the largest vendor of this service has been the National Foundation for Consumer Credit (NFCC) with its more than one hundred Consumer Credit Counseling agencies. Formed in early 1960, the NFCC has greatly influenced the characteristics of local credit counseling organizations, including the small number of family agencies offering financial counseling as an individual service.[13] These nonprofit programs are funded on a sustaining basis by local business and industry. The major thrust of their service is to help establish a workable budget that allows for part of the family income to be brought to the credit counseling office to be distributed to creditors. It generally takes from twenty to thirty-six months to complete this payment adjustment plan, also referred to as prorating.[14] No work is done with the family aside from the one or two interviews required to set up the plan. Although these programs certainly have met an enormous need, their major drawback lies in their spending too much time (and money) in budgeting and prorating, and too little time in helping with family and personal problems that often underlie the financial problems. Prorating creates the secondary problem of removing the client from the reality of his situation. Thus the experience is of minimum future value. As Frances L. Feldman points out, "Inherent in the counseling process . . . is the recognition that the troubled individual will arrive at a more satisfactory solution . . . if he does most of the thinking and planning and if he accepts responsibility for bettering the solution."[15]

Even when credit counseling agencies recognize related emotional problems and refer problem-ridden families to social agencies for further help, there is little follow-up to determine if the family gets there. This cooperation between the two services has other weaknesses. Many families do not easily reveal their underlying problems, and a professional person is needed to help such families face their problems. In addition, families in heavy debt generally project the blame for their situations onto outside events much as a parent of a delinquent may place blame for the child's problem on bad companions. Credit counseling that does not involve the family in a serious consideration of the total situation not only misses the opportunity to help the family understand why they got into debt in the first place, but fails to furnish them with the means to control themselves better in the future.

A New Approach

Nassau County, adjacent to New York City, has a population of about one and a half million people. Although it is suburban in appearance, it contains much industry and a large number of blue-collar people (40 to 45 percent), the group most heavily pressured by debts.

Family Service Association of Nassau County was established twelve years ago on the recommendation of the local Health and Welfare Council, as a priority need in the social service field. The agency has developed a county-wide counseling service for family problems. In response to special needs, it has also launched several demonstration projects. In 1967, after two years of study, a blue-collar project was initiated in heavily industrial eastern Nassau County. The objective was to reach out to the largely unserved working-class families and provide a more effective form of help through (1) planned short-term treatment (a maximum of fifteen interviews), (2) no waiting list and prompt service to all applicants, (3) an active approach in treatment, geared toward helping clients resolve their pressing problems, (4) availability of service in the evening and on Saturday for the convenience of employed persons, and (5) reaching out to blue-collar groups through contacts and printed matter to unions, factories, stores, and churches.

The project uncovered a pressing need for a debt-counseling service. In the first few months, several families who came for family counseling began to report that they were unable to manage their financial matters. It was decided to test a new approach to this problem by combining short-term therapy and debt counseling. This experience indicated that such counseling must be initiated by a professional social worker skilled in evaluating the total family needs. The actual budgeting and handling of creditors was handled by nonprofessional volunteers, without assuming the client's responsibility to make such payments himself. The caseworker provided short-term family counseling, with some clients referred to psychiatric facilities. It was found, however, that when the initial interview was conducted by a nonprofessional, the crucial family difficulties were not uncovered. As a result, the effectiveness of the debt counseling was jeopardized without the subsequent efforts of the caseworker. It was also learned that periodic follow-up with clients is essential if they are to maintain their repayment plans.

To date, forty families have come to the office specifically for debt counseling. It is difficult to appreciate the plight of families who fall so far behind in their payments that creditors begin to hound them. Usually, family problems already exist, but they are severely compounded by the financial situation. The hardships are great, and the anxiety over what might happen next is even greater. A number of clients who had small children in the home had their electricity and telephone service turned off and neither heat nor cooking facilities available during the severe winter months; cars that were urgently needed for work were repossessed during the middle of the night. In order to help these families with their problems, a program was developed to train volunteers in debt counseling. It has been found that they can approach the problem more practically and economically than can a professional social worker. The agency began with one woman who had had considerable experience in volunteer work in social agencies and has expanded to a corps of four volunteers who meet bimonthly to discuss cases and develop new techniques of dealing with financial problems.

During the past twelve months, they have conducted fifty-one debt-counseling interviews with clients. The trained volunteers work under the supervision of a professional social worker. They work on a budget with the clients and help them decide on appropriate steps to meet their financial obligations. They make special arrangements with the creditors for repayment of debts and in addition follow through to see that the family does not revert to the former pattern.

The assumption in working with these families has been that in addition to the exercise of poor judgment in handling credit, there probably are other underlying factors that cause the family to fall behind in their payments. Accordingly, preceding debt counseling, a caseworker explores the family situation in detail. Such factors as marital discord, illness in the family, severe personality disturbances, and gambling have been found to be causes of indebtedness. The conclusion, therefore, has been that family counseling must go hand-in-hand with debt counseling; if the underlying problems are left untouched, these families will either go into debt again or find themselves confronted with other problems.

After the initial diagnostic interview, the family counselor continues to see the family on a short-term basis—five to eight interviews—to help the family members understand the underlying causes for their distress, while the volunteer assists in following through on repayment plans and offers continued budget and financial counseling. Weekly contact is maintained until the clients are ready to carry on by themselves. Additional support is offered by way of periodic follow-up.

Training Program for Volunteers

A training program was developed that uses group process to teach volunteers the principles of credit counseling and human behavior. It began with teaching the concepts of self-determination, respect for differences in individual life styles, and the need to listen. It gradually progressed to some theoretical understanding of defensive patterns in personality and of the nature of resistance and how to deal with it through motivational forces.

The general understanding of individual psychological needs was emphasized, for this concept is more alien to volunteers than the application of money principles. Although the credit counselor's main responsibility lies in helping clients to repay their debts, she must have some grasp of the underlying emotional factors that can push even a financially secure family to the point at which they are caught in the spiral of borrowing from Peter to pay Paul.[16] Without this knowledge, the counselor has no appreciation of her role in the rehabilitation process.

Soon after the basic issues are covered, each volunteer is assigned to a client and training comes alive. The volunteer must strive now for the client's participation in the repayment process as a necessary and fundamental step in insuring his growth and development. Thus, although all practical aspects of money management are considered—budgeting, scaling down of payments, wife working, additional jobs, refinancing mortgage, and so forth—each client is encouraged to explore and select the method best suited to his own life style.

During this phase, the volunteer may find that the difficulty she is having with a particular client is due more to her reaction to that client than to the complexities of repaying his debts. For example, one rather timid counselor found herself losing interest in an aggressive, manipulating client whose financial problems were tied up with his need to prove his masculinity. At first, all she could see was an ungrateful man who would not listen to the best advice she had to offer. At the other extreme, an aggressive volunteer had to be helped to develop the same understanding of how her impatience with some clients caused her to lose sight of the process, thereby pushing them beyond what they could accept.

Group sessions and supervisory conferences focused on individual client behavior and the particular difficulties experienced by volunteers, such as the repeated threat volunteers initially felt in dealing with an irascible creditor who refused to go along with a scale-down of payments. The conferences also served as an opportunity for caseworker and volunteer to exchange information about what was happening to a certain client at a specific time. Whatever the particulars, the cultivation of teamwork forms the backbone of the program. In fact, its success is predicated upon the belief that this teamwork must include the client, for it has been amply demonstrated that only then can the client's inner resources be strengthened and mobilized so that effective patterns are established and future financial disasters averted.

Case Illustrations

One of the first clients was referred by an ill-fated consumer credit counseling service that went out of business after a year and a half.[17] Mr. and Mrs M were in debt for $2,500 to eighteen creditors. They applied for counseling, indicating that their only problem was a desire for material goods and an inability on their part to control spending. Outward appearances seemed to give credence to their statement that poor judgment was their only problem. Mr. M was a skilled technician earning $9,500 a year with good prospects for the future. Mrs. M was supportive of her husband, and there seemed to be excellent rapport between them and a great willingness to cooperate with the credit counselor.

Deeper probing by the social worker, however, revealed an entirely different picture of their situation. Mrs. M was depressed; in fact, she had contemplated suicide in the past year and had consulted two psychiatrists who had prescribed tranquilizers for her. Mr. M initially denied any personal problems, but the caseworker elicited the fact that he came from a family in which there had been absolute tranquility between his parents; his father had made all decisions and was considered the personification of perfection. Without being consciously aware of it, Mr. M had been carrying this inner image of perfection into his present situation. He could not allow his wife to question his judgment, for to admit mistakes would indicate a weakness that did not fit his mental picture of himself. To please and placate his wife, he took her to expensive restaurants and insisted on spending more than they could afford for furniture and clothing.

Mrs. M came from a family in which there had been many arguments, and she was striving to avoid a repetition of this situation in her present home. As she continued to suppress her own resentments about her husband's spending and poor management, she became increasingly depressed, which resulted in a marked lack of communication between them.

Under the guidance of the caseworker, they became aware of the patterns of interaction in their relationship. Mr. M was able to relax more and spend less, and Mrs. M began to participate in family budgeting, to her husband's delight and relief. The caseworker encouraged both partners to participate more actively with the debt counselor, who was planning their budget and aiding them in acquiring a consolidation loan to cover many small debts. Once the family saw their problems realistically, Mrs. M's depression began to lift, and Mr. M became more free in his dealings with his wife. The family's financial situation was readjusted toward a new outlook, which meant living within a budget that allowed for adequate living expenses and paying off debts over a period of time.

Actual contact which this family covered a four-week period with eight casework sessions and three credit-counseling interviews. A telephone follow-up after six months revealed that they were continuing to pay off their debts and were feeling more relieved and happy.

To reemphasize an important point, it is often difficult to assess the root cause. According to the Family Service Association of America study cited earlier, the basic reasons for indebtedness are poor judgment, unemployment or reduced income, and health problems.[18] In this age of easy credit, indebtedness caused by "poor judgment" can cover a multitude of possibilities, such as sexual inadequacy, marital discord, need for love and security, sense of power, and self-punishment.[19] Indebtedness may be a result of one's need to keep up with the Joneses, or it may express the severe pathology of the alcoholic, the compulsive gambler, and the psychotic.

Mr. and Mrs. P applied for debt counseling when Mr. P's income ($5,000 in the previous year) was not adequate to meet minimal living expenses for their family. Their debts amounted to $3,500. They asserted that Mr. P, a construction worker, had been out of work a great deal during the past year because of poor weather conditions. Although this explanation was plausible, there seemed to be some unexplained elements in this specific situation.

Initially, the caseworker helped the family establish eligibility for public assistance and Medicaid because there was only minimum income at the time of application and there were three small children to care for. The Department of Social Services helped the family financially with such items as electricity and rent while Mr. P worked sporadically.

Meanwhile, with careful questioning and much reassurance during several interviews, the caseworker learned from Mrs. P that her husband was a chronic gambler. At this time, because of tremendous pressure about debts, guilt about his gambling, and threats from loan sharks, Mr. P was suffering a severe panic reaction in which he actually felt that his head would "blow off." For a period of many days, he refused to come to the office and withdrew into his home. Recognizing the seriousness of his reaction, the caseworker—with the assistance of Mrs. P—was able to help Mr. P agree to referral to a psychiatrist. He was taken into treatment immediately for his compulsive gambling problem.

As Mr. P's mental condition improved, he began to work more regularly. He was also encouraged to advertise in a local newspaper to obtain private work during the off-hours, and their income increased accordingly. The credit counselor was then able to prepare a budget for the family, to arrange with their creditors for lower monthly payments, and to help the family live on their current earnings. Contacts with the family included a total of fifteen interviews during a six-month period.

A follow-up a few months after termination revealed an even higher level of functioning. The family was paying off all its debts and living within the prescribed budget. Best of all, Mr. P had gained control of his gambling. The familial and financial situation had improved greatly.

The importance of challenging a client's explanation of what has contributed to his indebtedness is well documented in the following example. Mr. and Mrs. D owed a total of $12,500, and although Mr. D was a professional man earning $15,000 a year, he was unable to meet his payments. They ascribed their indebtedness to a great deal of sickness in the family: Mr. D's, his mother's, the children's. The caseworker wondered about this statement, being aware that the D family had a medical plan, which, although it might not cover all the bills, did pay for most of them. Mr. D also continued to receive his salary while he was sick.

After careful and considerate probing by the caseworker, facts emerged that revealed Mr. D's tremendous psychological need for punishment. Although his better judgment told him he could do without many items of furniture and clothing that were being purchased, he would continually buy more because his children and wife requested them. Then he would complain about the tremendous financial burden he was forced to carry and blame the family for the money they were spending.

On the other hand, Mrs. D was suffering from a severe depression that was caused initially by her mother's death five years earlier but that continued because of the stress and strain in the home. It was difficult to get her to come to the office because she was somewhat afraid of traveling, and she also had a hopeless feeling about their situation.

With a confrontation of the situation, the husband and wife were able to see how each was pulling the other down—Mrs. D with her inaction and morbidity and Mr. D with his constant complaints. They had been barely talking to each other, and when they did, each looked the other way.

With the recognition of their problem and a reawakening of hope, Mrs. D was able to go out and obtain a part-time job. This action lifted her depression somewhat and also added revenue toward their debts. Mr. D gained some psychological understanding of his inability to manage money. In conjunction with the casework contacts, the credit counselor prepared a budget, called their creditors, made new arrangements for lower monthly payments, and pointed out ways to save money in vaious areas.

Six months later, Mr. D telephoned to say that he had been ill and had fallen behind in one payment. He asked help in resolving this problem, and he was reassured that he could call the creditor to make a new agreement. He confided that despite his illness, he had kept up all his payments except this particular one. He also stated that, although many problems still existed, the relationship between his wife and himself had improved considerably.

Implications for the Field

The number of families affected by severe money problems is reaching epidemic proportions. If the estimate is correct that for every bankrupt family twenty more are on the brink of bankruptcy, then nearly three and a half million people are facing financial crises.[20] Although the increasing consumer credit counseling services are easing some of this pressure, for the majority of cases they are not sufficiently equipped to tackle the incipient causes that lead many families to recurrent indebtedness. As one of the largest counseling services reports in its new training manual: "Statistics reveal... that 80 [percent] of all those filing for bankruptcy are back in trouble within five years, and 10 [percent] will file for bankruptcy again as soon as the six year required waiting period has expired."[21]

Despite the dimensions of this problem, in particular its impact on family breakdown, it has remained conspicuously unnoticed by the social work profession. Its consequences are not only reaped in the divorce courts, but on the public assistance rolls as the result of long-term, problem-solving failures.[22] The very fact that indebtedness has reached such extremes is not only an indictment of society's ostrich-like response but a signal to social work agencies to fill the void. Some agencies have already assumed responsibility for setting up advisory boards and enlisting the support of the interested business community.[23] Still others can do their part by meeting with representatives of the local credit counseling office or such credit-granting institutions as banks, finance companies, and credit unions to develop guidelines for cooperation. Some agencies could go a step further by conferring with the chief bankruptcy referee and impressing upon him the importance of casework services as an integral part of his office. They might even persuade him to ask for funds to employ a caseworker who could work in conjunction with their agency.

Short-term casework counseling, which is central to any such program, can be further enhanced by the addition of such services as group therapy for those families with problems requiring group counseling methods; self-help groups, modeled after Alcoholics Anonymous and Gamblers Anonymous, whose members can be encouraged to keep up payment plans, and which will seek out those who are faltering or dropping out and also bring in new members; and consumer life education groups similar in structure to family life education groups, in which the emphasis would be on developing good consumer practices and whose services would be restricted to those who had already gone through more intensive counseling for financial problems. Another, perhaps more important, adjunct to any counseling service is tackling the broader aspects of indeptedness by setting up the mechanism within agencies to work for the elimination of those legal and institutional structures that may have been more responsible for clients' indebtedness than their pathology. As Schneiderman says, "Too often his [the client's] situation or reality is one to which he should not be forced to adjust himself."[24]

Commitment to clients must go beyond helping them accept their reality; we must work with them and others in evolving strategies to change the mass array of regulations, laws, guidelines, rules, and practices that define that reality.[25] In the Nassau County program, for example, it is planned to process individual complaints of consumer fraud or credit abuse through the Family Advocate Division whose staff will compile complaints and will document general abuses. These complaints will then be taken to the board-appointed Public Issues Committee that is geared to form coalitions with other community groups to take action and, in connection with credit problems, to work closely with the Nassau County Office of Consumer Affairs.

In fulfilling this role of advocate, we must broaden our understanding of many regulations affecting the consumer, for without this knowledge our effectiveness is limited. Although there are too many regulations to note here, a few of the more common ones are worth mentioning.[26] In 1968 "the truth-in-lending" law was enacted to require lenders to tell their customers exactly what the total annual borrowing charge would amount to. Some individual states have gone further. So-called cooling-off laws allow customers to rescind contracts made with door-to-door salesmen within twenty-four to seventy-two hours. The "holder in due course" laws are in for heavier public scrutiny and have already been repealed by several states. Under such laws, merchants can sell their installment contracts to finance companies, thereby allowing the customer no recourse should the merchandise prove faulty. A fourth important credit law that may soon fade from the books is one that permits creditors to garnishee the wages of debtors.[27]

Although several states now forbid garnishment firing, it is estimated that between one hundred thousand and three hundred thousand workers are fired each year because of garnishments.[28] To protect his job, a person facing garnishment may enter bankruptcy as a way to avoid being fired. One strategy offered by Julius S. Hobson, head of the Washington, D.C., civil rights group called Associated Community Teams, calls for using bankruptcy as a social protest. "If every poor person who is being gouged would file [for] bankruptcy, it would be more devastating than any riot you ever saw."[29] Some installment buyers either do not read or do not understand the fine print buried in contracts. Items like the "add-on clause" allow the purchaser to add additional purchases under the initial contract. The catch, however, is that if he misses the last payment, the seller can repossess all merchandise purchased under that contract. The "acceleration clause" makes all future installments due if one payment is missed; the "balloon contract" allows for a blown-up final payment. If the buyer does not realize to what he agreed, he can very easily wind up in a credit trap. The number of loopholes is legion. Our obligation to the families we serve, or should be serving, depends upon our understanding that the problems that may result from credit buying jeopardize the very foundations of family life.

In this article we have dealt with the near-monumental problem of family indebtedness, to which insufficient attention has been paid. We have discussed one agency's approach as a guide to others wishing to set up programs aimed at assisting families caught in a morass of financial woes. The value of this program lies in its adaptability for family agencies. With a slight reorientation to the problem of indebtedness, a similar program can be implemented without significant change in existing staff. When the program is supported by paraprofessionals or volunteers, the staff is freed of the details of budgetary procedures and can concentrate on helping the client solve his problem.

In conclusion, let us consider an important point made by Alvin Toffler in his book, *Future Shock*, which explores the possible consequences for those caught up in unharnessed and accelerated change. Too frequently individuals subjected to too much change in too short a time suffer a shattering stress and disorientation that severely impedes their functioning.[30] One example of this impeded functioning seems to be the increasing number of families who are unable to cope with their financial realities and who find themselves plummeting in a direct line onto the welfare rolls. Unless family counseling agencies meet their obligation to these unassisted families and develop specific programs tailored to the problem, they not only forsake those whom they should be serving, but they risk potential replacement by other organizations, as evidenced by what has happened with the Office of Economic Opportunity and is now happening with the growing number of Consumer Credit Counseling Services. If the agencies continue in their immobility and inadaptability to meet change head on, they leave themselves wide open to the possibility that frequent criticism of casework as being inflexible and irrelevant will eventually exert adverse influence on those who control the agencies' financial lifeline. One small example of this problem can be seen in this area, where an influential labor union that contributes heavily to the United Fund is trying to prove that establishment agencies cannot respond adequately to the need of immediate family counseling.

The intent of this article goes beyond simple description of a new use of staff to meet an enlarging social and family problem. It will have meaning only if it stimulates others to realize the need to intervene and in their own way assist families threatened by overwhelming debts. The opportunity exists to prevent the kind of attacks justly leveled against so many institutions, but we must be willing to risk change within ourselves and our agencies.

References

1.   Leonard Schneiderman, The Practical and Cultural Significance of Money, *Public Welfare*, 23:199 (July 1965).

2.   Ibid., pp. 197–98.

3.   The Troubled American: A Special Look at the White Majority, *Newsweek*, October 6, 1969, p. 32.

4.   Herbert Bienstock, Employment, Prices, and Living Standards in Nassau and Suffolk Counties (Paper presented at the annual meeting of the Health and Welfare Council of Nassau County, East Meadow, New York, May 20, 1970), p. 13.

5.   These points are discussed in greater detail in The Troubled American, pp. 29–75; and The Blue Collar Worker's Lowdown Blues, *Time*, November 9, 1970, pp. 68–78.

6.   U.S., Congress, House, *Congressional Record*, President Johnson's Message to Congress, 90th Cong., February 16, 1967, Vol. 113, pt. 3, p. 3528.

7.   *Wall Street Journal*, April 16, 1968, p. 1.

8.   Worry Grows: Paying Personal Debts, *U.S. News and World Report*, June 22, 1970, pp. 66–68.

9.   Family Service Association of America, *Family Credit Counseling—An Emerging Community Service*, Summary Report (New York: Family Service Association of America, 1967), p. 9.

10. *Newsday*, February 5, 1970, p. 96.

11. It is important to recognize the close relationship that exists between marital adjustment and proper consumer practices. See Reuben Hill, Judgment and Consumership in the Management of Family Resources, *Sociology and Social Research*, 47: 446–60 (July 1963).

12. Schneiderman, p. 199.

13. *Family Credit Counseling*, pp. 13–14.

14. Commercial prorating where fees are charged for counseling services has been outlawed in a large number of states because of widespread exploitation.

15. Frances Lomas Feldman, *The Family in a Money World* (New York: Family Service Association of America, 1957), p. 84.

16. Geoffrey G. Rankin, Debts and Family Casework, *Case Conference*, 14:22–26 (May 1967).

17. The social characteristics of the families assisted were similar to those studied elsewhere: usually in their mid-thirties with three to four children and with low to moderate incomes, with their formal education ending around the tenth grade. See Max Siporin, Bankrupt Debtors and Their Families, *Social Work*, 12:51–62 (July 1967); *Family Credit Counseling*, pp. 17–18; Robert O. Herrmann, Family in Bankruptcy—A Survey of Recent Studies, *Journal of Marriage and the Family*, 28:324–40 (August 1966); David Caplovitz, The Problems of Blue-Collar Consumers, in *Blue Collar World: Studies of the American Worker*, ed. Arthur B. Shostak and William Gomberg (Englewood Cliffs, N.J.: Prentice-Hall, 1964), pp. 110–20.

18. Interviews with sixty-five families revealed that medical bills represent only 10 percent of bills: however, the relationship between illness and loss of income is hard to determine. *Family Credit Counseling*, p. 19.

19. For excellent discussions on the psychological implication of money, see William Kaufman, Some Emotional Uses of Money, *Pastoral Psychology*, 16:43–56 (April 1965); and Norman M. Lobsenz and Clark W. Blackburn, *How To Stay Married: A Modern Approach to Sex, Money, and Emotions in Marriage* (New York: Cowles Book Company, 1969).

20. The former Consumer Credit Counseling Service of Long Island reported a waiting list of more than three hundred families in Nassau County alone in 1966. If the present counseling is expanded to a county-wide basis, the need will probably exceed one thousand families a year.

21. Credit Counseling Centers, *Credit Counseling Training Handbook* (Southfield, Mich: Credit Counseling Centers, 1970), p. 70.

22. Siporin, *Bankrupt Debtors*, p. 52; Alvin L. Shorr, The Family Cycle and Income Development, *Social Security Bulletin*, 29:14–25 (February 1966).

23. Recently, the Consumer Credit Counseling Service of Greater Charlotte, North Carolina, merged with the Family and Children's Service with the encouragement of the local branch of the United Appeal.

24. Schneiderman, *Significance of Money*, pp. 200–201.

25. In this connection, see Robert Sunley, Family Advocacy: From Case to Cause, SOCIAL CASEWORK, 51:347–57 (June 1970).

26. Fur further information on this subject, see Sidney Margolius, *The Responsible Consumer*, Pamphlet no. 453 (New York: Public Affairs Committee, 1970); and The Hard Facts About Easy Credit Points to Remember Before You Buy or Borrow, *Changing Times*, November 1970, pp. 27–30.

27. According to a July 15, 1970 news release from the New York State Attorney General's office, effective September 1, 1970, salaries of less than $85 a week can no longer be garnisheed.

28. Steve Schlossberg, Protest Lack of Notice, Hearing: Garnishment Test Case Before Supreme Court, *UAW Solidarity* (April 1969), p. 11, as reported in Credit Counseling Centers, *Credit Counseling Training Handbook* (Southfield, Mich.: Credit Counseling Centers, 1970), p. 67.

29. *Wall Street Journal*, April 16, 1968, p. 1.

30. Alvin Toffler, *Future Shock* (New York: Random House, 1970).

21
Counseling and Treatment of the Poor Black Family

David Hallowitz

A review of the periodical literature over the past fifteen years can leave one with the discouraged feeling that effective clinical counseling and treatment of poor black clients are rendered almost impossible by the social and environmental burdens of these clients. Consequently, there seems to be a strong tendency to curtail and devalue such services. Martin A. Silverman and Eva Wolfson state:

> Individual psychotherapy... is the most effective method of treatment we have for producing lasting change in a child's attitudes and the use he makes of his resources. As such, it would appear to be aptly suited to the needs of the ghetto child. For varying reasons, it is little used in programs for the disadvantaged.... There are centers, in fact, in which mental health workers are implored to abandon their professional skills altogether and devote themselves entirely to social action.[1]

Carol M. Brooks makes the observation:

> The goal of adaptation should no longer be the goal of the worker. The social work profession, particularly, has been accused of focusing too long on patching up the afflicted and ignoring the primary causes of trouble. The conditions that generate the major trauma experienced by minority people grow out of society's basic structures. Social workers, therefore, should concentrate on intervention strategies that seek to change these structures.[2]

Similar points of view have been presented by other writers.[3]

The purpose of this article is to show that there is a need and place for professional clinical services to poor black clients; to delineate the range of potentially effective counseling and treatment modalities and methods; and to present some of the substance of such clinical practice.

Source: From *Social Casework* 56 (October 1975), pp. 451–459. Copyright © 1975 by the Family Service Association of America. Reprinted by permission.

Singling out poor black clients for separate examination could be misinterpreted as discriminatory. In truth, most of what is discussed here applies also to poor white families and to families of all socioeconomic groups. It is also a shortcoming of this chapter that poor black families are placed in a single category; in actuality, there are many differentiations and subgroupings within that category—too many to formulate here. The intentions of this article is to express profound respect for poor black families and to urge that clinical services of the highest quality be made fully available to them.

There is significant evidence of the validity of professional clinical services for poor people generally—including, of course, many black families. Discussing the issue of casework with the poor, Florence Hollis concludes:

> There are, indeed, differences between casework with the average low-income, poorly educated client and casework with the average middle-income, well-educated client. But these are differences in specific techniques and in emphases rather than in basic casework *method*. Work with impoverished families involves the use of all the procedures valued in work with more advantaged groups.[4]

Silverman and Wolfson observe that:

> An entirely different source of opposition to the use of psychotherapeutic techniques with disadvantaged populations is the claim that the lower classes are unable to make good use of such techniques. Our own experience indicates that this view is fallacious. Although obstacles exist, we have found that symptoms and developmental disturbances in this population [ghetto children] can be ameliorated . . . [We have also found that]a number of popular ideas regarding poor people's motivation for treatment and [their] ability to cooperate in a long-term venture with the goal of future rather than current satisfaction are either exaggerated or incorrect.[5]

Obstacles to Providing Counseling Services

There is no doubt that the socioeconomic conditions in which poor black families live create great impediments to their seeking and using clinical counseling and treatment services. Among these conditions are a preoccupation with the struggle for survival; the absence of a father in many families; the power of the delinquent gang, from which the youngster seeks the emotionally gratifying relationships he does not receive from his family and which also provides an outlet for pent-up anger and frustration; and the considerable difficulty core-area schools have in providing educational and growth experiences. Because of emotional deprivation and lack of parental interest and stimulation, many children become poor students and resort to disruptive and antisocial behavior in school. School faculties often have to look to their own safety and survival.

The problem of providing professional clinical services is compounded by the fact that the settings in which they are offered often are identified as serving the white, middle-class population. Poor black families tend to shy away from such settings for fear of further rejection and frustration. Similarly, there is an inherent distrust of the white, middle-class professional, yet, regrettably, there is a dearth of well-trained black professionals, and even they are confronted with technical difficulties in trying to work effectively with black clients.[6]

There is an undeniable question as to whether the white therapist can be effective with the black client. All writers on this subject agree that this issue is a real one and must be reckoned with in one form or another, to a greater or lesser degree.[7] The white therapist must examine with self-awareness, and try to resolve, subtle, subconscious prejudicial feelings about working with poor black clients. The white therapist-black client issue must be kept in mind by the therapist. In many instances, his basic acceptance of the poor black client as a person and a human being may be sufficient to dissolve the initial distrust and resistance on the client's part—perhaps not completely, but sufficiently to allow for constructive treatment and counseling work on both parts. In this connection, Peter Cimbolic found that black students did not show a preference for a counselor as a function of the counselor's color but of his level of experience.[8] In other instances, it may be necessary for the therapist to initiate discussion with the client of the color and ethnic differences between them. Shirley Cooper cautions:

> In short, in clinical work with minority patients, an overbalanced stress on difference, on ethnicity and its concomitant psychological meaning can distort the helping process. It may lead a therapist to focus so centrally on ethnic factors that individual problems and individual solutions become obscured.[9]

Reviewing numerous studies, Alfred Kadushin concludes that:

> although non-white workers may be necessary for non-white clients in some instances and therapeutically desirable in others, white workers can work and have worked effectively with non-white clients . . . although race is important, the nature of the interpersonal relationship established between two people is more important than skin color and . . . although there are disadvantages to racially mixed worker-client contacts, there are special advantages. Conversely, there are special advantages to racial similarity and there are countervailing disadvantages.[10]

New Approaches in Clinical Practice

In the face of the enormous socioeconomic obstacles and technical difficulties inherent in the white therapist-black client relationship, it is understandable that a tendency to curtail and devalue clinical services has developed. It is also understandable and highly commendable that certain needed programs have been developed—for example, outreach, crisis intervention, and social action services.

One should not lose sight of the fact that there have been exciting, innovative approaches in clinical practice—for example, the provision of clinical services in neighborhood settings which black clients can more naturally, comfortably, and conveniently attend and which provide the same help within the home.[11] Family therapy and counseling are also being increasingly used, with flexible modifications to meet the differing needs and circumstances of the black family.[12] Indigenous paraprofessionals play a vital role in helping families move into therapy and counseling programs, as well as assisting directly in these programs.

This article is based on the experience of The Psychiatric Clinic of Buffalo, New York, which serves children and adolescents up to the age of eighteen and their families. It can be characterized broadly as part of the Establishment, and its professional staff is almost entirely white, not by choice but because of the paucity of black professionals.

Several years ago, scarcely any black families were being served because of subtly rejecting attitudes on the part of the professional staff, not just toward poor black families but toward the lower socioeconomic group in general. Such clients did not provide gratifying experiences for the therapists. Traditional psychotherapy was extremely difficult to conduct in the face of family disorganization, extreme family pathology, and the inevitable preoccupation of the client with issues of survival. However, as the staff honestly faced their subconscious rejecting attitudes and became more accepting of such families, a new message was somehow communicated to poor families, including the black families, so that they increasingly applied for and received treatment and counseling services. The positive resolution and change in staff attitudes also constituted a vital dynamic in treatment and counseling effectiveness. Now, nineteen percent of the clinic clientele is black, although the proportion of black people in the community is only nine percent.

Principles of Effective Clinical Practice

It is vital that the agency and the practitioner have conviction about providing quality treatment and counseling services. Clinical services for all members of the family include crisis intervention, brief treatment, guidance and education, individual therapy, parent treatment, family therapy, and group therapy. The mental set of the clinician should be related to diagnostic and differential thinking toward determining particular treatment plans and goals—doing whatever is necessary effectively to help the client in relation to the presenting problems and the underlying dynamics.

People in distress should be seen without delay in the office or the home, dispensing with conventional intake and diagnostic procedures. Attention should be given, first and foremost, to the immediate problems for which the client is seeking help. The practitioner should reach out to the family when appointments are not kept and should meet with the client even if the latter is late or comes on the wrong day or at the wrong time. The process should not be viewed in terms of regular weekly interviews and the conventional fifty-minute hour, but as a continuum of contact whether it be by regular interviews, irregular interviews, home visits, or telephone communication. The telephone can be a powerful means of maintaining and enhancing the process.[13]

It is important to discover and work with the strengths in individuals and families without becoming overwhelmed by social pathology and psychopathology. Many black families, even if fatherless, show considerable strength and cohesion, which is augmented by the interest and involvement of relatives and friends.

Use should be made of such clinic resources as psychological testing, psychiatric evaluation, medication, and the arranging of neurological and other medical studies.

Family interviews and family process should be used to ameliorate or resolve intrafamilial relationship conflicts and strengthen the family. The practitioner should find and draw into the process relatives and close friends who can play a constructive role with the individual and family. Methodology should be modified to meet the special characteristics of poor black families.[14]

A problem-solving component[15] must be developed in the treatment process, and assertive leadership and direction should be provided for the family.[16]

Focus should be on the specific behaviors of the child in the context of the treatment process, the intrafamilial relationships, and the child-teacher relationship. Such a focus has been found effective with both young children and immature young adolescents. Concretizing their behaviors with task-oriented goals makes it easier for them to grasp and work on the problems that create difficulties for them in the family and the school. The incentives spelled out by the therapist are the winning of the good feeling, the liking, and the love of those persons who are important in the child's life and the gaining in self-esteem.

The practitioner should play an advocacy role in relation to organizations with authority and power over the clients' lives, but only when clients do not have the capacity to take independent action or when it would be of no avail. This kind of intervention by the therapist has to be carefully considered in the context of the total treatment process and undertaken with the full participation of the client.[17]

The practitioner must collaborate with teachers and the school faculty toward meeting the child's educational and socialization needs.[18]

After termination, the practitioner should be ready to provide additional help when the need is discovered by direct follow-up or because the family has called the therapist or agency. Poor black families, like other low-income families who have sought clinical assistance, usually need help from time to time over the years, mostly on a crisis-intervention basis but at times for resumption of treatment and counseling.

Black mental health workers should be involved as assistants in counseling and treatment programs; where possible, those who possess the interest, the basic qualities, and the potential should be helped to become full-fledged counselors and therapists.[19] Such help would entail in-service training, supervision, and, eventually, formal professional education.

Case Vignettes

The following vignettes illustrate most of the above principles and concepts. In each one, the therapist is white and the client is black.

The first case illustrates a commonly used form of therapy. The only difference was that the therapist was white and the adolescent black.

Michael, a fourteen-year-old boy, was an only child and lived with his mother. He spent most of his leisure time alone in the house. His teachers reported him to be quiet and withdrawn, and he applied himself minimally to his work. He had no friends in school or in the neighborhood.

Michael was found to be very depressed and bordering upon a psychosis-like withdrawal. Although the mother was loving and caring, she had to work full time. Michael's disturbance stemmed not from the relationship with his mother but from the divorce five years earlier which left him without a father figure in his life. Individual therapy with Michael and periodic interviews with the mother of a guidance and supportive nature made up the treatment plan.

Individual interviews with Michael continued for seven months. He walked a considerable distance from school for each appointment, yet he scarcely expressed himself verbally. Most of the therapy hour was spent playing sedentary games or with a football outdoors. The therapist would express in a modeling way his own feeling reactions to what was taking place in the activity and make comparable expressive remarks from Michael's standpoint. Little by little, Michael came forth with spontaneous expressions of his own. They had fun together, and through the play and verbally the therapist communicated his liking for Michael. From time to time, the therapist would talk with him about the original problems for which he came to the clinic: his feelings about the divorce, the loss of his father, and his relationship with his mother, and his interests and activities at home and in school. Michael became a happier person, played on the school basketball and football teams, made friends, and improved his schoolwork.

A second case is indicative of individual therapy for a black mother by a white therapist: the latter's advocacy role with respect to a serious environmental problem; and therapy with the boy by the black mental health trainee who provided an important relationship experience for Donald at the same time he helped him adjust better within his family and the school. The involvement of the teacher was an important aspect of the treatment program.

Donald, an eight-year old boy, and his three siblings were living with their mother who had been divorced from the father several years earlier. His teacher reported that Donald paid scarcely any attention to her or to his schoolwork.

In the clinic, Donald was seen as emotionally immature and insecure. He was reacting to his mother's insecurity and inconsistency in relating to him, and to the loss of his father. The mother, who cared deeply for Donald, was unhappy and often depressed about being on public assistance and living far from her own mother and family. She was in conflict about becoming emotionally and sexually involved with men in general and one friend in particular. These personal problems made it difficult for her to meet Donald's needs.

The initial treatment approach consisted of the therapist and a black mental health trainee—a young man—meeting in family therapy sessions with the mother and Donald. The trainee and Donald quickly took a liking to each other, and the treatment approach, therefore, was changed to that of the therapist working individually with the mother and the trainee, under the therapist's supervision, meeting in play sessions with Donald. There were times when the latter also visited Donald in his home. The mother's therapist and the boy's therapist held a conference with Donald's teacher to involve her as part of the treatment team.

A self-exploring person, the mother made excellent use of the therapeutic situation, gaining insights into her relationship with Donald and her personal problems. A reality environmental problem arose which she could not solve. She wanted desperately to move from the housing project in which she lived because of the prevalence of gangland violence and because a murder had actually been committed nearby. Her appeals to the housing authorities went unheeded. With her permission, the therapist intervened in her behalf and the desired result was achieved.

This third vignette illustrates the importance of the therapist's reaching out to the resistive client; his dealing directly with the white therapist-black client issue; his drawing upon the psychological evaluation and group therapy resources of the clinic; his working with the school; and the extension of the clinic-client relationship beyond the point of termination.

Gerald, a ten-year-old boy, was truanting from school and doing failing work. In addition, he did not cooperate with his mother in regard to household responsibilities. Gerald revealed that he was unhappy and angry that his mother had to work and could not spend much time with him. The mother was having difficulty in carrying the responsibility of earning a livelihood for, and trying to raise, her two children. She, herself, was a most unhappy person. Deserted by her husband when the children were young, she was bitter toward men and frustrated that she had no social life. Gerald was reacting to past and current emotional deprivation in a passive-aggressive manner. Psychological testing found him to be of average intelligence, capable of doing satisfactory school work.

When the mother and boy failed to come for the third appointment, the therapist called the mother. Angrily, she asserted that there was no point in continuing to come to the clinic because it was not helping her child. The therapist explained that a problem of this kind could not be solved immediately, and he invited her to come in and discuss it with him more fully. She accepted.

In the interview, the mother expressed her anger at the therapist for not bringing about a change in the child. Sensing that her anger and hostility had other causes, the therapist asked if her anger had anything to do with his being a white person. Without answering the question directly but, significantly, not denying its implications, she expressed herself vehemently and at length about how people like the therapist, to whom she had gone for help, were always blaming her, not really listening to her, and "pushing [her] around." In retrospect, it occurred to the therapist that the mother might also have been reacting in part to his being a man. Her experiences with men were negative, and she no longer trusted them. The therapist accepted her anger without having counteraggressive feelings. In fact, in his feelings and verbally, he expressed understanding and empathy. By the end of the interview, her anger had subsided and she agreed to continue.

The treatment process entailed individual work with Gerald and the mother; family sessions, mostly with Gerald and his mother but also, at times, including his older sister; and a close collaborative working relationship between the therapist and the teacher. At a later point, Gerald also took part in a boys' therapy group so that he could learn to relate to his peers.

The treatment program continued for about one year, with good progress made. Subsequently, there were occasional crises for which the mother turned to the therapist for help.

This fourth vignette illustrates the value of a focus upon specific behaviors of the child in the context of the treatment process; the use of psychiatric evaluation and medication; and collaborative work with the school. Treatment of the mother was mostly of a guidance nature. An unsophisticated, uneducated but intelligent person, she used the suggestions of the therapist.

Richard could not be contained in school because of his hyperactivity. This eight-year-old constantly jumped out of his seat and ran around the room, disrupting the class. Consequently, he was placed on half-day sessions. At home, he would not obey his mother, was destructive, and wandered from the neighborhood.

Diagnostically, it was thought that Richard was reacting to a weak family situation in which there was no father and the mother was overwhelmed by trying to raise four young children on a public welfare allowance. In addition, Richard had minimal brain damage.

The four children were born of different fathers, out of wedlock. The mother conscientiously tried her best to give good care to the children and came regularly with Richard, bringing her younger children along with her, even though it meant taking two buses to make the trip.

The clinic's psychiatrist who was involved in the evaluative process placed the boy on medication, which helped partially, but Richard was still difficult to manage in school and at home. In an individual interview, the therapist said to Richard: "Would you like to get along better with your mother and teacher? If you could do this—do your part—your mother and teacher would not be angry with you so much and could really get to like you. Your mother would be able to give you the love you need." Richard wanted to try. The therapist suggested making a game of it. Together, they drew up a chart for each day of the week, one for home and one for school. Richard listed the behaviors upon which he would try to improve: at home, listening to his mother, not breaking things, putting his things away, and so forth; at school, not jumping out of his seat, not bothering the other children, listening to the teacher, and so forth. The mother and Richard, and the teacher and Richard, together would fill out the chart at the end of each day and record a mark: A for excellent, B for good, C for not good. The mother and teacher were asked to discuss each item with Richard. Richard would bring the charts to the therapist each week. The therapist and Richard developed an individualized relationship so that there was an element of his wanting to put forth the effort in order to please the therapist, as well as to his mother and teacher. The A's and B's eventually predominated and Richard was proud of his achievements.

This last vignette illustrates again the possibility of conducting intensive therapy with a black person by a white therapist; arranging for medical studies; the use of medication; and the limitations of clinical treatment because of the chronicity of the individual and family psychopathology and the nearly overwhelming environmental hardships.

Vera, a nine-year-old girl, had frequent abdominal pains, headaches, and other physical ailments, although in-hospital studies revealed no physical basis for the symptoms. The psychiatric opinion was that Vera was developing a neurotic pattern of reaction to the mother's emotional disturbance and past history of mental illness, particularly to the latter's intermittent anxiety states. Vera would then become visibly worried, count the mother's prescribed pills for fear she might take an overdose, and look in on her mother when asleep. The mother had similar psychosomatic symptoms herself, had attempted suicide, and had been in a psychiatric hospital a few years earlier because of a mental breakdown.

In addition to Vera's problems, the mother was beset by the physical problems of her seven-year-old son who had a history of petit mal and grand mal epilepsy. The children were born of a marriage in which she was cruelly treated by her husband and often physically beaten in the presence of the children. Her husband had also been unfaithful to her, and she had obtained a divorce. Growing up as a child, Vera's mother had witnessed terrible fighting between her own parents who separated when she was seven years old. There were other traumatic and tragic episodes in the immediate family: the mother's sister had been murdered by her husband who, in turn, committed suicide.

The initial treatment plan was individual therapy for Vera and the mother by two therapists. The child's psychiatrist, however, found that Vera's symptomatology was reactive to the mother's upset states and that the key to the helping process would be therapy with the mother. The mother readily understood and accepted the termination of therapy for Vera and the continuation of hers.

Early in the mother's treatment process, the therapist arranged for psychiatric evaluation. The psychiatrist met with her and arranged thorough medical studies with respect to the physical symptoms. When it was found that the symptoms were psychogenic, the psychiatrist placed her on medication as an adjunct to therapy.

The mother was able to reveal to the therapist a great deal about herself and her significant life experiences, her current fears of men, her anxieties about embarking upon a course of study toward becoming a registered nurse, her anxieties and upset feelings about her children, and the financial hardships entailed in being dependent upon public assistance.

Feeling a lack of self-confidence in peer relationships, she joined a mothers' therapy group in which there were black and white members. She participated in helping others with their problems and revealed her very personal problems and feelings as well. She found that the members liked and accepted her and provided her with much-needed help as well.

The mother made progress through the individual and group therapy. She began going out with men. She had a need for companionship as well as sexual gratification, all of which she discussed openly with the therapist and in the group. As the mother improved, the child's symptoms subsided. Yet, the mother had setbacks from time to time and then the same would happen with Vera. The case has been in treatment for two years. Although overall the mother's progress has been substantial, and so has Vera's, it is doubtful that the two will ever achieve complete stabilization. Periodic interventions over a period of many years seem to be the future perspective.

Discussion and Summary

By chance, in none of the vignettes was there a father in the family, although a number of intact black families have come to the clinic. However, a large proportion of poor black families in need of clinical services seem to be without fathers. On the other hand, cohesion and strength are often found in the nuclear and extended family.

The outcome in the cases described was generally favorable. But in other cases, the results have been unfavorable, in large part because of the obstacles created by the adverse socioeconomic conditions that beset black families. Yet, the psychological and emotional diagnostic determinants must also be considered.[20] Many poor black children suffer extensive emotional deprivation, and they often do not have the limits, controls, and supervision by loving parents that they need for normal psychosocial development. Children and parents may have developed severe personality and characterological impairments. The child's poor ego and superego development, inadequate capacity for reality-testing, and impulsive acting-out behavior may have reached such proportions that it is impossible to treat him effectively on an outpatient basis, even with the variety of counseling and treatment modalities that have been developed.

Such unfavorable outcomes are also found in work with poor white families in which there has been a great deal of disorganization and chaos, thereby creating conditions for disturbed emotional development in the children. Middle-class and upper-class white families in which, despite economic affluence, there is marital strife, mental illness, and other conditions also produce inadequate emotional nurturance of children, leading to emotional disturbance and mental illness later on in life. Yet, it can not be denied that, by and large, poor black families suffer much more stress, hardship, and disorganization than white families of the various socioeconomic groups.

The thesis of this article is that professional counseling and therapeutic services are needed and wanted by poor black families. Among the technical problems involved in the white therapist-black client therapeutic relationship and process are the need for the therapist's being aware of and dealing with his own subtly prejudicial attitudes and the distrust and hostility which the black client may have toward him. Although working with poor black families is different from working with poor white families, there is also a great similarity: basic counseling and treatment principles, concepts, and methods apply to both groups. The same holds true for all families, regardless of racial origin and socioeconomic status, in which conditions precipitate maladaptive behavior, emotional disturbance, and mental breakdown.

The segment on the spectrum of clinical services that can be used by poor black families may be the same as or narrower than a comparable segment on a spectrum for white families. If narrower, it does not mean that these families should be denied professional clinical services. Moreover, it is possible that what has been learned about the principles and concepts of effective clinical practice with poor black families can be extended to many more such families. Establishing more clinical centers in their neighborhoods and in other settings that would not be forbidding and threatening constitutes one avenue of approach. Professional clinical services for poor black families must be developed and extended at the same time that the range of other services and programs, aimed at ameliorating and correcting the adverse social conditions under which they live, are also being developed and extended.

There is a need to discover how more black people can be enabled to become trained professionals. Continuation and extension of the use of black paraprofessionals as clinical assistants has validity, in any event. There is a great need for such workers to provide relationship experiences for emotionally deprived children of fatherless families. They can also be of help in enabling black families to take the step of going to a clinical center. Certain of these paraprofessionals, with the interest and basic qualities and potential, can become full-fledged therapists through in-service training, supervision, and eventual formal professional education.

References

1.   Martin A. Silverman and Eva Wolfson, Early Intervention and Social Class, *Journal of the American Academy of Child Psychiatry*, 10:603 (October 1971).

2.   Carol M. Brooks, New Mental Health Perspectives in the Black Community, *Social Casework*, 55:491 (October 1974).

3.   William G. Mayfield, Mental Health in the Black Community, *Social Work*, 17:106-10 (May 1972); and Charles Hersch, Mental Health Services and the Poor, *Psychiatry*, 29:236-45 (August 1960).

4.   Florence Hollis, Casework and Social Class, *Social Casework*, 46:170 (October 1965).

5.   Silverman and Wolfson, Early Intervention and Social Class, p. 604.

6.   Maynard Calnek, Racial Factors in the Counter-transference: The Black Therapist and the Black Client, *American Journal of Orthopsychiatry*, 40:39-46 (January 1970): and LaMaurice H. Gardiner, The Therapeutic Relationship under Varying Conditions of Race, *Psychotherapy: Theory Research and Practice*, 8:78-87 (Spring 1971).

7.   Jean S. Gochros, Recognition and Use of Anger in Negro Clients, *Social Work*, 11:28-34 January 1966); Evelyn Stiles et al., Hear It like It Is. *Social Casework*, 53:292-99 (May 1972); Alfred Kadushin, The Racial Factor in the Interview, *Social Work*, 17:88-98 (May 1972); and Shirley Cooper, A Look at the Effect of Racism on Clinical Work, *Social Casework*, 54:76-84 (February 1973).

8.   Peter Cimbolic, Counselor Race and Experience Effects on Black Clients, *Journal of Consulting and Clinical Psychology*, 39:328-32 (October 1972).

9.   Cooper, A Look at the Effect of Racism, p. 78.

10. Kadushin, The Racial Factor in the Interview, p. 98.

11. Dorcas D. Bowles, Making Casework Relevant to Black People: Approaches, Techniques, Theoretical Implications, *Child Welfare*, 48:468-75 (October 1969); Ar-

thur Pierson, Social Work Techniques with the Poor, *Social Casework*, 51:481–85 (October 1970); and Mildred G. Edwards and Edith R. Schmidt, "Downtown" Is the Office, *Social Casework*, 52:634–42 (December 1971).

12. Salvador Minuchin and Braulio Montalvo, Techniques for Working with Disorganized Low Socioeconomic Families, *American Journal of Orthopsychiatry*, 37:880–87 (October 1967); and Geraldine E. McKinney, Adapting Family Therapy to Multideficit Families, *Social Casework*, 51:327–33 (June 1970).

13. Norman Epstein and Anne Shainline, Paraprofessional Parent-Aides and Disadvantaged Families, *Social Casework*, 55:230–36 (April 1974).

14. Minuchin and Montalvo, Techniques for Working with Disorganized Families; and McKinney, Adapting Family Therapy.

15. David Hallowitz, The Problem-solving Component in Family Therapy, *Social Casework*, 51:67–75 (February 1970): and idem, Problem Solving Theory, in *Social Work: Interlocking Theoretical Approaches*, ed. Francis J. Turner (New York: The Free Press, 1974).

16. David Hallowitz, Ralph Bierman, Grace P. Harrison, and Burton Stulberg, The Assertive Counseling Component of Therapy, *Social Casework*, 43:543–48 (November 1967).

17. David Hallowitz, Advocacy in the Context of Treatment, *Social Casework*, 55:416–20 (July 1974).

18. David Hallowitz and Catherine Van Dyke, The Role of the School as Part of the Treatment Program, *Child Welfare*, 52:392–99 (June 1973).

19. Carter Umbarger, The Paraprofessional and Family Therapy, *Family Process*, 11:147–62 (June 1972); and Kermit B. Nash and Victoria A. Mittlefehldt, Supervision and the Emerging Professional, *American Journal of Orthopsychiatry*, 45:93–101 (January 1975).

20. Barbara E. Shannon, The Impact of Racism on Personality Development, *Social Casework*, 54:519–25 (November 1973).

22
Counseling Engaged Couples in Small Groups

Dorothy R. Freeman

The prodigious advances in science and technology made in this century have had their impact on family life, and former guidelines for role behavior of husbands, wives, and children are no longer valid in our society. However, there is general agreement that the family's central function—child-rearing and socializing youth to find its place in society—remains. If the family is the primary agent for the molding of adults to live in our society and achieve personal satisfaction, the new pattern of the democratic family creates a challenge for the isolated young couple. The absence of norms—what to expect in marriage—and the fact that yesterday's parental family no longer serves as a suitable model for many young couples in our large cities have contributed to the confusion and relative inability of couples to create a set of values on which to build a sound and healthy family life.

The modern "companionship" marriage calls for freer communication (more open sharing of experiences) and joint decision-making between husband and wife. It demands skills, adaptation to change, and a willingness to give and take for which young couples are often ill prepared. Recognizing "the present high rate of marriage failure as a constant source of infection to the mental health of the community," the Marriage Counselling Centre of Montreal was set up in 1955 as a community mental health service with emphasis on premarital counseling.[1]

John J. O. Moore has emphasized the need to see marriage counseling as part of a spectrum of interdependent community services supported by such basic institutions as schools and churches and by related professional groups, stating: "In the language of war, we can perceive of preparation for marriage as one line of defense."[2] He saw premarital counseling as being related to parent, youth, family life, and professional education. The center

Source: From Social Work 10:4 (October 1965), pp. 36–42. Copyright © 1965 by the Family Service Association of America. Reprinted by permission.

agrees that preparation for marriage and counseling of engaged couples in groups cannot be isolated from a community-wide program to strengthen the family.

The present paper will focus on this line of defense—group counseling for engaged couples—recognizing the limitations inherent in this approach. It is viewed as a primary preventive service: promotion of healthy marriages and reduction of the risk of marital breakdown. This aspect of primary prevention is also in operation in a number of marriage counseling centers in the United States.

Group counseling of engaged couples was initiated by the writer in 1955 through the Extension Department of the McGill University School of Social Work. In 1956 it was added to the services provided by the Marriage Counselling Centre of Montreal for individual couples before and after marriage. The center has experimented with the small-group discussion method and has limited counseling sessions to ten and sometimes to six two-hour periods. Groups are limited to five or six couples to permit effective participation and interaction.

For operational purposes, the Marriage Counselling Centre of Montreal distinguishes between group counseling and group therapy, particularly in terms of aims and goals of the group. The center agrees with the distinction made between therapy and guidance groups by Slavson and others, i.e., that therapy groups are concerned less with the group process than with the individual's problems and dynamics and encourage transference, catharsis, and insight.[3] In a group that meets for only six or ten sessions, it is important for the leader to avoid activating early emotional conflicts of unconscious content. In keeping with Slavson's ideas, the clinic has accepted the importance of focusing on current reality in counseling engaged couples in groups and of relating group content to marital role expectations.

Aim of the Group

The aim of the engaged couples' group is not to set up a single model of the "good" marriage, but to make each couple aware of the kind of marriage appropriate for them—one that would meet their individual needs. The center accepts the view of a healthy family as one that is able to work out its problems, rather than one that is problem-free.[4] Its belief is that marriage is not a ready-made affair; each person in the partnership has a responsibility to contribute to its growth, development, and endurance. The objective, therefore, is to help the young couple understand the stresses, as well as the satisfactions, that are part of all family life.

Slavson's experience with guidance groups indicates that individuals with "a not too neurotic pattern can effect constructive attitude-change in four to twenty sessions." Rutledge has also expressed the conviction that in fifteen sessions significant behavioral and attitudinal change can take place.[5] The center has found that counseling young couples in groups can provide a constructive learning experience, involving clarification of reality expectations of themselves and their prospective mates, within the limitations of ten or even six sessions. Although the primary focus of these counseling groups is educational, at the same time attitudes and behavior have been modified through the group experience. There are limitations, however: all couples cannot profit from this experience to the same extent, and ongoing counseling for a couple is sometimes required when the sessions are completed. The fee charged includes a final separate interview with the counselor and, if indicated, further counseling sessions may be arranged for the couple.

The couples are usually self-referred, responding to a newspaper or radio announcement. Parents (usually the mother), a doctor, a clergyman, or a couple who had previously attended the course are additional referral sources. These couples are highly motivated to develop a good marriage. Therefore, the important ingredient of group cohesiveness is almost a built-in factor. Bach has pointed out that the cohesive group is a laboratory conducive to reality-testing in a way individual counseling cannot provide.[6]

Screening Process

Screening of the couples prior to the opening session is an essential aspect of this type of group counseling. Each couple is asked to complete the premarriage inventory form, adapted from that used by the Marriage Council of Philadelphia (the work of Dr. Emily Mudd). This provides information about their education, religion, marriage plans, period of acquaintance, previous marriage or engagement, and present relationship to parents, siblings, in-laws, and so on. Later, in an individual interview with each partner, the group leader utilizes this information so that a tentative social diagnostic assessment of each person is established. Then, each couple is seen in a joint interview in which the aims of the course and the couple's expectation of the group experience are discussed. This interview provides a picture of the couple's patterns of communication and interaction (who talks the most, who leads, who follows).

The screening process attempts to separate those couples who can use the group to advantage from those whose neurotic patterns, severe problems, or crisis situation prevent them from benefiting from the group experience. The latter are offered separate premarriage counseling.

Individual diagnostic assessment is not enough to ensure effective group life.[7] This is an application of Kurt Lewin's theoretical concept that a group is more than the sum of its carefully selected individual members.

Slavson has also emphasized that selection is as important in guidance groups as it is in therapy groups. In practice it has not always been possible to carry out the kind of selection that may be considered ideal. However, it has been possible to do a fair amount of selection when two groups with two group leaders are functioning at the same time.

In developing criteria for group composition it should be noted that the purpose of the group and its goals are the essential factors. The following criteria have been helpful:

1. *The heterogeneous factor.* By combining couples from different social, economic, religious, and occupational backgrounds an opportunity is provided for couples to understand and accept differences in others, as well as in each other. It has been found that intimate friends do better in different groups.

2. *Avoidance of isolated group members.* A couple should not find itself too different from the others in the group. There should be at least one couple with whom they can readily identify.

3. *Intelligence.* This has proved to be a particularly important factor. Too great a disparity in intellectual interest and ability hinders communication. For example, a young couple with one or two years of high school education will not be comfortable with or easily accepted by a group of university graduates.

4. *A variety of complementary roles.* Contrast and balance are useful principles in group composition. For example, combining the "doubting Thomas," the peacemaker, the pseudo-sophisticated man of the world, the shy young lady, the highly conventional, the opinionated, and the assertive member provides the ingredients for a lively and meaningful group experience, taking into account the process of group interaction and effective leadership.

Techniques

In both training and practice, caseworkers are becoming increasingly involved in working with groups and are equipped with an understanding of individual dynamics and behavior as well as of group process and interaction. A sound knowledge of all aspects of marriage is also necessary. Important, too, is social work experience in listening with respect and interest, and creating an atmosphere of acceptance and freedom to express ideas and differences in the group.

Since there are as many varieties of groups as clients in a case load, the group leader must be flexible in adapting himself to the needs of different groups. He may apply many familiar techniques commonly used in casework, such as restating and simplifying, reflecting back group communications, interpreting manifest group feelings, summarizing and clarifying the pros and cons of an issue, and providing information that is lacking in the group. In other words, he plays a variety of roles; catalyst, supporter, challenger, at times the frank information-giver and at other times the group member.

In short-term counseling it is essential to develop a structure in order to avoid the anxiety aroused in a vaguely defined situation. While the leader is responsible for setting up the structure of the group in relation to its purpose, it is important to establish the principle of group participation from the start and encourage the members to isolate the major themes of group interest. These major themes are decided upon by the members at the first session. However, they are not held to rigidly and may sometimes overlap. The group leader will occasionally need to make connections with the central theme or between themes. This technique has been described as "linking."

The screening interviews will provide the group leader with cues for "starting where the group is." It is usually the girls who initiate the request for group counseling, while the boys reluctantly tag along. One young man said in his screening interview, "I don't want anyone telling *me* how to run my marriage." Another said sheepishly, "I hope I won't be asked any embarrassing questions."

Casework experience and the technique of verbalizing for the client his feelings of discomfort in accepting help may easily be adapted to the group situation. For example, at one first session the men stood around awkwardly and the girls shyly, until the group leader said, "All you men, I know, have one thing in common—you didn't want to come in the first place!" A light touch and a little humor help to reduce initial embarrassment. Settling down without delay—in an informal seating arrangement around the table or using easy chairs in a circle—also helps to put the group at ease.

At a typical opening session, members are asked to introduce themselves by first name only. They are given large name badges, and are asked to tell a little about themselves. This is an example of the technique of "going around." The group leader then introduces himself and spells out the aims of the course and its limitations. The leader guides the discussion, rather than lecturing the group. It is pointed out that these sessions do not offer a prescription for lasting happiness, but aim to increase the group members' understanding of themselves and their partners; thus enabling them to develop the kind of marriage that will meet their individual needs.

At this point a short film may be shown, highlighting the modern concept of marriage. The following took place at one group session following the showing of a film.

> The men warmed up by pulling the film to pieces; one complained, "It is all so smooth and easy." One of the girls defended the film, saying that love is what makes marriage work. Then they began to define love, the men intellectually, the girls sentimentally. One girl said, "Love is the gift of oneself to another—

the other should *always* come first." This had a silencing and sobering effect on the group. The group leader then asked whether someone wished to challenge this statement, which evoked more realistic reactions—the need, even the right, to be an individual as well as a marriage partner. Someone timidly asked, "Does this mean that we should have separate as well as common interests?" Soon they began talking about their own interests and activities and how their respective partners felt about them. One young man described how he loves to go hunting, but his fiancée is afraid of guns. Suggestions came from all sides. They found that they had common as well as individual interests. Perhaps, they considered tentatively, there is room for separateness as well as together-ness. Here the group leader offered a reinforcing comment, such as, "All healthy people occasionally become a little weary of belonging, of cooperation and perfect agreement."

Later Sessions

Before the close of a first session, the group leader suggests that they decide on subjects for forthcoming sessions. Frequently topics suggested overlap, and the leader groups them into themes. Typical themes are as follows: expectations of love and marriage, the working wife, relationships to parents and in-laws, attitudes about money (budgeting and credit-buying), sexual adjustment and the honeymoon, becoming parents, and a family faith and value system. Then the group establishes priorities for discussing these subjects.

As stated earlier, themes are not rigidly held to. For example, while discussing relationships to in-laws, one man declared that his in-laws were fine, but that he was struggling with a bossy widowed mother. He and his fiancée "could not even look at bedroom furniture without her tagging along." Another man had foster parents who resented his imminent marriage and refused to attend the wedding. A third man said, "The same thing has happened to me. I know just how it feels but I stuck to my guns, and my parents came around when they realized that I was determined." This is typical of the kind of group support, followed by suggestions about different ways of coping with the problem, that the peer group effectively provides. As Rutledge said, "Changes in thinking and feeling come about with group support, which might be resisted if suggested directly by the counsellor."[8]

Sometimes the group leader uses role-playing to help the group members understand how they contribute to a difficult situation. The week after a role-playing session, the group asked the man with the bossy mother what had happened. He replied, "Radar must have been operating, as my old lady has really improved since we role-played her!" One group member told him that perhaps he had learned not to "stick his neck out," and another that he had learned not to apologize for every move. He agreed that he tended to do both of these, but still expressed concern that his mother would be lonely. The group was sympathetic and accepted the fact that she would need to feel that she was gaining as well as losing by his marriage. The leader here generalized that parents, too, have adjustments to make and that the role of an in-law is not always easy. Several groups have suggested that preparation for in-laws in groups should be made available at the center.

The group leader must be sensitive and alert when using such devices as role-playing. Otherwise, one group member may be unduly exposed. Timing is also important in generalizing problems, so as to encourage the individual group members to share personally meaningful material. For example, feelings of discomfort about working wives are often initially denied by the men in the group.

In later sessions, the group becomes increasingly free to agree and disagree. The group leader will at certain points indicate what is happening in the present interaction, will point out that conflict is an inescapable part of life and that married couples can differ, express anger, and learn to deal with it without fear of disaster. As the group "jells" they draw from and share their own personal concerns more freely, and the initial tendency to intellectualize disappears.

In discussing the members' future roles as parents, the group leader will be able to link some of the problems of growing up expressed in earlier sessions. This enables the group to see how these experiences may influence their own feelings and behavior as parents, and sometimes their expectations of the marital partner. The natural tendency to compensate through their children for what they have missed or to repeat the family pattern is discussed, and can be understood at least intellectually. Sometimes they can express the fact that their marriage will be unlike that of their parents, and that their children will be different from themselves. The group leader will reinforce these ideas.

The need to understand themselves, their partners, their patterns of communicating and interacting, and their ways of expressing or not expressing positive and negative feelings are brought out into the open. The need to communicate openly with each other in all areas of married life—including sex—is a recurrent theme, as is their mutual responsibility for developing problem-solving skills. The pamphlet *Sexual Harmony in Marriage* is used.[9] Couples are asked to discuss it together before the session on sexual adjustment, to which a gynecologist is invited. A premarital physical examination, methods of birth control, and the range of normality in sexual behavior are freely discussed and surprising misconceptions are clarified.

In the last evaluatory session the usual reactions are: "We feel closer together as a couple, more tolerant of people and ideas we formerly resented." "We thought when we began this program that marriage would be either very good or very bad. Now we see that it depends on us." "We intend to make our own kind of marriage." "It was most helpful and encouraging to learn that others had similar needs and problems, and that we were not exceptions."

The center tries to hold a reunion with each engaged couples' group a year after completion of the course. This has not always been possible. However, a majority of the couples do get together, and many intimate friendships have resulted from this brief group experience. They have reviewed and discussed material from the group, and felt the experience had been helpful in developing a better marriage. With a few exceptions, all couples proceeded with the marriage.

Although an adequate follow-up has not been possible, five couples with problems are known to have returned to the center. One of the five couples separated, another divorced, and three couples used counseling to advantage. It would appear that contact with the center made it easier for them to accept help in the early phase of married life, before they had children.

Conclusions

Although work with engaged couples in small groups is still in the pioneer and experimental stage, it is apparent that despite its limitations it fulfills a useful function by clarifying the expectations of young people before marriage. With a skilled group leader and appropriate safeguards, some relearning and modification of attitudes and behavior are possible, within the time limits of the course.

The potential in short-term help is far greater than has generally been recognized. In this connection, Caplan and Parad have stressed—in their development of "crisis theory"—the principle of timing.[10] That is, if help is given quickly and at the right time, it may be brief yet effective. Hopefully, there are few who see impending marriage as a crisis situation. However, marriage does involve elements of stress common to role transition, and the crisis principle can be related to premarriage counseling.

As mentioned by Garcea and Irwin, the high proportion of "dropouts" in the initial phase of casework treatment led a family agency to experiment with offering a limited number of sessions (four to six interviews) to hesitant clients, with surprising results.[11] The writer appreciates the need for lengthy services in specific areas, for example, the multiproblem family. The question is whether they are not too often offered indiscriminately by the social work profession.

Finally, it may be of interest to note that the program for counseling engaged couples in groups has led to other developments in Montreal. The Marriage Counselling Centre, in collaboration with McGill University School of Social Work, has provided extension courses for members of the clergy, doctors, and lawyers on premarriage counseling related to their specific professional activities. This has become an additional source of referral for the center's engaged couples' course, as well as for pre- and post-marriage counseling.

For the inevitable extension of the program described and for related programs, more intensive evaluation and thoughtfully designed research projects will have to be undertaken. From such efforts, more definitive guides and procedures should emerge.

References

1. "The Marriage Counselling Centre of Montreal" (Montreal, Canada: Quality Press, 1956).

2. John J. O. Moore, "A Community Meets the Need for Marriage Counselling." Paper presented at the annual meeting of the Montreal Marriage Counselling Centre, Montreal, Canada, March 1964.

3. Samuel R. Slavson, "Clinical and Dynamic Differences Between Therapy and Guidance Groups." Paper presented at the American Group Psychotherapy Association meeting, New York, New York, January 1953.

4. John Levy and Ruth Monroe, *The Happy Family* (New York: Alfred A. Knopf, 1938).

5. Aaron Rutledge, "Group Preparation for Marriage." Paper presented at the annual meeting of the Montreal Marriage Counselling Centre, Montreal, Canada, April 1962.

6. George R. Bach, *Intensive Group Psychotherapy* (New York: Ronald Press, 1954).

7. Florence B. Powdermaker and Jerome D. Frank, *Group Psychotherapy* (Cambridge, Mass.: Harvard University Press, 1953).

8. Rutledge, *op. cit.*, p. 2.

9. Oliver M. Butterfield, *Sexual Harmony in Marriage* (New York: Emerson Books, 1953).

10. Gerald Caplan, MD, "An Approach to the Study of Family Mental Health," *U.S. Public Health Reports*, Vol. 71, No. 10 (October 1956); and Howard J. Parad, "Brief Ego-Oriented Casework with Families in Crisis," in Parad and Roger R. Miller, *Ego-Oriented Casework, Problems and Perspectives* (New York: Family Service Association of America, 1963).

11. Ralph A. Garcea and Olive Irwin, "A Family Agency Deals with the Problem of Dropouts," *Social Casework*, Vol. 43, No. 2 (February 1962), pp. 71–75.

PART IV
The Individual-Psychological Facet

Introduction

This section deals with the troubled individual in relation to the family as well as to various societal institutions.

The article by Murphy, Pueschel, and Schneider describes the problems families face after discovering that a newborn child has Down's syndrome. The authors report their work with such families in groups, including insights into the dimensions of the crisis, the range of responses to the crisis, and the kinds of support professionals and the community can provide.

Hersh reports the changes that occur in a family once a retarded child is separated from them by institutionalization. The author covers the impact of institutionalization of the child on the family functioning through exploring seven behavioral dimensions of personal response, marital interaction, parent-child interaction, children's response, family management, family transactions, and family development.

With the development of sophisticated medical technology, new legislation mandating social work treatment for certain chronic illnesses, and the prolongation of life through medical treatment, new areas of practice are emerging for social workers. Hickey discusses developments in the treatment of kidney disease and their implications for social work practice. Abramson describes a hospital program of group work established to help the families of burn-injured patients. While both articles deal with specific problems, they also yield many generic concepts that can be applied to other health-related problems.

Mueller provides guidelines for casework with the family of the male alcoholic. The author emphasizes the importance of helping the wife understand that alcoholism is a treatable disease and the importance of letting the alcoholic suffer the consequences of his drinking. He shows how self-help groups can be a valuable resource to the alcoholic and his family.

Krupp explores maladaptive reactions to the death of a family member and how these are affected by societal and familial attitudes toward death. He covers pathological responses to death, effects of religion on bereavement, techniques for dealing with reactions, and preventive techniques.

Lindahl reports reactions of families to the illness and death of a child following hospitalization, particularly the parental responses of grief, anger, guilt, turning away from religion, and replacement of the dead child. The role of the worker in these circumstances is described.

Spitzer, Morgan, and Swanson believe that the ways in which the family responds or fails to respond to deviance are crucial determinants of the career of the deviant member as a psychiatric patient. The authors use as "sensitizing concepts" the level of expected performance and the propensity for action to deduce pathways to hospitalization, readiness to accept the sick role, extent of adjustment to hospitalization, attitudes toward treatment staff, and likelihood of readmission. They provide a typology that can be useful in planning patient care, predicting readmission, and making decisions with the patients and their families before, during, and after hospitalization.

Individual responses to mental illness have frequently been studied but little attention has been given to the reactions of family members to an individual's mental illness. Raymond, Slaby, and Lieb present a sequential pattern of a family's response to psychiatric illness. By developing an understanding of the variety of these responses, the worker is better able to make appropriate and effective intervention.

The article by McKamy addresses the problem of working with wealthy families when one member has been hospitalized. This article is included not only because it deals with the problems of the institutionalized individual but also because it treats the special problems faced by the social worker assigned to work with people who are used to exercising power and being in control of their environments. Most social workers do not come from wealthy backgrounds, are not accustomed to working with people from these backgrounds, and have been trained to work primarily with poor and powerless families and individuals. McKamy provides some helpful guidelines for dealing with the unique dynamics of situations involving upper-class clients.

23

Group Work with Parents of Children with Down's Syndrome

Ann Murphy
Siegfried M. Pueschel
Jane Schneider

Social workers are increasingly stressing their role in prevention of social maladjustment. Frequently, however, they lack access to groups of people sharing a common crisis. Children with birth defects do not ordinarily come to the attention of social workers unless the family manifests some adjustment problem or there is need for specific social planning. Even then, contact is apt to be limited to resolution of a particular issue with selected families. Patterns of coping which are maladaptive have been identified. Retrospectively, they would indicate that if help had been available to the family when attitudes were being formed, the current problems might not have developed.

For one and one-half years, the authors had an opportunity to meet families coping with the impact of discovering that their newborn child had Down's syndrome. This is a chromosomal aberration resulting in a characteristic physical appearance and mental retardation. It is more commonly and incorrectly known as mongolism. Following closely nearly seventy families of infants with Down's syndrome in a group experience provided insights into the dimensions of such a crisis, the range of responses, and the kinds of support professional people and the community can offer. The group also served as a therapeutic resource for the participating families in working through the trauma of giving birth to a defective child.

Source: From *Social Casework* 54 (February 1973), pp. 114–119. Copyright © 1973 by the Family Service Association of America. Reprinted by permission.

Background of Study

In September 1970, the developmental evaluation clinic of the Children's Hospital Medical Center in Boston received a grant to evaluate the effect of a drug (L-5-hydroxy-tryptophanpyridoxin) upon the motor, language, and intellectual development of young children with Down's syndrome.[1] A multidiscipline team of anthropologist, neurologist, nurse, pediatrician, physical therapist, psychologist, speech therapist, and social worker was organized to document the progress of newborn children on all major parameters of development. One-half the children received the medication and the other half a placebo, but the identity of the members of each sample was unknown both to the parents and to the professional staff involved in the evaluation. The parents of all the children were instructed in motor and sensory stimulation. They were cautioned that all of these efforts would, at most, facilitate the development of the child and were not expected to be curative. Appointments were initially scheduled at three- to four-week intervals, and as the child's health and family were stabilized, the frequency decreased. Comprehensive evaluations were to take place every six months during the first three years. Children were recruited for the program by informing all pediatricians and maternity hospitals within a 150-mile radius of Boston of the existence of the project and by encouraging referrals of newborn infants. The babies ranged in age from one week to three months at the time of the first appointment, but typically they were about two weeks old. The clinic program was unusual because of the high proportion of fathers who attended, in contrast to other clinics in the hospital.

The social worker's original plan was to interview all families at the first appointment, when the baby was six months old, and again at one, two, and three years of age, to assess their responses as the different dimensions of the handicap became apparent. The objective would be to study factors which influence a family's adaptation to a child with this type of birth defect.

Common Initial Concerns of Parents

The birth of a child with Down's syndrome places a great stress on the parents. What has been anticipated as a joyful occasion is characterized by a sense of loss, grief, and mourning.[2] The medical staff handle their own disappointment by suggesting institutionalization, by avoiding the parents, or by exhorting them to love the child, thereby betraying their underlying negative feelings. Specific facts on what the diagnosis entails or how the child may develop are frequently lacking, and there is little opportunity for the parents to check their fantasy that they have given birth to a monster against a more objective reality. Many are afraid to look for what they might see; a common expectation, for example, is that the infant will have a very large head. It is not surprising that a number of parents misinterpret the term *mongoloid* to mean mongrel. When they do look it is difficult for them to reconcile what they have heard with the rather normal appearance of the baby.

A typical assumption is that the child will be an object which they will feed, while he in turn will do nothing but lie there. Some parents resist touching the child because they fear becoming involved by claiming the child as their own. Friends and hospital personnel contribute to the unreality by not sending greeting cards, not photographing the baby, or failing to list the birth in the community newspaper. Some parents illustrate their feelings of low self-esteem by expressing surprise that friends would want to come and see them. Often they do not know anyone else with such a child, and their grief and mourning is compounded by a sense of isolation. Up-to-date reading material is not readily available in the maternity hospital or even in the local library, and what exists is often based on experiences with institutionalized children with this defect.

All the families studied expressed positive feelings about the opportunity to participate in a program in which their child would receive some help and they themselves would receive some support and would participate in activities which might be remedial in nature. In only three of the families was there sufficient indication of disorganization or acute emotional disorder to indicate need for intensive casework treatment. However, all were struggling with feelings of sadness, depression, concern as to cause, and a need for information; these feelings rather than focused conflicts are part of the process of living with a child with a defect. What seemed indicated was a continuing experience which would allow for discharge of feelings, examination of fantasies and fears, and development of constructive adaptive patterns. Since all appointments for the program had been scheduled on the same day of the week for the convenience of the staff, there were at least five or six families present in the waiting room at any given time. It seemed appropriate to consider whether a group experience might offer the additional support such parents appeared to need.

Formation of the Group

All families were informed at the time of their first visit to the clinic of the opportunity to meet with other parents. Parents who were still questioning the accuracy and finality of the diagnosis usually deferred participation until their second visit. Although they placed a varying value on group attendance, all but two families elected to participate. The meetings were held in a small conference room within the clinic area. The atmosphere was informal and coffee was served. Parents usually preferred to bring their babies into the group, although facilities were available for child care. The group composition varied but there was usually a nucleus of people who had been enrolled in the program for some time and who knew each other from previous group meetings. The pediatrician joined the group for the last half hour to answer questions on Down's syndrome, expected development, medical complications, and genetics. The group meetings usually lasted one and one-half hours, although sometimes parents remained in the room to talk after the meeting was over.

The function of the social worker was to facilitate introductions, assist the group in identifying topics for discussion, and encourage participation by the more reserved members while limiting the more aggressive ones. When individuals denied negative feelings or worries which might have been appropriate, the worker verbalized these for the group, allowing others to bring such topics into the discussion. She also assisted the group in exploring fears and questions at a somewhat deeper level than they might have done spontaneously and in functioning as a resource person in terms of information about the diagnosis and clinic and community programs. Typically, the parents related quickly to one another, volunteered data about themselves, and directed personal questions to others. They usually felt free to disagree or to correct one another's misconceptions. Members were particularly supportive and protective of new group attendees; a number of parents formed friendships outside the group. They frequently referred to the fact that the availability of the group and the clinic program diminished their feeling of isolation.

> I look forward to coming; it must be like psychotherapy. I don't feel so alone. It recharges me so I feel strong enough to continue. . . . If I couldn't come here, I would get depressed and then it might affect my baby's development and I would not be able to give to him in the way that I should.

Working Through the Diagnosis

The group experience served as a vehicle to work through feelings regarding the diagnosis. Each new member was usually asked how he was told about the diagnosis; this query gave him an opportunity to describe the experience and to express his feelings of shock, anger, disappointment, and fear. "I was so elated after the birth, then it was as though I had nothing at all. It took me a while to realize I still had a baby, a husband, and a home." At this point the longer-term members reviewed their own experiences, usually with diminishing intensity of feeling as time passes. They discussed freely what they had feared their child would be like, for example, a monster who would be able to do nothing, out-of-control, or dangerous. They then described their relief at the child's actual responsiveness and development as a person. All parents used the group to assist them in comprehending what the diagnosis meant in their child and to reconcile the word and its stereotypes with his presence, a process which usually requires four to five months.

> Sometimes he looks it, sometimes he doesn't. When he's awake his tongue sticks out and then you really notice it.

> I don't know whether to pick him up or not when he cries. He stops crying if I do. He has caught on already and they say he is retarded.

> I feel so much better when I am with the baby. When we are apart my imagination takes over.

For some parents, discussing feelings about the diagnosis in the group was a preparation for talking about the diagnosis with relatives and friends. On each occasion when they had to speak of it to another acquaintance the original sadness and anxiety were reawakened. The group was utilized to clarify their thinking about how and whom to inform about the diagnosis and what terms to use that would be understandable while avoiding the stereotypes that would be conjured up by the word *mongoloid.* "People are curious. They seem to think you have a monster or a freak. When you hear *mentally retarded* you imagine it will be different from normal." Before moving to a new neighborhood, one parent asked the group whether she should introduce herself by saying that she had a child with Down's syndrome, as though this were her most important characteristic. The group members discussed the mourning reaction of their friends who were unsure of how to approach them and the parents' need to take the initiative to help friends relate comfortably to them and to the baby. Advice was solicited and given on how to discuss the child's handicap with their other children and how to anticipate their questions.

The behavior of the professional staff in maternity hospitals was discussed in detail during the group meetings. All members agreed that any person who broke such news to a family was likely to become the target of angry feelings. A few parents described sensitive and supportive experiences with hospital staff. "They let the baby stay with me longer and let my husband hold him." A majority complained about lack of information, avoidance by hospital personnel, and hindrance of their contact with their child.

> My baby suffered the first social rejection at the hands of his obstetrician.

> The nurse in the hospital told us we should put our baby's name on a waiting list for an institution in case she should turn out to be severely retarded. When I asked her what this meant, she said, "Well, if she becomes dangerous to others."

The group allowed the parents to gain some perspective on what kind of people have children with Down's syndrome. Group members varied in age from seventeen to the mid-forties and were from various socioeconomic and educational levels and ethnic backgrounds. For some parents the involved baby was their first child; some had as many as nine other children. Sometimes they speculated on what they all had in common that caused them to create such children. There was much interest in research to identify causal factors and in physical characteristics or attitudinal factors as possible precipitants.

Obtaining Perspective on Child Development

The group allowed the parents to compare the development of their baby with that of his peers.

I wouldn't want to compare him with a normal child. It only discourages the parent.

I can't live in a void, I need to talk with other mothers. That's why it's good to get together because you can compare with other kids like him.

They held one another's children and discussed how the characteristics of Down's syndrome were manifested differently in each child.

There was much mutual questioning regarding growth and development, feeding and sleep patterns, temperament, and level of responsiveness. They offered one another advice on specific methods of effective management. This information was particularly supportive to those group members who were parents for the first time and who would ordinarily have used friends, relatives, and literature as guides to develop competence in child care. Those who had other children were sympathetic to parents whose first child was the involved child; the new parents suggested that perhaps it was easier for them because they had no point of comparison. All the group members shared their excitement and joy at each accomplishment of the child. A few parents avoided their peers with normal children of the same age because they resented those children's normal development. Sometimes friends avoided them out of guilt because their own child was normal. Those group members whose children had cardiac lesions compared notes on diagnosis and prognosis, and those whose children had had diagnostic procedures prepared the parents whose children were about to undergo them. A vital aspect of the clinic's program was that the parents felt that the clinic was a place where their child was valued as a person; in general, the experience seemed to enhance their self-esteem, sense of adequacy, and normalcy.

A frequent topic was what the future will bring in terms of the child's development and the parents' ability to cope with his special needs.

Will I still love him the way a parent should when his handicap shows more?

It's fine now, for me it's later, people staring. I don't know whether I will be able to cope with a child who won't be toilet trained or walk until late. . . . I also fear the future, but I shut my mind.

I worry who will take care of him after I am gone. Will other children be cruel to him and tease him?

Some parents were more oriented to the future than others, but after a few months most parents concentrated on the present and anticipated only the next phase of the child's development. Anxieties about the future were handled in the group by discussions of the hope that social attitudes would change and resources become more available.

Another major concern of the younger couples was in planning future pregnancies. The attitudes varied from plans for another child very soon to refusal to accept such a risk although adoption might be considered. One couple whose child was critically ill with heart disease conceived another "in case he died." A pregnant woman could not imagine herself bearing a normal child.

The Value of the Group Experience

The literature on crisis theory emphasizes the vulnerability or accessibility of the individual under stress to the influence of significant others in his environment. Lydia Rapoport describes stress as associated with a rise in tension, some personality disorganization, reactivation of old unresolved conflicts, a general feeling of helplessness, and some cognitive confusion. She identifies three aspects of a healthy resolution of a crisis: correct cognitive perception of the situation, management of affect through awareness of feelings and appropriate verbalizations leading toward discharge of tension, and development of patterns of seeking and using help.[3] What forces come into play during the crisis period may be more influential than previously existing personality characteristics of the individual in determining his ultimate adaptation to stress.

Parents of a newborn child with Down's syndrome described themselves as being in a state of shock, lacking in self-esteem, and beset by fantasies and fears. They were actively looking to those around them for emotional support and information in order to reorient themselves. "One of the most frightening things is the process of finding direction." They wanted facts about what such babies are like, what they can do, and whether they will be able to function like other children in such activities as walking, communicating, and caring for themselves.

Reading material which contains these facts, preferably supplemented by pictures of such children in natural settings, is a basic need. A notable example is *David,* a book that describes the experience of a couple who have a child with Down's syndrome, their initial ambivalence, and subsequent resolution of their concerns during the early years of their child's life.[4] Many of the parents in the group saw themselves as potential leaders in making such resources available to others.

Meeting other people undergoing the same stress can provide an invaluable opportunity to test reality. The immediacy and intimacy stimulated by the common experience is of a different quality from that characteristic of contact with a professional person. The closeness of the bond to the group mitigates feelings of isolation and depression. Members could see how the other children appeared and acted. The discovery that other parents had similar feelings and fears reassured them of their own adequacy and sanity. Some parents served as role models to illustrate that it is possible to survive such an event. The group provided them with an opportunity to test themselves in a protected environment preparatory to dealing with the stresses of the larger community. The parent of an older child with Down's syndrome commented, on meeting the group of parents, that she was impressed with their openness and degree of comfortableness in discussing the problems of their children in contrast to her own experience at that stage.

The development of any child poses certain stresses for his parents, and typically these are more intense for the parents of handicapped children. Each new crisis reactivates unresolved issues of the past. As the child approaches the age of school entrance or of adolescence, patterns of coping may become increasingly maladaptive. The opportunity to work through the grief of bearing a defective child at the time of diagnosis and to receive support in building a positive relationship with the child can provide a more secure foundation for dealing with the future conflicts which will inevitably arise.

The opportunity for social workers to meet with groups of families having a common stress focuses attention on those common needs which are not being met by professional people. Although the staff of maternity hospitals have nearly abandoned advising institutionalization for children with Down's syndrome, they apparently have not substituted adequate supportive services to families. This fact stimulated the staff of the developmental evaluation clinic to enlist the help of these families and others in designing a more constructive approach to discussing the diagnosis of Down's syndrome with a family as a basis for an educational program for professional people. Siblings also are in need of information and supportive services. With the assistance of these parents, such a program has been implemented for them.

Although the experience described in this article concerned families of children with Down's syndrome, some of the conclusions may apply also to families of children with other birth defects which have a disruptive effect on the evolution of the parent-child relationship. Some of the clinic experience paralleled the descriptions of David M. Kaplan and Edward A. Mason as well as Lydia Rapoport in their studies of families of premature infants.[5] Other life-threatening neonatal problems—those requiring prolonged initial hospitalization or those where the infant's appearance or functioning is predictably deviant—undoubtedly interfere with the parents' ability to accept the child as their own and threaten their self-esteem or sense of adequacy. More thought should be given to the therapeutic potential of a group experience for such parents in the setting which supplies treatment to the child.

Such a group experience can be instructive to the professional because it focuses attention on major themes and the needs of a group of people rather than on the unique stress and adaptation of individuals. Two developments which emerged from this group work were an educational program for professionals on the needs of parents who had given birth to a child with Down's syndrome and a program of information and support for the siblings of such children.

References

1.   This work of the clinic was supported by National Institute of Child Health and Human Development (Bethesda, Maryland) Grant HD-05341-01 and Maternal and Child Health Service Project No. 928, U.S. Department of Health, Education, and Welfare.

2.   Simon Olshansky, Chronic Sorrow: A Response to Having a Mentally Defective Child, *Social Casework*, 43:191 (March 1962).

3.   Lydia Rapoport, The State of Crisis: Some Theoretical Considerations, in *Crisis Intervention: Selected Readings*, ed. Howard J. Parad (New York: Family Service Association of America, 1965), pp. 22–31.

4.   Nancy Roberts, *David* (Richmond, Virginia: John Knox Press, 1968).

5.   David M. Kaplan and Edward A. Mason, Maternal Reactions to Premature Birth Viewed as an Acute Emotional Disorder, *Crisis Intervention*, pp. 118–28; and Lydia Rapoport, Working with Families in Crisis: An Exploration in Preventive Intervention, *Crisis Intervention*, pp. 129–39.

24
Changes in Family Functioning Following Placement of a Retarded Child

Alexander Hersh

Separation of a retarded child from his family by institutionalization, long a culturally supported phenomenon, has been the subject of much interest but of little systematic investigation.[1] Recently, however, there has been a trend away from random institutional placement toward selective placement based on therapeutic and habilitative goals. In view of this hopeful trend, the effects of separation on all those involved assume new relevance.

Placement of a retarded child introduces new patterns of living for all the principals. The child is called on to adapt to the school, and the parents, who until placement had been intimately involved with the child's care on a daily basis, must establish new patterns of relationship with the school, which is now a partner in caring for the child. Hence these new patterns of living are direct consequences of the decision to place the child. This paper reports a study of the separation experience of families placing a retarded child in a private state-aided residential school.

The purposes of this exploratory and descriptive study were to ascertain, record, and conceptualize changes in family functioning accompanying the placement of a retarded child in a residential school; to test a design for later use with larger samples; to develop hypotheses for further study;[2] and to develop guidelines for families considering placement. The study involved a systematic investigation of what a family experiences as it responds to placement of a child and the child's subsequent adjustment to his new environment. Families placing a child were observed for three months following

Source: From *Social Work* 15:4 (October 1970), pp. 93–102. Copyright © 1970 by the National Association of Social Workers. Reprinted by permission.

placement with respect to changes in their functioning, their reactions to the child's placement and the program planned for him, and their relationships to the child and the school.

Research Method

The case study method was utilized in this study so that the varieties of reaction to separation from a child could be explored and recorded in depth and family living and processes of interpersonal adjustment could be analyzed. Data were collected by four means:

1. Tape-recorded semistructured interviews with fifteen sets of parents who enrolled a child in Elwyn Institute, a private institution in Pennsylvania serving eleven hundred residents and two hundred day students. The parents were interviewed at the time of enrollment and then monthly for three successive months. The investigator gave them a brief progress report on the child at each interview following placement.

2. Extracting information from the case records of the fifteen children.

3. Interviews with the students' housemothers at the end of each of the first three months following enrollment.

4. Interviews with the director of education or the students' teachers at the end of each of the first three months following enrollment.

Criteria for inclusion in the study were as follows: either sex, no restriction as to IQ, under 21, Caucasian only (a preliminary survey showed that few black students entering the school would meet the study criteria; actually, no black families enrolled children during the period in which the subjects were being selected),[3] and first-time placement (family dynamics and motivation may be quite different once a family has experienced placement of a child).

Of the new students enrolled in Elwyn during a ten-month period, fifteen who met the study criteria were selected in chronological order. Those families that met the established criteria were asked if they wished to participate in the study, which was outlined to them verbally so that they had a sufficient basis on which to make a decision. Each family approached volunteered; none rejected the opportunity to participate. When fifteen subjects had been accumulated, no additional ones were solicited.

The study design centered on collection of data regarding family functioning prior and subsequent to the placement of the retarded child, in the form of the following carefully defined variables:

1. Antecedent variable.
   a. The children and their families at the time of the placement.

    b. The effects of the retarded child on family functioning according to seven dimensions.

      1. Personal response
      2. Marital interaction
      3. Parent-child interaction
      4. Children's response
      5. Family management
      6. Family transaction
      7. Family development

2. Characteristics of the separation experience.
    a. Relationship between the family and the school.
    b. Relationship between the family and child.

3. Consequences of the separation, according to seven dimensions of family functioning (see 1.b, 1–7).

The data comprising the antecedent variable were treated in three ways: (1) Tables were prepared to show the characteristics of the children and their families at the time of the study and the relation of these characteristics to the families' experiences over the three-month postplacement period was determined. (2) Data on the effects of the mentally retarded child on the family's functioning were collected according to seven dimensions of family functioning and ratings were made of the degree of effects so that gross associations with the consequences of the enrollment could be determined and clues to the responses to separation obtained. (3) Documented case summaries were prepared for the fifteen families so that the cause-and-effect aspects of the research question could be examined in the change process experienced by the families. The characteristics of the separation experience were analyzed in terms of the relationships between the family and the school and between the family and the child from the standpoint of how the experience affected the feelings, attitudes, and actions of the parents.

Finally, the consequent variable was examined in the following ways: (1) Documented summaries were drawn up on the fifteen families so that the effects of the placement according to the seven dimensions of family functioning could be examined for the change process. (2) Ratings were made of the degree of change in family functioning and then placed in association with the characteristics of the families and ratings of the effects of the retarded child on their functioning prior to the separation. (3) These gross findings were used to determine patterns and find clues to cause-and-effect relationships, which were then followed up by examination of the detailed individual case histories. (4) The research questions were posed and analyzed. The range of phenomena derived were described, common denominators of experience determined, and patterns of response traced.

To objectify possible sources of bias in the interview techniques and determine the reliability of the interview guide, the definitions used as criteria for the variables, and the investigator's ratings, the independent judgment of another professional social worker was obtained. This worker was presented with an outline of the study design, the interview guide, and the defined dimensions and then listened to eight tape-recorded interviews that had been completed at that point. From these she made seventy ratings of three variables, which were then compared with the ratings made by the investigator. The overall agreement rate was 96 percent. Since agreement was so high, it was deemed reasonable to proceed with the study relying on the investigator's judgments alone.

Study Population

The study group consisted of fifteen children, ten boys and five girls. As a group the girls were slightly older than the boys; the mean age of the total group was 13 years, with an age range of 6–19. The bulk of the children were mildly mentally retarded, but borderline and moderately retarded groups were also represented. The mean IQ was 59. Ten of the children were presumed to be brain damaged and all but a few were multiply handicapped, that is, in addition to being mentally retarded, other associated conditions such as sensory deficits were present. Several were emotionally disturbed and two were clearly diagnosed as having Down's Syndrome.

The study group was typical of the range of students enrolled in Elwyn. The school's intake procedure involved four steps: (1) initial response to an inquiry and filing of an application for enrollment, (2) careful screening of professional reports on the child by the director of admissions (those ruled out at this point included children who had a history of profound mental retardation, psychosis, serious behavioral difficulties, or primary sensory deficits), (3) interviews with the child and parents by professional and dormitory staff, (4) review and recommendation by the Admissions Committee. Acceptance was normally based on the cited exclusionary factors, matching a child's needs with available programs, and the review of other relevant factors such as motivation, lack of community resources, and capacity of the family and/or agency to support placement.

Because of space limitations voluminous analytical data obtained on the families, all of which were analyzed in relation to the placement-separation phenomenon, have been highly condensed throughout this report. For example, the following additional data were obtained: parental occupation, length of marriage, religion, place of birth, financial basis for meeting the cost of placement, family size, ordinal position of the placed child, family life cycle index, operational definition and ratings of the effects of the retarded child on family functioning, effects of separation on family functioning, and patterns of family functioning following placement.[4]

The families in the study group, while not statistically representative of the population at Elwyn or possibly of any other specific universe of families, were, in the opinion of the investigator, typical in the sense that their problems, experiences, and feelings are probably shared by most families that have a mentally retarded child and decide to place him in a school for retarded children. With the exception of one retired couple the parents were mature, but still relatively early in their economically productive years, ranging from 33 to 71 years of age. Almost half of the fathers were in the 40–49 age group and twelve of the mothers were in the 30–39 and 40–49 age groups. Nearly three-quarters of the parents were under 50 years of age. In five of the families the oldest child was between 6 and 13; in eight, the oldest was between 13 and 20. They represented families that were no longer expanding, were accumulating material goods, were settled in their homes, and were rearing their children and solidifying their family lives. In two families the retarded child was the only child. Because the families differed in their makeup and experience following separation, no significance can be attached to the only-child factor.

As a group the parents had a high educational level. All but five had completed high school and ten had completed college. The mean gross annual income of the group was $14,126, and the income range was $7,000–$45,000. Fourteen of the fifteen families owned their own homes, with the mean length of residence in their present homes being 7.7 years. According to the Hollingshead Two-Factor Index, the following distribution was obtained: two families were in Class I, five in Class II, three in Class III, and five in Class IV. There were no families in Class V.[5]

In this group the presence of a retarded child in the home was viewed as a disruption of some aspects of family life. In instances when a program could not be worked out for the child at home, he had come to represent a threat to family solidarity in the form of an emotional drain on the parents or by having a retarding effect on the careers of family members.

The Separation Experience

This segment of the inquiry dealt with the characteristics of the separation experience as it was related to the cause-and-effect aspects of the process by which a family established a relationship with the school, its new partner in caring for the child.[6] A combination of factors, including the parents' physical and emotional weariness, the lack of adequate community facilities for the mentally retarded, most families' lack of experience with residential schools, and the positive reputation of Elwyn, produced in parents an inordinate degree of trust in the school. They usually spoke so highly and at times so optimistically of Elwyn that staff members feared parents would expect results that the school could not produce. With the exception of two families in upper income brackets Elwyn represented an oasis to the parents. They gratefully regarded the school staff as experts and authorities. Whatever doubts and reservations they had were in the beginning left unexpressed. All the parents stated that they trusted the staff to "tell us what to expect." With the exception of the parents of two children who were entering the vocational program, the parents stated that they were not told except in the most general terms of what their child's program would consist, yet this did not reduce their trust. When asked about their reaction to this practice, virtually every parent said that he "knew" the school would do whatever was necessary and would advise him accordingly.

Since none of the families had prior experience with residential schools, their basis for formulating roles for themselves was limited and they were largely unclear about what role to assume. Beyond the passive general notion that the school would direct them, each family identified itself as performing one of four roles: (1) providing encouragement to the child ("keeping up his morale," "keeping him as happy as we can at this distance"), (2) maintaining family ties ("keeping him part of the family" and "He's still a member of the family"), (3) cooperating with the school ("We'll do whatever is expected of us," "We want to cooperate"), (4) holding the school accountable for the child's care—a supervisory or service-consumer role ("our part will now be supervisory," or "The school has taken a big responsibility off our shoulders").

At the outset many parents felt a sense of uneasiness, as if they were "losing their way." Since no formal structure was arranged for reacting, questioning, clarifying, and exchanging ideas with the staff, a majority of parents felt they had been left to their own initiative. Relinquishment of the intimate aspects of child care such as feeding, dressing, and bathing the child, putting him to bed, and playing with him were experienced most keenly in the first month, at a time when no clearly defined new role was yet available to them.

Although all the parents delighted verbally in the child-centeredness of the school's approach, they had not anticipated clearly the newness and strangeness of their relationship to the school. It was not surprising, therefore, that more than half of the parents reacted to the uncertainty they felt to such a degree that they spontaneously requested "something in writing" from the school that would outline what was expected of them. Several felt that their uncertainty was due in part to their lack of familiarity with the school's customs, practices, and mode of operation. By contrast, whenever the school informed the parents of anything such as notifying them when their child was physically ill and receiving treatment, they were reassured and felt trust in and kinship with the staff.

Although during the admissions process the school's procedures were studiously outlined to parents in relation to letter-writing, visiting, vacations, and the like, parents universally claimed a degree of vagueness and uncertainty about these procedures, which suggested that their anxiety in their original encounters with the staff may have been great and, possibly, that the newness of the total situation was overwhelming to them. As a result their recall of the details presented to them was inconsistent. They requested considerable reinforcement of these directions in the period following placement. These responses coincided with feelings of loss, which all the parents experienced at the outset.

The loss of role owing to the absence of the child created a vacuum that did not remain static. A shift in the parents' relationship to the school began to take place, usually in association with their expectations and the degree of their need for personal engagement with the staff. In this phase direct encounters between the family and school occurred that served to test realistically the families' trust in the school and to give them an opportunity to delineate their new role and their responsibility to the child and school. The interactions that occurred between parent and school staff were varied, ranged widely in scope and intensity, and highlighted the relationship between the school and the families in the early months. The interactions clearly pointed up the school's expanded and the family's contracted caretaking role.

In thirteen of the fifteen families interaction with the staff did not clarify the parents' role in relation to the school or child. That is, of the fifteen families only two felt they had gained some expanded or clearer idea of how to proceed in adapting to their child's absence or in working cooperatively with the school. Hence it could be said that aside from these two, the families studied maintained the role-types with which they began the placement.

Ten of the families acted unilaterally concerning their children and either did not seek the staff's advice or, having received it, went ahead on their own. Five families clearly received advice from the school either spontaneously or on request. In one case in which the placement was not progressing well, the family sought advice but did not agree with the counsel they received. Some of those acting unilaterally seemed to wish no counsel, while others were disappointed at not receiving help from the school staff spontaneously. For the most part these encounters shaped a loose, nondirective—yet at times authoritarian—relationship between school and parents. This caused the inordinate degree of trust felt by parents at the outset of the placement to undergo some modification, usually becoming firmer but more realistic.

The manner in which parents maintained direct contact with their children in the first three months—visiting, family vacations, telephoning, sending packages, and writing letters and cards—was carefully surveyed. The consequences of these contacts appeared to have many meanings to parents that were linked to the subtle personal and psychological meaning the children held for them. The most common configuration of the parent-child relationship following placement was one in which parents visited regularly and on their own initiative supported any personality developments their child showed as a result of his new environment.

Contacts with the children answered four questions uppermost in parents' minds: Is my child happy? Is my child healthy? Is my relationship with my child in jeopardy? Is Elwyn the right place for my child? In the first month following placement the parents relied heavily on staff members' opinions regarding these questions. Thereafter they tended to rely more on their own direct contacts with the child. However, parents often wanted help with these questions from the staff even after they had established visiting patterns and could themselves make some evaluation of the child's progress. If the child's adjustment as perceived by the parents was good—as it was in thirteen instances—the family was able to feel less guilty and ambivalent, to develop a sense of fulfillment and well-being about the placement, to improve its functioning, and to continue the placement. If the child's adjustment was perceived as poor, parental anxiety was great and the placement was jeopardized or terminated.[7]

Consequences of the Separation

The inquiry into changes in family functioning following placement explored the reactions of the families to their child's placement and progress, patterns of family response to the separation in the context of the frame of reference utilized in the study, and the effects of separation on family functioning. Prior to analyzing in detail the responses of each family studied, a comprehensive picture was obtained of the patterns of changes in family functioning of the study group as a whole. The overall picture was one of an initial profound reaction followed by gradual achievement of greater equanimity on a different level of organizational functioning, so that by the end of the third month following placement there was generally a balanced response. Some of the salient features of the results are presented according to the seven dimensions of family functioning.

PERSONAL RESPONSE

There were more changes over the three-month period in this dimension than in any other. A high degree of adjustment had not been reached by the families at the end of three months, yet there was enough decline in parental response to reveal a pattern of reduced anxiety and beginning adjustment. Certain parental responses in this dimension were so repetitive as to suggest a new universality of response for the group studied. The central themes were identified as loss, relief, guilt and ambivalence, and fulfillment and a sense of well-being.

A paradigm of common response was observed that could be stated in this way: Parents experienced feelings of loss and relief after the placement. If either feeling (or both) promoted ambivalence or guilt about the placement that could not after a reasonable length of time be resolved into a belief that the child was being provided with something the home and community had not been able to provide, parental adjustment and placement were both in jeopardy.

MARITAL INTERACTION

The families reacted least of all in this area of family living. Since in those studied a relatively high degree of intactness and harmony existed, this finding was not unanticipated. The effects of removal of the child were revealed by patterns in two aspects of marital interaction.

In the decision-making aspect, highly individualized responses were found. The general pattern was one in which parents were at first often ambivalent about the placement. If the placement went well, the marital partners resolved their ambivalence, closing ranks in a sense of togetherness. If the placement did not meet with their approval or expectations, they either terminated it or closed ranks without feeling a sense of fulfillment of purpose in the placement.

The second aspect dealt with change in the marital organization. Following an original response to the separation, the marriages remained essentially the same, developed critical modifications, or were relieved from tension, so that their functioning improved. Whether the marriage improved was found to be related to individual factors, the psychological place of the retarded child in the marriage, and the definition and purpose of the placement established by the parents.

PARENT-CHILD INTERACTION

Parent-child responses followed similar patterns of declining, yet continuous, responses over the period studied. With the changes in family structure and the relief from guilt about the burden under which normal children were thought to have lived with the retarded child in the home, a clear picture of modification in parent-child interaction emerged. Less diverted by the retarded child and with more time available to them, parents turned their attention to their remaining children. The normal children's needs, which heretofore were not fully appreciated or remained unmet, now came under greater parental scrutiny. As parents became more insightful about their normal children, they moved into closer and more satisfying relationships with them.

NORMAL CHILDREN'S RESPONSE

The normal children followed a similar pattern of declining, continuous response that was balanced at the conclusion of the study period. The children seemed to be more adaptable to the retarded sibling's removal than their parents.

Parents wished their normal children to feel emancipated, but three months was too short a time for them to formulate a clear idea of how they wished the normal children to relate to the retarded child now absent from the home. All the children reacted to their sibling's removal to some extent. Most parents reported that these reactions took place in the first month, after which the children showed improvement in temperament, were less restless and tense, felt emancipated, and were resigned about the placement.

FAMILY MANAGEMENT

Management changes were most noticeable in the first and second months, then declined to a point of limited change by the end of the third month. Changes in this dimension occurring in the first month were almost as great as those occurring in the personal area, highlighting the great impact of the separation on management aspects of living.

A complete spectrum of response was found, from slight change to total deterioration of family routine owing to the loss of the retarded child, who may have acted as a keystone in family organization. The majority of the families found their routines easier and gradually adjusted to the change. The "relief from burden" theme once again was echoed by universal reporting of a considerably quieter atmosphere and reduced turmoil in the home. Shopping, food preparation, mealtimes, bathing, and care of clothing were noted as being easier, less hectic, less rushed, smoother, quicker, or less burdensome. A quick decline in interest in these areas by most parents, however, suggested that the physical aspects of the earlier turmoil were quickly minimized and the gaps filled with other activities.

FAMILY TRANSACTION

Transactional changes occurred in most of the families, generally following a pattern of greatest change in the first and second months following placement and then achieving a balance by the end of the third month.

However, the primary finding was that these three months were a period of adjustment and experimentation owing to the emotional and geographic considerations involved in arriving at a satisfying and balanced degree of contact with the placed children. A continuum of "no change" to "total relief and exhilaration" was directly related to the personal dimension described earlier, as well as to the family's economic circumstances. Many families undertook a flurry of social activity—the most dramatic evidence being vacation trips, which half of the families took. Such trips appeared to be symbolic representations of physical and psychological liberation from the burden associated with caring for a retarded child.

In addition to quantitative differences, qualitative differences in social activities were often reported as an expression of a family's feeling of well-being. The qualitative aspects of a family's social experiences may be a predictor of how the family will fare later in the placement. A few showed martyrlike responses, that is, claiming neither willingness nor ability to enjoy the freedom that they acknowledged now existed.

FAMILY DEVELOPMENT

The pattern of changes occurring in the family development dimension was in reverse order of the others, showing more change in the third than in the first month. The separation of a retarded child from his family obviously constitutes a major financial step in a family's planning and development; therefore one might expect a reorganization of family financial planning to follow closely after this important event. Several families showed important changes in career-type activities and goals. A near-total response of this group was the energizing effect of the placement on parental concern about the place of the retarded child in the family's future. The families appeared to organize themselves around three possibilities: doubts about what the future would hold, inclusion of the children in the family's future, and exclusion of the children from the future. Placement seemed to influence a family's perception of its own future course, with placement freeing some families and not others. In most instances it could be said that the placement served to free normal siblings to develop socially and emotionally. Significantly, a liberating effect was not felt by families that regarded the placement with uncertainty.

Recommendations

In spite of the limitations of the study that might be attributed to the short time period and the small number of families, certain implications for social work practice emerged clearly. The results obtained, especially concerning personal responses, support the principle that parents are in need of supportive, sympathetic relationships after as well as before placement of their retarded children. Of special significance were the feelings of loss parents experienced in the early phases of placement. In his own way each parent asked that the school's services be extended to him.

There were clear indications that families needed (1) further opportunities to understand the school's practices, (2) explanation of practices and procedures in writing, which might prove supportive until parents could become better acquainted with the procedures and establish trusting relationships with staff members in a way that would enable them to contend with the school's size, and (3) professionally directed opportunities to share experiences with other parents in circumstances similar to theirs. Several parents, it seemed, spoke to parents of children already in the school to obtain counsel from them. The advice that they received was supportive, but not always appropriate for their own situation. This advice and support could probably be better obtained through an appropriate service provided by the school.[8]

It was the investigator's impression that the relief from burden and the loss of parental role that parents experienced in the placement of their retarded children may be a determining factor in the reduction in parents' involvement with their placed children later in the placement. With the children absent from the home, the relief from daily tensions seemed to reduce the level of anxiety and engagement that might be necessary for the continued motivation of parents toward the resolution of conflicts between themselves and their retarded children.

The implications of this finding may be especially great for those children who have a potential to return to the community but who are unable to do so because of lack of sufficient parental support. If parents are to remain significantly engaged with their placed children, ways would have to be found to keep them from feeling so relieved that they transfer authority and responsibility for their children to the school or institution. In later life the children, when habilitated, partially trained, or sufficiently developed to return home, may need parental support and understanding. The school should therefore define with parents their joint responsibilities and encourage parents' active participation in their children's lives so that they continue to be parents in fact rather than in name only. Volunteer services and parent-staff association activities provide means for continued parental involvement. The nature of parental participation in these activities was, however, beyond the scope of the present study.

The need for a structured means by which parents could continue to express their anxiety, ask questions, seek reassurance, clarify their roles, gain in understanding of their children, obtain progress reports, and learn ways of supporting their children's placement so as to reduce the trauma of the separation was strikingly apparent. Although all parents may not need such services, many do. The provision of additional services, while costly, is in the interest of families and staff and should be provided.

Finally, certain suggestions for further study emerged from the inquiry. It was shown that the placement of a retarded child in a residential school is a complex phenomenon. It seems clear that placement holds different meanings for different people and that the term placement probably represents an overgeneralized concept that could be defined with greater specificity. In order to throw greater light on family functioning in the context of the separation of one of its members, the definition should probably include an understanding of a family's motivation for choosing separation as a tension-reducing strategy.

The frame of reference utilized in the present study provides a comprehensive picture of family functioning. With the further refinement of ratings of changes in family functioning in the dimensions devised, it might be possible to design a project that measures the changes in family functioning more precisely and over a longer period of time.

The present study emphasized the process of separation and some of the cause-and-effect aspects of the placement experience. The three major findings can be investigated further. The first finding was conceptualized as a paradigm of common response noted in almost all the families studied. This four-step response of (1) loss, (2) relief, (3) guilt and ambivalence, and (4) fulfillment and well-being, although phenomenological as it is presently understood, has service implications too. It is important to know and even predict, at least in a general way, the usual and expected direction that parental responses following placement may take. To do so in no way reduces respect for the individual or denies that human behavior is both purposive and spontaneous. In a large school, however, individualized services are costly. The ability to predict categories of parental response would enable administrators to identify readily parents who have the greatest need for service. It cannot, however, be assumed on the basis of the small numbers in the present study that the response pattern of all families is the same. It may be that there are many different patterns; hence further investigations into changes in family functioning accompanying the placement of a retarded child in a residential school are needed.

The second major finding dealt with the response of parents in relation to the school. It was noted that parents came to the school with expectations of the role they would play, and the loss of an active parental role created much anxiety for them. Further investigations into the complexity of such interactions are needed.

The range of strategies of schools in relation to parents warrants further study. This school established with parents a loose, nondirective, yet at times authoritarian, relationship. Soon after placement began it became clear to parents that the school's program was child rather than family centered. It was noted that the families were left with uncertainties about the placement and their own roles in relation to the school and their retarded children and that, except in certain cases, the effect of these uncertainties on the families was not clear. It is likely that further study over a greater time span might reveal that the school takes different postures and different strategies at different times with different effects.

In conclusion, the findings of the present study suggest that unless residential schools serve families, the families' understanding of their children may lag and family members' development as parents and as individuals may also be arrested. Therefore improved services to families and further investigation into the effects of these services on families and their retarded children are needed.

References

1.   *See* Bernard Farber, *Effects of a Severely Mentally Retarded Child on Family Integration*, "Monographs of the Society for Research in Child Development," Vol. 29, No. 2 (Yellow Springs, Ohio: Antioch Press, 1959); Betty Caldwell and Samuel B. Guze, "A Study of the Adjustment of Parents and Siblings of Institutionalized and Non-Institutionalized Retarded Children," *American Journal of Mental Deficiency*, Vol. 54, No. 5 (March 1960), pp. 845–861; John R. Thurston, "Attitudes and Emotional Reactions of Parents of Institutionalized Cerebral Palsied Patients," *American Journal of Mental Deficiency*, Vol. 55, No. 5 (September 1960), pp. 227–231; Laura L. Dittman, "The Family of the Child in an Institution," *American Journal of Mental Deficiency*, Vol. 66, No. 5 (March 1962), pp. 759–765; and William C. Adamson, Dorothy F. Ohrenstein, Delores Lake, and Alexander Hersh, "Separation Used to Help Parents Promote Growth of Their Retarded Child," *Social Work*, Vol. 9, No. 4 (October 1964), pp. 60–67.

2.   Marie Jahoda, Morton Deutsch, and Sturar Cook, *Research Methods in Social Relations* (New York: Dryden Press, 1951), p. 42.

3.   With the development of new programs by Elwyn relevant to the needs of blacks, a substantial number of black students have since been enrolled.

4.   Data not presented are available from the author.

5.   August B. Hollingshead, *Two Factor Index of Social Position* (New Haven: printed by the author, 1957).

6.   Owing to space limitations, only the most important findings will be presented.

7.   One family terminated the placement because of a lack of fulfillment and a sense of well-being. In a follow-up telephone interview the mother described her disappointment in the placement because it had not progressed to her satisfaction. She rejected the medical staff's opinion that her daughter's physical condition warranted curtailment of activity and decided that if her daughter could not participate in planned activity, there was little point in keeping her away from home.

8.   Following completion of the study, these findings led to the development of two innovations at Elwyn. A written guide for parents was developed and each parent of a newly enrolled student was provided with a copy at the time of his child's acceptance. In addition monthly group meetings were initiated for parents of newly enrolled children.

25
Impact of Kidney Disease on Patient, Family, and Society

Kathleen Hickey Read

The National Kidney Foundation estimates that over seven million Americans now suffer disease of the kidney. More than 125,000 people in the United States die from kidney disease each year. If transplantable kidneys were available, seven thousand of these persons could be saved.

The long periods of chronic illness, repeated hospitalizations, and the overwhelming amount of stress placed on patients and families have implications for social work. It is the purpose of this article to provide information about kidney disease and methods of treatment and to point out some of the social problems in order that social workers might be better prepared to assist clients with kidney disease. The material in this article is drawn from experience at the Kidney Transplant Service of the University of Minnesota Hospitals, a teaching facility of 826 beds, with 125,000 outpatient visits each year. The Kidney Unit has 25 hospital beds and 220 patients attending the Transplant Out Patient Clinic.

The person who is faced with the loss of kidney function manifests a state of crisis. Permanent kidney failure formerly resulted in death; choices today are limited to implantation of another person's kidney, kidney dialysis, or death. Two methods of treatment offer a chance for life—hemodialysis (use of artificial kidney machine) and kidney transplantation.

Hemodialysis has shown itself to be a feasible means of prolonging the lives of people with permanent kidney failure. The treatment procedure involves implantation of tubes (cannulas) into the arm or leg of a patient. The cannulas are inserted into the artery and vein and are connected by a shunt that lets the blood flow from one cannula to the other between treatments. When a patient comes in for treatments, the cannulas are connected to tubes

Source: From Social Casework 53 (July 1972), pp. 391–397. Copyright © 1972 by the Family Service Association of America. Reprinted by permission.

leading to the artificial kidney machine that removes the impurities from the blood. The patient must spend several hours lying in bed attached to the machine, as a dialysis may take from four to twelve hours and is required two or three times a week.

Kidney transplantation, which involves grafting of an organ from one individual to another of the same species (homograft), has now advanced to the stage in which it is the treatment of choice for persons with permanent renal failure. Successful transplantation removes the patient from the "sick role"; dialysis does not. He feels better, sources of stress are lessened, and he is able to assume a functioning role. The aim of transplantation is to restore the individual to a normal functioning life.

Physicians have intensified research and study on kidney transplantation as a method of treatment for several reasons. (1) Deaths were numerous among young people; (2) kidney transplantation is technically the easiest method to perform; and (3) the kidney is the only vital paired organ of which a human being can lose one and still survive well. Also, if the body does reject the new kidney, the patient can be maintained on the artificial kidney machine. It is anticipated that improved immuno-suppressive drug therapy, organ preservation, and more accurate tissue typing will, within the next few years, greatly reduce rejection reactions and increase the chances of longer life.

The University of Minnesota Hospitals has a liberal admission policy. Although a patient must meet certain medical criteria, social and economic factors do not play roles in a patient's acceptance. Patients also do not have to be state residents. Those rejected by other centers and those with disease or complications, such as diabetes, are accepted. Because of these factors, social problems are perhaps more prevalent and severe.

In 1971, eighty patients received kidney transplants; of this number, sixty-three were adults, and seventeen were children under sixteen years of age. Of the group, thirty-four received cadaver (deceased, nonrelated donor) transplants. All the children and twenty-nine of the sixty-three adults received kidneys from blood-related donors. When a patient receives a kidney of a related donor, his chances for survival with a functioning kidney are much greater.

Surgical illness is a "human experience" and produces new adaptations that may or may not be pathological. The dramatic character of transplantation surgery diverts attention from social problems inherent in the medical procedures, such as failure of the operation to meet expectations of the patient and family, disruption of family equilibrium, and investment of public funds to meet these costs. Renal failure and transplantation precipitate a crisis that may be defined differently by the patient and family. The crisis situation may mobilize or it may incapacitate them.

The discussion that follows will be based on the experiences of the social worker assigned to the Kidney Transplant Unit. The social worker assists the staff by obtaining detailed information in the form of social histories concerned with the impact of the disease on the patient and his family. The major functions of the social worker are to help the patient face his current environment and work through his feelings, fears, and attitudes and to help him strive toward a realistic adjustment and plan for his future life after discharge. The social worker explores the interaction and dynamics of members of a family—their attitudes, ways of communicating, and patterns of coping. Adherence to the patterns of a past life is not always indicative of the future but may identify specific problem areas. The focus is on helping families retain their integrity and functions.

The social work role varies with each patient. It consists of (1) helping the individual to understand the extensive treatment plan, (2) counseling with the patient and family in working out acceptance of the medical problem and methods of modifying some of its aspects by exploring ways for more satisfying relationships, (3) assessing readiness for acceptance of help from community and similar resources, (4) acting as a resource person and liaison with community agencies, (5) providing casework services to assist the patient and family, and (6) offering public education.

In order to coordinate information to assist the physician so that the patient can receive maximum benefit of treatment at University Hospitals, the "Hospital Team Conference" was initiated and is concerned with a comprehensive program for total care. The team attempts to alleviate forces that interfere with the patient's ability to receive and accept medical care. There is also considerable interaction and intense involvement among patients and between patients and staff. Social systems that characterize hierarchy among the patients are evident. Codes and rules are established, and patients redefine these roles and set up new expectations and responsibilities of which the staff must be aware in order to meet the needs. A therapeutic environment is encouraged by the staff through team conferences, physical therapy, occupational therapy, and diversional activities.

The Chronically Ill Patient and Hemodialysis

Hemodialysis prolongs the life of patients by the use of the "artificial kidney." Patients unable to receive a kidney transplant, those awaiting a cadaver donor, and patients who have had rejected transplants are maintained on dialysis. The treatment procedure can return a patient to a reasonably normal existence but presents some physical side effects and psychological complications. Although hemodialysis alleviates the uremic syndrome and the patient generally feels better, there are diet restrictions, problems with blood pressure, feelings of weakness, impotence, periodic hospitalizations, and shunt complications (clotting), any of which may prevent participation in living activities. Most patients experience some degree of apprehension before dialysis and tend to become most anxious at the beginning and end of the treatment when the shunt is disengaged or when technical difficulties arise. Attention span is often short, and it has been noted that some patients defend themselves against their anxiety by intellectualization or through sleep. Dialysis can be a frightening experience as a patient is able to observe his blood leaving and returning to his body. He may experience various degrees of fantasies and distorted body imagery, and he may view himself as not wholly human. The dialysis technician and nurse, who are particularly close to the patient, must deal realistically with the patient's anxieties concerning the machine. After dialysis, temporary weakness and nausea from salt and water loss is present; this weakness is often accompanied by lethargy.

Thus, hemodialysis does not completely alleviate difficulties of renal failure, and patients may be faced with a future of chronic illness. Patients, however, may function adequately in the "sick role." The passive dependent person probably will make an adjustment to dialysis but may have difficulties in long-term adjustment after a successful transplant. Patients on dialysis are also placed in a dependent situation and may never accept the shunt as an integral part of themselves. The cannula is a constant reminder of their condition and dependence on the dialyzer. A state of mental depression is not uncommon and follows the general grieving sequence of stages. At first patients tend to use denial; then they go through a period of grief and mourning, followed by anger and frustration, which may give way to depression or regression. Then constructive attempts are made to adjust to the illness and treatment plans. (A temporary depressive phase is also noted immediately following transplant.)

It is not uncommon for the patient on dialysis to violate a dietary or fluid restriction. Patients are carefully taught about permitted and forbidden food and its significance in relation to their illness and life. Nevertheless, patients frequently refuse to eat designated foods, request foods they know they are not allowed, or eat in the hospital canteen. Food can assume great importance for the patient under stress. The traditional methods for relieving anxiety and tension, other than food, are often not permitted for the dialysis patient. He may be advised to stop smoking or restrict alcoholic and fluid intake. He may not be allowed lengthy trips or participation in rigorous activity. These prohibitions may result in hostile feelings, and the patient may attempt to use his diet to control his situation, seek gratification, and release his stress. Another form of behavior that might be interpreted as an act of resentment, denial of illness, or desire for self-harm is the patient's neglecting to take care of his shunt.

Long-term dialysis requires sacrifices on the part of the patient and his family because of the special requirements and frequent trips to the hospital for dialysis. The patient and family members may resent this intrusion on family life and display open hostility and guilt, often directed at the staff. The patient's self-image and role can change greatly during this period.

The time of dialysis (day or night) and the distance to the center are important factors in the patient's total rehabilitation and his ability to be gainfully employed or perform household duties. Thus, chronic hemodialysis has a profound psychological impact on the patient and his family.

The Transplant Patient and His Family

The transplant patient must plan to remain under medical supervision for an indefinite length of time. The prospect of transplantation presents freedom from pain and provides an opportunity to engage in meaningful activity. Conflict may arise between the patient and family. The patient may feel more threatened by new independency in assuming the "healthy role" than by facing death. The choice of a kidney donor requires family decisions that can produce a high degree of stress. This decision-making crisis in kidney transplantation is unique; all the members of the family know that one could be saved by the sacrifice of another. The act of donation may be inconsistent with other life patterns and may not follow a rational decision-making process. Man is used to identifying with a model, and the lack of norms and customs to use as guidelines would appear to cause a great amount of tension and stress. The patient knows that if he receives a kidney from a family member, his chances for survival are twice as good as they would be from a cadaver kidney. Reactions to receiving a cadaver kidney have not been studied extensively; however, from observation, attitudes vary from curiosity about the person who donated and how his death occurred to indifference and relief that the patient does not have to be concerned about family responsibilities or obligations to the donor. Some relatives reveal a sense of grief about the inability of the family members to contribute toward saving the patient's life. The attitude regarding the donated cadaver organ seems to differ between recipient families and donor families, the latter probably viewing donation as a gift and sacrifice.

The length of the interval between the first knowledge that a transplant is needed and the time of the surgery influences psychological attitudes. The patient exhibits various degrees of psychological decompensation pertaining to the donated kidney, based on intrafamilial relationships and personality makeup. Particularly if the recipient is an adult, he will look beyond his immediate family for a potential donor. Role obligations for family members (siblings, aunts, or other close relatives) are unclear in our culture with the possible exception of parents' donation to children. Parents who donate seem to feel that their donation is not so spectacular or extraordinary but something natural to do for their child. Siblings appear unclear about this obligation to donate a kidney. Realistically, the donation of a kidney would cause the donor discomfort, loss of work time, and a small risk of kidney loss for himself later in life. Some families are subjected to many pressures, and the decision to donate a kidney may be a very stressful process. Many of the patients do not approach the entire family but request another member to do so, and this member may play a key role in the recruiting of donors. The patient usually has a good idea if a family member will not volunteer because of ambivalent family relationships; he accepts this fact and is satisfied to wait for a cadaver donor. However, in less close relationships, decision making can be very difficult. Studies are currently being conducted by Dr. Roberta Simmons of the Sociology Department at the University of Minnesota on the nature of this crisis, focusing on the extended family and on the relative who does not donate a kidney. It has been observed that some relative donors, however, may question their responsibility for the recipient's life; likewise, the recipient may feel threatened in taking the kidney. There is also some indication of feelings of greatness versus hypochondrism on the part of the recipient and donor. In general, donors postoperatively display pride and increased self-esteem and handle their emotions and physical discomfort well.

Patients, both adult and child, become quite sophisticated and knowledgeable about their medical conditions. The patient takes an active part in his treatment program and is able to understand and speak the medical terminology. He learns about the detailed functions of the kidney and about the complex medications and their purposes. "Dialysis and transplantation" are explained thoroughly to him. The kidney disease patient understands his medical diagnosis and prognosis and the reasons for his renal failure in more detail than do most chronically ill patients. The medications given after transplant are essential for the life of the new kidney and the patient's life. The patient knows this and must accept the medications, which may produce observable side effects and impose psychological implications. The first year posttransplant is probably most crucial; problems such as rejection of the organ will most likely occur during this time period. Thus, even after discharge from the hospital, patients often must be readmitted for rejection episodes. This threat, which continues to cause work and home disruptions, adds to the patient's fears.

The high level of emotional involvement in regard to the donation and possible rejection of the new kidney may arouse great anxiety, grief, and disruption of family equilibrium. Rejection of a transplanted kidney produces changes in relationships and a breakdown in defenses. Changes in roles and in the patient's total life situation may be consequences of chronic illness or kidney rejection. Successful transplantation, however, also may produce new life situations and adaptations that do not automatically insure total social and psychological rehabilitation.

The changes in total life situation and attitudes of the transplant recipient may, for example, influence women to change their attitudes in regard to childbearing as against adoption of a child. Marital and sexual relations that have been altered drastically because of the patient's uremic condition during dialysis treatment may make the posttransplant adjustments difficult. Employment retraining may be indicated. Conflicts or problems existing prior to transplantation, on the other hand, may be resolved following a successful transplant.

Teen-agers who receive a transplant have special problems. Absences from school, loss of friends, and conflicts in regard to sex and dating appear to be common. The adolescent is apt to find his body image and identity more of a problem than he can handle.

The social problems a child with kidney disease faces differ from those of the adult. His lack of knowledge and immaturity make the medical treatment plan less well understood and more frightening. Often the child's personality is formed during lengthy and recurrent hospitalizations. The parents' fears and concerns and the limitations of the illness influence the child's development.

Children frequently identify very strongly with a kidney that has been received from a parent donor. For example, a thirteen-year-old boy who received a kidney from his father stated, "I have the only kidney for a boy my age that flew forty missions over Germany."

The parents of a child who has a successful kidney transplant must learn a whole set of new adjustments. Their general concerns and over-protection must be modified to enhance the child's normal development. Siblings who have had competitive feelings and resentment because of special favors and privileges accorded the ill child may add to the difficult readjustment of parents and patient. At times, even the marriage itself must be rebuilt and the entire family relationships recast, requiring assessment, time, and work. Most families need the services of a caseworker during this process.

The social workers in hospitals need to be sensitive to the reactions of patients and relatives so that they can provide guidance and support when needed. During the patient's hospital course, he usually seeks out other patients and compares progress. Strong friendships may form, offering each other a great deal of support. On the other hand, inaccurate information is often exchanged. Relatives, too, may misinterpret another patient's medical status and assume that the same fate is in store for their relative. When a patient becomes acutely ill or dies, the other patients generally become agitated, withdrawn, and depressed; feeling tones are easily picked up and transferred one to another and should be discussed. Because of the critical nature of the illness, the social worker must be able to understand and recognize his own feelings about death and have substantial medical knowledge so that he can empathize with and relate to all patients' families.

Financial Costs and Community Responsibility

The cost of medical care for kidney transplant patients ranges from $10,000 to $80,000. The average cost at the University Hospitals is approximately $16,000 for total inpatient care exclusive of professional fees. Chronic dialysis treatment may amount to between $5,000 to $15,000 on a yearly basis, whereas it is hoped that transplantation is a one-time expense. Eventually, these costs will decrease because of shorter hospital stays and medical advances. The principal sources of financial help at the present time are private insurance, federal research grants, and public welfare programs. Thus, the financial costs entailed by chronic hemodialysis and transplantation impose a problem for the patient, his family, and society. Loss of economic, social, or personal status can become a serious problem and can greatly affect the patient's adjustments and capacity to function. Economic variables directly influence family attitudes as do those of culture, religion, sex, age, and length of illness.

The middle-class patient, who may have insurance coverage and a fairly adequate and stable salary prior to hopitalization, may be required, when his insurance coverage is less than his expenses, to apply for welfare assistance—a plan difficult for many to accept. Furthermore, because they own property and have financial assets, many are ineligible for public assistance until legal income requirements are met. The tragedy is compounded for farm patients who are faced with the necessity of selling their land and sacrificing their livelihood and financial independence. For patients residing outside the metropolitan area, there is the additional financial strain of transportation and maintenance costs. Most welfare departments and communities are not able to authorize funds to meet these expenses.

Major financing for the medical expenses of these patients comes from public funds under Title XIX of the Social Security Act. The provisions of the act make it possible to provide complete care for these patients. However, state plans, the interpretation of the act, and procedures by local community agencies impose limitations that create difficulties. The large amount of money required to provide medical care for patients who have severe renal disease, moreover, may be more than a community considers justifiable for one individual. The alternatives are for those in medical practice to refine technical methods to reduce costs and for the federal government to grant financial assistance to institutions involved in development of new methods of medical care. Kidney disease is a major community health problem and thus has serious implications for every community whose social agencies cannot offer constructive services to help these patients.

Among men and women under twenty-five, kidney diseases are the second highest cause of work loss in the United States today. From age twenty-five on, these kidney-related diseases are the fourth highest cause of work loss. The Kidney Foundation, the only major voluntary agency relating itself to the total problem, states that one of every twenty-five persons in any community suffers from some form of kidney disease. Thus, in order for the patient to receive maximum benefit from medical care, his financial, social, and psychological needs must also be met by the community and society.

Employment

Generally, when the patient who has had a successful kidney transplant is ready for discharge from the hospital, he has no vocational restrictions imposed upon him. Ideally, the patient can return to his former job. Realistically, however, his former job may not be available. The prolonged treatment and hospitalization, the financial costs, complexity of medications, periodic checkups at the hospital, and drastic changes in the patient's life situation may have interfered with work performance and resulted in loss of his job. Overprotection is often manifested by family members; it impedes the patient's return to work and independency and interferes with his rehabilitation. Patients, too, fear that harm may come to the new kidney if they engage in strenuous work or extracurricular school activities. Because the majority of patients receive Social Security Disability or county assistance, it is difficult for them to relinquish this aid until they are secure in a new job. Employers hesitate to hire persons who receive Social Security Disability. Many employers do not understand the nature of kidney transplants and do not wish to risk employing someone who might be readmitted to a hospital at any time. Thus, patients may be rejected because they have received an organ transplant. The primary reason generally given is the restrictions imposed by insurance and union policies of large companies.

Physical side effects produced by medication, such as cushioned face, may also prevent patients from seeking the type of employment they want or from resuming past activities. Family relationships and support are important in determining the patient's successful rehabilitation and his return to a level of activity that is equal to, or surpasses, the level prior to the onset of kidney disease.

Vocational rehabilitation and counseling services should be enlisted prior to the patient's discharge from the hospital. Studies focused on defining "rehabilitation" and "adjustment" pretransplant and posttransplant would be useful with the recognition that definitions vary. The mere fact that a person has returned to work following transplantation does not automatically conclude that he is "rehabilitated." The quality of the individual's functioning must be explored. When the gainful employment he has returned to is satisfying to him and to his needs, employment can be used as an indicative factor of rehabilitation.

Moral and Ethical Aspects of Transplantation

Transplantation of human organs is a new era in medical history. The availability of new surgical techniques that prolong and save the lives of thousands of individuals makes it necessary to examine current beliefs concerning the use of organs from the bodies of other people. There are fears within the population regarding the donation of organs, as evidenced by the customs and the mass media. The value of the body, fear of mutilation, sickness, and future health are all considerations and should be correlated with religious beliefs, socioeconomic status, sex, age, race, and culture.

The development of living organ banks is an attempt to institutionalize societal fears. The signing of a donor card may represent a wholesome impersonal aspect, although it is questionable whether people view this action realistically or view it as socially desirable. In the past it has been thought that people who sign cards donating vital organs to a medical center to be used for others are from the better educated, higher socioeconomic groups and view this act as humanitarian. Recent studies, however, indicate that people in the lower socioeconomic groups also wish to make a donation of parts of their body—possibly as a contribution to society or from religious motivation.

The use of organs from the body of a healthy, functioning individual raises moral questions. The extent to which one individual may impose on another is an ethical consideration. The rights of people to safeguard their own bodies can never be denied. In some of these instances the moral and family pressures on donors impose obligations that deny this right.

Another ethical aspect of the procurement of organs involves the purchase of organs for transplants when immunological techniques are perfected. More organs would then be available on a cash-negotiation basis. Because American culture is based on paying for what one receives, this action might not be disturbing to the population. If purchase of organs were authorized, the use of family and cadaver donors would be less of a necessity. However, purchase of organs raises the difficulty of determining price. A high price for organs would certainly discriminate against the poor. The selling of organs might also be interpreted as a partially suicidal gesture. Through laws, it is likely that attitudes and customs regarding transplantation and donation may change, and donation may come to be viewed as a social obligation rather than as a gift or sacrifice.

At the University of Minnesota Hospitals the criteria used for selection of people to receive a renal tranplant or to be maintained by hemodialysis are based primarily on medical decisions. As yet, the quality of life the patient will be able to lead or the contributions he can make cannot be determined or defined without enlisting value judgments. Transplantation provides a "potential" life with a new organ. The moral issue is, "Are we doing what we are supposed to do?"

26
Group Treatment of Families of Burn-Injured Patients

Marcia Abramson

Probably no injury causes more physical and psychological trauma than a severe burn. Both the injury and the treatment that follows are frightening and painful, and the patient is often left with residual deformities that can radically alter his life. Varying degrees of fear, depression, grief, loss of hope, and psychotic reactions during the course of the treatment and during the long recovery period have been reported. In addition, the burn-injured person and his family are faced with the prospect of enormous medical costs and extensive hospitalizations that mean long separations from home and community. It is no wonder that a severe burn creates a severe crisis situation for patients and their families.

Interest in the psychological reactions of burn patients was first aroused at the time of the Cocoanut Grove fire in Boston in 1942. It was found that many of the persons burned at that time suffered from persistent and serious emotional problems.[1] Subsequent literature on the subject has supported these earlier findings.[2] One of the significant outcomes of a study at the University of Iowa Hospitals and Clinics, previously reported in Social Casework, was that the relatives of burn patients undergo many of the same stresses as do the patients.[3]

During the early, acute stages of treatment, when the patient is faced with the initial physical and psychological shock to his system, the relative is often stunned and depressed. As the patient begins to cope with the active demands of the convalescence and the rehabilitation processes, the relative must also adjust to these changes. Because the focus of the medical staff must be on the patient, the relative often faces his anxieties about death and deformity and his boredom with a prolonged hospital stay without the active

Source: From Social Casework 56 (April 1975), pp. 235–241. Copyright © 1975 by the Family Service Association of America. Reprinted by permission.

support of the professional staff. In addition, the families are faced with the trauma of watching a loved one suffer, often without being able to intervene in a meaningful way.

As a result of these findings,[4] it was recommended that a group be organized at the burn unit of the University of Iowa Hospitals and Clinics to help relatives cope with the stresses of being supportive to a seriously burned patient. It was apparent that relatives who remain for long periods of time with their burned family member form a natural group on the ward. They orient one another to procedure, offer each other support at times of stress, and develop an informal grapevine to disseminate information. It was anticipated that with the added leadership and participation of a social worker and a nurse to help focus the group's attitudes, feelings, and beliefs, the natural group could be utilized to achieve certain educational and counseling goals.

The original plan was to include only those persons who planned to remain with their relatives for the duration of the hospitalization and who would therefore be available to come to weekly meetings on a regular basis. It soon became apparent, however, that relatives who are not able to stay for the duration of the hospitalization are equally in need of support from the group and can contribute to the other members. It was also decided to include the relatives of patients who were returning for follow-up checks or reconstructive surgery. Recovery from a severe burn takes two years or more; the relatives can benefit from the continued support of the group and can help those persons whose relatives are still hospitalized to appreciate the problems that occur after discharge.

Group Structure

Initially, a sign was posted just outside the nurses' station announcing a weekly meeting and asking relatives to sign up if they were interested in attending. Subsequently, during the week following each patient's admission to the burn unit, the relatives were approached and asked whether they would like to attend the group.

The meetings were co-chaired by a social worker who was knowledgeable about the problems of families of seriously ill patients and a nurse who was familiar with the burn unit's medical and nursing procedures. The physical therapist and chaplain from the unit attended a few meetings in which the focus of group concern was on issues relevant to their services.

At the beginning of each group meeting, the purpose of the group was reiterated by the social worker: to help orient the relatives to the burn unit and give them the opportunity to share common concerns and questions with others undergoing similar stresses and to help the burn unit staff better understand these problems in order to be more helpful to them and to other families in the future. Although group members often already knew one another and were familiar with the patients, the social worker usually asked each member to introduce himself and describe the circumstances of the burn and the patient's current condition. Coffee was served, and group members were encouraged to talk with each other about their experiences in the hospital.

A notebook was kept on nursing care issues and made available to the rest of the unit nursing staff. Periodic meetings of nursing staff and the group leaders were held to share information and help the nursing staff understand and deal with the emotional reactions of family members. During a two-year period, meetings were held at weekly intervals, whenever there were two or more relatives present on the burn unit who wished to attend. In all, thirty-eight group meetings were held.

Initial Reactions

It was found that at meetings in which there was a preponderance of re-tives of newly admitted patients, there were many specific questions about the medical and nursing care. Questions relating to shock, intravenous medications, diet, debridement, burn rounds, the use of silver nitrate, and the timing of procedures were raised, and relatives of patients who had been in the hospital longer were encouraged to share their relevant experiences. Only when the emotional implications of the procedures had been discussed did the nurse answer the specific question. If more experienced relatives were not present, the social worker would attempt to have the group members discuss the psychological implications of the various procedures before specific responses were given.

The need for specific information about procedures seemed to be closely related to the initial shock the relatives suffered during the early weeks of the hospitalization. At the same time that he had to begin to face the severity of the injury that had occurred to the patient, the family member had to get used to the sights, smells, sounds, and procedures of the unit. Explanations about the procedures often were not understood and had to be repeated; the relatives had to be helped to know what and whom to ask when they had questions. The group acted as a forum and catalyst for this procedure.

> Mrs. L's husband was injured after suffering a seizure while burning trash. Mrs. L complained at the meeting that she never had an opportunity to talk with the doctor about her husband's condition. As she spoke to the group about her husband, it became clear that she had many misconceptions about his condition and his need for posthospital care. Underlying her inability to

formulate questions for the medical staff was the fear that they would tell her that he was in an even worse condition than she imagined. The group helped her to talk about her fear that her husband had suffered permanent mental deterioration from a recent seizure and would therefore require twenty-four-hour supervision upon discharge from the hospital. She responded well to the group's suggestion that she talk with the unit social worker about these fears and enlist her aid in formulating the questions to ask of the medical staff.

Group Support

More experienced members of the group have been able to share their experiences and solutions to problems with newer members in a way that can be highly supportive to the new members, as well as therapeutic to themselves.

At the first meeting he attended, Mr. P, whose two children were burned in a house fire two weeks earlier, spoke of how other persons who had relatives on the burn unit had welcomed him to the unit, informed him about procedures, helped him to ask questions and understand what the doctors and nurses were telling him, and encouraged him to attend the group for further support and clarification. He discussed his children's different reactions to their burns. The group began to prepare him for the fact that his daughter, who was the more badly burned of the two but much more stoical than her brother, would probably begin to feel more pain and become increasingly depressed as treatment progressed. In later meetings, Mr. P spoke of how this discussion had helped him to understand his daughter's withdrawal and depression when it did occur and to deal with it as part of the normal reaction to a severe burn.

Among the problems discussed in the early stages of hospitalization were the primary relative's discomort at being torn between the patient and the family at home, his need for support from other family and friends, and the visits from other family members, especially small children whose imagination about the burn was often much worse than the actual injury.

A phenomenon that occurred in the group was the mobilization of group effort to help a particular relative or patient. Sometimes it was a person like Mr. P, who needed information and support during the early stages of hospitalization. Other times it was someone who needed help in coping with the demands of a patient and could accept advice from the group more easily than from the staff.

Mrs. K, whose fifteen-year-old son was hospitalized with severe burns for several months, had promised her son at the time of his admission to the unit that she would remain with him throughout his hospitalization. After many weeks of constant attendance at his bedside, she was becoming emotionally and physically exhausted by the strain, and it was clear that she would end up a patient herself if she did not leave. All the encouragement, direction, and advice of the medical and nursing staff was to no avail until other members of the group decided that it was time for her to take a few days of rest away from the hospital. They convinced her, and then her son, who later believed that it had been his idea to send his mother home.

Sometimes the group served as surrogate family for a patient who had no relatives available.

Carl, a fifteen-year-old who had been burned in a gasoline explosion, had no relationship with his family. As his sixteenth birthday approached, different members of the group expressed concern that the day not go uncelebrated. They spent part of two group sessions planning a party and delegated a group member to involve the staff and take up a collection. The party turned into a gala event for staff, patients, and relatives and clearly demonstrated the burn unit group's interest in one another.

Often relatives who were having difficulty coping with the patients, procedures, or staff were able to express some of their own feelings by focusing on the problems of others.

Mrs. D, whose husband was burned in a farming accident while working as a migrant laborer, came a great distance to stay with him. She spoke little English, had few financial resources, and had much concern about her two small children who had been left at home with relatives. The usual problems experienced on the unit were compounded by her inability to communicate and her resulting isolation. The group spent several meetings giving her practical advice about financial resources and emotional support to cope with her husband's demands. The group also suggested ways to communicate better with the staff and activities that could help her become more involved with other people. Other patients who were having problems with finances and communication difficulties with staff and were also suffering from isolation were able to express their own needs indirectly while they were helping Mrs. D.

From Acute Care to Rehabilitation

One of the most stressful periods for burn patients and their relatives seems to occur when the focus changes from acute care to rehabilitation efforts. From being immobilized for days at a time, dependent, cared for by staff and relatives, and encouraged to express his feelings freely when in pain, the patient is suddenly faced with new instructions to be independent, take care of his own eating and toileting needs, do a prescribed number of exercises a day, and control his expression of negative feelings. The relative who has been so important in feeding, entertaining, and encouraging is often asked to leave if the patient continues to ask for assistance with tasks the patient is expected to do himself. For many patients, especially children, who have felt that the family member will stay only as long as he participates actively in the treatment process, and for their relatives, who suddenly seem to have no purpose, rehabilitation can be an anxious time. Patients complain about the nurses and physical therapists who are pushing them, or else they cooperate with staff instructions and take their frustrations out on the family member. Relatives find themselves caught between concern for the patient and fear of alienating the staff.

Mrs. R, whose ten-year-old daughter, Marie, was burned when her dress caught on fire, found herself distressed by her daughter's expression of pain and the staff's expectations that Marie exercise control over her screaming. Believing that Marie's extreme fear increased her inability to cope with the pain of the exercises, Mrs. R became overwhelmed with the strain of being supportive while trying to keep Marie and herself from alienating the staff by too much expression of concern. She expressed to the group her feelings that the staff wanted her to leave the burn unit.

The group was able to be helpful in a number of ways. It provided a place for Mrs. R to express her anger, not only toward the staff but also toward Marie for putting her in such an uncomfortable position. She continued to receive support and acceptance from the group despite her expression of angry feelings. She was able to express her anger directly to staff in the persons of the co-leaders without fear of retaliation. The co-leaders and group were able to help her examine and better understand her daughter's behavior and her own and the staff's reactions to it in a way that lent itself to the formulation of new solutions to the problems.

Relatives often use the group to express their pleasure in the fact that the burn crisis had made them appreciate strengths in themselves, the patient, and other family members that they did not know existed. A wife who had thought of herself as the dependent, helpless partner found she could assume the role of caring for the family farm and operating the machinery. She amazed the male members of the group when she described how she had changed the clutch on a tractor. One mother was delighted at the way her burn-injured adolescent boy, who previously had expressed a great deal of dissatisfaction with school and family life and had threatened to drop out of school, seemed to be able to redirect his energies toward finishing high school. Other mothers found that their teen-age children at home were willing and able to assume new responsibilities for themselves and younger children when a burned sibling kept the mother away from home for long periods of time. The expression of these strengths in the group and their positive reinforcement by other group members encouraged the participants to continue their efforts to cope effectively with the crisis.

Preparation for Discharge

As the time for discharge from the hospital draws near, family members experience anxiety about how they will manage the patient at home. While the patient becomes increasingly concerned about returning to home, school, work, and other activities, the relatives begin to realize that at home they will be responsible, without the help of the physicians, nurses, and physical therapists, for exercises, wrappings, and dressing changes. The group experience permits the family member to express a natural ambivalence about taking on this responsibility alone. Returning relatives can share experiences and solutions to problems with those who are about to face them.

Evaluation of the Group by Participants

A few weeks after the patient's discharge from the hospital, every relative who attended two or more meetings was sent a questionnaire asking for his evaluation of the burn unit's relatives' group. Of the thirty-three letters sent out, twenty-three were returned. These relatives had participated in from two to twelve meetings of the group, with an average of four meetings per person.

When asked to indicate how helpful they found the group sessions, seventeen checked "very helpful," four "helpful," and two "not too helpful." When asked to comment on the ways in which they found the group helpful, many said the group meeting was a place to share problems with others who understood—both relatives and staff. One wife commented, "It was good to just be able to discuss some of my fears regarding my husband's condition with people who understood so well because they were going through the same ordeal." A mother added, "The nurse and social worker listened to everything I had to say. They were very reassuring when I needed it. I felt I could talk about any problem." Relatives indicated that they had come away with increased understanding of what patients go through physically and psychologically and had a better understanding of procedures and staff problems. The group meetings had helped them feel closer to one another and had relieved some of their tensions. Several commented that it was good for both the relative and patient for the family member to get away from the burn unit to talk. A husband commented, "I was able to release tension and ask questions about my wife's case without feeling like a nuisance."

When asked to comment on how the group failed to be helpful to them and what could be done to make it more valuable for relatives in the future, most replied that the group had fulfilled all their expectations, although there were some comments about the fact that a few relatives monopolized the conversation. Suggestions were made about timing, including making the meetings longer, scheduling them at a time when more relatives could attend, having more frequent meetings, and involving relatives as soon as the patient is admitted to the unit.

Relatives were also asked to comment on the problems that they and the patient faced on return home for which they had not been prepared. A number said that the most difficult adjustment was to the patient's moods and irritability. According to one mother, it was "mostly the change in personality which lasted—stubbornness." A wife said, "The only problem we had was getting adjusted to his moods, because mentally he was very unstable and at times he is very despondent." Another mother commented, "I didn't realize the full strain I was under. I did a lot of worrying and wondering if I was doing all of it right—the wrapping and such of my son."

Observations from the Ward

In addition to what happened within the group and the reported benefits from group members after discharge, certain observations were made about the effect on the ward of the establishment of the relatives' groups. In the past, when many severely ill patients required much staff attention, relatives often reacted to the feeling that their patient was being neglected by expressing hostility toward one another or toward the staff. Cliques would form and one or two relatives or staff would become recipients of all the hostile feelings. With the advent of the group, the scapegoating of one another diminished. The relatives appear to have gained a greater understanding of why nursing and medical efforts need to be concentrated on certain sicker patients. The family members fill in with care and support for patients who do not need as much nursing attention, patients who would previously have felt neglected and uncared for. Furthermore, group meetings provided an opportunity for members to examine the emotional forces operating within the close-knit family of burn patients and their families. Some scapegoating of staff continued, but the group leaders were much better able to offer the relatives the opportunity to handle their anger and complaints in a manner conducive to productive change.

The group meetings also gave one member of the nursing staff the opportunity to share nursing concerns with the relatives, and other nurses were able to share their concerns with the nurse leader who brought them to the group. The group's reactions could then be conveyed to the rest of the nurses individually, by means of the group notebook and in staff meetings. The periodic meetings that the social worker and nurse co-leader held with the nursing staff permitted the sharing of information about patients' and relatives' psychosocial problems and needs and how these could best be met by nursing staff. As a result of these meetings, the nursing staff expressed a desire for more social work coverage so that they could have a better understanding of the patients and families as early as possible in the hospitalization.

The use of a nurse who was part of the burn unit staff and a social worker who had no direct responsibility on the ward seemed to be particularly effective. The nurse was knowledgeable about patients, procedures, and individual problems and in continuous communication with the rest of the staff. She demonstrated to the relatives the interest and concern that the staff must have for them, as shown by sending her. The social worker, on the other hand, because she was not identified as a member of the burn unit, could ask questions about issues that others took for granted and could focus primarily on the needs of the relatives, unlike other professional staff for whom the patient is the primary person. Thus, she brought a different point of view.

Recommendations

Although burn injuries are particularly stressful because of their suddenness, intensity, painfulness, and duration, there are many other medical problems that create significant stress for patients and families. Any illness that results in drastically altered life-styles or that causes temporary alteration in the patient's ability to cope can produce stress and crisis for the patient and his family. Cancer, chronic renal disease, cardiac illnesses, neurological problems, and birth defects are just a few of the medical problems that cause significant stress for patients and relatives. Relatives as well as patients need support from others who understand and who can provide some relief from the demands of the illness and treatment process. A group especially designed to provide such support for family members can ultimately help the patients and the medical and nursing staffs responsible for the care of such seriously ill patients.

References

1.   Stanley Cobb and Erich Lindeman, Neuropsychiatric Observations, *Annals of Surgery*, 117:814–24 (June 1943); and Alendra Adler, Neuropsychiatric Complications in Victims of Boston's Cocoanut Grove Disaster, *Journal of the American Medical Association*, 123:1098–1101 (December 1943).

2.   David A. Hamburg et al., Clinical Importance of Emotional Problems in the

Care of Patients with Burns, *New England Journal of Medicine*, 248:355–59 (February 26, 1953); David A. Hamburg, Beatrice Hamburg, and Sydney DeGoze, Adaptive Problems and Mechanisms in Severely Burned Patients, *Psychiatry*, 16:1–20 (February 1953); Helen L. Martin, J. H. Lawrie, and A. W. Wilkinson, The Family of the Fatally Burned Child, *Lancet*, 295:628–29 (September 14, 1968); Helen L. Martin, Antecedents of Burns and Scalds in Children, *British Journal of Medical Psychology*, 43:39–47 (March 1970); idem, Parents' and Children's Reactions to Burns and Scalds in Children, *British Journal of Medical Psychology*, 43:183–91 (June 1970); and N. J. C. Andreasen et al., Management of Emotional Problems in Seriously Burned Adults, *New England Journal of Medicine*, 286:65–69 (January 13, 1972).

3.   Gene A. Brodland and N. J. C. Andreasen, Adjustment Problems of the Family of the Burn Patient, SOCIAL CASEWORK, 55:13–18 (January 1974).

4.   Ibid.

27
Casework with the Family of the Alcoholic

John F. Mueller

Recent estimates of the number of persons suffering from alcoholism and alcohol abuse in the United States place the figure at approximately 9 million.[1] Further, it can be assumed that every alcoholic adversely affects the mental health of two or three family members, thus adding another 20 to 30 million persons who feel the destructive impact of the illness.

The cause of alcoholism is not known. There are many theories, some stressing physiological aspects, some highlighting psychological factors, and others focusing on sociocultural components. None has been sufficiently substantiated to warrant its acceptance as *the* cause.

Similarly, no cure has as yet been discovered—cure in the sense of a combination of therapies that enable the alcoholic to return to controlled social drinking. However, several reasonably effective treatment modalities have been developed for helping the alcoholic arrest his illness and lead a normal, constructive life without alcohol.

It is important that the social worker and the alcoholic's family understand the natural progression of the illness from a psychological to a psychological-physiological dependence on alcohol. Jellinek's significant study revealed a sequence of symptoms that the typical alcoholic goes through unless therapeutic intervention alters it.[2] He identified the following steps that partly reflect the progressive aspect of the illness: occasional and then constant drinking as a result of increased alcohol tolerance, memory blackouts, growing preoccupation with alcohol, surreptitious drinking, guilt about drinking, inability to discuss the problem, occasional loss of control of drinking, rationalization of drinking behavior, persistent remorse, repeated failure to control drinking, trouble with family and friends, job

Source: From *Social Work* 17:5 (September 1972), pp. 79–84. Copyright © 1972 by the National Association of Social Workers. Reprinted by permission.

problems, self-pity and unreasonable resentment, protection of alcohol supply, tremors and morning drinks, prolonged periods of intoxication, physical
and more deterioration, impaired thinking, undefinable fears and anxieties,
and an obsession with drinking.

Jellinek makes it clear that "not all symptoms... occur necessarily in
all alcohol addicts, nor do they occur in every addict in the same sequence."[3]
Nevertheless, knowledge of this typical sequential development can be a
useful diagnostic, therapeutic, and educational tool to the social worker,
whether working with the alcoholic or his family.

Wives of Alcoholics

Jackson, in searching the literature, found that much research on wives
of alcoholics is concerned with their psychopathology. Gliedman and his colleagues thought that the wives were better organized than their husbands in
the marital pairs they studied.[4] Ballard found them less disturbed than wives
in control pairs caught up in marital conflict.[5] Most investigators, however,
found them disturbed.

In exploring this disturbance, some researchers conclude that the alcoholic's wife unconsciously encourages her husband's alcoholism because
of her own needs; they suggest that if the husband becomes sober, the wife
often begins to show neurotic symptoms.[6] Others acknowledge that the wife
tends to be psychologically disturbed during the husband's active alcoholism, but observe that typically her adjustment seems to improve with
his sobriety. Should there be any increased disturbance when he becomes
sober, they contend it is only temporary.[7] As Jackson points out:

> This is not to deny, however, that the onset of sobriety precipitates additional
> disturbances on the part of all family members.... When the onset of sobriety
> is viewed in the context of the total family crisis, rather than as an isolated
> piece of family history, one may suppose that much of the behavior on the part
> of the wife which appears to be dysfunctional for the recovery of the alcoholic
> plays an important part in maintaining the intergration and stability of the
> family as a social unit. An example of this is the wife's reluctance to relinquish
> her dominance until sobriety is well established and appears to be permanent.[8]

Without question, certain types of women marry alcoholics to satisfy
deep unconscious needs to be married to weak, inadequate, and dependent
males. However, the generalization about the neuroticism of alcoholics'
wives is difficult to accept. Rather, the observations of those who postulate
that the wife's disturbance is derived essentially from the cumulative stress
of living with an alcoholic seem more credible. Jackson, examining the impact of this stress, notes that just as the alcoholic goes through progressive

phases, so too the wife may go through phases in attempting to adjust to the crisis of the developing disease. She categorizes this process in seven stages, as follows:

1. Initially there is denial of the problem. Intermittent drinking episodes occur, with both husband and wife seeking to explain these early symptoms as normal behavior: he is tired, worried, bored, nervous, or pressured, and so on. Since drinking for these reasons is perfectly acceptable in our culture, these explanations are quite credible.

2. The wife finally recognizes that the drinking pattern is not normal. She feels that her husband's alcoholism emanates from lack of will power and so she goes through endless so-called home remedies to persuade him to quit or at least cut down his drinking. She is still trying to maintain the family structure; conceal the problem from outsiders, employer, and friends; and protect him in other ways from the consequences of his behavior. But the family structure is becoming shakier, the children are beginning to show signs of emotionally upset.

3. Family equilibrium almost completely breaks down, with disorganization and chaos characterizing family functioning. The children exhibit more pronounced signs of upset. The wife no longer tries to conceal the alcoholism. She simply aims to relieve immediate tension rather than achieve long-range gains. Family finances are usually in a precarious position. The wife questions her own sanity and her ability to salvage anything from the situation. She may begin to seek outside help.

4. The wife tries to minimize the disruptive force of the alcoholic husband by reorganizing family life. As she gradually assumes increased responsibility, he is frequently relegated to a recalcitrant child's role. When she brings some order out of chaos, she begins to regain her self-confidence.

5. The wife may separate from her husband or obtain a divorce if she can work out the problems surrounding such a move. Or she may continue with him indefinitely.

6. The wife and children reorganize as a family without the husband.

7. If the husband achieves sobriety, the family may reunite and try to function as a unit again. This attempt to realign the family structure and reinstate the father in his original role is doubly difficult because everyone had assumed that with sobriety all problems would be magically resolved.[9]

A few of the home remedies that the wife—not understanding alcoholism—attempts in persuading her husband to do something about his drinking are common. They also serve at times as a mirror that reflects the interaction, poor though it may be, between the alcoholic and his wife.

One early remedy is the wife's saying in effect, "If you really loved me and the children you would do something about your drinking. Don't you realize what you are doing to me and the children and yourself?" To the alcoholic this merely communicates her lack of understanding about how he feels. No one is more painfully aware of what he is doing. His wife's comments intensify his guilt, self-hatred, and sense of loneliness and rejection.

Or she may ask, "Why don't you be a man? Use your will power." One can imagine how helpful that plea is for someone already overwhelmed with feelings of inadequacy, who probably has tried using his will power many times and failed.

The wife invariably coaxes her husband not to drink exacting promises that he will remain sober, promises readily and even sincerely made but not kept. This failure in turn aggravates his guilt and further lowers his self-esteem.[10]

She may hide or destroy his supply of alcohol or she may buy the alcohol for him, hoping to control the amount he drinks. She may drink with him, thinking he may then exercise more control and also that they may be able to communicate better.

She may use sex as a weapon to reward or punish—"bedroom blackmail" as it were. Kisses become sobriety tests.

She pacifies him, fearing that any incident may increase his drinking. Finally she explodes and then feels guilty about her own anger and resentment. She threatens: "I'm going to take the children and leave." More often than not, she will not do so. If she does, she soon returns. She insists that he develop hobbies to take his mind off drinking—gardening, bowling, woodworking, stamp collecting, golf, fishing, and so forth. Or she tries to control the social situation, deciding where they will go according to how much drinking there will be.

When the alcoholic's wife first comes to the social worker, she probably views her husband's drinking in a simplistic way, as a behavior pattern subject to rational control or will power. She may express anger and self-pity, feeling he has failed her as a husband and father. Or she may exhibit guilt and defensiveness because, admit it or not, she is apt to feel responsible for his drinking. She may say: "Didn't I love him enough?" or "If I had been an adequate wife, mother, and homemaker, he wouldn't have this need to drink all the time." Frequently she alternates between these two sets of feelings. The worker must enable her to express these feelings. But for this to occur, he must show her that he understands the pain, confusion, and uncertainty she is feeling.

Disease Concept

The worker should also begin to introduce the disease concept of alcoholism. This offers the wife hope because she begins to accept the idea that her husband has a treatable illness. Also, it usually helps reduce her feelings of guilt and responsibility for his excessive drinking and thereby frees her for constructive action. Timing is vital in introducing the disease concept. Its premature mention could cut off the cathartic expression of resentment and anger.

The wife's gut-level acceptance of alcoholism as an illness is most important because one of the social worker's goals is to help her view her husband's actions as symptoms of that illness, not just as weak, vindictive behavior. Achieving this is extremely difficult. Fever, chills, nausea, headaches—these are readily accepted as disease symptoms. But deceit, alibis, resentment, apparent lack of concern for family, drunkenness—can these be symptoms of illness too?

Accepting them as such is the goal toward which the worker must strive. In that direction lies the wife's recognition that she did not cause the illness and that she is not capable of or responsible for curing it. Once freed of that burden, she can drop her ineffective coping and rescue operations. She can learn to stop nagging, making threats without carrying them out, and protecting her husband from the consequences of his drinking. And these measures are best for her and potentially for her alcoholic husband.

Letting the alcoholic suffer the consequences of his drinking is an important step toward rehabilitating both wife and husband and stems from the wife being freed of guilt feelings about causing the husband's excessive drinking. Then she no longer feels compelled to interfere with her husband's drinking or its consequences. She no longer feels obligated to cover up for him with his employer, pay off his bad checks, clean him up and put him to bed, and bail him out of jail. Her consequent lack of action should not emanate from anger and retaliation but rather, so far as possible, from a sense of objectivity and detachment.

This approach is part of a broader concept encompassing surrender and release. Clinebell describes a case in which the wife's determination to help her husband become sober had become almost an obsession.[11] The more she failed, the more frantically she tried. Her sense of worth as a person had somehow become bound to her husband's sobriety. He sensed this and it gave him tremendous power over her. Finally, after years of futile struggle she surrendered and accepted the fact that nothing she could do could make him stop excessive drinking. For the first time in years she experienced peace. This surrender enabled her to release the alcoholic. Facilitating such surrender and release in the alcoholic's spouse is a major goal of the caseworker. And helping her to see this release as an act of concern rather than rejection may make its accomplishment easier.

An excellent contribution to the rehabilitation of the alcoholic's family can be made by Al-Anon and Ala-Teen groups—fellowships of, by, and for family members. In these groups the family learns that others are traveling the same road and have made the same mistakes—that they are not alone. They can learn to let go. Both the alcoholic and his wife can learn to follow the good counsel of the Serenity Prayer: "God grant me the serenity to accept the things I cannot change, the courage to change the things I can, and the wisdom to know the difference."[12] They can learn, with the support of these groups, that there is hope and a path the family can travel through understanding the illness. The social worker should be familiar with these valuable community resources.

Impact on Children

Jackson's search of the literature regarding the impact of a parent's alcoholism on children indicates that the effects are varied and far reaching.[13] In an enlightening comparison, Newell suggests that the situation of alcoholics' children is not unlike that of experimental animals who are lured toward rewards and then repeatedly frustrated, who have no control over a constantly changing environment.[14] She notes that animals undergoing such experiences often have nervous breakdowns. These children frequently feel more affection for the alcoholic than the nonalcoholic parent, probably because the former tends to reward them when sober, while the latter may well be irritable and reject them at times because of the emotional strain created by the situation's constant pressure.

Jackson notes that in the home adults who play their roles in a distorted fashion are the behavior models of these children.[15] The alcoholic demonstrates little adult behavior. He acts one way toward his children when sober, another way when drunk, and still another during a hangover. The nonalcoholic parent tries to function as both mother and father, frequently failing to do either well. All too often the children are used in the parents' battles. The alcoholic's wife finds herself disliking, depriving, or punishing the child preferred by or resembling the father and, in the reverse situation, the father reacts similarly. If the child tries to stay close to both parents, he is trapped in an untenable position, since each parent resents the affection the other receives. As Jackson notes:

> When neighbors ostracize them, the children are bewildered about what they did to bring about this result. Even those who are not ostracized become isolated; they hesitate to bring their friends to a home where their parent is likely to be drunk. Moreover, the tendency of the child to examine his own behavior for reasons for parental alcoholism is very often reinforced inadvertently by his mother. When it is feared that the father is leading up to a drinking episode, the children are put on their best behavior. Then when the drinking episode occurs, it is not surprising that the children feel that they have somehow done something to precipitate it.[16]

Some children of alcoholics seem relatively unharmed by this pathological environment. Damage seems least when the nonalcoholic parent has insight into her problems with the alcoholic, recognizes the children's problems and gives them emotional support, behaves with reasonable consistency, and refrains from using the children against the alcoholic. If the wife accepts alcoholism as an illness and explains it as such to the children, this is also most helpful. And, as indicated earlier, Ala-Teen can be invaluable in providing information, understanding, emotional support, and perspective.

In working with the family of the alcoholic, the social worker should keep in mind a common pitfall. Because of the all-encompassing nature of the illness, both the alcoholic and his family members tend to associate all their problems with his drinking. Conversely, they assume that once he achieves sobriety, all will revert to normal and there will be no problems. The family will get along smoothly, and there will never be any relapses. Obviously, this rarely happens. When he becomes sober, the alcoholic immediately wants his early role back and tries to accomplish everything at once, at the same time using up most of his energy simply trying not to take a drink. The wife is reluctant and distrustful about relinquishing portions of her newly acquired role. All the necessary adjustments take time; both the alcoholic and his family should be aware of this in advance and be given continuing support and guidance.

Conclusion

Although the etiology of alcoholism is still unknown, treatment modalities for the alcoholic have emerged that yield a reasonable degree of success. Similarly, although views differ on pathogenetic aspects of problems of the alcoholic's wife, helpful therapeutic approaches have been developed. This paper has presented guidelines for counseling the wife, but the same principles can be readily adapted for working with the husband of the alcoholic wife.

Frequently when the wife first sees the caseworker she asks: "Do something to make my husband stop (or cut down) drinking" or "Help me do something to make him stay sober." These are not realistic requests. But by placing the emphasis on the alcoholic, they open the door to two contraindicated therapeutic approaches: (1) relegating the wife to a collateral contact seen in conjunction with treating the real patient, the alcoholic, or (2) unconsciously allowing her to step into a role she may mistakenly try to assume, that of cotherapist in treating the alcoholic husband. These roles are neither appropriate nor effective.

Because the wife is a legitimate client, treatment must be guided by her needs. Therapy should be used to help her find a more productive and satisfying solution to her situation, not to get her husband sober. For example, if she is considering separating from her husband, the worker should help her understand that such action ought to be based on the feeling that she can no longer live with him, not the hope that "it will bring him to his senses." True, his sobriety is a hoped-for by-product of her improvement, but as far as her treatment relationship is concerned, it is just that—a by-product.

In summary, when counseling the alcoholic's wife, the social worker's primary focus should be on helping her acquire knowledge about alcoholism and its behavioral manifestations and then achieve the emotional strength and courage to translate that knowledge into effective action. In essence this means that the social worker should help her walk the middle ground between punishing and pampering, support her in letting the alcoholic suffer the consequences of his drinking, and reinforce her perception that doing so expresses concern rather than rejection.

References

1.   U.S. Department of Health, Education, and Welfare, Alcohol and Health: First Special Report to Congress (Washington, D.C.: U.S. Government Printing Office, December 1971).

2.   See Elvin M. Jellinek, "Phases of Alcohol Addiction," in David J. Pittman and Charles R. Snyder, eds., Society, Culture, and Drinking Patterns (Carbondale: Southern Illinois University Press, 1962), pp. 356–368.

3.   Ibid.

4.   Joan K. Jackson, "Alcoholism and the Family," in Pittman and Synder, op. cit., pp. 472–492. See also Lester H. Gliedman et al., "Group Psychotherapy of Male Alcoholics and Their Wives," Diseases of the Nervous System, Vol. 17, No. 3 (March 1956), pp. 90–93; and Gliedman, "Group Therapy of Alcoholics with Concurrent Group Meetings of Their Wives," Quarterly Journal of Studies on Alcohol, Vol. 17, No. 4 (December 1956), pp. 665–670.

5.   See Robert G. Ballard, "The Interaction Between Marital Conflict and Alcoholism as Seen Through MMPI's of Marriage Partners," American Journal of Orthopsychiatry, Vol. 29 (July 1959), pp. 528–546.

6.   See Samuel Futterman, "Personality Trends in Wives of Alcoholics," Journal of Psychiatric Social Work, Vol. 23, No. 1 October 1953), pp. 37–41; and Donald E. MacDonald, "Mental Disorders in Wives of Alcoholics," Quarterly Journal of Studies on Alcohol, Vol. 17, No. 2 (June 1956), pp. 282–287.

7.   See Marion M. Kalashian, "Working With Wives of Alcoholics in an Outpatient Clinic Setting," Marriage and Family Living, Vol. 21, No. 2 (May 1959), pp. 130–133; and Jackson, op. cit.

8.   Jackson, op. cit., p. 481.

9.   Ibid., pp. 472–492.

10.   See John E. Keller, Ministering to Alcoholics (Minneapolis, Minn.: Augsburg, 1966), pp. 124–137.

11. Howard J. Clinebell, Jr., *Understanding and Counseling the Alcoholic* (Nashville, Tenn.: Abingdon Press, 1968), pp. 266–293.

12. Written especially for Alcoholics Anonymous by Reinhold Niebuhr, 1938.

13. Jackson, op. cit.

14. See Nancy Newell, "Alcoholism and the Father Image," *Quarterly Journal of Studies on Alcohol*, Vol. 11, No. 1 (March 1950), pp. 92–96.

15. Jackson, op. cit.

16. Ibid., p. 477.

28

Maladaptive Reactions to the Death of a Family Member

George Krupp

The social worker confronting a child who has lost a parent, a wife who has lost a husband, or a widower with children faces an inevitability that he has probably avoided subjecting to any but the most superficial scrutiny. Death is so integral a part of life that it is remarkable that the event itself and the emotional forces surrounding it have withstood empirical study for so long. With the growth of literature exploring man's feelings about death and with death being removed from taboo topics by frank discussion, the professional worker, in dealing with people in crisis, will find it advantageous to examine the subject anew. It is becoming apparent that awareness and recognition of adaptive or maladaptive reactions to death are essential to sound counseling and therapy.

It is now known that mourning can remain unresolved for years and that adults who have suffered bereavement in early childhood are more disposed than are others to mental illness.[1] Professionals working with families and family members are discovering that unresolved reaction to loss has a deep influence upon the personality and that it may reveal itself in damage many years later—in poor choice of mate, in marital discord, in the behavior problems of children, and in irrational behavior of parents. Despite this awareness, bereavement—especially early bereavement—is often overlooked in the therapist's search for causes of mental illness.

Grief and mourning, however, are not simple emotions. The pain of loss and its attendant yearning for a deceased loved one are merely the more familiar external facets of a highly complex reaction. In its primary sense, grief over death is fettered anger—anger at the injustice done to the self—not only through the actual loss, but through the dependence, the loneli-

Source: From Social Casework 53 (July 1972), pp. 425–433. Copyright © 1972 by the Family Service Association of America. Reprinted by permission.

ness, and the inconvenience it may bring. The angry bereaved attempts to regain equilibrium, while he combines strong feelings of guilt with a reactivation of old emotions connecting him with the lost one. Denial fantasies and longing help temporarily to ease the pain. These emotions are not constant. They shift and intermesh, ebb and flow, as the bereaved attempts to cope with the loss; and their interaction may serve either to abet or retard the resolution of his grief.

In an attempt to clarify the dynamics of depression, Freud elucidated the mechanism of bereavement. The mourner, according to Freud, clings to the loved object, now lost but still represented by many separate memories of the past.

> Reality passes its verdict—that the object no longer exists—upon each single one of the memories and hopes through which the libido was attached to the lost object and the ego, confronted as it were, over a decision whether it will share this fate, is persuaded by the sum of its narcissistic satisfactions in being alive, to sever its attachment to the nonexistent object.[2]

Mourning, therefore, is not simply reaction to the loss of a loved person, but a process of extricating interest from that person and transferring it elsewhere. It is a painful and difficult task to carry out the "work of mourning." The bereaved one resists, sustaining the illusion that the lost one still lives.

Whereas the term *bereavement* implies the external appearance and behavior, as well as attitudes and feelings, of someone who is engaged in the severance of ties necessitated by death, the word *grief*, although not entirely exclusive of external appearance and behavior, basically refers to the inner emotions, attitudes, and thoughts of the mourner. Mourning also often tends to be applied to the external rites, customs, or conventions. When death occurs, the ensuing crisis brings into play individual and cultural mechanisms that have been developed to defend the ego and critically tests their efficacy.

John Bowlby views the bereavement process as one consisting of three stages: (1) protest and denial, (2) despair and disorganization, and (3) reorganization.[3] Denial and anger are paramount in the early stages, although these feelings for the most part may be unconscious. Originally, anger is directed at the loved one for leaving the individual, as if the deceased had willed himself to die. There is often displaced anger at the hospital, the doctor, or God for having allowed the loss to occur. It is almost as if the fact might be undone if a cause could be found.

The external world is not the only object of the bereaved person's anger. There is also anger toward self for real or imagined wrongs done the deceased; for death wishes, for secret relief, and for the triumph he experiences that he, at least, is still alive. During the first stage there is a desperate effort to recover the lost object in fantasy, which is expressed in an unconscious denial of the death and is almost always revealed in dreams of the loved one's return.[4]

These feelings incur and ultimately commingle with the second phase of despair and disorganization,[5] until finally the individual reorganizes himself and his surroundings and transfers his love and interest from the deceased to a new object or objects. The role that the deceased person had played in the family is assumed by one or more family members or by others, and life goes on. It is only when this three-stage process is not completed—when the mourner remains in an early stage—that pathological or unresolved mourning endangers the individual's subsequent adjustment. Before scrutinizing the symptoms any further, however, it is necessary to examine some of the reasons that maladjustments in the bereavement process are able to influence later adjustment to such a degree.

Familial Attitudes Toward Death

Several basic, and in some ways contradictory, facts about present-day American familial customs have great significance for the "work of mourning." Big cities and rapid and efficient communication and transportation have combined with other social forces to eliminate the extended family (several generations living together under one roof) in preference to the present nuclear family consisting only of parents and their children. The strength of the extended family has been in the maintenance of its identity and its property as well as in its collective sense of responsibility when a member dies. In such a family, the trauma of death was not likely to be fully disruptive; the parent-child and husband-wife relationships have often been extended to other relatives. It is not implied here that strong emotional ties and intense relationships are lacking, but rather that the availability of substitute objects and many supportive family members tend to lessen the pain of separation. In the nuclear family, however, the individual who suffers a loss is thrust upon his own resources. There is an absence of socially sanctioned familial supports present in preliterate societies or in other cultures with strong, emotionally binding extended family relationships.[6] There is no compensation in this type of family structure for the "thinning out" of interpersonal relations. It is rare that the role of the deceased (especially in the case of a deceased parent) is assumed by a relative. Following a period of high involvement by relations, the nuclear family must usually fend for itself socially and psychologically.

The nuclear character of the family is not the only factor affecting bereavement; one must also consider the trend toward greater freedom for the individual within the family.[7] In all social realms the family has less control. The mass media provides behavioral sanctions which are often inimical to family solidarity. Ease of mobility augments exposure to influences outside the family. Family ties loosen; the family weakens as a source of comfort.

At the same time, society emphasizes a long period of child-parent dependence as well as the uniqueness and worth of the individual. Intense, meaningful interpersonal relationships are encouraged. Less and less are people thought of as members of an amorphous mass; more and more are individuals regarded as significant in and of themselves. Thus, when loss occurs, the sense of grief deepens in proportion to involvement, dependency, and belief in the worth and value of the individual.

Often the depth of the loss is not manifested until the child becomes a parent.

At that time the loss is revived and while he fights to protect his child from the same hurt, he also repeats to the child the hurt. . . . While he wants to give to the child, he also desperately wants to be given to. . . . In addition they (parents) were particularly prone to fluctuations between indulgence and over-solicitude at one time and extreme harshness at another; this seemed related to alternation between longing and craving to give what they would have wanted to receive, and jealousy and envy towards the child who was getting what they had craved. They possessed an excessive need to satisfy their own unsatisfied longings in the careers of their children.[8]

Mrs. A, thirty-nine years old, sought treatment for her nine-and-a-half-year-old daughter. The child had not been in school for six months because of school phobia. Several visits revealed that the root of the daughter's phobia was separation anxiety and the unconscious reluctance of the mother to let go.

Mrs. A began analysis and soon revealed that her home life had not been unusual until she was nine, when her seventeen-year-old sister died of leukemia. This sister had protected her and loved her dearly. She described her mother as being unaffectionate and busy.

The sister's death depressed the whole family. Her mother handled her grief by going to work. The patient handled it by phantasying, "My sister is not really dead. I will carry her around with me and not let her die." Like her sister who had been kind to others, she became a good samaritan. "I was good to everyone, just as she was," she said.

On occasion, she developed symptoms that her sister had had—burning sensations and pain in the legs. Although she was an excellent student, when she reached the senior year in high school she began failing and did not graduate. It had been during the senior year that her sister had died. She also reported that she could not finish her job.

Four years before she came into analysis, following increasing tension and before moving into a new house (the family was to have moved into a new house before the sister died), she "said" to her sister, "Goodbye. You have to go now. I cannot take care of you any more." She then went into an acute depression. During this time, she felt that she was getting leukemia and had "burning sensations of being on fire" and would wake up at night frightened.

After her hospitalization and recovery from depression, and when her own daughter was nine—the same age she had been when her mother went to work—she purchased a store. Analysis revealed that this decision allowed her to reenact the role of her rejecting mother. But because she could control her own work hours, she was able to play a second role simultaneously; she could play the role of the protective and loving older sister by remaining at home whenever her daughter refused to go to school. Consequent recognition of the indentification factor aided her in coping with the separation anxiety.

Bereavement becomes more difficult as ambivalence increases. As the core of anxiety and neurosis, ambivalence consists of the alternation of positive and negative feelings. They may be partially concealed from awareness or only one polar feeling may be conscious. Although object relations are always more or less ambivalent, problems in adjustment ensue when the relationship with the deceased was characterized by excessive hatred accompanied by guilt.

Mr. B, thirty-eight years old, sought counseling for what seemed to be a marital problem. His relationship with his wife had deteriorated, and the couple was considering divorce. In treatment, it was revealed that Mr. B frequently had been in conflict with his father, who had been a dominating person. The father had suffered from a respiratory ailment which caused him to wheeze audibly. From time to time, when he heard the labored breathing at night, Mr. B would yell to his father to "shut up."

In college, Mr. B had fallen in love and had contemplated marriage. Because one of the girl's parents was of another religion, Mr. B's father forbade the marriage. While he was traveling to his seriously ill father's bedside, the young man wished that his father would die. His father was dead when Mr. B arrived. He felt no particular reaction immediately, although at the cemetery he broke down with severe crying.

Subsequently, Mr. B devoted himself to his mother rather than to his girl friend, apparently feeling a strong obligation to take care of her. He told the girl that if they married, they would have to move in with his mother. When the girl refused to marry him under those circumstances, he felt somewhat relieved.

At twenty-eight, Mr. B. married a thirty-two-year-old professional woman who was willing to move into the house with him and his mother. Two years later, however, the wife persuaded the mother to move out. Two children were born, and on the surface, everything seemed fine. The wife did complain repeatedly, however, that Mr. B cared more for his mother than he did for her.

Some months before Mr. B came for therapy, his mother had suffered a thrombosis that necessitated leg amputation. Mr. B insisted that she move back into his home and his relationship with his wife deteriorated until she insisted upon a divorce. At this time, Mr. B came for help. His wife had agreed to stay with him on condition that he sought therapy.

In treatment, Mr. B recalled the experience of his father's death and began to acknowledge the unresolved bereavement and the feelings of guilt connected with it. He began to understand how they had caused him to devote himself *excessively* to the care of his mother, thus taking his father's place. Reactivated by his mother's illness, the oedipal conflict reinforced his feeling that his wish was responsible for his father's death. Fortunately, his wife's demand for a divorce started him on the way toward resolution of his conflicts. When he became aware of his chronic, unresolved bereavement and his feelings of guilt, Mr. B was able to develop a more mature relationship with his wife and mother, whom he was able to help to live away from his home.

In the foregoing illustration, ambivalent feelings toward the deceased made the "work of mourning" extremely difficult. Guilt feelings about someone's death are often the result of powerful, unexpressed hostility toward the person. Because it is too threatening to acknowledge the hostility openly, the mourner is often unaware of it and feels only guilt and depression. Guilt focuses attention back upon the mourner himself, thus preventing objective contemplation of the loss of its open acknowledgement. For Mr. B, the development of a mature marital relationship was made virtually impossible by his oedipal desires and guilt.

Effects of Religion on Bereavement

In addition to the changes in family structure and the changes in the positions of the individuals in it, a shift in the role of religion has had important effects on bereavement reactions. The leave-taking of a loved person has throughout history been a source of concern for all people; at best it is the "sweet sorrow" of those who anticipate swift reunion, at worst, the despair of those who know the finality of death. In order to deal with the emotional problems that arise in the wake of death, man has developed rituals, group ceremonies, and culturally accepted patterns of behavior. Rituals of death and mourning channel and legitimize the normal expression of grief and rally friends and relatives to the emotional support of the bereaved. They also publicize and formally establish new statuses and roles necessitated by the loss and help the bereaved to explore and accept philosophically the relationship between this occurrence and the natural progression of events.

In modern society, however, the influence of norms established by religion has progressively weakened; the culture is secular. Conflicting theological systems, unrealistic ethical dogma, and liberal theology have made it impossible for religion to continue in the role of universal panacea. There are no unequivocal answers to our moral questions; there is no solace in seeking explanations.

In view of these juxtaposed societal influences, it is to be expected that many persons fail to adjust adequately to the stress of bereavement. People are enmeshed in conflict—dear ones have become fewer and less easily replaced, yet opportunities to express and resolve intense emotion have also diminished.

Pathological Responses

Mourning in itself is a normal reaction to loss; it is only when unconscious factors predominate and hostility, guilt, anxiety, and depression are extreme both in degree and duration that the reaction becomes pathological. Unresolved bereavement—the failure to complete the "work of mourning" successfully and transfer interest from the dead love object to the living world—must be recognized because, if the maladjustment can be perceived, adjustment can be nurtured.

A universal phenomenon of bereavement is, in this culture, accompanied by a wish to deny death. For most poeple, it is a wish that evaporates swiftly and painfully in the light of reality. Grief may be considered healthy when it gradually diminishes in intensity, and when the bereaved gradually accepts the absoluteness of this final separation and commits himself once again to the mainstream of life. Grief that becomes fixed in despair, that surrenders to apathy, is a symptom of illness. It is therefore important to understand it and to guide and direct it so that the bereaved emerges from his ordeal with an increased awareness of his own capacities for living.

Fantasies that promulgate denial of the loss, maintenance of the lost object in awareness, or attempts at union with the lost object are indicative of pathological mourning responses. There is less complete admission of death here; there is only a change in communication with the deceased. Symptomatic or personality identifications are attempts to recover the lost object, and they act to prolong the mourning process by not permitting the relinquishing or restitution fantasies which occur in normal mourning.

There are several forms of pathological mourning. It should be noted, however, that one or all of the symptoms delineated below, exhibited in a mild form, may be part of normal mourning.

EXAGGERATION

One of the most common pathological mourning reactions is the prolonged, intense one in which the bereavement reaction becomes chronic and leads to a true depression. It may be accompanied by nightmares, outbursts of fear and anger, and strong feelings that the mourner has no right to be alive. Intense guilt gives rise to the conviction that the mourner must be punished—that he must make amends by dying too. This guilt may lead to suicide. Shakespeare's *Hamlet* describes a bereavement containing elements of ambivalence, oedipal guilt, murder, psychosis, and suicide.[9]

COMPLETE EGO BREAKDOWN

Intense rage that is projected outward may erupt in paranoid and persecutory delusions. Such panic is related to the ego's fear that the very object it mourns will return and harm it. Ego boundaries disintegrate and distinction between self and object becomes less clear. The individual's hallucinatory world of attack and counterattack by internal and external evil objects may dominate him, waking and sleeping.

PATHOLOGICAL IDENTIFICATIONS

An intense reaction in which the mourner assumes the symptoms of the deceased permits him to retain the dead one in fantasy as if he were alive. This reaction is usually pleasurable in one sense, but it also represents a punishment for real or imagined wrongs done the deceased. One patient developed chest pains, anxiety, and fear of heart disease following his father's heart attack and death. These symptoms returned intermittently during periods of tension when, for one reason or another, he wished his father back.[10]

ARRESTED PSYCHOSOCIAL DEVELOPMENT

A form of neurotic mourning that prevents maturation of the individual occurs when there is a fixation of the bereaved individual at an immature level. He has difficulty in developing beyond the stage at which he was when the loss occurred. This inability to mature may happen because the loss occurs at a time in the child's life when the dependency needs are very great. The need to stay at the same age seems to be a way of denying the death, and the absence of the socializing influence of the deceased parent makes it extremely difficult for the child to grow either intellectually or emotionally. The following illustration shows this symptom of mourning.

> Miss C, a twenty-two-year-old woman, was referred for consultation because of increasing fears, anxiety, depression, and difficulty in leaving her home in order to go to work. Miss C's father, a successful manufacturer, had died when she was thirteen. She had had a relatively good relationship with him during her early life, but there had been conflict with her mother. At the time of her father's death, she had been slim and pretty, but she was now

heavy, infantile in her appearance and demeanor, and her tone of voice was querulous. She had found it necessary to leave college and could not keep a job. From time to time she seemed to exhibit her father's coronary symptoms; she had chest pains and difficulty in breathing.

Her father used to tell her that he wanted her to grow up to be a model and that he would then give her a job. Now that he was dead, she could not grow up. Her greatest pleasure at the time of counseling was to go to the beauty parlor, which she said was the only place in which she was relaxed. In the beauty parlor, she was a model. She felt safe there. Her entire demeanor was characteristic of a fourteen-year-old, and her behavior was, in fact, an attempt to keep herself fixated at that level. She said that it seemed as though her father had just died a few days before. She wrote poetry to "someone sitting above" and worshipped and idealized that someone. In Miss C's case, therapy required separation from this ideal one. An acceptance of her father's death enabled her to grow up and accept herself as a woman.

ABSENCE OF MOURNING

Denial or postponement of emotion is one of the most frequent defense mechanisms utilized by the individual against anxiety or psychic pain. It is a component of the first stage of the healthy bereavement reaction and acts as a safeguard against complete disintegration of the individual. However, if it is not overcome and if the mourner remains in the first stage and does not seem to react to the loss at all, then the situation must be regarded as pathological.

Helene Deutsch observes:

First, that the death of a beloved person must produce reactive expression of feeling in the normal course of events; second, that omission of such reactive responses is to be considered just as much a variation from the normal as excess in time or intensity and, third, that unmanifested grief will be found expressed to the full in some way or other.[11]

Mrs. D, thirty-three years old, was referred to a family service agency because of her children's maladjustment. Her father, to whom she had been deeply attached, had died overseas in combat when she was fifteen. At that time, she had felt no grief and could not believe that he was really dead. A few months later, however, she had become promiscuous, and, shortly thereafter, she married. For the next eighteen years she continued to look for her father in restaurants and other public places. Meeting a man who reminded her of him, Mrs. D entered an intensely emotional, but platonic, extramarital relationship with him. At the time of referral she was excessively preoccupied with it and was neglecting her children.

After a therapeutic rapport had been established with the caseworker, Mrs. D discussed her feelings about her father and began, emotionally, to accept the idea that he was dead. She cried for the first time over her loss and finally began the "work of mourning." Although postponed for eighteen years, her cathartic bereavement reaction, when resolved, brought about a more mature approach to her problems.

Inability to cope with loss may be characteristic of an entire family. Denial may be a family pattern acquired by individual members in a milieu in which other family members share similar feelings and attitudes. Norman Paul and George Grosser report that in families the reaction to loss which was characteristic of one of the significant members of the group permeated the attitudes of the other members as well. In families in which a denial pattern existed, a change of job, the possibility of moving to a new community, marriage, college, the maturation of a child were all seriously threatening to the family unit, and "major changes in family homeostasis, such as those which might result in separation or independence of its members, were often resisted."[12] This means that in its efforts to maintain a sense of stability, the family as a whole may prohibit change which may be necessary for the growth of its individual members.

When a loved one dies, the family functions of the deceased individual must be redistributed among other members of the family. One source of friction arises when the surviving members are unable or unwilling to take on the functions to which they fall heir. In their incomplete adaptation to a loss, a family may encourage an individual member to assume the role of the deceased as though he were still alive, rather than dividing the duties evenly. For the individual involved, the task may conflict gravely with his own ego-fulfillment. On the other hand, in many cases an individual will attempt to cope with a loss by identifying with the deceased and taking over his functions. This serves two purposes: the individual is able to deny his loss by keeping the deceased alive through the identification and also to maintain "normal" activity after the interruption caused by the death.

The following case illustration is that of a thirty-six-year-old widow whose identification with her dead husband, although apparently constructive, led to an abnormal extension of the mourning period and disrupted family functioning.

Two years before she came for consultation Mrs. E had been widowed. During her marriage she had been dependent on her husband, leaving all extrafamilial affairs to him. After his death, however, she found herself capable of speaking to auto mechanics, gardeners, and repair men in an authoritative tone. To her surprise, she was also able to pay the bills and balance the check book—tasks she had never been able to do before. On a superficial level, it appeared that she had finished mourning and was successfully applying herself to reentering the mainstream of life. Months after her husband's death, however, she could not consider removing his clothes from the closet. Every day, at about the hour he had usually come home, she would feel chest pains similar to those he had suffered during his heart illness.

The prolongation of her bereavement and identification with her husband had a deleterious effect on Mrs. E's family life. Her preoccupation with the deceased drained time and energy that should have been allocated to the effective raising of her children. In addition, her failure to accept the loss prevented her from looking for another mate and reestablishing a normal family situation.

It is clear, then, that unresolved mourning has a serious effect on both the individual and the family. The task of helping to resolve the maladjustment falls to the professional.

Techniques of Resolving Unresolved Mourning

Paul and Grosser have developed the term "operational mourning" to describe a corrective mourning technique employed by many professionals.[13] Designed to help both the individual and the family, the technique involves a directed inquiry about reactions to actual losses sustained by specific members of the family. The other members of the family witness the ensuing expression of feelings of grief by a specific member and they react to it. Children, often for the first time, are able to observe the expression of intense feelings by their parents, and the family shares a critical affective experience.

Grief reactions of a similar nature can be induced by individual psychotherapy. The expression of grief by the individual, although it may be a belated one, will, in turn, affect the family relationships of that individual. The patient, by means of directed probing by the therapist, is put through the bereavement experience again, but this time he is encouraged to complete the process. The positive effects of this technique can be recognized in each of the case illustrations described earlier. After the mourning process has been completed, regardless of how long it has been delayed, the individual is able to accept and confront his conflicts and problems on a more effective level.

One of the most useful tools available to a therapist in reaching this goal is empathy, which here may have to exceed its normal limits in psychiatry. The bereaved feels an absence of judgment in an empathic counselor. He does not have to fear being pitied, nor does he have to feel beholden to someone who is expressing only sympathy. Rather, the patient realizes that, for the moment, the counselor feels as he does, and the two effectively share the experience of grief. This empathy allows the bereaved to express his emotions fully in a nonhostile environment while being assured of complete understanding.

Preventive Techniques

It is important to be able to treat cases of unresolved mourning. It is also valuable to consider ways in which such maladjustments may be prevented.

In American society today, the average person has little firsthand experience with death. Whereas years ago it was a rare individual who had not been present at least once at the death of a relative, today deaths usually occur in hospitals and the bodies are immediately removed to funeral homes. Children thus have little, if any, contact with death or the dead person; frequently they are not allowed to go to the funeral parlor and so inevitably hear about death secondhand. Death thus becomes something fearful, mysterious, and unnatural.

An interesting suggestion for preparation for bereavement is that of early "immunization" to later life stresses, much as one is immunized against physical disease. According to Gordon D. Jensen and John G. Wallace, the medical models of most psychiatric conditions are being viewed afresh as family processes, which suggests that exposing young children to small doses of painful life experiences may aid in building a kind of immunity against later stressful experiences.[14] Thus the death of a household pet or classroom turtle would be brought out into the open and followed by a discussion of larger tragedies, such as the death of a grandparent. This discussion would help to prevent the development of morbid fantasies and would build strength to face later losses. By emphasis on death as a part of life, the child is educated against a fear of death. Marjorie McDonald's study of a nursery school class tells of Wendy, a little girl who lost her mother. Told of the death by their own parents, Wendy's classmates were most concerned about what would happen to Wendy. All of the children then defended themselves against the knowledge of the death by denying it in one way or another. They all exhibited new anxiety about separation from their parents and behaved more childishly than usual.[15]

After a while, though, different kinds of reactions could be distinguished. Some of the children were able to take a second, very important step: they were able to talk about the possibility that their own mothers or they themselves might die. It is with precisely such imaginative leaps that children reach for reality in the process of maturing. Moreover, it is hardly accidental that the children who were able to take this second step were encountering death for the second time, because each of them had already lost a grandparent and so had begun to master his feelings about death.

Perhaps, then, the time has come to expose children to the facts of death in small, controlled doses. In this way perhaps they can be prevented from devastation by later experiences of bereavement.

Another preventive measure that might be useful to some families, is the strengthening of religious and moral values. This method is helpful in providing the family with something on which to depend other than itself and a framework within which to place the death. In time of crisis the role of religious and other social institutions is an important one. Ceremonies tend to dramatize the interest of the group by marking the event and to clarify the role and status changes occasioned by it. The ceremonies become occasions during which group strength is mobilized both for the protection and maintenance of the group and for the support of the individual.

Another counterforce to the devastation often occasioned by bereavement is the recognition and encouragement of interdependence of autonomous families—an interdependence that, in time of stress, assures the nuclear family of emotional and practical support. The de-isolation of the American family in today's society is a difficult task, but an important one.

Summary

To deal with the emotional problems that arise in the wake of death, man has developed culturally prescribed rituals, group ceremonies, and patterns of behavior unique to the individual. Some of these actually do help him to cope with loss; some, however, do not.

American society with its movies, television, and mores represents a supreme effort to preserve youth and deny aging and death. Although death cannot be eliminated, it has been postponed by the progress of modern medicine, and human death today, in most cases, no longer occurs in the home. Individuals have less and less contact with nature, with the death of livestock, and with the slaughtering of animals for food. Death has become frightening, mysterious, and repugnant, yet the bereaved person is supposed to behave well and keep his emotions under control.

Even after death has occurred, denial manifests itself in the funeral parlor, in the banks of flowers heaped around the coffin, in the makeup used on the deceased, in the music, and in the words spoken by many clergymen. Friends look at the corpse and describe the dead as "so lifelike." Society, then, makes it more difficult in many ways for the individual to accept and adjust to bereavement when it occurs.

Individual mechanisms too may either help the bereaved to reconcile himself successfully to the death and reorient himself to the new life circumstances occasioned by it, or they may, under the influence of neurotic ambivalent conflicts, secondarily provoke depressive and other pathological conditions. It is the professional's task to discern these pathological tendencies in individuals and in society and to attempt to minimize them, as well as to redirect the misguided emotions of mourning, so that the bereaved individual is enabled to redevote himself to making his own life a rewarding and fulfilling one.

References

1. See George Krupp, Identification as a Defence Against Anxiety in Coping with Loss, *International Journal of Psychoanalysis*, 46:303–14 (July 1965); David M. Moriarity, ed. and comp., *Loss of Loved Ones* (Springfield, Ill.: Charles C. Thomas, 1967); and John Bowlby, Grief and Mourning in Infancy and Early Childhood, in *Psychoanalytic Study of the Child*, vol. 15, ed. Ruth S. Eissler et al. (New York: International University Press, 1960).

2. See Sigmund Freud, Mourning and Melancholia, in *Collected Papers*, vol. 4, ed. Joan Riviere (London: Hogarth Press, 1950), pp. 152–70.

3. Bowlby, Grief and Mourning.

4. Sigmund Freud, *Interpretation of Dreams*, trans. James Strackey (New York: Basic Books, 1955).

5. The second stage of mourning is characterized both for animals and human beings by apathy, depression, and withdrawal. Dogs, chimpanzees, jackdaws, and geese become listless and may refuse to eat. The renowned ethologist, Konrad Lorenz, tells of a greylag goose that, after a frantic but futile search for its lost mate, sank into lethargy and turned sickly in appearance. "These deserted, solitary geese," Lorenz notes, "show a decreased readiness for any social contact. . . ." See Konrad Lorenz, *Man Meets Dog* (London, Methuen, 1956).

6. See George Krupp and Bernard Kligfeld, The Bereavment Reaction, A Cross-Cultural Evaluation, *Journal of Religion and Health*, 1:223–46 (April 1962).

7. William J. Goode, *World Revolution and Family Patterns* (New York: Free Press, 1970).

8. Rita Rogers, The Influence of Losing One's Parents on Being a Parent, *Psychiatric Digest*, 29:29–36 (May 1968).

9. Ella F. Sharp, The Impatience of Hamlet, *International Journal of Psychoanalysis*, 10:270–79 (April-July 1929).

10. George Krupp, Identification as a Defence.

11. Helene Deutsch, Absence of Grief, *Psychoanalytic Quarterly*, 6:12–22 (January 1937).

12. Norman L. Paul and George H. Grosser, Operational Mourning and Its Role in Conjoint Family Therapy, *Community Mental Health Journal*, 1:339–45 (Winter 1965).

13. Ibid.

14. Gordon D. Jensen and John G. Wallace, Family Mourning Process, *Family Process*, 6:56–66 (March 1967).

15. Marjorie McDonald, A Study of the Reactions of Nursery School Children to the Death of a Child's Mother, in *Psychoanalytic Study of the Child*, vol. 19, ed. Ruth S. Eissler et al. (New York: University Press, 1964), pp. 358–76.

29
Families in Grief: The Question of Casework Intervention

Mary W. Lindahl

THE DEATH OF a child is a tragic blow to any family. When the child dies in a hospital, however, there are additional burdens: constant, exhausting visits to the hospital, helpless watching while doctors attempt to save his life, anxiety about the effect on other children at home, and ever mounting hospital bills. When the child dies, his parents have to cope not only with their own grief, but also with the reactions of the other children in the family.

Existing limitations on the knowledge of grief reactions and techniques of therapeutic intervention are in large part owing to the frightening nature of the subject, which brings with it an awareness of individual mortality and feelings of guilt and helplessness about the death of others. For these reasons, a dying child and his distraught parents often evoke a partial withdrawal of cathexis in doctors, hospital personnel, and social workers.

Purpose and Scope of Study

This report is based on a study conducted by the author at the Massachusetts General Hospital in 1964–1965. Concerned with the reactions of parents and siblings to the illness and death of a child on the hospital's pediatric ward, its goal was to determine whether casework intervention might be warranted in such situations.

The information was obtained from two-hour interviews with the

Source: From Social Work 12:4 (October 1967), pp. 40–46. Copyright © 1967 by the National Association of Social Workers. Reprinted by permission.

families in their homes, which took place from 5 1/2 to 11 months after the child's death. The sample included all families willing to be interviewed who had two or more children under 14, one of whom had died during a six-month period in 1964. Of a possible thirty-seven families, five were interviewed, five refused, and the remainder were excluded because they were not available, the siblings did not fit the age criterion, or, in the case of private patients, the family's private physician refused the interviewer permission to talk with the family. A letter was sent to the ten families who fit the criteria for selection, expressing the hospital's concern for parents who had lost a child and asking them to discuss their experience and offer ideas of how the hospital's services to them could have been improved.

All of the parents in the sample were white Roman Catholics ranging in age from the middle twenties to early forties. The children's ages ranged from 36 days to 12 years and they had been ill from eighteen days to seven months. Three of the children died from a blood disease and two from brain damage. None of the five families had been known to the hospital's social service department previously.

Concepts of Grief

In "Mourning and Melancholia," Freud examined both healthy and pathological processes of grief and described its symptoms, which were found to persist until the "work of mourning" is completed.[1] Lindemann described grief as a "definite syndrome with psychological and somatic symptomatology," which is often distorted and prolonged in the absence of psychiatric intervention, especially in male mourners.[2] He also noted "anticipatory grief" reactions in cases of expected death.

Hamovitch found that parental participation in the care of the dying child can help families adjust to the child's death, presumably because it enables them to grieve before its actual occurrence.[3] In addition, his results indicate that parents do not want to be left alone by friends and professionals in the months immediately following the child's death.

The question "Do children mourn in the same way as adults?" is a controversial one. Bowlby claims to demonstrate "the reality and duration of grief and of the psychological processes of mourning in even very young children" who are separated from their mothers.[4] Freud and Deutsch, however, think that for their own protection children do not mourn as adults, and Hilgard, Newman, and Fisk note "an extreme sensitivity" to their mother's grief rather than personal grief in children who have lost a father before they were 9.[5] Nagy and Gesell and Ilg have described children's concepts of death, observing that before the age of about 9, these concepts are largely personalized, distorted, and unrealistic.[6]

Parents' Expression of Grief

Although a sample of five families, each of whom discusses experiences that took place at least five months before, does not permit broad generalizations about the grief of parents, some common features may be noted. Strikingly, three of the mothers in the study expressed an intense need to talk about the child and his death; their husbands, however, were unable to speak of it and even refused to allow the child's name to be mentioned.

All of the parents denied the possibility of death during the child's illness, a reaction that was partially realistic for the three children whose illnesses were not diagnosed until autopsy. The one mother whose child's death was inevitable "postponed" the depressive affect connected with her grief during his seven-month struggle with leukemia.[7] While manifesting other symptoms of grief (anger, somatic distress, and guilt) and verbally acknowledging the inevitability of death, she remained cheerful. She stated that the doctor had advised her to tell the diagnosis to as few people as possible so that the child would not find out. Thus, she shared the knowledge only with her husband and her mother, who lived in the South. After the boy's death, however, she experienced the full measure of grief with appropriate affect, and could not stop talking about it. Her reaction became intolerable to her husband, who had been more dejected than she during the child's illness, but after his death attempted to avoid expressing his grief.

Two other mothers also experienced an intense need to talk about the death; one felt she would "burst" if not allowed to do so. The mothers' grief at this time, when the ego's hypercathexis to the lost child was at its height, was one step ahead of their husbands', who resisted expressing their emotions.[8] Three of the fathers were not interviewed (one woman went to elaborate lengths to conceal the interviewer's presence and her tears when her husband telephoned). The two fathers who were interviewed were better able to verbalize their bereavement but admitted to persistent difficulties in discussing the subject.

Two fathers reacted strongly to tangible reminders of their sons. One man closed the door to his child's room and had not entered it since the death five months before. He also removed all pictures of the child from his house and wallet. The other father, attempting to deny the reality of death, left the child's room exactly as it had been when the boy was alive—with the door open. He did not let his wife convert it into a nursery for the new baby until nine months after the death—one month before the baby was due.

The mothers tried various methods of fulfilling their need to talk; they spoke to neighbors, kept in close contact through letters and visits with the hospital staff and mothers of other patients, and consulted priests. Four of the five mothers felt strongly that they would have been interested in talking to someone at the hospital, "to express what I was going through." One mother, who regularly ate lunch with other patients' mothers, described pathetically that she had no one with whom to eat on the day her son died.

The mothers also expressed the wish that someone could have helped their husbands, who were grieving silently. The fathers, when asked in the interview whether they would have liked help with their feelings, seemed hesitant, although one father said he would have welcomed advice but was too "proud" to ask for it. The other father expressed interest in talking to someone near his age rather than to an older person.

Guilt and Anger

All of the parents interviewed, with the exception of one mother (who admitted only to "disappointment" at the loss of a newborn) expressed some feelings of guilt. These were focused on etiology (e.g., "Was the measles vaccine, given months before the death, a possible cause of death?"), diagnosis (delay in recognizing the initial symptoms), and treatment (inability to afford private treatment, which they considered to be of superior quality). One couple, who thought that their daughter had "pushed away" her father before her death, felt vaguely responsible for this and attributed it to something they had done, such as leaving her in the hospital at night.

All of the families expressed anger. One object of their anger was the physician who made the initial diagnosis. He was variously described as tactless, blunt, insensitive, and incompetent, and one couple accused their doctor of giving "incompatible blood" to the child (a charge discovered by the interviewer to be inaccurate). One mother said that the doctor did not care about her daughter and was only interested in learning something from her case. These hostile feelings did not seem to be so intense toward the doctors who treated the children after diagnosis; in fact, several of these latter were respected by families who expressed anger at their first doctor.

Although some physicians, owing to the intensity of their own feelings of helplessness, may not be tactful enough, the universality of the parents' anger seemed to indicate that it was a displacement of their basic anger at being singled out for such an unfortunate occurrence.

The anger was also displaced onto the hospital: "The Massachusetts General is such a great hospital; why couldn't it save my son?" Several families were concerned and angry that the doctors had "experimented" on their child. This was revealed by such slips of the tongue as: "Joan's experiment, or experience, or whatever you want to call it, was agony." Most of the children had suffered physically, both from painful medical procedures and from the symptoms of the disease.

To understand these reactions, it is necessary to remember that the parents were desperate during their child's illness, and that they wanted their child to be diagnosed properly and cured. After death, however, they were overwhelmed by guilt over what they considered to be the extra pain caused by these unsuccessful procedures and this guilt was expressed as anger toward the medical staff.

Two of the families, both of whom expressed little conscious anger toward the hospital, did not pay their bills (or work out terms to pay them), even though the hospital sent many follow-up letters, including one that threatened legal action. Economic hardship did not seem to account for these failures. Moreover, the families were mystified as to why they had ignored the letters, and one mother described her prompt payment of a larger bill for her first child who had lived. Although the other parents paid their bills, several expressed resentment that the hospital did not help to pay them. In one case, a father went deeply into debt, which seemed to alleviate in part his sense of guilt. Whatever the explanation, the hospital bill seemed to be an emotionally laden issue.

Also, some anger was displayed toward the interviewer, even in families who expressed relief at the opportunity to talk about their experience. The anger ranged from a mild curiosity as to why the families were being interviewed at that time to strong expressions of resentment that the hospital had failed them by sending the interviewer then instead of earlier, when they so badly needed someone.

Religion

The religious faith of the families, all of whom were Roman Catholic, was variously affected by the child's death. For three, faith became stronger and religion more meaningful. For the other two, inability to understand why the death occurred greatly decreased the comfort they derived from faith. They found it difficult to understand why they had been chosen to suffer when they had been "so good" to their children.

In families in which religious faith was strongest, and in which it was perhaps least permissible to blame God, anger seemed to be intensified. They blamed either the doctor or the hospital, and in one case, the mother turned her anger inward.

Replacement

Four of the five families expressed a need to replace their dead child. One mother became pregnant the month after her son died. Another couple adopted two girls nine months after their child's death. Two families were anxious for another child; one mother put the live child's bed where the dead child's had been, as though to replace the lost child with the living one. The fifth family, who lost an adopted 8-year-old son after a seven-month illness, expressed no desire for another child; perhaps they could not emotionally cope with another at that time.

Sibling Reaction

Although the siblings' reactions were reported by their grieving parents (and, therefore, may be exaggerated), it does seem evident that the younger siblings reacted strongly to the family's disequilibrium, while the older siblings showed a capacity for independent grief that increased with age.

Two siblings were under 3. They were separated from their mothers during the illness and death and were cared for by their grandparents. One child was 20 months old and previously had a close relationship with his grandmother. His mother did not seem depressed by the death of her newborn infant and the child had never seen him. There seemed to be no observable change in this child's behavior during this period or afterward. The mother of the other child, a 2 1/2-year-old boy, was preoccupied with her older son's illness. When she picked up the younger child each night she was depressed and tearful, and felt guilty about her "neglect" of him and her concern for the ill child. After her son's death, she desperately needed to talk about it, but her husband could not bear to hear the child's name mentioned. During the patient's illness, the sibling was frightened and clinging; this behavior persisted at the time of the interview eight months later.

A 3-year-old sibling also seemed to react strongly to the family's disequilibrium. At first, her parents thought she accepted her sister's death; then she began to talk about her incessantly, "conversed" with her in heaven, and asked many questions, such as when her sister would return. At this time her mother was tearful and depressed and needed to talk about the death but could not speak about it to her husband. Evidently, she talked to this sibling, who when her mother cried and said, "Mommy misses Anne," responded with the apparently comforting words, "I have a *very* beautiful Mommy."

The oldest sibling in the study, a 13-year-old boy, seemed to react with signs of genuine grief: sadness, depression, loneliness, withdrawal from family life for a time, and irritability. He began to recover from these symptoms months later when his parents adopted two girls.

A most interesting reaction was described by the parents of a 9 year-old girl. They had not told her of the serious nature of her brother's long illness, and a cheerful attitude was maintained in the house until the boy's death. Suddenly she was included in the whole spectrum of her family's grief, except the funeral. (Because they wanted to spare her feelings, her parents sent her to a carnival instead.) Also, her mother used her as an outlet to verbalize her grief because her husband could not tolerate its expression.

After her brother's death she became nervous and frightened, expressed feelings of intense loneliness and sadness, and began to sleepwalk. She worried that she would "catch" leukemia and whether her brother had gone to heaven. Also, it may be noted that her parents kept her present during the entire interview although the interviewer told them it was not necessary.

Undoubtedly, children's reactions to the death of a sibling are composed of many elements. The younger child's response is usually complicated by the concomitant separation from his mother. This separation elicits a stronger reaction than the loss of a sibling because the mother fulfills basic needs and the sibling is a companion and competitor. It is difficult to determine which is more important in understanding a child's reaction—family disequilibrium or independent grief; it does seem, however, that the former is most important to the younger child. As the child becomes older, his reactions seem to become more of a mixture of the two elements, which are both quite important.

Refusal to be Interviewed

Five families declined to be interviewed. Two would not discuss their refusal. One mother consented at first because she felt a sense of duty to the hospital, which had given large free care allowances in the long illnesses of her two children who died, but reconsidered when the interviewer, sensing her deep reluctance, advised her to consent only if she thought the interview would help her.

Two families' reactions showed signs of pathology. One father accused the interviewer of making a spot check because he had not paid his bill (he paid it immediately after receiving the request for an interview). When she denied his accusation, he told her that he did not want any "baskets of fruit" from the hospital. His excessive suspicion masked a deep anger at the hospital, which was revealed further by his remark that he had "absolutely no complaints" about the hospital, and felt the doctors had done everything possible to save his newborn child—"or at least I *hope* they did!" The fifth family at first agreed to be interviewed, but declined when called for confirmation. The mother seemed more concerned about her marital situation than her child's death, and completely denied grief over the death.

Conclusions and Recommendations

Unfortunately, because of the small size of the study sample, it is impossible to make any comparisons of response to a child's death based on differences in religion, ethnic group, education, or age. It did seem that the death of a child was an equally difficult experience whether the death was relatively sudden or expected, the child was natural or adopted, or there had been previous deaths in the family.

Although it is necessary to have more complete data gathered at the time of death to determine whether the reported reactions are predominantly normal or pathological, it can be said that each family had difficulties with which it could have used help. All parents did not react in the same way and, therefore, cannot be helped in the same way. Mothers, especially, needed to talk about their experience during the child's hospitalization and afterward; some fathers needed help in expressing their grief, too.

The caseworker must be skilled enough to judge the place of the individual reaction, and must be sensitive to which issues can be handled at each stage. Furthermore, it would be much easier on the caseworker and the parents if they had a relationship before the child's death.

During the child's illness, the caseworker may talk with him to help alleviate some of his anxieties and make the time before death as emotionally bearable as possible. Social work is still in the theoretical dark as to how to do this. In addition, when parents are helped to experience anticipatory grief, it may simultaneously increase their withdrawal from the child, which may be frightening and difficult for him.

The parents in the study also seemed to need help with their other children. They worried about what to tell them and when, and how to answer their questions. They wondered whether their children's reactions were normal, and how to help them cope with death. In addition, there were severe difficulties in disciplining the sibling; many parents suspended it entirely because of their guilt feelings toward the dead child.

It is crucial that social workers attempt to fill the family's unmet needs, which range from practical services (financial assistance, transportation, and babysitting) and temporary escape from the oppression of the situation to emotional support and help with expressing grief. Social workers must learn to determine what techniques to use at what times. To do this, we must build not only on theories and experience, but also must strive for increased understanding of our own reactions to death—and this is perhaps the most difficult task of all.

References

1.   In Ernest Jones, ed., *Collected Papers*, Vol. 4 (London, Eng.: Hogarth Press, 1925), pp. 152–170.

2.   Erich Lindemann, "Symptomatology and Management of Acute Grief," *American Journal of Psychiatry*, Vol. 101, No. 2 (September 1944), pp. 141–148.

3.   Maurice Hamovitch, *The Parent and the Fatally Ill Child* (Duarte, Calif.: City of Hope Medical Center, 1964).

4.   John Bowlby, "Grief and Mourning in Infancy and Early Childhood," *Psychoanalytic Study of the Child*, Vol. 15 (New York: International Universities Press, 1960), p. 49.

5.   Anna Freud and Dorothy T. Burlingham, *War and Children* (New York: International Universities Press, 1943); Helene Deutsch, "Absence of Grief," *Psychoanalytic Quarterly*, Vol. 6, No. 1 (January 1937), pp. 12–22; and Josephine R. Hilgard, Martha F. Newman, and Fern Fisk, "Strength of Adult Ego Following Childhood Bereavement," *American Journal of Orthopsychiatry*, Vol. 30, No. 4 (October 1960), pp. 788–798.

6.   Maria Nagy, "The Child's View of Death," in Herman Feifel, ed., *The Meaning of Death* (New York: McGraw-Hill Book Co., 1959), pp. 79–98; and Arnold Gesell and Frances L. Ilg, *The Child From Five to Ten* (New York: Harper & Brothers, 1946).

7.   For a discussion of postponement of affect *see* Otto Fenichel, MD, *The Psychoanalytic Theory of Neurosis* (New York: W. W. Norton & Co., 1945), pp. 162–163.

8.   For an elaboration of the ego's hypercathexis in grief *see* Sigmund Freud, *op. cit.*

30

Determinants of the Psychiatric Patient Career: Family Reaction Patterns and Social Work Intervention

Stephan P. Spitzer,
Patricia A. Morgan,
and Robert M. Swanson

The use of typologies to conceptualize and augment social work knowledge is becoming more prevalent. This paper focuses on a typology developed to describe familial reactions to mental illness and the evolution of the psychiatric patient career.* Through examination and evaluation of the various familial reactions, it may be possible to determine the extent to which social work intervention is needed by particular types of families, as well as to determine the kinds of intervention most appropriate to a specific family type. If these two objectives can be attained, the goals of social work intervention may be more effectively reached. These goals are to insure that (*a*) the family supports the patient's hospitalization, (*b*) the family encourages the patient to return for treatment if symptoms reappear, and (*c*) the family both urges and expects the patient to function at an optimal level.†

In addition to its etiological significance in the initial development of illness, an increasing amount of evidence points to the family as a crucial

Source: From *Social Service Review* 45 (March 1971), pp. 74–85. Copyright © 1971 by the University of Chicago Press. Reprinted by permission.

*Funds for this investigation were made available from the Research Fund of Iowa, through Dr. Paul E. Huston, Director, Psychopathic Hospital, University of Iowa. The authors have expressed appreciation to Robert K. Lehr and Cheryl Phelps for their help in classifying the case histories.

†These are only a few of the goals that might necessitate social work intervention based on specific needs of a certain case situation.

factor in the evolution and outcome of mental illness. The family plays a major role in the identification of psychiatric deviance (16, 24, 33), determines the type of help source sought (19, 32, 33), contributes to the stabilization of deviance (15, 23, 25), and influences case outcome (8, 9, 14, 21). The family also provides socialization into the sick role (20, 26), contributes to feelings of alienation and stigma on the part of the patient (1, 4, 7, 31), and alters the course of hospitalization of family members (5, 18).

Also, through analysis of family reactions, it may be possible to predict at least some of the pathways that the psychiatric patient career takes, depending upon who the audiences are, what their actions are, and how they respond to deviance.

A Typology of Family Reactions

In the course of preparing an investigation concerned with changes in self-identities, attitudes, and interpersonal relations among psychiatric patients, it became evident to the authors that different career patterns evolved (6, 27, 29). For some persons, treatment was initiated shortly after mental illness was detected, while for others years elapsed before they entered a psychiatric hospital. Similarly, some were readmitted to hospitals almost immediately after discharge, others returned within ten years of discharge, and still others had not been rehospitalized for over a decade.*

To an extent, these observations could be attributed to a number of commonly recognized variables, e.g., diagnosis, initial severity of illness, prognosis, rate of improvement, or accommodation to the hospital regime. Family reactions to deviance, however, seemed to account for much of the residual variance, for, when the histories and characteristics of various patients were inspected, the impression was that case outcome was associated with the attitudes prevailing in the families from which the patients came.

In order to explore this hypothesis, 79 first-admissions patients with functional disorders admitted to a university teaching and research hospital were selected for investigation. The patients and a family member were interviewed before admission in an attempt to learn what brought the patient to the hospital. The patients were followed throughout the course of their hospitalization (averaging forty days) and also for about two years after discharge from the hospital. As a consequence, two "sensitizing concepts" associated with directions of career paths were identified. One is "Expected level of performance"; the other is "Propensity for action." Although appear-

---

*"Readmission" is used here as an indication of case outcome rather than as a measure of the success of treatment.

ing under varying terminology in the literature, both are substantiated by theory and empirical findings. They are largely summary indicators of probable attitudes toward the sick role, toward psychiatry, and toward reacting to deviance under the rubric of mental illness.

"Expected level of performance" refers to what the family expects of its members on various dimensions: economic, interpersonal, community relations, conformity, and so on. In short, just what does this family require for participation and membership? Freeman and Simmons found that families set up certain expectations for the "deviant" in terms of stability of employment and associative patterns, and the expected performance level accounted for higher recidivism rates in some families (8, 9). In another investigation, performance-level expectations were found to be associated with the deviant's family position; higher performance levels were set for persons having a key role in the family (14). Gordon's study of the sick role also disclosed marked variations in expectations regarding the rights and obligations to be assumed once this role has been described (10).

The second dimension, "Propensity for action," refers to a family's differential readiness to ascribe a psychiatric label and prescribe psychiatric treatment for a family member. What is regarded as mental illness in one family is not necessarily recognized as such in another. Investigations concerned with the process of recognizing psychiatric problems disclose noticeable variations among families (3, 13, 17, 24). Families also differ in their tolerance for accepting deviation from normative patterns before taking action. Myers and Roberts, Clausen and Yarrow, and Mechanic report large differences in the degree to which family members are willing to support and tolerate deviance (3, 17, 19). Moreover, even within a given family, tolerance limits established for different family members tend to vary (11). Finally, families differ in their ability to tolerate or withstand stress. In some families the deviant serves an integrative function, helping to maintain stability by fulfilling a needed role (2, 16, 30). Hence, the family is able to withstand considerable stress before initiating plans for action.

By regarding families as either high or low on the dimensions of "Expected level of performance" and "Propensity for action," four "ideal" family types, as shown in Table 1, are discernible. Sometimes more than one family type is entered in a cell of the table. This is because families are characterized by dimensions in addition to those on which the typology is based. The additional dimensions include attitudes toward psychiatry, the kinds of explanatory concepts employed to understand human motivation, and modes of interpersonal conduct.

Seventy-six of the 79 cases could be classified. In the three remaining cases the patient either had no family or he had separated from the family before the onset of deviant behavior. Not all cases fit perfectly into the taxonomy, but there was sufficient correspondence between the characteris-

TABLE 1.   Types of Family Reactions

| | EXPECTED PERFORMANCE LEVEL | |
PROPENSITY FOR ACTION	High	Low
High	Stipulators Altercasters	Authoritarians
Low	Stoics Poltroons	Pacifists Happenchancers Do-nothings

tics of the observed cases and the "ideal" cases that all could be classified with substantial agreement.*

High Level of Performance Expected

Four types of families seemed to expect a high level of performance of family members.

STOICS

The family designated as "stoic" is characterized by a "philosophical" outlook on life. Its propensity for action is low when deviation of a family member is observed. Family members have a high tolerance level for deviant behavior and a marked ability to tolerate or withstand stress. They believe that painful experiences can be endured and that illness does not necessarily lead to progressive deterioration. Their expectations for performance are high, but their demands on the deviant are minimal. They are silent and uncomplaining.

"Stoics" rarely play a major part in initiating treatment for their deviant members. The deviant behavior often comes to the attention of outsiders,

*Four judges working independently were instructed to assign each case to that one of the eight categories which it most closely approximated. The criterion for "agreement" was consensus among at least three of the four judges. This criterion was met for 60 of the 76 cases. Differences in opinion were resolved without undue difficulty through group discussion for the remaining 16 cases. This was possible because total disagreement was never found among all judges; at worst, the judges split evenly between two categories. Moreover, when discrepancies in classification occurred, it was almost always between categories that had common characteristics. The judges had the greatest difficulty in discriminating between "stipulators" and "authoritarians" and between "happenchancers" and "do-nothings."

who may come to play an active role. In such instances family tolerance limits are finally exceeded, and plans for treatment are initiated. During the inpatient phase family members visit the patient frequently but do not attempt to influence his attitudes and behavior in any appreciable way. They may temporarily accept a psychiatric definition of illness, but during the postpatient phase they revert to their old behavior patterns. Although family members may be disappointed that the patient fails to perform at a satisfactory level, their demands on him remain low. Action is rarely initiated for rehospitalization, although it may come about at the urging of outsiders.

POLTROONS

The family designated as "poltroon" feels the necessity for removing the deviant, but is reluctant to undergo a direct confrontation with him. Because family members desire to avoid strains in their relationships with the deviant, their ability to tolerate stress is high. Fear of stigma associated with mental illness adds to their reluctance to take direct action. The course taken is to operate behind the patient's back. Under false pretenses the deviant is often referred to the family physician, who has been requested to recommend psychiatric hospitalization. If the family doctor does not fulfill their expectations, a member of the extended family, such as an uncle, may be recruited to act as "complainant." Thus, when the deviant member is removed, any animosity he may experience is misdirected.

Once the patient has been hospitalized, family members align themselves with the hospital. If called upon, they cooperate fully with the hospital staff. The postpatient in this kind of family has a high potential for readmission. Family members can justify readmission on the basis of their obligation to the hospital.

As might be expected, even though all judges agreed on how particular cases should be classified, the cases did not always fit the descriptions perfectly. For example, while all judges might agree with certainty that a case should be classified as "stoic," they were also aware that it contained certain characteristics not found in the description of the "stoic" type of family. Thus, although statistical agreement among judges was substantial, a certain looseness in fitting the cases to the category descriptions is undeniable. Because a typology as simple as the one presented here is obviously inapplicable to all families, it will be necessary to incorporate additional dimensions of family reactions. In addition to the three suggested earlier, another pertains to family reactions as determined by the patient's role in the family. For example, there are probably fundamental differences in the ways in which families react to a sick mother and to an adult child, and these differences may influence how, when, and why the recipient arrives at a treatment setting. See also Lefton et al (14).

An extended version of this taxonomy, with slightly different labels (the labels used here are simply shorthand designators; they are temporary, and they were chosen with no attempt to be flippant) and illustrative case histories, as well as a more complete description of the methods and procedures, is given elsewhere. See Spitzer et al (28).

STIPULATORS

Members of families designated as "stipulators" are willing to inform the deviant that he could be mentally ill and that his behavior is disruptive to the family. Because of their value orientations, the patient is expected to perform at a high level. Deviance is intolerable on the basis of principle or because it is threatening to family integration. Moreover, the family may believe that, in the interests of the patient's welfare, illness should be treated as soon as possible. Attempts are made to evoke conformity through interpersonal pressures, but, as it becomes evident that attainment of conformity is improbable, the deviant is presented with the ultimatum of "shaping up or shipping out." If this threat does not produce the desired result, arrangements are made for psychiatric treatment.

Family members are not overly concerned with the prepatient's attitudes toward them, since he has been repeatedly warned of the consequence of continued deviation. In addition, they can subscribe to the moral justification that hospitalization would benefit both the patient's health and the family's welfare. They hope that psychiatric treatment will be successful, but they anticipate returning the postpatient to the hospital if problems recur after discharge.

ALTERCASTERS

The family designated as "altercaster" has many of the characteristics of the "poltroons" and the "stipulators." Family members desire to avoid direct confrontation with the deviant and attempt to conceal from the deviant that they are responsible for his removal from the family. However, they are more subtle than the "poltroons." Rather than forming a coalition with the family physician or psychiatrist, they present the help source with the deviant, casting him into the position of making a treatment decision. Or they altercast the patient by convincing him that his symptoms are indicative of psychiatric illness. If the patient internalizes this definition he is obliged to seek psychiatric help. Hence, the family has accomplished the same end as if the patient had been taken to the help source. Often what seemingly appears to be a self-made decision to seek psychiatric treatment is actually an outcome of the altercasting process.

Punitive and threatening attitudes are absent, but, like the "stipulators," these families have high expectations for performance and a high propensity to initiate action. If family members have been particularly successful, further actions are unnecessary, since the patient will automatically carry out their wishes. In such instances, rehospitalization is self-perpetuating.

Low Level of Performance Expected

PACIFISTS

Other families have very low expectations of the patient. The family designated as "pacifist" tends to accommodate to the deviant member. As a consequence, family members have lowered their expectations for performance and their propensity for initiating any sort of action to remove the patient from the home. At one time they tried to evoke conformity by the use of a variety of mechanisms such as pleading, nagging, threatening, or extending rewards. Because these techniques have proved to be ineffective, the family accommodates to the deviant, who then receives greater latitude for deviation. While this strategy may precipitate additional problems, rejection of the deviant is not an absolute necessity. Concern is shown that the patient's "illness" may grow progressively worse, but still the family is slow to initiate action. More than the "stoics" or the "poltroons," such families subscribe to the belief that the deviation may be "outgrown" or that spontaneous recovery might occur. Rehospitalization of the patient is relatively improbable.

HAPPENCHANCERS

Members of the family designated as "happenchancer" recognize departure from typical functioning of other family members and are ready to seek clarification of the problem. Deviance is invariably interpreted as resulting from physical causes. Contact is made with a medical practitioner who is then likely to recognize the problem as psychiatric. As these family members are generally passive and uninformed persons, professional judgment is acted upon. Sometimes the physician makes arrangements for hospitalization without consulting the family.

Psychiatric treatment is not what family members had in mind, and they are dismayed to find that control of the situation has passed into other hands. The inpatient is urged to do whatever the treatment authorities deem necessary, but the family makes no attempt to persuade the patient to accept the attitudes and orientations of professional staff. Later, the activities of the family may become directed toward facilitating the deviant's release from the hospital.

It is difficult to predict the evolution of the patient career in this type of family. One course of action is to avoid rehospitalization; by accident the family has chanced upon a path to treatment, and this mistake is not likely to be repeated. Another course of action results from an uncritical acceptance of the professional definition; further deviation on the part of the patient will be cause to seek out the old authority for clarification and advice.

DO-NOTHINGS

In the family designated as "do-nothing" psychiatric deviance may be unrecognized or may be classified under some other rubric (troublemaker, criminal, and so on). If the deviation is recognized as mental illness, the question of utilizing psychiatric treatment is not considered. Opposition to psychiatric care occurs, but indifference predominates. A minimal level of performance is required, perhaps no more than contributing sporadically to the economic needs of the family or carrying out simple household tasks.

Because of a modicum of social control within the family, the deviant may begin to act increasingly aberrant. As frequency and intensity increase, the deviation becomes more salient to the outside community. If a recommendation for psychiatric treatment is made through outside intervention, little is done to implement treatment.

Because of a rapid transition between unrecognized and recognized deviance, and/or because of a carry-over of prior attitudes of indifference, family members are reticent to accept a psychiatric definition of the situation. Thus, the family remains uninvolved as the patient enters the hospital. After the patient returns home, the likelihood that the family will initiate rehospitalization is small, although the possibility of outside intervention remains.

AUTHORITARIANS

Families labeled as "authoritarian" are characterized by a severe, stern, and harsh atmosphere. Even slight deviations are not tolerated. Unlike "stipulators," "authoritarians" adhere to only one or a few expectations. On those occasional instances when expectations are enumerated, family members actually anticipate superficial performance on the specified dimensions. In some instances the intent of hospitalization is to punish the deviant member.

Little indecision or remorse is shown when arranging for hospitalization. The patient is often committed with no forewarning. Occasionaly family members dispose of the deviant through the same techniques used by "altercasters" or "poltroons," but they act more out of convenience than out of temerity. If an outside agency intervenes, "authoritarians" refrain from interfering with efforts to remove the deviant from the home. Persons are moved into treatment rapidly from this type of family, and rehospitalization is highly probable.

Implications for Social Work

It is commonly recognized that involvement with families by social workers is not uniform. Overall need for services and type of services needed vary according to specific case situations. By viewing families according to the typology presented, it is possible to illustrate how the extent and nature of involvement of the social worker can be determined by family type. If the differential need for social work involvement based on specific family reaction patterns is recognized, social workers can more appropriately direct their efforts toward carrying out hospital goals.

REDUCING RESISTANCE TO SERVICE

Efforts of social workers to reduce resistance to service are particularly critical with family members whose propensity for action is low. These familes are most typically resistive to social work intervention as they do not view the patient as "ill" within the medicopsychiatric model. Since their perceptions often deviate from those of the hospital staff, social workers find it difficult to help family members discuss the patient's behavior or their own role in the patient's illness. "Happenchancers" are perhaps the most difficult in this respect. Efforts to develop a relationship with them may necessitate a great deal of time and effort in order to work through the anger felt due to loss of control over the patient and his future. Although this anger may be displaced onto the social worker, it may be possible to utilize the family's feelings in a constructive manner.

"Do-nothings," because they are typically unmotivated for service, will rarely, if ever, come into contact with the hospital staff. Consequently, they will probably deny the total process of hospitalization. It would be beneficial for the referring agency to deal with such families before referral so that family members can be sensitized to the importance of their participation during hospitalization and treatment. Another goal for the social worker is to involve these families after hospitalization. Moreover, as stated previously, because these families may need the patient to maintain equilibrium of the unit, toleration for deviance is high. Although this type of family is among those who need the most service, it is often among those who receive the least. Accordingly, social work intervention is rarely accomplished.

CRISES INTERVENTION

Once a patient is admitted, relatives often experience emotional crises.* Hill has depicted institutionalization for mental illness as a family

---

*As defined by Rapoport (22:24), a crisis is "an upset in a steady state."

crisis of the gravest order, wherein family members suffer demoralization as well as loss (12). They are often overwhelmed with feelings of helplessness, fear of the future, and guilt for not having somehow averted the patient's "breakdown." They may also feel guilty for going behind the patient's back and placing him in a hospital against his will.

Social workers in mental health facilities need to be especially available on a crises-intervention basis with family members characterized as "happenchancers," "stoics," and "do-nothings." These families, because they are most resistive to admitting to pathology in the patient, also experience the greatest emotional shock when the patient is hospitalized.

It has been noted that families prepared for a traumatic event will adjust better to the crisis (12). In order that these families can most effectively support the patient's hospitalization, immediate intervention is necessary. Early support is also essential to forestall any possible family disintegration stemming from the crisis and, in the case of the "happenchancers," to prevent behavior aimed at undermining treatment, such as signing the patient out of the hospital against medical advice.

ONGOING INTERVENTION

Specific intervention will vary in terms of family reaction patterns. The goals of intervention emphasized here are that the family (a) receives and accepts education regarding a medicopsychiatric model of illness, (b) supports the patient's hospitalization, (c) urges the patient to return for further treatment if symptoms reappear, (d) communicates an expectation for the patient to function at an optimal level, and (e) refrains from stigmatizing the patient and supports him in spite of his disability. Some families achieve these goals without extensive intervention. However, the implications are negative for patients from families wherein propensity for action and expectation levels for performance are low. This is especially probable for patients with chronic illnesses, such as schizophrenia, in which there is continued remission and exacerbation of illness. A majority of these patients can function at a relatively high level if an expectation and a structure for future treatment are provided by the family. The following denotes those goals that require outside intervention and suggests the types of social work activities that could be utilized in order to increase the probability that these goals will be attained.

Families that are the most resistive and in need of immediate action, e.g., those with low propensity for action, are among those that need the most thorough and intensive ongoing intervention. Although not all of these types harbor hostility toward the hospital and staff, they characteristically view the patient's behavior differently than do the professional personnel.

The "stoic" family needs preparation in order to return the patient after discharge, should symptoms recur. This goal might be accomplished by sensitizing family members to the meaning of symptoms and their relationship to mental illness. Perhaps awareness that prompt psychiatric attention can avert the development of more severe symptoms will give impetus for seeking treatment if and when minor symptoms reappear. "Stoic" families are often unaware that the patient is capable of functioning at a higher level and that raising expectations might automatically lead to this result. One strategy in supportive casework is to aim at reducing the passivity of family members toward the patient's behavior. Another strategy is to heighten their ability to view the patient's potentiality in a more realistic fashion.

In dealing with the "pacifist" family, efforts could be profitably directed toward helping family members to support hospitalization, to return the patient if symptoms reappear, and to raise their expectations regarding the patient's functioning. Involving family members from the first day of admission is important; orientation to the hospital routine and frequent progress reports will involve these families in the hospitalization process, thereby helping them to view mental illness from a perspective similar to that of the hospital staff. Education about the awareness and meaning of symptoms will aid family members to decide when and how to seek assistance for the patient if problems recur. Family treatment may also be indicated in order to deal with the extreme tolerance of aberrant patient behavior. Discussion of the patient's potential may also include sharing the results of vocational rehabilitation consultations with family members.

Discharge planning is crucial for "pacifist" families, especially if little or no progress is evident in achieving the previously mentioned goals. The social worker may be successful in preparing some family members for faster action in the future and in raising their expected level of performance for the patient, and should strive to achieve these ends during the patient's first admission. These families are needful candidates for posthospital supervision. Social workers from community agencies and affiliated visiting nurses could be informed of the patient-family constellation so that rehospitalization can be accomplished if relapse occurs.

It can be argued that the lack of social control found among "do-nothings" indicates a multiproblem situation in an uncohesive family, and thus, in exceptional circumstances, discharge planning might include arranging for the patient to live apart from the family. However, since it is typical for the postpatient to resume his prior family position, community agency cooperation may be considered in order to help motivate members of this type of family to raise their expectations for the patient's behavior, as well as their readiness to take necessary remedial action. Direct confrontation with such family members during the inpatient phase might serve to dispel apathy, but the success of this technique is probably dependent upon continuing education about mental illness and increased involvement with psychiatric hospital goals and functions.

Families designated as "happenchancers" not only need immediate emergency service at the time of admission, but also need continuing intervention during the inpatient phase of the patient career. Of the various family types, "happenchancers" are most taken aback at the loss (albeit temporary) of a family member. Involvement in hospital activities and frequent contact with the social worker during visiting hours may help to decrease the initial shock and fear of mental illness. Few of these family members have other than a traditional medical framework for interpreting illness. Motivational determinants of psychopathology are not part of their conceptual scheme. Thus, education about mental illness and explanations of the relationship of symptoms to emotions are extremely important.

If expectation levels are raised without a corresponding decrease in propensity for action, "authoritarian" families will become even more rejecting of the patient. In order to circumvent this problem an often-tried technique is to encourage family members to view the patient as an individual with strengths as well as weaknesses. A collaborative review of the patient's social history could function as a point of departure to engender commitment to the hospital and to aid in developing latent empathic abilities. Reflective discussions of the implications of interactions with the patient for family dynamics could represent a second step in the socialization process.

Providing ongoing services for the "stipulator" type of family presents a less delicate problem. Casework devoted to bolstering relatives' awareness of the patient's strengths and needs for affiliation, in conjunction with mutual examination of the consequences of family interaction on patient behavior, may lead to increased tolerance of the patient.

The extent of need for ongoing services for families designated as "poltroons" and "altercasters" is less than for the other family types, since these families normally achieve at least some of the five goals without special services. However, each is amenable to specific kinds of intervention. Intervention with "poltroons" could reasonably be aimed toward alleviating guilt for the deception perpetrated and helping family members accept responsibility for the patient's welfare. Similarly, "altercasters" can be expected to work openly and actively with the patient only if their characteristic mode of interpersonal conduct is modified. Sometimes change can be effected simply by interpreting their behavior to them, but in those instances in which family members have determined the effectiveness of the technique and use it intentionally, striving to identify and to remove the underlying causes will be necessary before maximum progress can be made. In any event, because of their low resistance to social work intervention, "poltroons" and "altercasters" are potentially the social workers' best clients. Consequently, there is a tendency to spend an inordinate amount of time with such families while labeling others as "unmotivated" or "unworkable."

Discussion

Social workers have been attempting to conceptualize the knowledge which heretofore was attributed to intuition or the "art of practice." The development of a typology based on characteristic familial reaction patterns of identifying deviance and subsequently seeking psychiatric treatment has been such an attempt. Since it is not feasible for social workers to become intensively involved with all families of hospitalized patients, an initial appraisal of each case situation is necessary to select families that are most in need of service. By thinking of a typology of family reactions in relation to certain social work goals, practitioners can better determine which cases require most involvement, which need immediate attention, and which might be postponed until time permits.

This paper has presented an initial formulation of how such a typology of family reaction to mental illness might be utilized within the field of social work. With more data, it might be possible to associate other variables such as family structure, patient symptomatology, or family class status with specific familial reaction patterns. Establishing the degree of association between these variables and family reaction patterns should allow greater predictability of case outcome and better determination of social work activity. Further investigation might also attempt to test whether the use of such a typology in determining the kinds of intervention necessary with certain kinds of family types does make a difference in the attainment of certain goals in behalf of the patient.

References

1.   Alivisatos, Gerassimos, and Lyketsos, George. "A Preliminary Report of a Research Concerning the Attitude of the Families of Hospitalized Mental Patients." *International Journal of Social Psychiatry* 10 (Winter 1964): 37–44.

2.   Bursten, Ben, and D'Esopo, Rose. "The Obligation to Remain Sick." In *Mental Illness and Social Processes*, edited by Thomas J. Scheff. New York: Harper & Row, 1967.

3.   Clausen, John A., and Yarrow, Marian R., eds. "The Impact of Mental Illness on the Family." *Journal of Social Issues* 11, No. 4 (1955): 3–65.

4.   Cumming, John, and Cumming, Elaine. "On the Stigma of Mental Illness." *Community Mental Health Journal* 1 (1965): 135–43.

5.   Deasy, Leila, and Quinn, Olive Westbrooke. "The Wife of the Mental Patient and the Hospital Psychiatrist." *Journal of Social Issues* 11, No. 4 (1955): 49–60.

6.   Denzin, Norman K. "The Self-Fulfilling Prophecy and Patient-Therapist Interaction." In *The Mental Patient: Studies in the Sociology of Deviance*, edited by

Stephan P. Spitzer and Norman K. Denzin. New York: McGraw-Hill Book Co., 1968.

7. Freeman, Howard E., and Simmons, Ozzie G. "Feelings of Stigma among Relatives of Former Mental Patients." *Social Problems* 8 (Spring 1961): 312–21.

8. _____. "Mental Patients in the Community: Family Settings and Performance Levels." *American Sociological Review* 23 (April 1958): 147–54.

9. _____. "Social Class and Posthospital Performance Levels." *American Sociological Review* 24 (June 1959): 345–51.

10. Gordon, Gerald. *Role Theory and Illness*. New Haven, Conn.: College and University Press, 1966.

11. Gurin, Gerald; Veroff, Joseph; and Feld, Sheila. *Americans View Their Mental Health*. New York: Basic Books, 1960.

12. Hill, Reuben. "Generic Features of Families under Stress." In *Crisis Intervention: Selected Readings*, edited by Howard J. Parad, pp. 32–52. New York: Family Service Association of America, 1965.

13. Hollingshead, August B., and Redlich, Frederick C., M.D. *Social Class and Mental Illness*. New York: John R. Wiley & Sons, 1958.

14. Lefton, Mark; Angrist, Shirley; Dinitz, Simon; and Pasamanick, Benjamin. "Social Class, Expectations, and Performance of Mental Patients." *American Journal of Sociology* 58 (July 1962): 79–87.

15. Lemert, Edwin M. *Social Pathology*. New York: McGraw-Hill Book Co., 1951.

16. Lidz, Theodore, et al. "Patients and Their Siblings." *Psychiatry* 26 (February 1963): 1–18.

17. Mechanic, David. "Some Factors in Identifying and Defining Mental Illness." *Mental Hygiene* 46 (January 1962): 66–74.

18. Moore, Kenneth B., and McCravy, N., Jr. "Family Interaction as a Factor in Prolonging Hospitalization." *Journal of Nervous and Mental Disease* 136 (May 1963): 485–91.

19. Myers, Jerome K., and Roberts, Bertram M. *Family and Class Dynamics in Mental Illness*. New York: John R. Wiley & Sons, 1959.

20. Parsons, Talcott, and Fox, Renee C. "Illness, Therapy, and the Modern American Family." *Journal of Social Issues* 8, No. 4 (1952): 31–44.

21. Paul, N. L., and Grosser, G. H. "Family Resistance to Change in Schizophrenia." *Family Processes* 3 (September 1964): 377–401.

22. Rapoport, Lydia. "The State of Crisis: Some Theoretical Considerations." In *Crisis Intervention: Selected Readings*, edited by Howard J. Parad, pp. 22–31. New York: Family Service Association of America, 1965.

23. Ray, Marsh B. "The Cycle of Abstinence and Relapse among Heroin Addicts." In *The Other Side*, edited by Howard S. Becker, pp. 163–77. New York: Free Press, 1964.

24. Sampson, Harold; Messinger, Sheldon L.; and Towne, Robert D. *Schizophrenic Women*. New York: Atherton Press, 1964.

25. Scheff, Thomas J. "The Role of the Mentally Ill and the Dynamics of Mental Disorder: A Research Framework." *Sociometry* 26 (December 1963): 436–53.

26. Spitzer, Stephan P., and Bealka, Richard J. "Family Influences on Psychiatric Patient Performance." *Child Welfare* 48 (November 1969): 545-51.

27. Spitzer, Stephan P., and Denzin, Norman K. "The Career of the Psychiatric Patient in Two Types of Hospital Settings." Progress report, Psychopathic Hospital, Iowa City, Iowa, June 1967.

28. Spitzer, Stephan P.; Swanson, Robert M.; and Lehr, Robert K. "Audience Reactions and Careers of Psychiatric Patients." *Family Process* 8 (September 1969): 159-81.

29. Swanson, Robert M., and Spitzer, Stephan P. "Social Attitudes among the Mentally Ill and Their Significant Others: A Study in Social Distance." Paper presented at the annual meeting of the Midwest Sociological Society, April 1968.

30. Vogel, Ezra F., and Bell, Norman W. "The Emotionally Disturbed Child as the Family Scapegoat." In *A Modern Introduction to the Family*, edited by Norman W. Bell and Ezra F. Vogel, pp. 382-97. Glencoe, Ill.: Free Press, 1960.

31. Whatley, Charles B. "Social Attitudes toward Discharged Mental Patients." *Social Problems* 6 (Spring 1959): 313-20.

32. Wood, Edwin C.; Rakusin, John M.; and Morse, Emanuel. "Interpersonal Aspects of Psychiatric Hospitalization, I: The Admission." *Archives of General Psychiatry* 3 (December 1960): 632-41.

33. Yarrow, Marian R.; Schwartz, Charlotte G.; Murphy, Harriet S.; and Deasy, Leila C. "The Psychiatric Meaning of Mental Illness in the Family." *Journal of Social Issues* 11, No. 4 (1955): 12-24.

31

Familial Responses to Mental Illness

Margaret E. Raymond,
Andrew E. Slaby,
and Julian Lieb

Although a fair amount of attention has centered on the patterns of individual response to a variety of crisis situations, there is little in the professional literature on a family's reaction to mental illness in one of its members. An understanding of the variety of responses can enable the therapist to make a more appropriate and efficacious therapeutic intervention. This article covers the sequential pattern of a family's response to psychiatric illness.

> Before Michael's death and perhaps to a good degree afterward, we *tried* [italics added] to learn more about the nature of his nightmare... we cannot comfortably assume that the outcome was foreordained and that what we might have said or done differently along the way might not have mattered.[1]

These are the words of the parents of a young schizophrenic who at the age of twenty-six committed suicide after ten years of varied psychotherapeutic approaches in which no cost was spared. Like many other parents who may not have had comparable financial resources or a similar ability to articulate their anguish, they had wanted to but did not succeed in either understanding their son's illness or participating productively in his treatment.

Since Erich Lindemann's classic description of the symptomatology and management of grief reported in 1944 after the catastrophic Cocoanut Grove fire,[2] there have been several reports of indiviual or family response to a variety of crisis situations. These studies include reactions to the diag-

Source: From *Social Casework* 56 (October 1975), pp. 492–498. Copyright © 1975 by the Family Service Association. Reprinted by permission.

nosis of chronic illness and impending surgery, premature birth, impending death, and stages in the course of a marriage which are particularly stressful.[3] Notably, however, there has been a paucity of descriptions of an individual's or a family's response to the development and diagnosis of mental illness in a relative or close friend. This lack is unfortunate because an understanding of the stages of reaction of a family to a relative's mental illness can facilitate treatment by enabling the therapist to initiate a particular therapeutic approach when it could have the most useful effect. Obviously, if family members are not able to admit that a relative is ill, it is generally impossible to involve them in treatment.

A mental health professional's approach to family involvement in treatment should rest to some degree on an understanding of the progression of emotional response that all family members, including children, predictably go through as they attempt to come to terms with psychiatric illness. Inevitably, the threatening and unfamiliar situation stirs up within family members disturbing feelings and questions about family relationships. Hidden guilts and hostilities surface. As defenses become weakened, family members may become amenable to psychiatric intervention. Growth and a more mature level of family interaction may evolve as relatives grope through their own feelings and attempt to find a way in which they may participate with some assurance and self-esteem in the treatment program.

An intellectual understanding of this process may not eliminate the pain but, as with a woman who has been prepared to understand and participate in the phases of natural childbirth, the pain can be handled better. As an individual feels less anxiety, there is a greater ability to understand what is occurring within himself and within a sick relative as each undergoes what he must.

The stages of reaction of the family are illustrated below. The phases usually overlap and often vary in intensity.

Beginning Uneasiness

Early in the course of a patient's illness, the relatives generally sense that all is not well, although misgivings are often dismissed as being just a phase, because overt recognition would be too disturbing or painful. An intermittent sense of uneasiness and puzzlement may lead family members to make comparisons with an individual's previous behavior or between the ill person's behavior and that of others.

> On entering her junior year in high school, Alice becomes afraid of getting hurt in gym. She is unwilling to undress and shower with her classmates. Pale and anxious, she stays in her room after school. Her parents

minimize any difficulty by reminding each other that she is underweight and growing fast and that she has always found the first week of school difficult.

At this time, suppression may be a key defense. A relative may tell himself, "I won't let myself think about it." Although something is obviously amiss, to think about it may have implications that family members are not yet prepared to accept. At a later stage, an individual may realize in retrospect that he knew it from the beginning.

> Bill, a young accountant, begins to leave cryptic formulas on the refrigerator as messages to his parents. He becomes impatient with his mother when she fails to understand and respond. She has always considered herself mentally slow compared to her quick-reacting husband and son and now wonders if she is not being stupid in failing to grasp the messages' meaning. Or is her son testing her with a joke? She dismisses the irritating dilemma, having diverted her attention from questions about implications of her son's behavior to her lifelong discomfort with her own inadequacy.

Need for Reassurance

When unusual behavior persists and the initial uneasiness increases to a concession of open doubts and misgivings, family members attempt to gain reassurance. This phase may be initiated by obtaining confirmation that although there is some problem, it is not serious or permanent. The family may try to reason the sick one out of complaints, or coax him to agree that he is all right. Aunts, uncles, and grandparents, from the perspective of many years' experience or knowledge about relatives in different generations, may offer opinions that the behavior under question has been inherited and is therefore normal.

> A middle-aged parent, recalling a period of his own mild youthful rebellion, discounted his son's hostile explosions of inappropriate rage and violent radicalism as "just a phase he's got to go through in growing up—I've been there myself."

Despite some similarities of behavior, this parallel often does not extend into basically different experiences of the mentally ill person. The reassurance, therefore, is without foundation.

Relatives often turn to a clergyman or family doctor for the reassurance that the mentally ill patient will outgrow the disturbing behavior. In this phase, families may resist and postpone seeking psychiatric evaluation because such a step risks such dreaded possibilities as confirmation of psychiatric disturbance or a professional opinion that the family is the cause of the difficulty. Relatives may equate the need for professional help with their own inadequacy and failure.

Sometimes people attempt to account for a family member's unusual behavior or mood by likening it to that of a successful but nonconforming individual. This tendency may be particularly the case if the individual has demonstrated some special talent. The family may overrate the degree of originality or quality of creativity that one of their members possesses.

With the greater psychological sophistication possesssed by many people today, writing off aberrant behavior as eccentric is difficult, and as the illness evolves it becomes increasingly hard to avoid recognition. Relatives may then begin to search for explanations in circumstances and surroundings, such as financial problems, overwork, or the season of the year. These environmental influences are less disturbing than the factors more intimately involving the sick one's personality or the pattern of family interactions. Solutions to external difficulties seem more manageable because they involve readily definable and less threatening changes, such as a new job with a more understanding boss or a change in geographic location.

Denial and Minimizing

Following ineffectual efforts to find reassurance, an unconscious delaying tactic appears—a minimizing of the symptoms or a complete denial that illness is present. A relative may insist that he does not experience anxiety. Magical thinking may play an important role at this point, and a family member may say to himself, "If I don't think about it, it may go away by itself." Much later, after the problem has developed clearly, the relative may recognize, not infrequently with self-reproach, that somehow he had a blind spot about a situation that was quite evident to others. After a suicide, a spouse may report that the event occurred entirely without warning. Recognition of another's suffering may entail acknowledgement of one's own possible responsibility for maintaining the distressed one's suffering.

The patient himself often reinforces this process, for he, too, may have a vested interest in keeping at bay open recognition that he is ill. This situation is graphically demonstrated by patients with organic brain disease.

A young woman, disconcerted by memory loss from an organic brain syndrome, tries to cover the lapses with playful joking. When pressed to perform, she reacts with rage and asks, "Why ask me such stupid questions?"

In *Father Figure*, Beverly Nichols portrays a chronic alcoholic father and a masochistic mother who unspokenly collude to maintain the fiction, through a forty-year marriage, that the father is "having trouble with his heart and is not himself." The author poignantly describes his anguished confusion as a young child between his real perception of his father's abusiveness and manipulations to obtain drink and his longing to accept his mother's idealized and quite false version of the situation.[4]

A man of fifty-five, previously decisive and actively involved in social causes, developed a depression after a mild stroke, although physically he recuperated well. He talked of life's being without enjoyment or meaning, feared being left alone, and showed a dependency quite different from his former self-sufficiency. His family and friends tried to cheer him with optimistic accounts of recoveries others had made and the favorable medical prognosis. They compared his situation favorably to those who had far worse handicaps. He felt shame and fear at not being able to respond. He tried to stifle his complaints and assume his former hearty manner. Neither he nor his family could give up easily their past image of him as a strong man and accept the change.

Anger and Blame

As the behavior and attitudes of the mentally ill person become more marked and more burdensome to his relatives and friends, they often begin to express criticism, resentment, and anger. They may engage in mutual recrimination or displace anger about the illness onto mental health professionals or other outsiders. Questions tinged with bitterness arise: "Whose fault is it?" "Do we deserve to have you behave like this after all we've done for you?" "Why can't you brace up the way other people do and stop feeling sorry for yourself?" Accusations are made which carry the extra weight of resented situations from the past. Projection and displacement, which play important defensive roles at this stage of the family's response to an individual's illness, represent a final attempt to resist open examination of the family members' own role in the genesis of a relative's illness; it is a last delaying tactic, albeit unconscious, to resist change in established roles and patterns of interactions.

An overconscientious, masochistic young woman with lifelong episodes of depression marries a volatile, critical husband who resembles her emotionally unstable father. Following any quarrel, she is overwhelmed with guilt, drinks, retreats to bed, and at times attempts suicide by drug overdoses. Her husband becomes furious at this behavior and beats her. At times, he declares that he will "put her away for good." He tells her therapist, "She doesn't have to be like this; she's got to be like she was when I married her, the good-time girl without a care in her head." The husband threatens to thrust her out of his life.

A twenty-nine-year-old man from an upperclass family, once a brilliant graduate student, begins to feel a deepening isolation and inability to fit in with other people. He travels aimlessly about the country. When he returns from time to time to his parents' prosperous home and complains of vague physical illness and an unusual series of minor accidents, his father makes it clear that his son's presence is disruptive and unwelcome to the family. The parents say that they are disappointed in their son's failure to make something of himself. They discredit his sister's suggestion of a psychiatric evaluation, maintaining, "He's got to learn to help himself." The parents find relief in the conviction of conservative contemporaries that radical groups were to blame for "corrupting the young."

Anger partly serves to camouflage the more disrupting emotion of fear. Great anxiety and confusion occur as family members faced with a severe emotional disorder attempt to look for help or advice. Should the relative permissively overlook the behavior or should he show authority with restrictions and directiveness? Should the sick member be expected to conform to the family's usual standards or be treated as an invalid? An undercurrent of uneasy self-questioning arises among the healthy family members about their own feelings and the security of the family itself. What does the illness of one family member imply about the health of the others? Could there be some contamination?

Guilt, Shame, and Grief

When defenses against recognition that a family member is mentally ill finally give way, feelings of guilt, shame, and grief arise. Spouses, parents, and other close relatives or friends go through anguished appraisals of their own possible roles in the situation. Sometimes these responses are painfully appropriate, but at other times they reflect inaccurate assumptions about the chain of events and factors from early cause to resulting illness. Especially in families with a genetic predisposition to manic-depressive illness or schizophrenia, the relatives' self-reproach adds needlessly to the burden of failure which the mentally ill member already endures.

In this phase, a relative may repeatedly ask himself questions for which he finds no answers. "What did I do wrong?" "Could I, in some way, have helped prevent this illness?" Tormenting doubts lead to a frightening distrust of a relative's own perceptions, instincts, and judgments. At a time when the mentally disturbed individual is confused and most needs reassuring steadiness from his family, the closest kin themselves feel shaken in confidence. A relative, at this stage, may suppose his help to be worse than useless. If the patient is in treatment, the relative may believe cure depends entirely on the therapist, and the clinician may collude in maintaining this impression. When the therapist recommends that the patient receive care apart from his family, the family members' unhappy misgivings that they are bad for the patient seem confirmed. One father, trying to cover his hurt pride with a semblance of a joke, stated that he was "now considered a monster."

Sometimes a degree of guilt and shame is realistic as spouse, parent, son, or daughter reviews events and the quality of relationship with the patient before the illness clearly emerged. Parents become aware of the pressure they exerted on children to achieve goals more meaningful to the parents than to the child's self-realization or of the hypocrisy that underlay their smug declarations that malicious or retaliating responses were for the child's good, for which he would ultimately be grateful. A husband and wife may correctly suspect that for years one of them has exploited the other's dread of rejection by inconsiderateness and wounding patterns of response in the face of the spouse's distress.

Professionals sometimes forget the extent to which some people still attach stigma to mental illness, viewing it as obscurely shameful or as evidence of a person's weakness and failure. This fact was vividly brought to the forefront when one of our country's senators was denied nomination to the vice-presidency when it became known that he had previously undergone psychiatric treatment. Negative societal reaction seems greatest when a patient's symptoms include violent or disoranized behavior, primitive impulsive acts, heterosexual or homosexual promiscuity, or alcohol or drug abuse.

Finally, the patient himself may stir up guilt in his family. He may oppose efforts to involve him in treatment, and blame and emotionally threaten relatives for bringing him to a mental health professional. The patient may be adroit at manipulating or, with the increased sensitivity that accompanies some forms of mental illness, use his awareness of his relatives' ambivalence to generate confusion and guilt in them about carrying out recommended psychiatric treatment.

> One menopausal woman, psychotically depressed and suicidal, loses over forty pounds in three months by refusing to eat. She paces the floor at night, recounting the sins of her youth. When her husband and daughter bring her to be hospitalized, she tells them, "I shall never talk to you again." Husband and daughter, in tears, need several hours before they can decide to go ahead with the necessary hospitalization.

Burdened with guilt and anxiety, families are tempted at this stage to withdraw from involvement or perceive the situation as hopeless. Mental health professionals should encourage family members to explore their feelings and remain involved. Particularly helpful is acknowledgement that these feelings are understandable and that ambivalence, painfully evident at such times, is a characteristic of all intimate relationships.

Confusion in the Changed Family

With the existence of mental illness openly acknowledged, relatives face a new and confusing situation. Problems that were unsuspected or hidden from view become exposed. The family members' new perception of one another causes previous balances in family relationships to become upset until they can work out new ways of communicating and relating to each other. The family's world is disordered, at least temporarily.

Although relatives may experience some relief after an obscurely troubled situation at last becomes defined, they may also feel dismay over their misinterpretation of the patient's condition. If a wife had believed her husband happy up to the time of his suicide attempt, how can she trust her ability to later assess his mood or, for that matter, that of anyone she knows? An anxiously guarded carefulness interferes with a family's ordinary spontaneity. The changed balance of relationships creates new problems for the patient and his family.

> A dictatorial husband is disconcerted when, following her successful recovery from a depressive illness, his wife insists that she intends to share in decisions formerly assumed by her husband. She has learned in therapy that to continue her self-denying submission is to imperil her potential for growth. Upset over the untried new relationship, he begs her, "Just go back to being the little girl I married."

Acceptance of Reality

Families undergo some or all of the previous phases as they come to terms with the presence of mental illness. Living through the ordeal may lead some families to a level of self-awareness, an ability to communicate, and a compassion for human suffering which they might never have reached if one among them had not suffered a mental illness. Other families may never understand or accept the mental illness and will be left with more or less permanent emotional scars. However, only after relatives' acceptance does it become possible to channel their concern and energy into an alliance with a therapist.[5] Sometimes, several weeks or even months are needed before a family can talk about themselves and the factors in the family situation that may have led to the illness of one of them. Mental health professionals need to offer families a combination of support and education in viewing mental illness from a perspective that will enable each person to lower his defenses and gain confidence in his ability to deal with strong feelings and intense conflicts. This educative process helps family members acquire some understanding of the family system, and a degree of objectivity toward the patient and themselves, an acceptance that reduces the need to blame.

The phases of a family's response to mental illness resemble the reaction of individuals to such other life crises as the impending death of a loved one. This relationship is consistent with some theories of human adaptability in which there is posited a relatively predictable response of a human being to stress. Gerald Jacobson and associates believe that there are recognized patterns of response in given crises and have labeled this conceptualization the generic approach.[6] This theory focuses less on individual variation and more on the unique nature of the crisis. For many families, the diagnosis of a mental illness, particularly of schizophrenia, can be as tragic as the announcement of impending death. This reaction is especially true when long-term hospitalization becomes necessary. Thus, as Elizabeth Kübler-Ross writes of an early stage of denial in the awareness of a person or his family of impending death,[7] so, too, there is often an initial denial and inability on the part of the family to recognize that one among them is mentally ill. This period of denial provides a respite for the family to develop strength to face some of the implications of mental illness. Similarly, the analogue to Kübler-Ross's stage of progressing through anger is the phase called anger and blame in this article. The tension of anger serves to ward off grief and mourning temporarily. Mental health workers need to be alert to the dynamics of this phase in order to avoid responding personally or critically to the relatives' hostility. In a therapeutic alliance with the family, mental health workers should strive to absorb some of the excessive reaction.

The bargaining stage in coming to terms with impending death parallels the phase in which a family searches for alternate explanations for a relative's disturbed behavior. Like denial, it allows for some delay, during which time a family may realign forces, but at this point there is recognition at some level that something is wrong. Temporarily, there is confusion and change in the balance of family roles. The stage of depression and mourning for the dying patient parallels the phase of guilt, shame, and grief of the psychiatric patient's family: Both involve the loss, actual or apparent, temporary or final, of a previously normal person. It is a bitter situation, for example, for the parents of an honor student to find that their child, after his illness, can function only as a gardener.

Although the theme of this article has been the response of families to psychiatric illness, a therapist, like a family member, may undergo similar reactions. A therapist who has worked diligently in therapy may have a vested interest, not unlike that of a parent, in a patient he is treating. He is not immune to minimizing or denying his patient's condition. Similarly, reactions based on anger, guilt, blame, and grief are often evoked in helping professionals, not only based on transactions with patients, but also on a defensive need to avoid recognizing how ill some patients really are.

References

1. James A. Wechsler, *In a Darkness* (New York: W. W. Norton & Company, 1972), p. 14.

2. Erich Lindemann, Symptomatology and Management of Acute Grief, *American Journal of Psychiatry,* 101:141–48 (September 1944).

3. Irving L. Janis, *Psychological Stress: Psychoanalytical and Behavioral Studies of Surgical Patients* (New York: John Wiley & Sons, 1958); David M. Kaplan and Edward A. Mason, Maternal Reactions to Premature Birth Viewed as an Acute Emotional Disorder, *American Journal of Orthopsychiatry,* 30:539–52 (July 1960); Gerald Caplan, *Principles of Preventive Psychiatry* (New York: Basic Books, 1964); Elizabeth Kübler-Ross, *On Death and Dying* (New York: Macmillan, 1969); and Rhona Rapoport, Normal Crises, Family Structure and Mental Health, *Family Process,* 2:68–80 (March 1963).

4. Beverly Nichols, *Father Figure: An Uncensored Autobiography* (New York: Simon and Schuster, 1972).

5. Margaret E. Raymond, Andrew E. Slaby, and Julian Lieb, *The Healing Alliance* (New York: W. W. Norton & Company, 1974).

6. Gerald Jacobson, Martin Strickler, and Wilbur E. Morley, Generic and Individual Approaches to Crisis Intervention, *American Journal of Public Health,* 58:339–42 (February 1968).

7. Kübler-Ross, *On Death and Dying.*

32
Social Work with the Wealthy

Elizabeth Herman McKamy

Social work education and practices equip social workers to deal with people who are primarily disadvantaged by their economic, social or cultural backgrounds, and secondarily disadvantaged by intrapsychic or physical handicaps. Psychosocial studies underline the fact that social workers are trained not only to consider a client's psychopathology, ego strengths, and immediate family situation, but also to evaluate these as assets and liabilities relating to capacity for *minimal* functioning within the community's socioeconomic framework.

Although a substantial number of social workers are recognized as competent psychotherapists and psychoanalysts, the deepest root of their identity is grounded in orientation toward alleviating poor people's distress. Gordon Hamilton, Annette Garrett, Helen Harris Perlman, Charlotte Towle, and others have illustrated the systems and conditions of human suffering of those who lack the basic resources for an equal position in society. Many social workers, along with some of their first clients, moved on: but the generic identity of social workers as helpers of the poor remains.

Oriented as he is toward helping the poor, how does the social worker approach work with the wealthy? Even though most people are adversely affected by a troubled world economy today, a small segment of the population regards money as no obstacle in seaching for and obtaining psychiatric care. Characterized not only by affluence, the wealthy patient and his family often have an impressive heritage of achievement. Dysfunction arises frequently from an acute or chronic psychodynamic conflict, rather than from social or economic stress impinging on a weak psychological structure.

In a traditional public or voluntary institution the multiproblem family might manifest social, economic, or educational malfunction in conjunction with psychiatric problems. Conversely, multiproblem families in private

source: From *Social Casework* 57 (April 1976), pp. 254–258. Copyright © 1976 by the Family Service Association of America. Reprinted by permission.

settings are usually characterized by a complexity of psychodynamic break-downs and few, if any, social, economic, or educational ones. Whatever purity of approach this fact may afford, it nonetheless demands that the social worker reassess some of the basic assumptions of his task.

The Social Worker's Role

As part of his role at The C. F. Menninger Memorial Hospital, the social worker usually functions as liaison between hospital and family. As a member of the patient's treatment team, the social worker is the primary interpreter of the history and current situation of the family for the team. While this information helps the team to better understand the patient, it also facilitates clearer insight into countertransference phenomena as they develop. Based on an overall understanding, the team recommends indi-vidual psychotherpy, group psychotherapy, or family therapy as adjuncts to the patient's milieu treatment program. The social worker communicates the team's concept of the problems and its recommendations to the family.

Whether intensive family therapy or planned periodic visits are rec-ommended during the course of hospitalization, the family is encouraged to become involved. Some families are amenable from the beginning to their own active participation in the process; others are resistant.

Affluence and successful management in business and social spheres characterize many of the families with whom the staff work. Such families are accustomed to and adept at controlling their environment. They rarely ex-perience situations where their own resources are not sufficient to solve their problems. In fact, such people seldom find themselves having to ask for help. The social worker, popularly thought of as a helper of the socially and economically distressed, finds himself in an unusual position.

He needs to defend himself and his professional task in an arena which is somewhat alien both to him and to his clients; he is not used to working with people of wealth and power, and his clients are unused to asking for help. Treatment difficulties arise involving families with means because of long-established patterns of resistance to placing themselves in a position seemingly controlled by others. The social worker too may experience con-flicts in relating to people whom society may deem more capable and influ-ential than he.

Wealth as Power

"You get what you pay for" is a maxim to which our culture has given credence. Depsite progress in social security and public and voluntary health and child-care services, the belief is still espoused that the more an individual pays, the higher the quality of service he gets. Accordingly, one might expect that where direct party payment for service prevails, there is also a greater demand for achievement and performance. The rich are people who do not have to knock on doors, deal with secretaries, or with middlemen of any kind. Indeed, they are people who can put pressure on the hospital administration regarding anything that is done or not done to the designated patient. Such pressure, filtered down to the clinician, can be a stimulus for excellence on the job, or it can be experienced as a constraint.

Although most hospitals support their workers in clinical decisions, whether they meet, or fail to meet, the immediate approval of the patient and his family, there still remains an atmosphere of concern: the call of the board member who attempts to persuade through threat if an acquaintance is not given the treatment that he or his family dictates; the angry removal by a family of its member who is a well-known writer; the elopement of a patient of national renown, as a consequence of disagreement with staff; the threat made to a hospital that a much-needed grant will be withheld if existing policy within, for example, the social work discipline is not altered to accommodate what an individual family feels are its particular needs at a given time.

Powerful, educated, wealthy families are accustomed to direct access and management over what they have bought. They are used to controlling business and, as they see it, payment for private hospitalization is not unlike an investment in a business. In not offering a precise prospectus, however, the psychiatric hospital business often stimulates anxiety in families and the concomitant impulse to want to dictate and control through familiar patterns, for example, demand and litigation. Currently, health services and practitioners are particularly sensitive to suggestions of or hints at litigation. A hospital may be known to support its employees in their clinical decisions, but the concern for legal consequence to the institution and the individual employee still exists. Such concern is a significant influence—for better or worse. Sometimes the accessibility of resources and information to families, coupled with direct party payment for service, facilitates communication and cooperation with the treatment team. At other times, however, the very assets that allow these people to choose "the best" can make delivery of "the best," as clinically determined, a tenuous and difficult task.

Rich or poor, most families defend themselves against the recognition that they, as well as the patient, are part of the problem. Pain, confusion, and fear of change are orchestrated in almost any troubled family into a complexity of defenses that resist intervention. At the time when hospitalization of the patient has become necessary, most families would prefer, consciously or unconsciously, that the problem, namely the patient, be treated and that they, the family, support such treatment but remain essentially outside of it.

Visits, encouragement, and assuming responsibility for things the patient can not do are among the many ways a family can help its sick member while he is in the hospital. Most often, though, when deep understanding and change of personality are the goals of treatment, families have to become more intensively and purposefully involved.

Resistances of the Wealthy

The wealthy sometimes present resistances to more active therapeutic involvement that are different from those of other kinds of families in other kinds of settings. "We're functioning just fine" is often heard from families of the patients treated in our hospital. Frequently, such a statement is difficult to confront.

Father, for example, may be operating at full capacity as a corporation lawyer while at the same time involving himself in a home and social life replete with every sign of success. Mother, with children grown beyond school age, may have returned to her earlier career as a drama reviewer for the city newspaper. She explains that this job has always allowed her a flexibility of hours so that she can maintain her home as the first priority in her responsibilities. The patient's oldest sibling may have just married, while another enters his second year of college. All members of the family, including the designated patient, state that the only problem is the patient's illness.

As the patient, who had seriously attempted suicide shortly after beginning college, gains confidence in his treatment staff, he evidences in his behavior anxieties about separation from the family that showed up initially in psychological testing. He has always feared leaving his parents because he sensed from an early age that there were deep marital problems that might emerge were he to move away from home. Crazy as these fears may be, this seventeen-year-old's suicide attempt might lend sufficient evidence of trouble in the family to induce the treatment team to recommend family therapy along with the hospitalization of the patient.

Involving the Family in the Therapy

By the time hospitalization is necessary, chronically ill patients and their families are often veterans of years of psychiatric care. A high level of general education and sophistication, coupled with multifaceted and often unsuccessful experience with doctors, psychologists, psychiatrists, and so forth, can form an impressive defensive structure. Some of these families and patients use diagnostic jargon with ease. They are skilled at anticipating interventions and interpretations. Moreover, they can intellectually acknowledge an understanding that they may not truly feel. They can take the therapist's seat literally and figuratively.

A physician father, for example, may insist that continuing to medicate his daughter is his effort to be helpful and expedient in the treatment process. A mother may defend herself against recognizing the family problems that are stirred up by her daily calls to her son. She explains that her psychoanalyst at home is encouraging a closer relationship between herself and her children. An entire family can lucidly explain the dynamics of family life as they relate to the patient's illness. They can even try to convince the social worker that this understanding is more than enough homework for them to think about while the patient is in the hospital.

Splitting away from the central focus of family treatment by intellectualization and bringing in auxiliary supports and other specialists can present formidable resistance to intervention by the social worker. Although putting forth parallel interpretations and offering alternative concrete supports to the family can be useful some of the time, more often the social worker finds that sharing his experience of the family process in action is the most effective means of engaging them in a working alliance.

"We'll support anything you do" is a position taken by some families. Years of struggle and pain with a chronically ill relative have brought them over the threshhold of frustration into hopelessness. Such families have come to feel that all they can offer their sick member is protracted financial security in a private hospital. In such a setting they hope that the patient will have the maximum of physical comfort while they themselves find a long-desired peace of mind. These families may experience difficulty in translating their passive despair into a sense of personal purpose in a treatment process. The unremitting illness of the patient has come to seem like an unremitting affront to the family's ability to cope and care. The very hope that the social worker communicates in his effort to engage the family can easily be taken by them as a further insult to their capacity to be good parents or caring people.

Difficulties in Establishing a Working Alliance with the Family

In a state hospital, the proposition of unlimited financial backing for any treatment approach would be unlikely and fairly extraneous to the administrative system. In a private hospital, however, where the treatment teams feel constrained at times by the presence and power of families, there can be a temptation to collude with a carte blanche proposal that full responsibility for the patient be left in the treatment team's hands, thus excluding the family from the therapeutic task.

The very fact that the family's wish to reject the patient seems so blatant can emulate in the team a counter wish to reject them; allowing the family to remove itself entirely from the arena of treatment. Yet, when the goal is to help facilitate an integration of the patient's past in a way that will enable him to function autonomously as an adult in the future, it is almost always advisable that the family be accessible to work with the treatment staff. In the ongoing process with such families, the social workers often have to deal with their own frustrations, anger, and temptation to assume a "better" parental role that by its nature might have them reenact the same pathological patterns that the patient and his family experienced among themselves.

In work with less advantaged people, a social worker is usually able to help a family see that there are areas of dysfunction within the overall structure of their lives. Financial difficulties are common concerns, as are frustrations about underachievement in school or community. An asset in establishing a working alliance with socially or economically disadvantaged families is the social worker's often-given position as role model. When the social worker is viewed by the family as someone who has achieved an admirable level of professional, economic, and social success, the family may feel that at least some learning may take place from their contact with him.

With wealthy, successful families whose apparent level of functioning is at the apex of our social structure, it can be more difficult to establish this necessary working alliance. The social worker may find himself relying more on symptomatology revealed in the process of a family meeting than in the factual information shared. There may be fewer nonverbal assets to rely on in his initial work with these people. There is less likelihood of the social worker being taken from the start as a role model in the classical sense. Moreover, with the affluent family comes the additional demand for the social worker to be in touch with his own feelings about assuming an authoritative position with people whose lifestyle connotes a formidable authority in its own right.

Countertransference

Most of those who work in a psychiatric setting—psychiatrists, nurses, psychologists, activities therapists, aides, social workers—are from lower to upper middle-class backgrounds, and have grown up with the injunction that in order to achieve or maintain a comfortable income for themselves they have to work. Most people on the staff of a private hospital do not come from backgrounds of wealth. Therefore, at the risk of being simplistic, one might say that the present achievements of the individual members of a hospital staff are based on individual resourcefulness and effort, and the staff members' future financial and social prospects are, relatively speaking, somewhat limited.

Most social workers bring with them to their jobs a professional image as it was originally hewn out of their predecessors' exclusive work with the poor. Like his colleagues, the individual social worker has to consider countertransference that may be stimulated by his contact with patients. He may envy and resent the wealthy. Furthermore, he may find difficulties in being assertive enough, or difficulties in being too assertive in trying to counter a tendency to appease. In a psychosocial paradigm, prominent patients and their families may well represent parental figures to the social worker. And, similarly, a recovered patient may threaten as yet another powerful figure in the social worker's environment. In fact, enabling the privileged patient to achieve, or regain, his potential level of functioning might well mean helping him to *exceed* the social worker within the socioeconomic framework of society.

Finding ease with the fact that one's patients and their families might, out of the context of their current distress, far outdistance one along the continuum of success that exists in our culture is a sobering thought. Yet this difference in status militates against the social worker's efforts only insofar as he is unaware of its importance.

In working with wealthy patients and their families, the social worker must exert care to maintain a sensitive and strong self-image. He may need to take extra pains to strengthen his professional identity while realistically accepting both his assets and limitations. Armed with such insights into both his personal and professional background, he can formulate realistic goals and keep a sense of perspective. Only then can he effectively manage his job, especially the tasks centering around work with wealthy patients and their families.

The treatment of people of means may be limited by their wealth just as treatment of the poor may be limited by their poverty. Nevertheless, along with the unique difficulties that such caseloads present, there exist some equally unique assets. Wealthy patients and their families can, by and large, afford a treatment program individually determined on the basis of their needs. If indicated, families can travel for scheduled appointments, as many do at The C. F. Menninger Memorial Hospital. Or they can pay for adjunctive treatment at home. Most of the people worked with are verbal and can become motivated toward a goal they think worthwhile. They are resourceful and can focus their energies over an extended period of time if it is necessary. Many of them have generations of security and comfort behind them, and can therefore envision regaining an overall peaceful existence which to less privileged people might be a Utopia unknown.

When these assets can be channeled into a therapeutic alliance, the rewards for all are considerable. Such an alliance, as a prerequisite for meaningful treatment, evolves from a sensitivity to the social worker's personal and professional feelings, awareness of the fears, anxieties, and defenses of the patients, and an acceptance of the unique strengths that each patient and his family, no matter how wealthy, bring to the private hospital setting.

Bibliography

ABRAMSON, MARCIA. "Group Treatment of Families of Burn-Injured Patients." *Social Casework* 56 (April 1975): 235–241.

ACKERMAN, NATHAN W. "Emergence of Family Psychotherapy on the Present Scene." In M. I. Stein (ed.), *Contemporary Psychotherapies*. New York: Free Press, 1961: 228–244.

ACKERMAN, NATHAN W. "Further Comments on Family Psychotherapy." In M. I. Stein (ed.), *Contemporary Psychotherapies*. New York: The Free Press, 1961: 245–255.

ACKERMAN, NATHAN W. "Family Healing in a Troubled World." *Social Casework* 52 (April 1971): 200–205.

AGUILAR, IGNACIO. "Initial Contacts with Mexican-American Families." In F. J. Turner (ed.), *Differential Diagnosis and Treatment in Social Work*. New York: Free Press, 1976: 512–517. Also in *Social Work* 17 (May 1972): 66–70.

BALSWICK, JACK O., and PEEK, CHARLES W. "The Inexpressive Male: A Tragedy of American Society." In W. C. Sze (ed.), *Human Life Cycle*. New York: Jason Aronson, 1975: 497–504.

BARDILL, D. R. "A Relationship-Focused Approach to Marital Problems." *Social Work* 11 (July 1966): 70–77.

BARDILL, D. R., and RYAN, FRANCIS J. *Family Group Casework*. Washington, D. C.: National Association of Social Workers, 1973.

BARKER, DIANA L., and ALLEN, SHEILA. *Dependence and Exploitation in Work and Marriage*. New York: Longman, 1976.

BARTEN, HARVEY H., and BARTEN, SYBIL S. (eds.). *Children and Their Parents in Brief Therapy*. New York: Human Sciences Press, 1973.

BAUBLITZ, JACINTH IVIE. Transitional Treatment of Hostile Married Cuples." *Social Work* 23 (July 1978): 321–323.

BEATT, BARBARA HAMBY, and WAHLSTROM, BARBARA BERG. "A Developmental Approach to Understanding Families." *Social Casework* 57 (January 1976): 3–8.

BECK, DOROTHY F. "Research Findings on the Outcomes of Marital Counseling." *Social Casework* 56 (March 1975): 151–181.

BECKETT, JOYCE O. "Working Wives: A Racial Comparison." *Social Work* 21 (November 1976): 463–471.

BELL, DANIEL. "The Coming of the Post-Industrial Society." *The Educational Forum* 40 (May 1976): 575–579.

BELL, NORMAN W., and VOGEL, EZRA F. (eds.). *A Modern Introduction to the Family.* New York: Free Press, 1968.

BELL, R. R. *Marriage and Family Interaction.* Homewood, Ill.: Dorsey Press, 1978.

BENGSTON, VERN L. "Generation and Family Effects in Value Socialization." *American Sociological Review* 40 (June 1975): 358–371.

BERGMAN, INGMAR. *Scenes from a Marriage.* New York: Bantam, 1973.

BERNARD, JESSIE. *The Future of Marriage.* New York: Bantam, 1973.

BILLINGSLEY, ANDREW. "Family Functioning in the Low-Income Black Community." *Social Casework* 50 (December 1969): 563–572.

BILLINGSLEY, ANDREW. *Black Families in White America.* Englewood Cliffs, New Jersey: Spectrum Books, 1977.

BIRDWHISTELL, RAY L. "The Idealized Model of the American Family." *Social Casework* 51 (April 1970): 195–198.

BLISTEN, DOROTHY R. *The World of the Family: A Comparative Study of Families in Their Social and Cultural Setting.* New York: Random House, 1963.

BLOOD, ROBERT O. *The Family.* New York: Free Press, 1972.

BOOTH, ALAN, and EDWARDS, JOHN N. "Crowding and Family Relations." *American Sociological Review* 41 (April 1976): 308–321.

BOSZORMENYI-NAGY, and FRAMO, JAMES (eds.). *Intensive Family Therapy.* New York: Harper & Row, 1965.

BRANDRETH, ALICE, and PIKE, RUTH. "Assessment of Marriage Counseling in a Small Family Agency." *Social Work* 12 (October 1967): 34–39.

BRIDGEMAN, JUDITH ANNE, and WILLIS, BEVERLY ANN. "A Divorce Workshop for Families." In John H. Hanks (ed.). *Toward Human Dignity: Social Work in Practice.* New York: National Association of Social Workers, 1978.

BRIELAND, DONALD. "Children and Families: A Forecast." *Social Work* 19 (September 1974): 568–579.

BRODEY, WARREN M. *Family Dance: Building Positive Relationships Through Family Therapy.* New York: Anchor Books, 1977.

BROWN, ROBERT A. "Feedback in Family Interviewing." *Social Work* 18 (September 1973): 52–59.

BURGESS, ERNEST W. "The Family as a Unity of Interacting Personalities." *The Family* 7 (March 1926): 3–9.

CAMPBELL, JOHN D. "The Child in the Sick Role: Contributions of Age, Sex, Parental Status, and Parental Values." *Journal of Health and Social Behavior* 19 (March 1978): 35–51.

CARR, GWEN B. *Marriage and Family in a Decade of Change.* Reading, Mass.: Addison-Wesley, 1972.

CHAIKLIN, HARRIS, and KELLY, GERALD R. "The Domestic Relations Offender." *Social Service Review* 49 (March 1975): 115–121.

CHAMBRE, SUSAN M. "Welfare, Work and Family Structure." *Social Work* 22 (March 1977): 103–108.

CHASKEL, RUTH. "Effect of Mobility on Family Life," *Social Work* 9 (October 1964): 83–91.

CHESTANG, LEON W. "Increasing the Effectiveness of Social Work Intervention with Minority Group Families." In John W. Hanks (ed.), *Toward Human Dignity: Social Work in Practice.* New York: National Association of Social Workers, 1978.

CHIANCOLA, SAMUEL P. "The Process of Separation and Divorce: A New Approach." *Social Casework* 59 (October 1978): 494–499.

CHILMAN, CATHERINE S. "Public Social Policy and Families in the 1970s." *Social Casework* 54 (December 1973): 575–585.

CHRISTENSEN, HAROLD C. (ed.). *Handbook of Marriage and The Family.* Chicago: Rand McNally & Co., 1964.

CLAVAN, SYLVIA. "Women's Liberation and the Family." In W. C. Sze (ed.), *Human Life Cycle.* New York: Jason Aronson, 1975: 531–540.

COLEMAN, JULES V., *et al.* "A Family Agency in a Community Project for the Hospitalized Mentally Ill." *Social Work* 12 (October 1967): 47–53.

CONSTABLE, ROBERT T. "Mobile Families and the School." *Social Casework* 59 (July 1978): 419–427.

COOPER, DAVID. *The Death of the Family.* New York: Vintage, 1971.

COSER, ROSE L. (ed.). *The Family: Its Structures and Functions.* New York: St. Martin's Press, 1974.

CRANO, WILLIAM D., and ARONOFF, JOEL. A Cross-Cultural Study of Expressive and Instrumental Role Complementarity in the Family." *American Sociological Review* 43 (August 1978): 463–471.

CROMWELL, RONALD E., and OLSON, DAVID, H. L. (eds.). *Power in Families.* New York: Halsted Press, 1975.

CROOG, SYDNEY H., and FITZGERALD, EDWARD F. "Subjective Stress and Serious Illness of a Spouse: Wives of Heart Patients." *Journal of Health and Social Behavior* 19 (June 1978): 166–178.

DAVIS, FRED. *Passage Through Crisis: Polio Victims and Their Families.* Indianapolis: The Bobbs-Merrill Co., Inc., 1963.

DEBURGER, JAMES E. (ed.). *Marriage Today: Problems, Issues, and Alternatives.* New York: Halsted Press, 1978.

DEBUSHEY, MATHEW (ed.). *The Chronically Ill Child and His Family.* Springfield, Ill.: Charles C. Thomas Publisher, 1970.

DEVIS, DONALD A. "Four Useful Concepts for Family Diagnosis and Treatment." *Social Work* 12 (July 1967): 18–27.

DINERMAN, MIRIAM. "Catch 23: Women, Work, and Welfare." *Social Work* 22 (November 1977): 472–477.

DUBERMAN, LUCILLE. *Marriage and Other Alternatives.* New York: Holt, Rinehart and Winston, 1977.

DUBERMAN, LUCILLE. *Marriage and the Family.* New York: Holt, Rinehart and Winston, 1979.

DUNCAN, PAUL R., and PERCUCCI, CAROLYN C. "Dual Occupation Families and Migration." *American Sociological Review* 41 (April 1976): 252–261.

DUVAL, EVELYN M. *Family Development.* Philadelphia: J. B. Lippincott Co., 1971.

EARL, LOVELENE, and LOHMAN, NANCY. "Absent Fathers and Black Male Children." *Social Work* 23 (September 1978): 413–415.

EPSTEIN, NORMAN. "Techniques of Brief Therapy with Children and Parents." *Social Casework* 57 (May 1976): 317–323.

ERICKSON, GERALD D., and HOGAN, TERRENCE P. *Family Therapy: An Introduction to Theory and Technique.* Monterey, Calif.: Brooks Cole, 1972.

ESHLEMAN, J. ROSS. *The Family: An Introduction.* Boston: Allyn and Bacon, 1974.

FAIRCHILD, ROY W., and WYNN, J. C. *Families in the Church: A Protestant Survey.* New York: Association Press, 1961.

FANTL, BERTA. "Casework in Lower Class Districts." In F. J. Turner (ed.), *Differential Diagnosis and Social Work Treatment.* New York: Free Press, 1976: 565–580. Also in *Mental Hygiene* 45 (July 1961): 425–438.

FERRIS, ABBOTT L. *Indicators of Change in the American Family.* New York: Russell Sage Foundation, 1970.

FIELD, MARTHA H., and FIELD, HENRY F. "Marital Violence and the Criminal Process: Neither Justice Nor Peace." *Social Service Review* 47 (June 1973): 221–240.

FRAMO, JAMES L. (ed.). *Family Interaction: A Dialogue Between Family Researchers and Family Therapists.* New York: Springer, 1972.

FREEMAN, DOROTHY R. "Counseling Engaged Couples in Small Groups." *Social Work* 10 (October 1965): 36–42.

FRENCH, ALFRED. *Disturbed Children and Their Families: Innovations in Evaluation and Treatment.* New York: Human Sciences Press, 1977.

FULLERTON, GAIL P. *Survival in Marriage: Introduction to Family Interaction, Conflicts, and Alternatives.* New York: Holt, Rinehart and Winston, 1972.

GEIST, JOANNE, and GERBER, NORMAN M. "Joint Interviewing: A Treatment Technique with Marital Partners." In F. J. Turner (ed.), *Differential Diagnosis and Treatment in Social Work.* New York: Free Press, 1976: 99–103. Also in *Social Casework* 41 (February 1960): 76–83.

GEISMAR, LUDWIG L., et al. *Early Supports for Family Life: A Social Work Experiment.* Metuchen, New Jersey: Scarecrow Press, 1972.

GEISMAR, LUDWIG L., and GEISMAR, SHIRLEY. *Families in an Urban Mold: Policy Implications of an Australian-U.S. Comparison.* Elmsford, New York: Pergamon Press, 1979.

GELLES, RICHARD J. *The Violent Home: A Study of Physical Aggression Between Husbands and Wives.* Beverly Hills, California: Sage Publications, 1974.

GILBERT, GWENDOLYN C. "Counseling Black Adolescent Parents." *Social Work* 19 (January 1974): 88–95.

GINSBERG, BARRY G., et al. "Group Filial Therapy." *Social Work* 23 (March 1978): 154–156.

GLENDENING, SUSAN E., and WILSON, A. JOHN. "Experiments in Group Premarital Counseling." *Social Casework* 53 (November 1972): 551–561.

GOLDBERG, RUTH L. "The Social Worker and the Family Physician." *Social Casework* 54 (October 1973): 489–495.

GOLDBERG, STANLEY B. "Family Tasks and Reactions in the Crisis of Death." *Social Casework* 54 (July 1973): 398–405.

GOLDSTEIN, MARK K. "Marital Communication Difficulties: Increasing Positive Behaviors in Married Couples." In J. D. Krumboltz and C. E. Thoresen, *Counseling Methods*. New York: Holt, Rinehart and Winston, 1976: 188–198.

GOLNER, JOSEPH. "Home Family Counseling." Social Work 16 (October 1971): 63–71.

GOODMAN, LAWRENCE. "Continuing Treatment of Parents with Congenitally Defective Infants." *Social Work* 9 (January 1964): 92–97.

GOODSELL, WILLYSTINE. *A History of the Family as a Social and Educational Institution*. New York: Macmillan, 1923.

GORDON, MICHAEL (ed.). *The American Family in Social-Historical Perspective*. New York: St. Martin's Press, 1978.

GREENE, B. (ed.). *Psychotherapies of Marital Disharmony*. New York: Free Press, 1965.

GROSS, LEONARD (ed.). *Sexual Behavior: Current Issues*. New York: Halsted Press, 1974.

GROSS, LEONARD (ed.). *Sexual Issues in Marriage*. New York: Halsted Press, 1975.

GUERIN, PHILIP J. (ed.). *Family Therapy: Theory and Practice*. New York: Gardner Press, 1976.

GUILLOT, ELLEN E. "Congress and the Family: Reflections of Social Processes and Values in Benefits in OASDI." *Social Service Review* 45 (June 1971): 173–183.

HALE, JOHN. "Gestalt Techniques in Marriage Counseling." *Social Casework* 59 (July 1978): 428–433.

HALEY, JAY. (ed.). *Changing Families: A Family Therapy Reader*. New York: Gruen and Stratton, 1971.

HALL, MARNY. "Lesbian Families: Cultural and Clinical Issues." *Social Work* 23 (September 1978): 380–385.

HALLECK, SEYMOUR L. "Family Therapy and Social Change." *Social Casework* 57 (October 1976): 483–493.

HALLOWITZ, DAVID. "The Problem-Solving Component in Family Therapy." *Social Casework* 51 (February 1970): 67–75.

HALLOWITZ, DAVID. "Counseling and Treatment of the Poor Black Family." *Social Casework* 56 (October 1975): 451–459.

HANDEL, GERALD (ed.). *The Psychosocial Interior of The Family*. Chicago: Aldine Publishing Co., 1967.

HAREVEN, TAMARA K. (ed.). *Family and Kin in Urban Communities, 1700–1930*. New York: New Viewpoints, 1977.

HARTMAN, ANN. "Diagrammatic Assessment of Family Relationships." *Social Casework* 59 (October 1978): 465–476.

HARTMAN, SUSAN S., and HYMES, JANE. "Marriage Education for Mentally Retarded Adults." *Social Casework* 56 (May 1975): 280–284.

HATFIELD, AGNES B. "Psychological Costs of Schizophrenia to the Family." *Social Work* 23 (September 1978): 355–359.

HAYNES, JOHN M. "Divorce Mediator: A New Role." *Social Work* 23 (January 1978): 5–9.

HERSH, ALEXANDER. "Changes in Family Functioning Following Placement of a Retarded Child." *Social Work* 15 (October 1970): 93–102.

HESS, ROBERT D., and HANDEL, GERALD. *Family Worlds: A Psychosocial Approach to Family Life.* Chicago: University of Chicago Press, 1959: 1–19.

HICKEY, KATHLEEN M. "Impact of Kidney Disease on Patient, Family and Society." *Social Casework* 53 (July 1972): 391–397.

HIGGINS, JOHN J. "Social Services for Abused Wives." *Social Casework* 59 (May 1978): 266–271.

HILL, REUBEN. *Family Development in Three Generations.* Cambridge, Mass.: Schenkman, 1970.

HILL, REUBEN, and RODGERS, ROY H. "The Developmental Approach." In Harold Christensen (ed.), *Handbook of Marriage and the Family.* Chicago: Rand McNally, 1964: 171–211.

HILL, REUBEN. "Generic Features of Families Under Stress." *Social Casework* 39 (February–March 1958): 139–150.

HILL, REUBEN. *Families Under Stress.* New York: Harper and Brothers, 1949.

HOLMES SALLY, et al. "Working with the Parent in Child-Abuse Cases." In F. J. Turner (ed.), *Differential Diagnosis and Treatment in Social Work.* New York: Free Press, 1976: 637–650. Also in *Social Casework* 56 (January 1973): 3–12.

HORWITZ, ALLAN. "The Pathways into Psychiatric Treatment: Some Differences Between Men and Women." *Journal of Health and Social Behavior* 18 (June 1977): 169–178.

HUDSON, WALTER W., and GLISSON, DIANNE H. "Assessment of Marital Discord in Social Work Practice." *Social Service Review* 50 (June 1976): 293–311.

HUNNICUTT, HELEN, and SCHAPIRO, BARRY. "Use of Marriage Enrichment Programs in a Family Agency." *Social Casework* 57 (November 1976): 555–561.

IRVING, HOWARD H. "Relationships Between Married Couples and Their Parents." *Social Casework* 52 (February 1971): 91–96.

JACKSON, DON D. "Family Therapy in the Family of the Schizophrenic." In M. I. Stein (ed.), *Contemporary Psychotherapies.* New York: Free Press, 1961: 272–287.

JANZEN, CURTIS. "Family Treatment for Alcoholism: A Review." *Social Work* 23 (March 1978): 135–141.

JAYARATNE, SRINIKA. "Child Abusers as Parents and Children: A Review." *Social Work* 22 January 1977): 5–9.

JAYARATNE, SRINIKA. "Behavioral Intervention and Family Decision-Making." *Social Work* 23 (January 1978): 20–25.

JOLESCH, MIRIAM. "Casework Treatment of Young Married Couples." In F. J. Turner (ed.), *Differential Diagnosis and Treatment in Social Work.* New York: Free Press, 1976: 90–98. Also in *Social Casework* 43 (May 1962): 245–251.

JUSTICE, BLAIR, and JUSTICE, RITA. *The Abusing Family.* New York: Human Science Press, 1976.

KAMERMAN, S. B., and KAHN, A. J. "Explorations in Family Policy." *Social Work* 21 (May 1976): 181–186.

KAMERMAN, SHEILA B., and KAHN, ALFRED J. *Family Policy: Government and Families in Fourteen Countries.* New York: Columbia University Press, 1978.

KANTOR, DAVID, and LEHR, WILLIAM. *Inside the Family: Toward a Theory of Family Process.* San Francisco: Jossey Bass, 1975.

KAPLAN, DAVID M. "Family Mediation of Stress." *Social Work* 18 (July 1973): 60–69.

KARSON, MARTHA A., and KARSON, ALBERT. "Counseling Couples in Their Sixties." *Social Work* 23 (May 1978): 243–244.

KAUFFMAN, M. "Short Term Family Therapy." In H. Parad (ed.), *Crisis Intervention.* New York: Family Service Association of America, 1965.

KAUFMANN, EDWARD, and KAUFMANN, PAULINE. *Family Therapy of Drug and Alcohol Abusers.* New York: Halsted Press, 1978.

KEITH, P. "A Family Service Agency in an Appalachian Community." *Social Casework* 51 (March 1970): 140–145.

KEPHART, WILLIAM M. *The Family, Society, and the Individual.* Boston: Houghton Mifflin Co., 1971.

KESHET, HARRY F., and ROSENTHAL, KRISTINE M. "Fathering After Marital Separation." *Social Work* 23 (January 1978): 11–18.

KIEREN, DIANNE, et al. *Hers and His: A Problem Solving Approach to Marriage.* New York: Holt, Rinehart and Winston, 1975.

KILGUSS, ANNE F. "Using Soap Operas as a Therapeutic Tool." *Social Casework* 55 (November 1974): 525–529.

KING, CHARLES H. "Family Therapy with the Deprived Family." *Social Casework* 48 (April 1967): 203–208.

KLEIN, ALAN F. "Exploring Family Group Counseling." *Social Work* 8 (January 1963): 23–29.

KNOX, DAVID. *Marriage Happiness: A Behavioral Approach to Counseling.* Ill.: Research Press, 1975.

KOHN, MELVIN L. "Social Class and Parent-Child Relationships." In W. C. Sze (ed.), *Human Life Cycle.* New York: Jason Aronson, 1975: 541–553.

KOMAROVSKY, MIRRA. *Blue-Collar Marriage.* New York: Vintage, 1967.

KREISMAN, DELORES, and JOY, VIRGINIA. "Family Response to the Mental Illness of a Relative: A Review of the Literature." *Schizophrenia Bulletin* 10 (Fall 1974): 34–57.

KRILL, DONALD F. "Family Interviewing as an Intake Diagnostic Method." *Social Work* 13 (April 1968): 56–63.

KRISTAL, H. F., and TUCKER, F. "Managing Child Abuse Cases." *Social Work* 20 (September 1975): 392–395.

KRUPP, GEORGE. "Maladaptive Reactions to the Death of a Family Member." *Social Casework* 53 (July 1972): 425–433.

LAING, R. D. *The Politics of the Family.* New York: Vintage, 1971.

LANCE, EVELYN A. "Intensive Work with a Deprived Family." *Social Casework* 50 (October 1969): 454–460.

LANTZ, HERMAN, et al. "The Changing American Family from the Preindustrial to the Industrial Period: A Final Report." *American Sociological Review* 42 (June 1977): 406–421.

LANTZ, JAMES E. "Cotherapy Approach in Family Therapy." *Social Work* 23 (March 1978): 156–158.

LASLETT, BARBARA. "Social Change and the Family: Los Angeles, California, 1850–1870." *American Sociological Review* 42 (April 1977): 268–291.

LAUGHLIN, JOHN L., and BRESSLER, ROBERT. "A Family Agency Program for Heavily Indebted Families." *Social Casework* 52 (December 1971): 617–626.

LAWRENCE, MARGARET. *Young Inner City Families: Development of Ego Strength Under Stress.* New York: Human Science Press, 1975.

LEADER, ARTHUR L. "Intergenerational Separation Anxiety in Family Therapy." *Social Casework* 59 (March 1978): 138–144.

LEADER, ARTHUR L. "The Place of In-Laws in Marital Relationships." *Social Casework* 56 (October 1975): 486–491.

LEADER, ARTHUR L. "Family Therapy for Divorced Fathers and Others Out of the Home." *Social Casework* 54 (January 1973): 13–19.

LEADER, ARTHUR L. "Denied Dependency in Family Therapy." *Social Casework* 57 (December 1976): 637–643.

LEBEDUN, MORTY. "Measuring Movement in Group Marital Counseling." *Social Casework* 51 (January 1970): 35–43.

LEDERER, WILLIAM J., and JACKSON, DON. *The Mirages of Marriage.* New York: Norton, 1967.

LEE, GARY L. *Family Structure and Interaction: A Comparative Analysis.* Philadelphia: J. B. Lippincott, 1977.

LEMASTERS, E. E. *Parents in Modern America: A Sociological Analysis.* Homewood, Ill.: Dorsey Press, 1970.

LEVANDE, DIANE I. "Family Theory as a Necessary Component of Family Therapy." *Social Casework* 57 (May 1976): 291–295.

LEWIN, KARL KAY. *Brief Psychotherapy: Brief Encounters.* St. Louis, Missouri: Warren H. Green, 1970. See Chapter 8, "Family Therapy."

LIPMAN-BLUMEN, JEAN. "The Implications for Family Structure of Changing Sex Roles." *Social Casework* 57 (February 1976): 67–79.

LIPMAN-BLUMEN, JEAN, and BERNARD, JESSIE (eds.). *Social Policy and Sex Roles.* Beverly Hills, Calif.: Sage Publications, 1978.

LOCKER, ROSE. "Elderly Couples and the Institution." *Social Work* 21 (March 1976): 149–150.

LUTHMAN, SHIRLEY G., and KIRSCHENBAUM, MARTIN. *The Dynamic Family.* Palo Alto, Calif: Science and Behavior Books, 1974.

MACNAMARA, MARGARET. "The Family in Stress: Social Work Before and After Renal Homotransplantation." *Social Work* 14 (October 1969): 89–96.

MALDONADO, DAVID. "The Chicano Aged." *Social Work* 20 (May 1975): 213–216.

MARTIN, J. P. (ed.). *The Violent Family.* New York: Halsted Press, 1978.

MARTIN, WALTER T. "Status Integration, Social Stress, and Mental Illness: Accounting for Marital Status Variation in Mental Hospitalization Rates." *Journal of Health and Social Behavior* 17 (September 1976): 280–294.

MARTINSON, FLOYD M. *Family in Society.* New York: Dodd, Mead, 1972.

MASTERS, WILLIAM H., and JOHNSON, VIRGINIA E. "Counseling with Sexually Incompatible Marriage Partners." In W. C. Sze (ed.), *Human Life Cycle.* New York: Jason Aronson, 1975: 469–480.

McCARY, JAMES L. *Freedom and Growth in Marriage.* Calif.: Hamilton, 1975.

McCLENDON, McKEE J. "The Occupational Status Attainment Processes of Males and Females." *American Sociological Review* 41 (February 1976): 52–64.

McKAMY, ELIZABETH H. "Social Work with the Wealthy." *Social Casework* 57 (April 1976): 254–258.

McKENNEY, MARY. *Divorce: A Selected Annotated Bibliography.* Metuchen, New Jersey: Scarecrow Press, 1975.

McKINNEY, GERALDINE E. "Adapting Family Therapy to Multideficit Families." In F. J. Turner (ed.), *Differential Diagnosis and Treatment in Social Work.* New York: Free Press, 1976: 109–118. Also in *Social Casework* 51 (June 1970): 327–333.

MEILE, RICHARD L., *et al.* "Marital Role, Education, and Mental Disorder Among Women: Test of an Interaction Hypothesis." *Journal of Health and Social Behavior* 17 (September 1976): 295–301.

MEYER, CAROL H. "Practice and Policy: A Family Focus." *Social Casework* 59 (May 1978): 259–265.

MEYER, CAROL H. "Individualizing the Multiproblem Family." In F. J. Turner (ed.), *Differential Diagnosis and Treatment in Social Work.* New York: Free Press, 1976: 595–603. Also in *Social Casework* 44 (May 1963): 267–272.

MILLER, EMILY. "Treatment of a Communal Family." *Social Casework* 54 (June 1973): 331–341.

MINUCHIN, SALVADOR. *Families and Family Therapy.* Mass.: Harvard University Press, 1976.

MITCHELL CELIA B. "Integrative Therapy of the Family Unit." *Social Casework* 46 (February 1965): 63–69.

MONTIEL, MIGUEL. "The Chicano Family: A Review of Research." *Social Work* 18 (March 1973): 22–31.

MORONEY, ROBERT M. *The Family and the State: Considerations for Social Policy.* New York: Longman, 1976.

MOST, ELIZABETH. "Measuring Change in Marital Satisfaction." *Social Work* 9 (July 1964): 64–70.

MOSTWIN, DANUTA, "Multidimensional Model of Working with the Family." *Social Casework* 55 (April 1974): 209–215.

MOYNIHAN, SHARON K. "Utilizing the School Setting to Facilitate Family Treatment." *Social Casework* 59 (May 1978): 287–294.

MUELLER, JOHN F. "Casework with the Family of the Alcoholic." *Social Work* 17 (September 1972): 79–84.

MURPHY, ANN, *et al.* "Group Work with Parents of Children with Down's Syndrome." *Social Casework* 54 (February 1973): 114–119.

NADELSON, CAROL C., *et al.* "Evaluation Procedures for Conjoint Marital Psychotherapy." *Social Casework* 56 (February 1975): 91–96.

NASS, GILBERT D. *Marriage and the Family.* Reading, Mass.: Addison-Wesley Publishing Company, 1978.

NICHOLS, BEVERLY B. "The Abused Wife Problem." *Social Casework* 57 (February 1976): 27–32.

NOLFI, MARY W. "Families in Grief: The Question of Casework Intervention." *Social Work* 12 (October 1967): 40–46.

NYE, F. IVAN, and HOFFMAN, LOIS W. *The Employed Mother in America.* Chicago: Rand McNally, 1963.

NYE, F. IVAN, and BERARDO, FELIX M. *Emerging Conceptual Frameworks in Family Analysis.* New York: Macmillan, 1966.

NYE, F. IVAN, *et al. Role Structure and Analysis of the Family.* Beverly Hills, Calif.: Sage Publications, 1976.

O'NEILL, WILLIAM L. *Divorce in the Progressive Era.* New York: New Viewpoints, 1967.

OPPENHEIM, KAREN, *et al.* "Change in U.S. Women's Sex-Role Attitudes, 1964–1974." *American Sociological Review* 41 (August 1976): 573–596.

OPPENHEIMER, VALERIE. "The Sociology of Women's Economic Role in the Family." *American Sociological Review* 42 (June 1977): 387–406.

ORADEI, DONNA M., and WAITE, NANCY S. "Admissions Conferences for Families of Stroke Patients." *Social Casework* 56 (January 1975): 21–26.

OXLEY, GENEVIEVE. "Short-Term Therapy with Student Couples." *Social Casework* 54 (April 1973): 216–223.

OZAWA, MARTHA N. "Women and Work." *Social Work* 21 (November 1976): 455–462.

PAPP, PEGGY (ed.). *Family Therapy: Full Length Case Studies.* New York: Halsted Press, 1977.

PEARLIN, LEONARD I. "Status Inequality and Stress in Marriage." *American Sociological Review* 40 (June 1975): 344–357.

PEARLIN, LEONARD I., and JOHNSON, JOYCE S. "Marital Status, Life Strains and Depression." *American Sociological Review* 42 (October 1977): 704–715.

PEEL, JOHN, and CARR, GRISELDA. *Contraception and Family Design.* New York: Longman, 1975.

PERRUCCI, CAROLYN C., and TARG, DENA B. (eds.). *Marriage and the Family.* New York: Longman, 1974.

PFOUTS, JANE H. "The Sibling Relationship: A Forgotten Dimension." *Social Work* 21 (May 1976): 200–204.

PINKSTON, ELSIE M., and HERBERT-JACKSON, EMILY W. "Modification of Irrelevant and Bizarre Verbal Behavior Using Parents as Therapists." *Social Service Review* 49 (March 1975): 46–63.

PLIONIS, BETTY M. "Adolescent Pregnancy: Review of the Literature." *Social Work* 20 (July 1975): 302–307.

PLONE, ANNE. "Marital and Existential Pain: Dialectic in Bergman's 'Scenes from a Marriage.'" *Family Process* 14 (September 1975): 371–378.

POLLAK, OTTO. "A Family Diagnosis Model." *Social Service Review* 34 (March 1960): 19–31.

QUEEN, STUART A., and HABENSTEIN, ROBERT W. *The Family in Various Cultures.* New York: Lippincott, 1974.

RAINWATER, LEE. "Marital Sexuality in Four Cultures of Poverty." In W. C. Sze (ed.), *Human Life Cycle.* New York: Jason Aronson, 1975: 481–496.

RANIERI, RALPH F., and PRATT, THEODORE C. "Sibling Therapy." *Social Work* 23 (September 1978): 418–419.

RATLIFF, BASCOM W., et al. "Intercultural Marriage: The Korean American Experience." *Social Casework* 59 (April 1978): 221–226.

RAYMOND, MARGARET E. "Familial Responses to Mental Illness." *Social Casework* 56 (October 1975): 492–498.

RED HORSE, JOHN G., et al. "Family Behavior of Urban American Indians." *Social Casework* 59 (February 1978): 67–72.

REISS, IRA L. *The Family System in America.* New York: Holt, 1971.

REYNOLDS, MARY K., and CRYMES, JOSEPH T. "A Survey of the Use of Family Therapy by Caseworkers." *Social Casework* 51 (February 1970): 76–81.

REYNOLDS, ROSEMARY, and SIEGLE, ELSE. "A Study of Casework with Sado-masochistic Marriage Partners." In F. J. Turner (ed.), *Differential Diagnosis and Treatment in Social Work.* New York: Free Press, 1976: 215–224. Also in *Social Casework* 40 (December 1959): 545–551.

RODGERS, ROY II. *Family Interaction and Transaction: The Developmental Approach.* New Jersey: Prentice Hall, 1973.

RODGERS, ROY H. "The Occupational Role of the Child: A Research Frontier in the Developmental Conceptual Framework." *Social Forces* 45 (December 1966): 217–224.

RODGERS, ROY H. "Toward a Theory of Family Development." *Journal of Marriage and the Family* 26 (August 1964): 262–270.

ROGERS, EVERETT M. *Communication Strategies for Family Planning.* New York: Free Press, 1977.

ROLLINS, B. C., and FELDMAN, H. "Marital Satisfaction Over the Family Life Cycle." *Journal of Marriage and the Family* 32 (1970): 20–27.

ROMNEY, LEONARD S. "Extension of Family Relationships into a Home for the Aged." *Social Work* 7 (January 1962): 31–34.

ROSE, SHELDON D. "Group Training of Parents as Behavior Modifiers." *Social Work* 19 (March 1974): 156–162.

ROSE, SHELDON D. "A Behavioral Approach to the Group Treatment of Parents." In F. J. Turner (ed.), *Differential Diagnosis and Treatment in Social Work.* New York: Free Press, 1976: 119–131. Also in *Social Work* 14 (July 1969): 21–30.

ROSSI, ALICE S. "Transition to Parenthood." In W. C. Sze (ed.), *Human Life Cycle.* New York: Jason Aronson, 1975: 505–529.

ROTTER, SHELDON. "Mary Richmond and Family Social Work Today." *Social Casework* 54 (May 1973): 284–289.

RUBIN, SUSAN. "Parents' Groups in a Psychiatric Hospital for Children." *Social Work* 23 (September 1978): 416–417.

SAARI, CAROLYN, and JOHNSON, STUART R. "Problems in the Treatment of VIP Clients." *Social Casework* 56 (December 1975): 599–604.

SANDBERG, NEIL. *Stairwell 7: Family Life in the Welfare State.* Beverly Hills, California: Sage Publications, 1978.

SATIR, VIRGINIA. *Conjoint Family Therapy: A Guide to Theory and Technique.* Calif: Science and Behavior Books, 1967.

SATIR, VIRGINIA. *Peoplemaking.* Palo Alto, California: Science and Behavior Books, 1972.

SAVELLS, JERALD, and CROSS, LAWRENCE J. *The Changing Family: Making Way for Tomorrow.* New York: Holt, Rinehart and Winston, 1978.

SAXON, WILLIAM W. "The Behavioral Exchange Model of Marital Treatment." *Social Casework* 57 (January 1976): 33–40.

SAXTON, L. *The Individual, Marriage and the Family.* Calif.: Wadsworth, 1972.

SCARR, SANDRA, and WEINBERG, RICHARD A. "The Influence of 'Family Background' on Intellectual Attainment." *American Sociological Review* 43 (October 1978): 674–692.

SCHERZ, FRANCES H. "Theory and Practice of Family Therapy." In R. W. Roberts and R. H. Nee (eds.), *Theories of Social Casework.* Chicago: University of Chicago Press, 1970: 219–264.

SHERZ, FRANCES H. "Maturational Crises and Parent-Child Interaction." *Social Casework* 52 (June 1971): 362–369.

SCHILD, SYLVIA. "Counseling with Parents of Retarded Children at Home." *Social Work* 9 (January 1964): 86–91.

SCHLACHTER, ROY H. "Home Counseling of Adolescents and Parents." *Social Work* 20 (November 1975): 427–428.

SCHUERMAN JOHN R. "Marital Interaction and Posthospital Adjustment." *Social Casework* 53 (March 1972): 163–172.

SCHUERMAN, JOHN R. "Do Family Services Help? An Essay Review." *Social Service Review* 49 (September 1975): 363–375.

SCHULMAN, GERDA L. "Myths that Intrude on the Adaptation of the Stepfamily." *Social Casework* 53 (March 1972): 131–139.

SCHULMAN, GERDA L. "Teaching Family Therapy to Social Work Students." *Social Casework* 57 (July 1976): 448–457.

SCHULZ, DAVID A. *The Changing Family: Its Functions and Future.* New York: Prentice-Hall, 1972.

SCHUYLER, MARCELLA. "Battered Wives: An Emerging Social Problem." *Social Work* 21 (November 1976): 488–491.

SETLEIS, LLOYD. "An Inquiry into the Moral Basis of the Family." *Social Casework* 59 (April 1978): 203–210.

SETLEIS, LLOYD. "A Philosophy of the Family as a Practical Necessity." *Social Casework* 55 (November 1974): 562–567.

SEWARD, RUDY R. *The American Family: A Demographic History.* Beverly Hills, California: Sage Publications, 1978.

SHELLHASE, LESLIE J., and SHELLHASE, FERN E. "Role of the Family in Rehabilitation." *Social Casework* 53 (November 1972): 544–549.

SHOTLAND, LEONARD. "Social Work Approach to the Chronically Handicapped and Their Families." *Social Work* 9 (October 1964): 68–75.

SIEFFERT, ALLAN. "Parents' Initial Reactions to Having a Mentally Retarded Child: A Concept and Model for Social Workers." *Clinical Social Work Journal* 6 (Spring 1978): 33–43.

SIMOS, BERTHA G. "Adult Children and Their Aging Parents." *Social Work* 18 (May 1973): 78–85.

SINGER, ELEANOR. "Subjective Evaluations as Indicators of Change." *Journal of Health and Social Behavior* 18 (March 1977): 84–90.

SKOLNICK, ARLENE. *The Intimate Environment: Exploring Marriage and the Family.* Boston: Little, Brown, 1973.

SKOLNICK, ARLENE, and SKOLNICK, JEROME H. *Intimacy, Family and Society.* Boston: Little, Brown, 1974.

SOTOMAYER, MARTA. "Mexican-American Interaction with Social Systems." *Social Casework* 52 (May 1971): 316–322.

SPEER, DAVID C. In W. C. Sze (ed.), *Human Life Cycle.* New York: Jason Aronson, 1975: 427–442.

SPIEGEL, JOHN P. "The Resolution of Role Conflict Within the Family." In W. C. Sze (ed.), *Human Life Cycle.* New York: Jason Aronson, 1975: 445–467.

SPITZER, STEPHEN P. "Determinants of the Psychiatric Patient Career: Family Reaction Patterns and Social Work Intervention." *Social Service Review* 45 (March 1971): 74–85.

STAPLES, ROBERT. "Towards a Sociology of the Black Family: A Theoretical and Methodological Assessment." *Journal of Marriage and the Family* 33 (February 1971): 119–138.

STEINMETZ, SUZANNE K., and STRAUS, MURRAY A. *Violence in the Family.* New York: Dodd, Mead, 1974.

STREIB, GORDON F. *The Changing Family: Adaptation and Diversity.* Mass.: Addison-Wesley, 1973.

STRYKER, SHELDON. "Symbolic Interaction as an Approach to Family Research." In J. G. Manis and B. N. Meltzer (eds.), *Symbolic Interaction: A Reader in Social Psychology.* Boston: Allyn and Bacon, 1972: 435–447.

SUNLEY, ROBERT. "Family Advocacy from Case to Cause." *Social Casework* 51 (June 1970): 347–357.

SUSSMAN, MARVIN B., *et al. The Family and Inheritance.* New York: Russell Sage Foundation, 1970.

TAYLOR, PATRICIA A., and GLENN, NORVAL D. "The Utility of Education and Attractiveness for Females' Status Attainment Through Marriage." *American Sociological Review* 41 (June 1976): 484–498.

The General Mills American Family Report 1974–75: A Study of the American Family and Money. Minneapolis: General Mills, Inc., 1975.

THOMAS, EDWIN J. "Coaching Marital Partners in Family Decision Making." In J. D.

Krumboltz and C. E. Thoresen, *Counseling Methods.* New York: Holt, Rinehart and Winston, 1976: 369–377.

TOMEK, AIDA K. *The Family and Sex Roles.* New York: Holt, Rinehart and Winston, 1975.

TRAVIS, GEORGIA. *Chronic Illness in Children: Its Impact on Child and Family.* Stanford, Calif: Stanford University Press, 1976.

TROPMAN, JOHN E. "The Married Professional Social Worker." *Journal of Marriage and Family Living* 30 (November 1968): 661–665.

TURRINI, PATSY. "A Mothers' Center: Research, Service and Advocacy." *Social Work* 22 (November 1977): 478–483.

URI, RUEVENI. *Networking Families in Crisis.* New York: Human Sciences Press, 1979.

VINCENT, CLARK E. "Familia Spongia: The Adaptive Function." In W. C. Sze (ed.), *Human Life Cycle.* New York: Jason Aronson, 1975: 555–568.

VOILAND, ALICE L., and BUELL, BRADLEY. "A Classification of Disordered Family Types." *Social Work* 6 (October 1961): 3–11.

WAITE, LINDA J. "Working Wives: 1940–1960." *American Sociological Review* 41 (February 1976): 65–80.

WALTZ, THOMAS H. "The Family, The Family Agency, and Postindustrial Society." *Social Casework* 56 (January 1975): 13–19.

WARD, MARGARET. "Large Adoptive Families: A Special Resource." *Social Casework* 59 (July 1978): 411–418.

WINCH, ROBERT F. *The Modern Family.* New York: Holt, Rinehart & Winston, Inc., 1971.

WISEMAN, REVA S. "Crisis Theory and the Process of Divorce." *Social Casework* 56 (April 1975): 205–212.

YOUNG, ALMA T., *et al.* "Parental Influence on Pregnant Adolescents." *Social Work* 20 (September 1975): 387–391.

YOUNG, LEONTINE. *The Fractured Family.* New York: McGraw-Hill, 1978.

YOUNG, MICHAEL, and WILLMOTT, PETER. *The Symmetrical Family.* New York: Penguin Books, 1973.

ZIMMERMAN, SHIRLEY L. "Reassessing the Effect of Public Policy on Family Functioning." *Social Casework* 59 (October 1978): 451–457.

ZUK, GERALD H. *Family Therapy: A Triadic-Based Approach.* New York: Human Sciences Press, 1971.

INDEX